DIANA PRESTON is an author and historian. Her recent account of Captain Scott's Antarctic expeditions, *A First Rate Tragedy*, was acclaimed both for her thought-provoking psychological portrait of Scott and her vivid depiction of exploration in the harshest of environments. Her first book, a biography of Bonnie Prince Charlie, *The Road to Culloden Moor*, was also well received for its verve and incisiveness. She is an avid traveller and when not on the move lives in London with her husband Michael.

Praise for *The Boxer Rebellion*

'[Diana Preston] writes with pathos and humour as well as with the astute eye of the objective historian.'

Literary Review

'Diana Preston's dramatic retelling of the summer-long siege of the Peking foreign district one hundred years ago – 'a pivotal episode in China's fractured relationship with the West' – does much to clarify China's enduring resentment towards foreign interference . . . Preston's account, compiled from many letters, diaries, and memoirs by European survivors of the siege, captures an odd strain of mordant humor.'

The New York Times Book Review

'A gripping new account of the deadly drama that shaped relations between China and the West one hundred years ago, and still has echoes today. The arrogance, ignorance, and 'yellow peril' fears that marked Western attitudes during the Boxer Rebellion still exist below the surface of today's more mutually respectful and interactive relationship. So does Chinese insecurity and xenophobia.'

Nicholas Platt, president, Asia Society

'[A] vivid and thorough account . . . Preston tells a riveting story about ordinary people placed under extreme pressure by events they could neither understand nor control.'

Publishers Weekly

D0188366

Other titles in this series

A Brief History of The Tudor Age
Jasper Ridley

A Brief History of The Druids
Peter Berresford Ellis

A Brief History of Fighting Ships
David Davies

A Brief History of The Great Moghuls
Bamber Gascoigne

A Brief History of The Royal Flying Corps
in World War I
Ralph Barker

A Brief History of British Kings & Queens
Mike Ashley

A Brief History of Science
Thomas Crump

A BRIEF HISTORY OF
THE BOXER
REBELLION

CHINA'S WAR ON FOREIGNERS, 1900

DIANA PRESTON

ROBINSON
London

Constable & Robinson Ltd
3 The Lanchesters
162 Fulham Palace Road
London W6 9ER
www.constablerobinson.com

First published as *Besieged in Peking*
in the UK by Constable and Co. Ltd, 1999

This paperback edition published by Robinson,
an imprint of Constable & Robinson Ltd, 2002

A copy of the British Library Cataloguing in
Publication data is available from the British Library

ISBN 1-84119-490-5 (pbk)

Printed and bound in the EU

10 9 8 7 6 5 4 3

To my husband,

MICHAEL

EXPLANATORY NOTE

To be consistent with the terminology in the primary sources, a modified Wade-Giles system has been used to romanize Chinese personal and place names where appropriate. Also, Beijing is shown as Peking and Tianjin as Tientsin.

CONTENTS

ILLUSTRATIONS

Between pages 94 and 95

ACKNOWLEDGMENTS

I am indebted once again to my husband Michael for his tremendous help and encouragement throughout, for his advice on concept and context, and his help with research and editing. I am also grateful to him for trudging with me from one end of Beijing to another during some hot and dusty August days as we looked for clues to the past.

I am most grateful to Ben Glazebrook for his help and guidance with this book and to the team at Constable & Robinson, in particular Nicola Chalton, the editor of this paperback edition. I must also thank my American publisher, George Gibson, of Walker & Company, New York, for his encouragement and support with the US edition, on which this revised edition is based.

This book is about the human experience of living through the Boxer rising. It could not have been written without the help and generosity of many people and organizations. I want to thank the staff of the London Library and the staff of the Bodleian Library, University of Oxford, in particular Peter Allmond, for tracking down many, sometimes very obscure, published sources; the staff of the British Library, and in particular Dr Frances Wood and Graham Hutt, for their help with unpublished sources and for showing me some fascinating Boxer posters; Emily Tarrant for her guidance through the Special Collections of the School of Oriental and African Studies (SOAS), University of London; and John Montgomery, Librarian of the Royal United Services Institute for Defence Studies in London, for Sir Claude MacDonald's article on the defence of the Legations from the Institute's Journal. I am also grateful to the National Army Museum in Chelsea for allowing me access to their archives, in particular to the diary of Captain Francis Poole; to the National Maritime Museum for allowing me to consult Earl Beatty's papers; to the Bodleian Library for permission to quote from the Backhouse memoirs; and to the Council for World Mission for permission to quote from the papers of the London Missionary Society. I am most grateful to Peter Trowell for the loan of letters written by his grandmother Mabel Read, a Baptist missionary in northern China in 1900.

I also want to acknowledge the kind help of a number of American librarians who went to great lengths to send me original source material in a range of formats from bundles of photocopies to microfiches: from the Hoover Library in Iowa, Dale C. Mayer in particular, for providing me with journals and correspondence of Herbert Hoover and his wife Lou and some of their acquaintances in China at the time; from the US Department of the Navy's Marine Corps Historical Center in Washington, D.C., especially Frederick Graboske, head of the Archives Section, and Leo Daugherty for their friendly advice, patience in answering my questions, and for providing me with access to the papers of a number of marines who fought in China in 1900, and in particular for arranging with the family of Oscar Upham for me to consult his lively and vivid diary. I am also grateful to the Houghton Library of Harvard University for extensive help and advice, and to Jennie Rathbone especially, for allowing me access to Luella Miner's extensive and fascinating diary and related material; and to the US Department of the Navy's Historical Center for assistance with information about Captain Bowman McCalla. I am similarly indebted to the Peabody Essex Museum in Salem,

Massachusetts, for permission to quote from the typescript of Paul Schlieper's 'The Seymour Expedition' (English translation), belonging to the Edward H. Seymour Collection, Phillips Library.

I was also given generous assistance by the Mitchell Library in Sydney, Australia, and Martin Beckett in particular, who went to considerable trouble to send me the papers of George Morrison and Edward Connor.

I am also most grateful to many individuals and would like to thank Earl Jellicoe for allowing me to consult his grandfather's journal; Frederick Sharf for his kindness and advice and for allowing me to quote from two documents belonging to the Jean S. and Frederick A. Sharf manuscript collection – the Journal of Captain Bayly and a translation of a report of the Seymour relief expedition by Commander Mori of the Imperial Japanese Navy; Lily Bardi-Ullmann for her unstinting research among the newspaper archives in New York and for tracking down a number of American publications; the Upham family for allowing me to quote from Oscar Upham's diary; Jim Hoare and Susan Pares for help and advice on the history of the Legation Quarter in Peking and kindness in sharing their own research material with me; Rod Wye of the British Embassy, Beijing, for showing me the surviving memorabilia of the period; David Warren for his insights into China today; Michael Thomas and Bill Hamilton of A. M. Heath, London, and Mark Chelius of Writer's House, New York, for their support and encouragement; and Chris Carduff whose guidance on US publications on the Boxers and generosity in sending me material I much appreciated.

Finally, I am grateful to Kim Lewison, Sharon Moross, and Neil Munro for advice at a key stage. I also much appreciated the loan of books by Ginny Covell and much-needed assistance with the Internet from St John Brown, Caroline Munro, and Joyce and Edmund Griffiths, and the encouragement of family and friends, especially Vera Faith and Helen Janecek.

PROLOGUE

The actual truth has never been written about any war, and this will be no exception. – George Lynch, journalist

'STANDING together as the sun rose fully, the little remaining band, all Europeans, met death stubbornly . . . As one man fell others advanced, and finally, overcome by overwhelming odds, every one of the Europeans remaining was put to the sword in a most atrocious manner.'[1] So read a dramatic dispatch in the London *Daily Mail* of 16 July 1900 from its special correspondent in Shanghai. Under the headline 'The Pekin Massacre', it confirmed in gruesome detail what the world already suspected – that hundreds of foreigners besieged in Peking's diplomatic quarter since 20 June had been murdered.

The news flew around the world, gaining in horrific detail. The *New York Times* dwelt on the fate of the Russian minister and his wife, plunged into boiling oil. It informed its readers that the besieged 'went mad and killed all their women and children with revolvers.'[2]

In the event, these reports proved false. They might so easily have been true. The summer of 1900 witnessed a pivotal episode in China's fractured relationship with the West – the Boxer rising. It was an event that left tens of thousands dead and touched the lives of millions more. It precipitated the end of the ruling Manchu dynasty. It tainted China's relationship with the wider world, and continues to do so even today.

The Boxer rising prompted an unprecedented international response. It saw the first steps in America's gradual assumption from Britain of the role of an often misunderstood, sometimes misguided and occasionally hypocritical world policeman. It brought home to Americans the moral compromises – and the cost in human lives – of becoming involved with diversely motivated allies in interventions against hostile populations in distant alien lands. It also revealed Japan's growing confidence and military prowess to a startled world. Soon she would become China's greatest tormentor.

The Boxers themselves were an unlikely catalyst for such far-reaching effects. An obscure, ill-organized sect that claimed to possess supernatural powers, it drew its members mainly from the poor and dispossessed of northern China. The foreigners called them 'Boxers' because of the ritualistic martial arts they practised. Their lives had long been a losing struggle against cycles of flood, drought and famine. The arrival in China of increasing numbers of foreigners had only deepened their misery. Some foreigners came in pursuit of commerce, and the new technologies they brought with them – steamboats and locomotives, telegraph systems and mining equipment – not only offended the spirits of earth, water and air but also robbed many Chinese of their jobs. Christian missionaries – fresh-faced and idealistic men and women from the American Midwest, bearded priests from Germany and France – came in search of souls. Often ignorant, dismissive or contemptuous of the native culture, they and their aggressive proselytizing threatened the very fabric of Chinese family and village life. The Boxers despised their Chinese converts as traitors, 'rice Christians' who had sold themselves for a square meal.

The Boxers' simmering resentment erupted across the northern provinces of Shantung, Shansi and Chihli in the summer of 1900.

Chanting mobs surrounded the mission stations and dragged out their terrorized occupants. Some they killed on the spot; others they took to Boxer temples to be slowly tortured to death. Tens of thousands of Chinese converts, Protestant and Catholic, were murdered – hacked to pieces, skinned alive, set alight or buried still living.

The Boxers attacked and murdered Western railway engineers and burned down stations. Reinforced by Imperial Chinese troops, they blockaded 600 foreigners and some 4,000 Chinese Christians in the international port of Tientsin. The foreigners in Peking – nearly 900 men, women and children from the eighteen most powerful nations in the world – were besieged in the diplomatic quarter.

Spheres of Influence in China, c. 1900

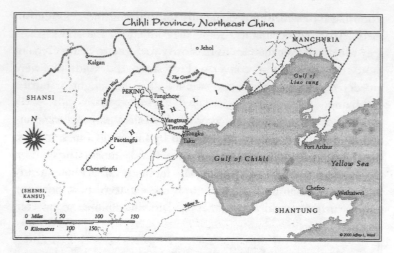

Established in the 1860s following China's defeat in the war with
Britain and France, the quarter was by 1900 a commercial as well
as a diplomatic district. Banks, shops and offices prospered along-
side the embassies – or 'legations', as they were then known – of
America, Britain, Russia, Japan and many of the countries of
Western Europe.

The siege forced the quarter's motley population – diplomats
and missionaries, academics and adventurers, soldiers and visiting
socialites, journalists and engineers – to cooperate despite differences of language and custom and a long history of petty rivalries.
The women sewed sandbags of expensive silks, and everyone,
from ambassadors' wives to Orthodox priests, filled them. Brave
men, both marines and civilian volunteers, fought and died
behind them. The cowardly hid in cellars on the flimsiest of
excuses. The besieged cooked and ate unappetizing, indigestible
meals of rice and horsemeat and were glad of them. Nearly everyone got dysentery. In the heat of the humid Peking summer, thick
swarms of black flies and the sickly sweet stench of rotting human
flesh were everywhere. The plight of the three thousand or so
Chinese converts sheltering in a carefully segregated part of the
compound was worst of all. Denied an equal distribution of the
food, they were soon reduced to stripping the bark off trees and

devouring crows and dogs bloated on human corpses in an effort to survive.

At first everyone listened for the sound of the relief force's guns. When it did not come some men made preparations to shoot their wives and children should the 'yellow fiends' overrun the complex. Others smoked cigars and swilled champagne from the well-stocked cellars. A few cracked under the strain and were locked up. The more phlegmatic wondered how they had got into a predicament that even the supposed experts had failed to foresee.

In the nearby Peitang Cathedral, a handful of French and Italian guards under the glinting eye of the martial French bishop Favier struggled against frightening odds and in even worse conditions to defend a community of nearly thirty-five hundred souls.

Watching and waiting on events from within Peking's fabled pink-walled Forbidden City was 'the Old Buddha', Tzu Hsi, the sixty-five-year-old Empress Dowager of China. In an otherwise totally male-dominated society, this extraordinary woman had held power, directly or indirectly, for nearly forty years. To many of the foreign community she was an Asiatic Catherine de Medici, a woman of unimaginable sexual appetites and political ambition who murdered anyone, including her closest family, who stood in her way. A reactionary to the core, she had recently incarcerated her nephew the emperor for daring to lead a reform movement. She shared the Boxers' loathing of the foreigners in China and was astute enough to realize two things: first, the Boxers could help her sweep the hated interlopers out of China, and second, their genuine social and economic grievances had to be harnessed or they might be turned against her and the Manchu dynasty. She therefore turned a blind eye to the Boxers' murderous activities, then gave them official support. It proved her greatest mistake.

Foreign troops relieved Tientsin in July while an international relief force eventually raised the sieges of the diplomatic quarter and the Peitang Cathedral in August. By then, however, over 200 foreigners had been killed or wounded in the diplomatic quarter and hundreds of Chinese Christians had perished, most from starvation and disease. In the Peitang over 400 Chinese and foreigners had died, including 166 children. In the Chinese hinterland, some 200 foreign nuns, priests, and missionaries and their families had been murdered while the death toll of Chinese converts ran into tens of thousands. The numbers of Boxers and Imperial troops who perished can only be guessed.

Both Tientsin and Peking were thoroughly and indiscriminately looted by all nationalities and all classes. Many innocent civilians committed suicide rather than face being raped and killed. Moats, rivers and wells became clogged with bodies. It had been a terrible bloodbath and it had backfired badly on Tzu Hsi. In her final years she was forced to embrace the very reforms she had earlier resisted and indeed to introduce them so quickly that they undermined the dynasty she had fought to preserve. The last emperor, Pu Yi, was deposed in 1911, just three years after her death.

It was an irony that the foreign powers that had cooperated to defeat China would soon be at war with one another. Indeed, the barely suppressed rivalries among them during the crisis in China had signalled to many the inevitability of an impending major conflict. Yet the allied action against the Boxer rising also set an important precedent, one that prefigures the relief and policing activities of the United Nations and NATO. It certainly caught the imagination of the many contemporaries who likened it to the Crusades. It had been, as British Prime Minister Lord Salisbury put it, 'an entirely new experiment.'[3] Nevertheless, it would take two world wars and one cold one to achieve such a widespread collaboration again.

The Boxer Rebellion was an extraordinary event – heroic and farcical, tragic and shocking, brutal and ridiculous, with far-reaching implications. Yet it was also a richly human story. The foreigners who survived wrote a great deal about the rising and its aftermath. Articulate, opinionated, often prejudiced, their accounts provide fascinating insight into what occurred during those traumatic months. Yet in order to understand why they felt and acted as they did during that terrible summer of 1900, we must first appreciate something of their world and their preconceptions.

*   *   *

The world at the end of 'the British Century' was a world very different from today's. The 1900 edition of *Whitaker's Almanack* quotes population figures for the many countries caught up in the Boxer rising. The UK population was around 40 million and that of the British Empire, covering a fifth of the world's surface, was 400 million. The population of the United States was given as only some 63 million, taken from the 1890 census. A new census in 1900 revealed that immigration had boosted the population to over 76 million, an increase of more than 20 percent in only a decade. Italy had 31 million people, France nearly 39 million, Japan 43 million, Germany around 52 million, and the Russian Empire 130 million. China was said to have over 300 million. *Whitaker's* dismissed claims of a Chinese population closer to 400 million with the haughty words 'it is generally thought that the so-called census returns of Chinese officials are untrustworthy.'[4]

The West, poised on the cusp of a new century, was in flux with new ideas and new technologies challenging the old and with intense international rivalry. Some were optimistic, believing in the unstoppable march of progress and civilization. H. G. Wells predicted a world of airplanes, air-conditioning and cosy suburban living but, like many others, he also foresaw wars. Some believed that a great international conflict was somehow close at hand. When the troubles broke out in northern China they wondered whether this would be the catalyst. One clear-sighted American missionary working in China, Luella Miner, described how 'the atmosphere is crackling with electricity' and asked anxiously, 'Are we on the verge of that long-dreaded European war?'

Darwin's theory of evolution gave additional force to the idea that rivals would eventually slog it out on the battlefield. To some, Darwinism seemed to legitimize distinctions between races and between individuals, and to justify the existence of social hierarchies and of rich and poor – indeed, of pecking orders of all sorts. Looking back over the nineteenth century, the well-known British journalist William Thomas Stead, later to go down with the *Titanic*, wrote: 'The doctrine of evolution . . . may be regarded as the master dogma of the century. Its subtle influence is to be felt in every department of life. It has profoundly modified our conceptions of creation, and it is every day influencing more and more our ideas of morality. Men are asking, Why hesitate in consigning to a lethal chamber all idiots, lunatics and hopeless incurables? And in the larger field of national politics, why should we show any mercy to the weak? Might becomes right . . . Wars of extermination seem to receive the approbation of nature.'[5]

Both Britons and Americans saw the Anglo-Saxon race as preeminent among the white races, which, in turn, rightly dominated the rest. One writer thought the Anglo-Saxons 'in perfect accord with the characteristic conditions of modern life.'[6] The Anglo-Saxon focused on physical interests and material possessions and consequently triumphed in world markets 'because he has supreme gifts as an inventor of material things which appeal to the average man of democracy.' His success in driving self-interest and ethical standards in double harness marked him out from others, but the writer believed the Anglo-Saxon to be 'supremely unconscious of this duality in his nature,' concluding smugly that 'there is a psychological difference between English-speaking men and others, which makes that which would be hypocrisy in others not hypocrisy in them. They are sentimentalists, and, as sentimentalists, not the best analysts of their motives and impulses.'

The perceived superiority of the westerner, and in particular of the English-speaking white male, dominates American and British accounts of the Boxer rising. They speak disparagingly of 'Continentals' lounging about, smoking and drinking and generally keeping out of harm's way, while the Anglo-Saxons got on with the hard work. One American missionary wrote: 'British and American boys can be told even in motley uniform by their manly bearing. It makes me proud of my race.'[7]

It was logical for Britain to look to America as 'the British Century' drew to a close and her responsibilities as global policeman and administrator of a vast empire were becoming too great to bear alone. It was to the United States that Rudyard Kipling addressed his plea to 'take up the White Man's burden.' To him and others like him, the white man's burden comprised all who were not white men. His appeal, with its flavour of selfless nobility, found a receptive ear among Americans about to embark on what would become their century and for whom events in China would pose fundamental questions about America's role in the world. The Republican William McKinley, who had been elected president in 1896, was, despite some personal misgivings, an expansionist. Hawaii was about to be formally annexed. Tension was mounting between America and Spain over the treatment of Cuba, then a Spanish colony. On 15 February 1898 a United States armoured cruiser, USS *Maine*, blew up and sank in Havana harbour. She probably exploded due to carelessness in storing combustible coal next to the powder room, but the American public instinctively blamed the Spaniards.

The American imperialist Albert Beveridge claimed, 'We are a conquering race, we must obey our blood and occupy new markets and if necessary new lands.'[8] The Pacific was 'the true field of our operations. There Spain has an island empire in the Philippines. There the United States has a powerful squadron. The Philippines are logically our first target.' War was declared on 25 April 1898, and five days later Commodore George Dewey attacked a Spanish fleet in Manila Bay. The war against the Spanish in Cuba ended with the defeat of a Spanish fleet off Santiago, four days before the ratification of the annexation of Hawaii. Cuba was given its independence and Spain ceded Puerto Rico and Guam to America.

The Philippines proved a more difficult problem. The leader of the Philippine independence movement, Emilio Aguinaldo, had been fighting the Spaniards for some time and sided with the Americans during the war. In return, Aguinaldo, who admired America and liked to be called 'the George Washington of the Philippines,' expected independence. He was to be disappointed. After some debate, America annexed the Philippines and Aguinaldo launched a bitter guerrilla war that was still being fought as 1900 dawned.[9] In the end, it claimed four times as many American lives as the war with Spain. 'I have been criticized a good deal about the Philippines,' President McKinley said, 'but I don't deserve it. The truth is . . . they came to us as a gift from the gods.'[10]

Problems in the Philippines did not, however, prevent a large body of American opinion, like that on the European continent, from backing the Boers in what was seen as their struggle for independence against the British in South Africa. The Boers were widely thought of as free white men, economically independent, fighting against a numerically larger and better-equipped enemy. The cause of the war was in part about rights for non-Boers in the Boer Republics, but perhaps even more about control over the diamond fields of the Rand. When the British eventually won, *Life* magazine summed up the struggle this way: 'A small boy with diamonds is no match for a large burglar with experience.'[11]

War had been declared in the middle of October 1899 and had from the start gone badly for the British. The army had not fought a major war since the Crimea forty years previously. Young officers, educated at public schools where sporting prowess was far more highly esteemed than academic excellence, proved easy prey for the older, more seasoned Boer commandos.[12] During 'Black Week', in December 1899, Britain suffered three major defeats – Magersfontein, Stormberg and Colenso.[13] By the beginning of 1900 the towns of Kimberley, Ladysmith and Mafeking were under siege and all Britain was in a state of shock at the poor performance of her armies. News of yet another disaster at Spion Kop was hardly the New Year's present that Britons wanted. It seemed to confirm their secret fears about incipient decline and imperial overreach.

Britain's continental rivals gloated. France was still annoyed at the thwarting of her African ambitions by the standoff with the British at Fashoda on the Nile in 1898. In January 1900 there were serious articles in the British press about the possibility that France would take the chance offered by Britain's distraction with the Boers to revenge herself by launching a combined-forces raid on London. Russia and Britain also suspected each other's motives, particularly in Asia. This was the time of 'the Great Game', when

British and Indian spies – like Kipling's Kim – kept watch among the nomadic tribes in the remote high mountains of central Asia in case Russian expansionism threatened British India. Relations with Germany were tense. Kaiser William, though fond of his grandmother Queen Victoria, believed that Germany's emerging military and commercial power entitled her to a fairer share of colonies. In pursuit of his aspirations he was determined to rival British naval supremacy. On New Year's Day 1900 he promised the rebirth of the German navy so that Germany might win 'the place which it has not yet attained.'[14]

In 1898 the tsar, Nicholas II, had recognized the danger posed by such rivalries between the powers and the resulting arms race and called an international conference to debate the issues. The conference opened in The Hague in May 1899 and agreed on a convention providing for voluntary arbitration of international disputes. Another convention defined the customs of war on land, including firm prohibitions on the seizure of private property by 'belligerents' – in other words, looting. A pious and toothless resolution stated that limitations on military expenditure and new types of arms were 'highly desirable for the moral and material benefit of humanity.'[15] All twenty-four delegations, except the United Kingdom and America, agreed to ban the use of the soft-nosed expanding dumdum bullet. Events in northern China would show that some of these agreements were more honoured in the breach than in the observance.

Japan was still something of an unknown quantity, although, like China, she too was represented at the Hague Conference. Since the Meiji restoration in 1868, Japan had been modernizing rapidly, combining Western science and engineering techniques with older values of patriotism and Eastern ethics.

The defeat of China in 1894–95 by Japan's army and navy, both organized and equipped along European lines, had shocked the world and prompted the kaiser to coin the expression '*die Gelbe Gefahr*' – 'the Yellow Peril.' The idea that an armed, ambitious Asia was turning its covetous gaze westward quickly took hold. In *The Yellow Danger*, a potboiler by M. P. Shiel published in London in 1898, the Chinese are portrayed as conspiring with Britain's Continental enemies to break Britannia's power in the Far East. Their real goal, however, is to forge a secret alliance between China and Japan to enable them to become masters of Europe and Asia. 'What appalling fate would be that of Europe if the yellow races in their hundreds of millions organized a westward march is beyond the imagination of man to conceive,' says one character. Nevertheless, the scenario is depicted for the reader. Screaming Chinese play ball with severed heads and limbs in the streets of Paris and 'the Oriental' indulges an almost natural penchant for cannibalism. 'The low hedge that divides the yellow man from omnivorousness was in Europe found to be very low indeed – where the flesh of men is not yellow, but pink, like the new-born mouse. At the first spur of hunger, the hedge was leapt with an easy bound.'

The Yellow Danger is peppered with phrases like 'fiendish love of cruelty' and 'devilish cunning' to describe the Oriental character. Exactly the same language is to be found in the letters and diaries of the foreigners trapped in Peking in 1900 and in articles in the international press. Raging against the supposed massacre in Peking, *The Times* warned of the danger of 'a universal uprising of the yellow race.'[16] A poem published in an American paper while the siege was still under way was typical:

> *Millions of yellow, pitiless, alien faces,*
> *Circle them round with hate;*
> *While desperate valour guards the broken places,*
> *Outside the torturers wait.*[17]

Many white Americans, particularly on the West Coast, felt the Yellow Peril was much nearer at hand in their own Chinatowns. They saw their local Chinatowns as threatening, hermetic enclaves – hotbeds of crime, drugs and prostitution, seemingly irreducible elements in the American melting pot. Chinese labour had been welcome in the early 1850s when it helped build the booming West and its railroads. However, with the economic downturn of the late 1860s and 1870s came resentment of the industrious and thrifty Chinese, prepared to work for low wages and often used to break strikes. While white Americans were prepared to pay fifty cents for entry to a Chinatown 'lookie show' to satisfy their curiosity about whether the genitalia of Chinese women differed, as rumoured, from those of white women, they were not prepared to see their wages and working conditions undercut.

Virulent anti-Chinese campaigns broke out. One of their milder manifestations was the 'pigtail hunt', in which innocent Chinese were chased and their pigtails roughly severed. Soon laws were passed aimed at restricting the influx of Chinese into the western states. Other laws forbade not only the immigration of Chinese women into America, but also intermarriage between Chinese men and white women. In 1882, a formal exclusion act prohibited the immigration of Chinese 'idiots', 'lunatics' and 'labourers' and placed the onus on all Chinese wishing to come to the United States to prove that they did not fall into these categories. Regularly reviewed, the act remained in force in 1900.

Darwinism appeared to give respectability to anti-Chinese fears and prejudices. It encouraged Westerners to think of Orientals as less highly evolved and more prey to savage animal instincts. In 1897 the *North China Herald* had published an article entitled 'Darwinism and China'. Citing the work of the Dutch scientist Eugene Dubois, who claimed to have discovered the 'missing link' in the shape of an ape-man in Java, the anonymous author argued that the Oriental was plainly less highly evolved than the European. Anyone who doubted this had only to walk down a street in China: 'Many Chinese have retained vestigial control of the feet which Europeans have lost . . . Observations of barefooted coolies on a damp road will prove plainly enough that the inner part of the sole never touches the ground.'[18] He went on: 'Man is never nearer to the beasts than when he is angry'; when a Chinaman was enraged his 'simian ancestry' returned, transforming him into 'a raging beast whose eyes glare, whose mouth foams

with almost as poisonous a secretion as that of a mad dog . . .
Watch him half bend himself downwards and then spring up with
a jerk, his gesticulating arm and twitching fingers hardly under
control . . . the very picture of an enraged anthropoid ape.'

The writer would have found it impossible to comprehend that
'the Chinese never appear to have entertained the smallest doubt
that, all things considered, they were incomparably superior to
any foreign people, and must in the end be victorious.'[19] This message was brought keenly home to the Reverend Timothy Richard,
a Welsh missionary travelling in Shantung.[20] He was asked by a
Chinaman where he came from:

'From Ch'ing-chow fu,' I replied.
'But,' he said, 'you are not a Chinaman; you are a foreigner.'
'Yes,' I replied, 'I am from England.'
'England!' he exclaimed. 'That is the country that
rebelled against us!' . . .
'She could never rebel,' I said, 'because she never
belonged to China.'
'But she did,' he retorted. 'Before that time she was one
of the nations that paid tribute to China . . . When England
revolted, it was the greatest rebellion since the world began.'

Far from seeing themselves as rebellious barbarians, most foreigners despised China's autocratic and closed system of government as anachronistic. Yet in 1900 Europe was still a continent of
kings and emperors. Only France and Switzerland were republics.
Of the countries that made up the international relief force sent to
Peking, only the United States, Britain and France had real claims
to democracy. The tsar, the Austrian emperor and the German
kaiser could dismiss their ministers as autocratically as the
Empress Dowager could dismiss China's.

Not surprisingly, this period was also the heyday of the anarchist
movement. Its philosophers had a vision of a stateless society where
man could be truly free, without government, laws, ownership of

property and the corruption of organized institutions. No man would live off the labour of another and human nature would produce natural justice. To reach this utopian state, however, there had to be revolution, since the ruling class would not voluntarily abandon its powers. The bomb and the assassin's bullet were the anarchist's tools. President Carnot of France was assassinated in 1894, President Canovas of Spain in 1897, and Empress Elizabeth of Austria in 1898. During the siege of the Peking legations, the Italians would learn of the assassination of their king by an anarchist.[21]

Meanwhile, in Russia in 1887, the young Alexander Ulyanov had been hanged with four other students for an attempted bomb attack on Tsar Alexander III. His brother Vladimir Ilyich swore revenge. In early 1900, on his release from three years of exile in Siberia, he made his way to Geneva and continued to plot a Marxist revolution more structured and organized than the spontaneous uprising beloved of the anarchist. Learning of the events in China, he called on the 'enslaved humanity in China to break its chains.'[22] In 1901 he began to use the pseudonym Lenin.

Socialist movements, revolutionary or not, gained widespread popular support: the Western world at the end of the nineteenth century was one of considerable inequality. In Britain at least fifteen landowners, all aristocrats, had income from land of over £100,000 a year. There were huge disparities in wages. The British minister to the Chinese Court, Sir Claude MacDonald, was paid £5,000 a year. A vice-admiral like Sir Edward Seymour, commander of the Royal Navy's China squadron, received £1,460 a year. However, a leading seaman on one of his ships could earn as little as £32 a year. While an infantry captain earned about £210, a private earned less than £20. Tradesmen, clerks and teachers could expect around £75 to £100 a year. In the United States half of the country's vast wealth was owned by 1 percent of the population. The Commandant General of Marines received $5,500 annually, a captain of Marines about $2,000, and a Marine private just $166. A clerk was paid $1,320 and a chambermaid $480 a year. (The exchange rate in 1900 was about $4.8 to one pound sterling.) In terms of buying power, £150 fully furnished a house in the United Kingdom. A bottle of whiskey cost 3s 6d, twenty-five cigarettes 5d and 'a steak and kidney dinner' 4d. In the United States a good quality suit cost $11, a bottle of whiskey about $2, corned beef eight cents a pound and a 'turkey dinner' twenty cents. During the sack of Peking, many ordinary soldiers and sailors lamented that they did not have the ready cash to pick up the looted bargains they saw their officers buying.

Technology was providing another stimulus for social change. The nineteenth century was the age of steam. Railways on land and steamships at sea had greatly increased the speed of travel, the mobility of the mass of the population and the volume of trade.[23] The steamer voyage from Britain to Shanghai took less than six weeks. The telegraph, the submarine cable and that new invention the telephone had rendered communication almost instant. In June 1897, Queen Victoria had sent her simple Diamond Jubilee message to the subjects of her empire by pressing a button in the telegraph room at Buckingham Palace. Within two minutes it had passed through Teheran and was well on its way to the farthest limits of the empire. At the outbreak of the troubles in China, 'all the appliances of modern civilization' were available to help the besieged. According to one, 'The telegraph has flashed the news of our distress beneath the waves of the ocean, and the navy yards and camps in the four quarters of the earth are set in commotion.'[24] Such inventions greatly increased the speed of military deployment to trouble spots. Motor transport, however, was still in its infancy,[25] and when railway and telegraph lines were cut, armies were once again, as allied troops in China discovered, as dependent as in the Middle Ages on the horse to carry messages and move baggage and field guns.

The guns themselves were becoming ever more powerful, quicker firing and more accurate. The first machine guns had been used as long ago as 1879, in the British war against the Zulus. Perhaps predictably, the two largest exhibits at the 1900 Paris International Exposition were Schneider-Creusot's long-range cannon and Vickers-Maxim's quick-firing machine guns. The

Chinese were extremely interested in the new weaponry and had been investing heavily with European armaments manufacturers. The fighting in China was one of the first occasions on which weapons were used against the nations that had supplied them. Hearing that a German gunboat had been fired on by Chinese outfitted with the latest Krupp cannon, an angry kaiser complained to Fritz Krupp: 'This is no time, when I am sending my soldiers to battle against the yellow beasts, to try to make money out of so serious a situation.'[26]

However, the 50 million visitors to the Paris Exposition received their greatest thrills from some other rapid technological advances. The main pavilion was the Palace of Electricity. Topped by the sparkling Fairy of Electricity, the palace was illuminated by 5,700 electric light bulbs, the most concentrated man-made light ever seen. Also, less than ten years after Edison's first public showing of a cinema film, visitors could see movies 'in the round', images produced by ten synchronized projectors – although they frequently broke down. Another great favourite was a 'trottoir roulant', a double moving sidewalk that wound round the grounds. There were also demonstrations of X-ray machines, the lack of which were bitterly lamented in the siege hospital in Peking.[27]

Elsewhere, Paris was continuing to live up to her reputation for nightlife. European gentlemen travelled there to indulge in more exotic sexual practices than were to be found at home. A brothel owner proudly displayed the chair where the Prince of Wales, the future King Edward VII, sat to select his girl for the evening. The can-can ruled at the Moulin Rouge.[28] Henri de Toulouse-Lautrec, though ill, was still painting his vivid scenes of the demimonde. A frail Oscar Wilde was living there in exile following his release in 1897 from Reading Jail.[29]

If Paris was alluring, how much more seductive were the soft beds of the East. Oriental women had an almost mystical fascination for Western men. As one Victorian wrote with unfettered enthusiasm, it was the common belief that Oriental women 'understand in perfection all the arts and wiles of love, are capable of gratifying any tastes, and in face and figure they are unsurpassed by any women in the world.'[30] One of the siege diarists described an encounter with Manchu women that was 'like a narcotic when a roar of fever still hangs in one's ears.'[31] Many men found local bed companions or 'sleeping dictionaries' an excellent and pleasurable way of learning the language. Something of this was captured in a story published in the American *Century Magazine* in 1898. It told the poignant tale of a young Japanese girl who marries but is then abandoned by an American naval officer. When dramatized, it became the inspiration for Puccini's *Madama Butterfly* (1904).

Decent Western women, on the other hand, were not supposed to enjoy sex. If they did they were considered natural harlots. One of Britain's first 'sexperts', Edward Carpenter, expressed in 1896 a widely held Victorian view that for a lot of women sex could be no more than 'a real even though a willing sacrifice.'[32] Lord Curzon, instructing his wife about lovemaking, reputedly told her 'Ladies never move.'[33] However, many accounts suggest that western life in Peking was enlivened for both sexes by frequent extramarital encounters.

At the same time, foreigners in Peking were fascinated by the apparently dominating figure of the Empress Dowager in a country where women were despised and subject. Yet, in none of the participating countries, despite the commanding presence of Queen Victoria, did women have full democratic rights.[34] Even in 1905, former US president Grover Cleveland could write that 'sensible and responsible women do not want to vote. The relative positions to be assumed by man and woman in the working out of our civilization were assigned long ago by a higher intelligence than ours.'[35] It does not sound so different from the doctrine of Confucius, which had defined the subject status of Chinese women many centuries earlier.

To be frail was thought to be ladylike, and in many ways white women were yet one further addition to the white man's burden, particularly when their honour had to be protected from revolting hordes of lesser races. This was why women missionaries travelling into the interior of China roused both concern and antipathy in nonmissionary circles. There were lively debates in the press about whether women should even play sports. The Duchesse d'Uzes argued that 'all sports are hygienic up to the moment when they cause too much fatigue.'[36] Dr Max Nordau, a well-known Hungarian-born social critic and moralist, believed that 'in sports, even of the most masculine character, [woman] has other ambitions and other aspirations than man. The question of dress preoccupies her. She tries to please by her prowess. It is another form of coquetry, it is always coquetry.' Certainly, few women played a martial role in the defence of the legations, though one or two appeared on the barricades and the Chicago-born wife of the manager of the Hôtel de Pékin rode out to rescue Chinese converts.

Smoking was just as controversial. According to the British *Lady's Realm* of February 1900, female readers were four to one in favour of women's smoking but with certain caveats. 'It depends how it is done and where it is done, and a lady will never do it when it is likely to annoy or give offence . . . Learn how to do it before making an exhibition of yourself; don't make faces; don't inhale, and avoid cheap cigarettes.' Among the women's comments against smoking was this acid remark: 'I think her [the smoker] a most horrid, unfeminine creature . . . and I hope men will shun her as she deserves: there is nothing more likely to bring her to her senses.' As late as 1908 in New York City the Sullivan Ordinance forbade women to smoke in public. However, during the siege of the Peking legations many women smoked heavily and publicly, partly to relieve stress and partly to mask the stink of decomposing bodies.

By 1900, women were also taking advantage of new educational opportunities. Colleges and universities were offering women degree courses in all subjects. Women were also beginning to look seriously at supporting themselves, not just from economic necessity but because of the greater freedom it offered. Women's magazines were full of advice on how to seek employment. Some women were entering the professions. By the time of the Boxer troubles there were over two hundred women doctors in Britain compared with only twenty-five in 1880. Five female doctors were among the besieged in Peking but all agreed without demur to serve as nurses under the male doctors.

This, then, was the world of the foreigners unlucky enough to find themselves in northern China in 1900. The events they experienced drove many to put pen to paper. Their vivid, at times passionate, accounts describe an extraordinary set of events that still resonate. George Lynch, an Irish journalist covering the Boxer rising for the British *Daily Express*, wrote: 'The actual truth has never been written about any war, and this will be no exception.'[37] He was right, but the fascinating and very human experience of the Boxer rising comes unerringly through.

I

The Poison in the Well

China on the Eve of the
Boxer Rebellion

1
A THOUSAND DEATHS

To have friends coming to one from distant parts –
is not this a great pleasure? – Confucius

I do not wonder that the Chinese hate the foreigner. The
foreigner is frequently severe and exacting in this Empire
which is not his own. He often treats the Chinese as though
they were dogs and had no rights whatever – no wonder
that they growl and sometimes bite. – Sarah Pike Conger

TURN-OF-THE-CENTURY Peking (Beijing) was the world's filthiest
city – or so foreigners thought. Their letters and diaries rail
about 'the worst smells imaginable,' 'the sickening odour,'
'dusty and malodorous streets' and 'dirt, piled in mountains of
dust in the summer, spread in oozing quagmires of mud after the
rains.' They complained it was 'impossible to avoid the foul
sights and smells' that made Peking 'superlatively disgusting
even for China' and that 'the European eye may perhaps become
more or less callous after years of education but the European
nose never.' They deplored 'an infragrant population ignorant of
the most elementary laws of sanitation, cleanliness, or decency,'

content to collect their sewage in great holes at the sides of the unlit streets into which at least one unwary foreigner had tumbled and drowned. The city was nicknamed *Pékin-les-Odeurs*.[1]

Yet many also wrote lyrically of a unique city that was the most fascinating in the East. Bertram Lenox Simpson, a twenty-two-year-old Briton employed by the Imperial Customs Service, was captivated by this 'capital of capitals' with its 'unending lines of camels plodding slowly in from the Western deserts laden with all manner of merchandise . . . curious palanquins slung between two mules and escorted by sword-armed men; a Mongol market with bare-pated and long-coated Mongols hawking venison; . . . comely Soochow harlots with reeking native scents rising from their hair; . . . water-carriers and barbers from sturdy Shantung; cooks from epicurean Canton; bankers from Shansi – the whole empire of China sending its best to its old-world barbaric capital.'[2] Even the fastidious Lord Curzon, despite complaining of Peking's 'myriad and assorted effluvia,' thought it a fabulous Babylon 'without parallel in the modern world.'[3]

Peking assaulted all the senses with its din and dust, filth and foulness, wonder and awe. Yet to foreign visitors and the five hundred or so diplomats, customs officials, academics and missionaries who lived there, it was above all a place of 'venerable and measureless bewilderment.'[4] They were just a tiny drop in the exotic ocean of humanity. Peking's population was nearly a million, and it was the heart of an empire of over 300 million souls. In 1900, *Whitaker's Almanack* quoted a total of 10,855 foreign residents in the whole of China, including 4,362 Britons, 1,439 Americans, 933 French, 870 Germans and 852 Japanese.

Hampered by language, culture and internal rivalries, foreigners and Chinese found each other's behaviour and motivation hard to interpret. Deep mutual suspicion was the result. Like spectators at a play enacted in a strange language and with an unknown plot, the foreigners watched the mandarins, the agents of the Imperial Chinese government, go about their business. The mandarins were striking figures in their long silken or sable coats. Their official hats displayed jewelled buttons or the coveted peacock's feather to denote their rank. Ivory chopstick holders and jewelled enamelled watches hung from jade clasps at their waists. 'Nodding behind saucer-like spectacles,'[5] some travelled swiftly through the streets in green or blue sedan chairs – the greater the dignitary, the faster the chair carriers had to run. Others rode flanked by outriders in closed Peking carts – springless wooden vehicles drawn by soft-coated mules in purple harnesses. Imperial messengers clad in red and yellow picked their way through the refuse-strewn streets bearing dispatches to and from the provinces.

Women of the ruling house – the Manchus – walked with their servants. Juliet Bredon, the daughter of Lenox Simpson's current mistress, described how 'they gathered in groups like birds of bright plumage, to gossip at temple fairs. They paid their visits . . . in carts or chairs, and a pretty face or a brilliant headdress might frequently be glimpsed through the window of a passing vehicle.'[6] They wore long, straight gowns that fastened at the shoulder and were in delicate hues of pink and lavender. Their faces were heavily powdered and rouged, and their long, dark hair was worn twisted in a high knot or mounted on a satin board, decorated with jewels, flowers and fringes of pearls. Their feet were unbound, unlike the Chinese women whose feet were broken in infancy to produce the tiny 'golden lilies' that so aroused the Chinese male.[7]

The streets of Peking were raucous with the calls of hawkers – the shrill blare of a brass trumpet announced the knife-grinder or the barber while the pedicurist clacked wooden castanets. Curio dealers hawking carved jade snuff-bottles or porcelain bowls jostled with charm sellers, acrobats and 'story-tellers enchaining an open-mouthed crowd.'[8] Such scenes conjured 'the half-fabulous days of Kubla Khan'[9] in the mind of a young American socialite, Polly Condit Smith, staying with relatives in the US legation. Yet the picturesque often mingled with the grotesque. Juliet Bredon recalled that 'repulsive sights were common. Masseurs, butchers and chiropodists plied their trades in the open while passers by obligingly made a detour to leave them room. Barbers shaved their customers on any convenient doorstep. Lepers and lunatics wandered about unchecked displaying their nakedness and their wounds.'[10]

The complexity and beauty of Peking's architecture, shaped by waves of successive invaders, were undeniable. The walls of the ancient Chinese City were thirty feet high and over twenty feet thick. The walls of the Tartar or Inner City, which adjoined it to the north, were even more massive – over forty feet high, fifty feet broad at the top and about sixty feet thick at the base, with six great iron-studded gates in the outer wall and three in the southern wall. Lenox Simpson thought Peking both alien and beautiful with its 'vast and magnificent works . . . weather-beaten though they be; the fierce reds, the wonderful greens, the boldness and size of everything speak to us of an age which knew of mighty conquests of all Asia by invincible Mongol horsemen.'[11]

Those Mongol horsemen had been succeeded by the Chinese Ming dynasty. Nervous of the energetic nomadic tribes in the mountains and valleys beyond the Great Wall north of Peking, they prudently established their capital on the Yangtze, calling it 'Nanking' or the 'southern capital'. The third Ming emperor felt sufficiently confident to move his capital back to Peking, the 'northern capital'. However, in June 1644, after seventy years of harassing raids from Manchuria, the Chinese generals finally lost faith in the ruling house and invited their northeastern neighbours to take the dragon throne. The last Ming emperor hanged himself in shame and despair from a tree that still clings to life in his former pleasure gardens. The Manchus moved into the Inner City and took stock of their new possessions.

Within the Inner City lay the Imperial City, a complex of palaces, temples, public offices and pleasure gardens. At its heart was the fabled Purple or Forbidden City – 'the Great Within' – begun by the Ming emperor Yung Lo in the early fifteenth century. According to legend, he received the plans from a priest who had descended from heaven specifically for that purpose.

The city was an exquisite private world of painted ceremonial gateways, lofty halls supported by vermilion pillars, ethereal bridges of glistening white marble, graceful pavilions and shaded courtyards. When the sun shone, yellow-tiled roofs reflected the light, creating a golden aura. Precious objects – carved jade, pieces of cloisonné, rare and delicate porcelain – were arranged with the same exquisite and symbolic symmetry as the Forbidden City itself. The dragon motif was everywhere, denoting that here lived the Son of Heaven – the emperor.

The emperor was the only man allowed on pain of death to remain within the Forbidden City after nightfall. His sexual needs were gratified by concubines, chosen from the Manchu clans or from the Manchu's Mongol allies. Intermarriage between the Manchu and the Chinese was prohibited to preserve the purity of the ruling elite. He was tended by an army of eunuchs, 'semi-men' whose entire private parts had been cut off with one sweep of the knife. A man could choose to become a eunuch at any age. Some even married and had children before taking this radical step. Their severed genitalia – known as 'the precious' – were carefully preserved in a pot. This served a dual purpose. The pot's contents could be presented as evidence of emasculation, but, more important, the eunuchs believed that if they took them to their graves they would become whole men again in the next world.

Castration brought certain physical inconveniences – many could no longer control their urine flow after the operation, giving them always a sour, offensive smell. Yet once their wounds had healed the eunuchs could become cogs in the elaborate machinery of court ritual. Some, like the Empress Dowager's favourite, the grand eunuch Li Lien-ying, achieved immense power and wealth through bribery and graft. However, advancement depended on the emperor's whim – mistakes could be punished by savage flogging, even death. Nevertheless, the loss of their manhood was treated with sensitivity. Courtiers considered it the height of tactlessness to mention tailless dogs or teapots with missing spouts in a eunuch's presence.

Foreigners found the workings of the Great Within, with its oblique pronouncements and innumerable opaque rituals, impenetrable. Dr Arthur Smith, an American missionary acknowledged as one of the greatest authorities on China and the Chinese then living, described the court as 'marsupial'. The struggles and strife within the pink-hued walls were as effectually concealed from the world 'as the squabbles of the young kangaroos in the pouch of their mother.'[12]

Nevertheless, the foreigners gossiped avidly and speculated wildly about what went on in palaces 'full of warm-blooded Manchu concubines [and] sleek eunuchs . . . and . . . always hot with intrigue.'[13] The secret life of the Forbidden City was custom-made to feed the imagination and fantasizing was irresistible. In his *Decadence Mandchoue*, Edmund Backhouse, eccentric scholar, literary charlatan and closet pornographer, described a lurid but illusory affair with the elderly and formidable Empress Dowager. During one encounter he claimed that the grand eunuch anointed his 'secret parts' with sandalwood scent and instructed him in the Empress Dowager's sexual preferences, informing him that she had 'an abnormally large clitoris', which she enjoyed rubbing against her lovers' anuses. Backhouse, clad only in a thigh-length cloak, was then led to the Imperial presence. The empress's bedchamber was ablaze with lights and lined with mirrors and she called to him to join her on her phoenix couch with the lascivious order: 'My bed is cold . . . now exhibit to me your genitals for I know I shall love them.'[14]

The Chinese found the diplomatic district – the 'Legation Quarter', as it was then known – as closed and mysterious as the foreigners did the Forbidden City, with customs and morals just as suspect and salacious. The Empress Dowager was said to believe that foreign women, once married, took lovers as a matter of course, and that 'no one seems to think ill of the matter, least of all the husband. They even have signals for this sort of clandestine arrangement. When the lover comes in during the absence of the husband, he leaves his hat and cane in the hall. When the husband returns, and finds the hat and cane, he knows that the lover is with his wife – *and goes away again until the hat and cane shall have been removed!*'[15]

The Legation Quarter covered an area some three-quarters of a mile square within the Tartar City. It was bounded by the massive Tartar Wall to the south and by the walls of the Imperial City to the north. Within the quarter lay the high-walled compounds of the 'ministers' – the diplomatic representatives – of eleven nations: Britain, America, France, Germany, Spain, Japan, Russia, Italy, Austria, Belgium and Holland. The compounds were interspersed with princely mansions, the gilded premises of wealthy Chinese merchants and the plain, one-storey houses and shops of ordinary Chinese with their tiny courtyards full of plants and songbirds.

Along the shady, tree-lined boulevards like the aptly named Legation Street, running east-west through the quarter, were stores like Imbeck's and Kierulff's, the oldest foreign shops in Peking. They stocked the latest delicacies from Europe, including plenty of Monopole champagne, and were enthusiastically patronized by Manchu princes. There was a post office and that mainstay of expatriate life, a club. There were the Russo-Chinese and Hong Kong and Shanghai banks, the offices of Jardine Matheson, and the premises of the Imperial Maritime Customs. Visitors could stay in the comfortable Hôtel de Pékin, managed by Auguste Chamot, an enterprising thirty-three-year-old Swiss, and his Chicago-born wife, Annie. A noisome canal, fetid and green but euphemistically known as 'the Jade River', flowed south through the Legation Quarter, out through a sluice gate in the Tartar Wall, and into the moat beyond.

The British Legation compound, on the western side of the canal and covering just over three acres, was easily the most imposing. It enjoyed a reputation for 'a generous and uniform hospitality.'[16] The minister's house, once a ducal dwelling, was 'a beautiful Chinese building with an imposing entrance' approached by a raised pathway 'passing under two stately porticoes.'[17] Its roof was covered with the green tiles reserved exclusively for the residences of high-ranking officials. Other

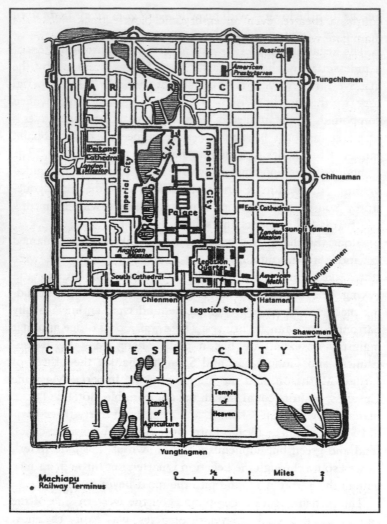

Peking in 1900.

legation staff, including the young student interpreters recruited
to the Consular Service, were housed in Chinese or European-
style buildings dotted about the compound. There was a chapel
and, for relaxation, stables, a tennis lawn, a bowling alley, fives

courts, a theatre, even an embryonic bicycle track. Near the main gate was also a handsome bell tower erected in honour of Queen Victoria's Jubilee. Mature trees pleasantly shaded the gardens and the whole complex had a look of comfortable permanence – rightly so, in fact, for the British had been there for nearly forty years.

The Western right to maintain a permanent diplomatic presence in Peking had been wrested from the Chinese after a bitter conflict in 1860. The war had concluded with the flight of the emperor and his court beyond the Great Wall, a punitive march on Peking by French and British troops, and the looting and burning of the exquisite Summer Palace under the direction of Lord Elgin. This was just one in the chain of mutually inglorious events that characterized China's relations with the West in the nineteenth century. The rot had begun with Britain's defeat of China in the Opium War of 1840 to 1842 and the ceding to her of Hong Kong Island. Foreign powers, greedy for cargoes of tea, silk and the rhubarb that the Chinese believed was essential to cure the foreigners' chronic constipation, had forced China to open her doors to trade. Initially at least these goods were purchased with money from the sale of 'foreign mud' – opium. As China's weakness became more apparent, she was coerced into making further territorial concessions. Shanghai, strategically placed at the mouth of the Yangtze, became a thriving international settlement, and the port of Tientsin, eighty miles from Peking at the mouth of the silted Peiho River, was opened to foreign trade.

As the century drew to a close, the Powers vied with one another for concessions in a kind of imperial feeding frenzy. One by one they wrested control over the satellite countries beyond China's borders. Nominally self-ruling, these countries acknowledged China as their effective overlord and sent tribute. She had already lost Burma to Britain in 1852. By 1885 the French, whose ambitions lay in southwest China, had secured a protectorate over both Tonkin and Annan (Vietnam) after a series of bloodthirsty encounters culminating in the destruction of almost the entire Chinese fleet.

The Japanese were becoming a particular threat. In 1878 they had intervened to prevent the king of the Loochoo Islands, between Japan and Formosa (Taiwan), from sending his customary tribute to the Middle Kingdom. The vigorous Japanese emperor Mutsuhito was particularly determined to end China's domination of Korea. The opportunity came in 1894 when a request from the Korean queen for help in suppressing a rebellion provided a pretext for both Japan and China to send troops into Korea. Finding the rebels already defeated, the two forces turned on one another and Japan emerged the easy victor. China was forced to sign the humiliating Treaty of Shimonoseki, which ended her control over Korea and compelled further territorial concessions to Japan, including that of Formosa and the opening up of four further river ports to foreign trade.

This disastrous defeat by the despised 'dwarf bandits' – as the Chinese contemptuously called the Japanese – sent shock waves throughout China. It also exposed her weakness for all the world to see. Arthur Smith wrote: 'China was shown to be a hollow sham, a painted gun on a wooden background, a giant manacled by a race of "pygmy dwarfs".'[18] Her unpaid, ill-fed, ill-armed, ill-drilled and badly led troops had simply fled at the sight of the enemy. Only three-fifths of the Chinese troops even had rifles – the remainder had to rely on pikes, swords and spears. China's defeat signalled something more fundamental than mere inadequacies in equipment. As Arthur Smith correctly observed, 'The necessity of making the appeal to arms was to the Chinese in many ways distasteful. They did not wish to fight, but merely to be let alone.'[19]

However, this was not an option. China's defeat by Japan prompted what Lord Salisbury disdainfully described as the 'Battle of Concessions'. Germany won concessions in Shantung, Russia demanded Port Arthur and the French, Kwangchouwan. The British, not to be left out despite their scruples, pressed for Weihaiwei and also secured a ninety-nine-year lease on a further part of the Chinese mainland opposite Hong Kong.[20] Sir Claude MacDonald, the British minister in Peking, described the whole episode as a 'general, and not very edifying, scramble'.[21] Many believed the partition of China to be only a matter of time. In March 1899 *The Times*'s correspondent in Peking, a thirty-seven-year-old Australian doctor called George Morrison, wrote to his foreign editor in London that it was coming nearer every day. Good imperialist that he was, he argued that Britain must stake her claim.

Many Britons agreed with him. They believed that China, with her enormous mineral resources and huge population, was more important to Britain commercially than India. Colonel Francis Younghusband, who later famously led a British military intervention in Tibet, wrote to *The Times* that 'the earth is too small, the portion of it they occupy is too big and rich, and the intercourse of nations is now too intimate, to permit the Chinese keeping China to themselves.'[22] Britain was particularly well placed to expand her influence if she so wished. In 1900, there were 672 foreign companies in China, of which more than half were British.[23]

The British government, however, was reluctant to take on yet further imperial commitments. This stance received a fillip when the American secretary of state John Hay issued his 'Open Door' note in September 1899 seeking equal trading rights for all within a sovereign China.[24] The Americans, or 'flowery flag devils' as some Chinese called them, had long been one of Britain's main rivals in the China trade. In 1784, the first American ship had arrived in China and by 1802 there was a thriving American 'factory' or trading station in Canton. One American merchant, William Hunter, amassed a mercantile fortune estimated in the 1830s as probably the largest in the world – a then staggering $25,000,000. As with the British, opium was a major early source of revenue. The Americans specialized in shipping Turkish opium to China, and in consequence the Chinese believed for many years that Turkey was part of the United States.

America's interest in China had, like Britain's, remained primarily commercial. She wanted trading opportunities rather than territory and by the late nineteenth century was better placed than ever to pursue this. Her recent victory in the Spanish-American War had given her the Philippines, an operating base a mere 400 miles or so off the coast of China, while industrial production at home was increasing rapidly. However, John Hay knew that this promising market would be prejudiced if other foreign powers established mutually exclusive spheres of interest in China. Hay's call for China's territorial integrity to be preserved and for commercial equality was therefore prompted as much by economic self-interest as by the political desire not to see China carved up as Africa had so recently been by the Europeans. The British supported Hay's call for reasons of equal self-interest.

Yet to the watching Chinese the situation looked desperate. Her foremost statesman, Li Hung-chang,[25] called it 'an unprecedented situation in the history of more than three thousand years.'[26] An Imperial edict of 21 November 1899 bemoaned the 'tiger-like voracity' of the foreign powers.[27]

Some foreigners shared that perception and their consciences were pricked. Journalist George Lynch summed the position up nicely: 'In the Punishment of a Thousand Deaths the criminal is bound up, and thus absolutely helpless, slices are quietly cut off his arms, his legs and so on. Now, although China has committed no crime whatever against the West, the Punishment of a Thousand Deaths is being inflicted upon that unfortunate country. Great Britain takes a bit, because the Chinese will not take to the consumption of a poisonous drug out of which Englishmen make money. Then France takes a slice, then the German Emperor comes along and carves out a bit from the tenderest portion of the anatomy. . . after Japan has had its piece. Now Russia is taking the big, fleshy, flabby slab of Manchuria.'[28]

Faced by such threats, China could no longer seek to remain aloof, 'wrapped in the mantle of a superb and paralyzing conceit,'[29] as Lord Curzon put it. But if the danger was clear, the solution was less so. In simple terms China appeared to have two choices – a process of modernization similar to that which had so recently transformed Japan or firm action to rid China of the 'foreign devils' and allow her to resume her isolationist path.

For a brief 100 days it had appeared that the choice would be reform. The twenty-seven-year-old emperor, Kuang Hsu, although quiet and shy, had developed an interest in foreign ideas as a stimulating escape from a life of relentless ritual. He had read the work of foreign missionaries like the Reverend Timothy Richard, which had been translated into Chinese, and Robert Mackenzie's influential book *The Nineteenth Century: A History*, which, thanks to Richard, had also been translated and become a major source of information about Europe. Prior to this, the West had been almost literally 'a closed book', with relatively few works translated into Chinese.

Kuang Hsu also began to listen to, and indeed to encourage the thinking of, a group of Chinese reforming scholars who had come into contact with foreigners in such places as Shanghai and Canton and had travelled abroad. They argued that China's only salvation lay in modernizing. He was particularly impressed by the ideas of Kang Yu-wei, a young man from Canton who had studied in Japan and written books about the West. Kang wrote to the emperor with the warning that 'China is confronted with the gravest danger in her history.'[30]

The emperor summoned Kang to an unprecedented two-and-a-half-hour audience. According to the scholar, who apparently knelt throughout the interview, the emperor complained that his conservative ministers were ruining China by their inaction. Kang agreed, arguing with passion that China's vulnerability to foreign aggressors resulted from her failure to embrace progress and that China would perish without radical change.

As Kang later told a journalist from the *China Mail*: 'I asked him to look at the difficulties Japan had to overcome before she could reform on modern lines. There the military or feudal party had more power than our present conservative Ministers, but the Mikado adopted the proper course by selecting young and intelligent men, junior officials, some of whom he set to work out the reforms in the country, while others went abroad to learn foreign methods, and returned to make Japan the powerful country which it is today. I repeated to him what Peter the Great did to make Russia powerful, saying, "You, the Emperor, I would ask you to remove yourself from the seclusion in which you live. Come boldly forwards."'

Kuang Hsu came forwards, embarking on a feverish programme of political and social reform aimed at revolutionizing China's administrative, financial, educational, military and industrial systems. There was to be a free press and a university at Peking, while the age-old examination system, which selected the imperial bureaucrats at the heart of Chinese government, was to be overhauled. He dismissed reactionary officials and threatened to sweep sinecures away. Between June and September 1898 he issued some forty decrees.

However, a strong conservative faction opposed the reformers. To some it was heresy to overthrow China's traditional laws and customs. Others felt personally threatened. A number even feared that the reform movement was being actively fostered by the foreign powers as a way of extending their control over China. The sheer speed of the changes alarmed many more moderate people who might have been attracted to them in theory.

Kuang Hsu's aunt – the aging Empress Dowager Tzu Hsi, who had twice been regent – had been watching events. Arthur Smith wrote of her: 'There is probably no human being now alive in regard to whom so much has been written upon such a slender basis of actual knowledge.'[31] Nevertheless, ignorance did not prevent this shadowy and enigmatic figure from being compared with an international 'rogues' gallery' of queens from the psychotic Empress Wu who ruled during China's Tang dynasty to Catherine de Medici and even 'Jezebel of Samaria, who slaughtered the prophets of the Lord and rioted with the priests of Baal.'[32]

Reginald Johnston, tutor to the last emperor of China, Pu Yi, described her as a kind of 'Queen of Wonderland' able to indulge her bloodthirsty caprices. 'When the "Venerable Buddha" [Tzu Hsi] said "Off with his head" there was no Alice to retort "Stuff and nonsense."'[33] Her powers of skilful procrastination and ability to play off competing factions make her perhaps closer to Elizabeth I of England as one of history's survivors. However, it was Queen Victoria whom she admired. Victoria's portrait hung in her apartments and Tzu Hsi was apparently intrigued by her relationship with her Scottish ghillie, John Brown, wanting to know whether he was 'cut off from the family,'[34] that is, a eunuch. Indeed, her fascination with Victoria was so strong that the first time she emerged from behind a gauze screen to allow herself to be seen by a foreign male was to greet Prince Heinrich of Prussia. He received this unprecedented honour purely because he was the British queen's grandson and Tzu Hsi wanted to take a close look at him.

Born in 1835, the Empress Dowager began life as the daughter of a minor Manchu official. By the age of sixteen her striking, piquant beauty had caught the appreciative eye of Emperor Hsien Feng. Selected as an Imperial concubine (third class), she rose quickly through the ranks by virtue of her looks, vivacious personality and a piece of good luck – she was the first of Hsien Feng's concubines to provide him with a male heir. Her reward was promotion to concubine of the first rank, making her second in status only to the empress.

Courageous, opinionated and genuinely gifted as a student of court politics, she developed a taste for power and a talent for retaining it, becoming one of the emperor's closest confidantes and a trusted consultant on affairs of state. A natural conservative with scant knowledge of the Western world, she had an overriding concern to protect her own position, and she never hesitated to act with ruthless opportunism when she felt under threat. She had a great love of the theatre and could herself assume different characters to suit the occasion. Many accounts describe her ability to manipulate people and she was no doubt speaking the truth when she told her lady-in-waiting: 'I can make people hate me worse than poison, and can also make them love me. I have the power.'[35]

This was certainly to prove true of the foreign community. One foreign admirer called her '*le seul homme de la Chine*' – 'the only man in China'[36] – and another described how she 'dominates everything and everybody in the Palace.'[37]

When Tzu Hsi's husband, the emperor Hsien Feng, died in 1861 she assumed the regency until her son Tung Chih – a libertine of dramatic sexual appetites – was enthroned in 1873. When Tung Chih died two years later, Tzu Hsi was instrumental in the selection of her own infant nephew, Kuang Hsu, as his successor. She was thus able to reign again until 1889, when, at the age of seventeen, Kuang Hsu came of age.

Tzu Hsi's reputation for political ambition also became inextricably intertwined with a reputation for sexual depravity and cruelty. There were persistent rumours among the foreign community that false eunuchs were smuggled into the palace to pleasure her and then promptly murdered. It was also rumoured that Tzu Hsi had personally supervised the debauching of Tung Chih. When he died of smallpox it was whispered that he had caught the disease from an infected face cloth sent to him at her behest and that she had then ordered his pregnant wife, the empress A-lu-te, to be murdered. Many believed that she had poisoned her rival, the co-Empress Dowager Tzu An, in 1881. Although there is no reliable evidence that she actually committed all, or indeed any, of these unnatural crimes, the stories gave a sinister, mysterious aura to Tzu Hsi and the Imperial Court.

At first the Empress Dowager appeared to acquiesce in her nephew's reform programme, but she was prudently biding her time and as usual weighing the balance of power. Once Kuang Hsu's reforms began to touch such sensitive areas as the abolition of sinecures, her instinctive conservatism was triggered. Kuang Hsu suspected, probably correctly, that she intended to move against him and made frantic plans to have Tzu Hsi imprisoned. However, his chosen agent, the shrewd and unscrupulous general Yuan Shih-kai, betrayed the plot. The Empress Dowager acted quickly. Eunuchs burst into the emperor's room and he was imprisoned on an island known as the Ocean Terrace in a lake by the west wall of the Forbidden City, a broken man. His brief bid to exercise real power, independent of his formidable, indeed intimidating, aunt, was over. Tzu Hsi regathered the reins of power, and arrests, executions and dismissals followed while many reformers fled – Kang Yu-wei escaping to Japan on board a British steamer.[38]

An Imperial proclamation stated that 'the emperor being ill, the empress dowager has resumed the regency.'[39] The reference to illness suggested only one thing to the foreign community – that Tzu Hsi had decided to dispense with Kuang Hsu and was politely 'notifying the world of his probable death at an early date.'[40] There even were rumours that Kuang Hsu had already been executed. Sir Claude MacDonald warned the Chinese that the foreign powers would view the emperor's execution 'with extreme disfavour.'[41] As a result of this foreign pressure, a French doctor was allowed to visit Kuang Hsu to confirm he was still alive. Although the visit may have saved his life, such interference in China's internal affairs with its consequent loss of face caused considerable anger. There were antiforeign riots around the Legation Quarter and the situation became so serious that the diplomats summoned to Peking marine guards from the foreign fleets lying off the North China coast for a period to defend the foreign community. This was the first time foreign troops had marched into the capital in peacetime and it caused further terrible offence.

To defuse the situation, Tzu Hsi invited some of the diplomatic ladies to call on her in December 1898 – an unprecedented honour. The guests were entranced by the exquisite embroideries, rich satins, silks and jewelled headdresses of the royal ladies. Sir Claude's wife thought the empress rather charming, genial and kindly, and that 'she might in another part of the world pass for an Italian peasant.'[42] The admiration was not mutual. The Empress Dowager thought the foreign women's feet very large, their shoes 'like boats',[43] and their faces hairy. She found the blue-eyed specimens among them particularly offensive. They reminded her of cats, which she loathed.

Meanwhile, with the emperor Kuang Hsu relegated to a twilight existence, the Empress Dowager was busily revoking his reform decrees. Then, in the spring of 1899, China had an unexpected diplomatic triumph. With no legitimate claim on the territory, Italy demanded Sanmen Bay as a naval station. China refused to yield and the Italians backed down. Arthur Smith believed, paradoxically, that 'the results to China were, perhaps, more serious than if the demand had been acceded to.'[44] Tzu Hsi began to believe that the foreigners might be resisted, even got rid of, and that China could 'revert to its old life again and do away with foreign intercourse, interference and intrusion.'[45] The problem was how.

2
BOXERS AND DEVILS

Support the Ching, destroy the foreigner. – Boxer slogan, 1900

A POSSIBLE ALLY had appeared on the scene in the form of an obscure peasant movement spreading across northern China like wildfire. Its members shared the same potent and explosive creed – they were virulently anti-Christian, antimissionary and antiforeign. Westerners called them simply 'Boxers' because of the physical exercises they practised en masse. But their origins were as complex as their rituals.

They first appeared in the northern province of Shantung. Calling themselves the I Ho Tuan, or Boxers United in Righteousness, they believed not only that they could make themselves invulnerable, but also that they could summon up thousands of spirit soldiers to their aid. Heirs to a long tradition of sects and societies in northern China, they fused religion, theatre, magic and martial arts in their rituals.

They were particularly influenced by two earlier groups that also had roots in Shantung. The first of these, the Big Sword Society, was essentially a vigilante group. It became prominent in southwestern Shantung in early 1895 in response to banditry and anarchy in the aftermath of the Sino-Japanese War, which had left China in a weakened state, unable to garrison her provinces adequately. The Big Swords filled the vacuum, protecting lives and property. They were convinced that a combination of deep-breathing exercises, magical formulas and the swallowing of charms made their bodies invulnerable to bullets, as if they were protected by a golden bell. They guarded their rituals of invulnerability jealously.

The other sect, which also emerged in the troubled mid-1890s, was the Spirit Boxers of northwestern Shantung. Unlike the Big Swords, who were principally landlords, farmers and peasants with property to defend and close links with the authorities, the Spirit Boxers were the ordinary people of the countryside, impoverished, with little or nothing to lose. They too practised martial arts and used spells and charms, but, unlike the Big Swords, they set up public boxing grounds and exercised openly in the villages. Their rituals, which were initially concerned with healing, were simple and deeply rooted in the popular culture. Their most striking feature was mass spirit possession. The Spirit Boxers would call on their gods to possess them, going into a trance that became a frenzy as the god entered. This mass spirit possession was their most important legacy to the charismatic sect the Westerners would know and fear as the Boxers and who were their direct inheritors.

The Boxer movement spread with extraordinary rapidity – a Chinese chronicler likened it to a whirlwind – despite its lack of an overall leader or organizational structure. It was in essence a loose coalition, spreading organically from village to village using the traditional grapevines of rural life. Like the Spirit Boxers, these new Boxers seemed to offer a lifeline to the poor and destitute of the countryside. They set up boxing grounds, often in temple precincts, where they drilled and these became the movement's focal points. Young men flocked 'to watch the excitement,'[1] as one of them described it, and stayed, mesmerized by the drama of mass ritual. The Boxers would call on a god to come down and possess them and then fall into a trance, whirling and dancing with their weapons in their hands, daring members of the crowd to attack them. The promise of invulnerability offered by these rites must have been irresistible, particularly to those who felt they had little power over their daily lives.

The Boxer ceremonies were also compelling because they were so closely intertwined with Chinese popular culture. The gods the Boxers called on to possess them were well known from the colourful and dramatic operas performed at temple fairs and village celebrations. These operas were frequently based on stories where heavenly beings transcended earthly boundaries. Deities such as 'Monkey', 'Sandy' and 'Pigsy' entered the mortal world to rescue the people from misery and subjection through a dazzling display of heroism and supernatural powers. When a Boxer invoked a particular god, he would take on its characteristics. If he had called on Pigsy, he would begin rooting about. If he had called down the God of War, he would strut and snarl in a suitably martial way.

People were captivated by the sheer glamour and drama of it all. Sometimes Boxers were injured during these wild displays but this did nothing to dispel public enthusiasm for the movement or belief in their powers. A Chinese magistrate later wrote, in despair at people's credulity, that the Boxers 'claimed swords could not injure or bullets penetrate. In practice, some got broken arms, others wounds in their chests. But it was claimed that these people's techniques were imperfect, and they continued to practise.'[2]

Herbert Hoover described the Boxers as 'one of those emotional movements not unusual in Asia,' He was right – the movement's meteoric rise was above all a heartfelt response to desperate and worsening conditions in northern China and an increasing sense of impotence. Shantung was a natural springboard for the Boxers. This already desperately poor, overpopulated province – the birthplace of Confucius – had been hard hit economically by the increasing tide of foreign goods flooding into China, particularly foreign textiles. New foreign technology was also wreaking havoc. The steamboats and steam launches, plying busily up China's rivers and canals, had put thousands of bargemen out of work, just as, in other provinces of northern China, railways were destroying the livelihood of camel-men, mule-drivers, chair bearers and innkeepers.

Shantung had also been wracked by successive floods and droughts. In 1898 the great Yellow River, 'China's Sorrow', overflowed its banks, flooding 2,500 square miles of country and destroying 1,500 villages. Plagues of locusts and bitter drought followed. Such economic and natural disasters made the province a fertile recruiting ground for the Boxers, who blamed foreign interference and the Christian converts for alienating China's traditional gods and causing them to punish the land and its people.

A further catalyst was the delicate political situation in Shantung. On the night of All Saints' Day 1897, two German Catholic missionaries from the aggressive and uncompromising Society of the Divine Word had been murdered by a small armed band. Seizing his opportunity, the kaiser had promised that hundreds of thousands of Chinese would 'feel the iron fist of Germany heavy on their necks.' He demanded and won Kiaochow Bay on the Shantung peninsula as a naval base, sparking the rush for concessions referred to earlier. He also demanded further concessions to the missionaries, including the construction of churches and cathedrals with Chinese government funds. At German insistence, the inscription above their doors read 'Catholic church constructed by imperial order.'

The kaiser's action understandably reinforced Chinese fears that the missionaries – or the 'primary devils' as they called them – were in political cahoots with their governments, which were using them as a pretext for intervention. It was little coincidence therefore that the first systematic persecution of Christian converts – the 'secondary devils' – by the Boxers broke out in Shantung. Boxers would send yellow cards to Christian households 'inviting' them to a meeting. The purpose of these meetings was to force them to recant and pay protection money. If they refused or could not find the money, their possessions were auctioned off and they were driven from their village.

Anti-Christian violence was nothing new. The peace settlement of 1860 had given foreign missionaries the freedom to rove deep into the Chinese interior in pursuit of converts. The 1860s and 1870s had witnessed violent riots in consequence. In 1870 a large-scale massacre took place in Tientsin as a result of rumours that the French Catholic Sisters of Charity, who ran an orphanage there, were cutting out children's hearts and eyes to make medicine. The flashpoint came when several Chinese children died of illness in the orphanage. A frenzied mob broke in and raped sixteen nuns, gouged out their eyes, sliced off their breasts and chopped up their bodies before throwing them into the flames of their mission. In 1891 terrible riots in the Yangtze Valley left a number of foreigners dead. In 1896 the brave and usually phlegmatic British lone traveller Isabella Bird was attacked in the city of Liang-shan by crowds who surrounded her with cries of 'foreign devil' and 'child eater' and nearly burned her to death. 'No one who has heard the howling of an angry Chinese mob can ever forget it,'[3] she wrote. She was lucky to live to remember it.

Now, however, in the worsening conditions, with large numbers of hungry, dispossessed and desperate refugees on the move, old grievances resurfaced with a frightening intensity. An American, Dr Robert Coltman, professor of surgery at the Imperial University in Peking and correspondent for the *Chicago Record*, understood why missionary activity was arousing such passion: 'For years it has been the practice of the priests and of many of the Protestant missionaries to assist their converts in lawsuits against the heathens, and to exert an unjust influence on their behalf. To "get even" with an enemy it is only necessary for a convert to tell his priest or pastor that he has been persecuted in some way for his religious belief, to induce the missionary to take up the cudgel in his defence. I have heard heathen Chinese often assert that these men [converts] appear good enough to their priests, who see very little of their ordinary behaviour, but behind the father's back they are overbearing and malicious to all their neighbours, who hate them because they fear them.'[4]

By the late 1890s, it appeared to the ordinary Chinese that the situation was getting out of hand. The Christian converts were becoming not only more numerous but also more demanding – in a famous case one Christian agricultural worker even forced his non-Christian employer to serve him a feast. The Empress Dowager Tzu Hsi certainly believed this and resented it: 'These Chinese Christians are the worst people in China. They rob the poor country people of their land and property, and the missionaries, of course, always protect them, in order to get a share themselves.'[5]

There were other factors as well. Their new religion debarred Chinese converts from participating in the ceremonies and festivals of their villages; neither did they share the costs. They were forbidden to practise ancestor worship, so fundamental and integral to Chinese life. This meant that the close-knit social fabric of town and village life was falling apart. As even a reforming Chinese scholar, writing under the pseudonym 'Wen Ching', put it: 'As soon as a man becomes a Christian he really ceases to be a Chinaman.'[6] Ostracized by their own communities, the converts became wholly dependent on the missions for their survival, working as servants and bearers. Many were from the poorest groups anyway and were disparagingly called 'rice Christians' in the belief that they had converted only to fill their stomachs.

Another source of grievance was that, since 1860, missionaries had had rights to build or rent premises. Some used this as an excuse to appropriate temples or halls or to build on sites where their high-spired churches collided with the geomantic beliefs of 'feng-shui' – an elaborate system bearing on the supposed effect on life and destiny of physical surroundings. This caused tremendous offence – Wen Ching likened it to the erecting of a stinking tannery next to Westminster Abbey.

If the Chinese had reason to detest the 'patronizing impudence'[7] of some of the missionaries, many foreigners also criticized their high-handed and insensitive behaviour. Lord Curzon castigated the 'irresponsible itinerants'[8] who roamed around rural China wearing Chinese dress and pushed in wheelbarrows, the conveyance of the Chinese masses. Some even adopted the Chinese pigtail or queue, impervious to the mirth of the Chinese and the disapproval of their fellow countrymen. Wilbur Chamberlin, an American journalist reporting for the New York paper the *Sun*, wrote scathingly that 'they braid their hair into pigtails, shaving the rest of the head like the Chinese, and they wear Chinese clothes. Maybe I'm wrong, but it seems to me that this is just a bit too far to go to save the heathen.'[9]

Their portmanteaus were stuffed with Bibles and most were implacably hostile to native religions and ethics. A. Henry Savage-Landor, another journalist, attended a lecture by a missionary whose opinion was that every Chinaman should be seized and given the choice of becoming a Christian or having his head cut off.[10] Savage-Landor would have sympathized with Tzu Hsi when she asked plaintively, 'Why don't these missionaries stay in their own country and be useful to their own people?'[11] However, by the end of the nineteenth century there were over 700,000 Catholic converts ministered to by more than 850 nuns and priests, mostly French. There were also about 85,000 Protestant Chinese under the earnest guidance of some 2,800 missionaries, mainly British and American, scattered far and wide across the country. Missionaries made up about a quarter of the foreign community and were the Westerners with whom the ordinary Chinese were most likely to come into contact.[12]

Against this background, Boxer propaganda – often a rehash of old stories – flourished, whipping up popular hysteria. Such propaganda projected people's anxiety about the present and fears for the future on to the foreigners and their Christian converts and demonized them both. The Christians' prayers were derided as 'the squeak of the celestial hog' and Christianity

was called 'the pig-goat religion'. Christ was shown as a cruci-
fied pig surrounded by fornicating worshippers. Stories
abounded about the vices practised and encouraged by missionaries – everything from mother–son incest to drug-crazed orgies
during religious services. Boxer pamphlets claimed that the
peculiar smell of Europeans came from drinking menstrual
blood and that missionaries used such blood, regularly daubing
it on their mission buildings, to keep Boxers at bay. A rumour
said that 'old women were sent out by the missionaries to put
dirty blood on the doors of some of the [Chinese] houses, and
that if it were not cleaned by the Boxers the inmates . . . would
all become fatally mad.'[13]

The Boxers also claimed that children taken into Christian
orphanages were mutilated and their hearts gouged out to
provide body parts for the medicines dispensed in the mission
stations. Stories spread of foreign ships seized off the coast of
China carrying grisly cargoes of human eyes, blood and female
nipples. Tzu Hsi apparently told one of her ladies-in-waiting
that she believed that Christian missionaries ate babies and
plucked out their eyes to make medicine. Some said that foreigners required human eyeballs – particularly children's eyes – for
their photographic work and stored them in jars. Such tales
amused Luella Miner. One day while singing hymns she 'could
hardly keep from shaking [with laughter] . . . because I had a
vision of a roomful of people with their eyeballs all rolling down
into their laps and around on the floor like marbles.'[14]

The fears and anxieties of the Chinese may have seemed
absurd to the foreigners, but such irrational and ill-founded
prejudice was also to be found in Europe at the time, leading
to violence there too. In 1900, the body of a German schoolboy was found dissected and bloodless in a Prussian town. This
prompted accusations that he had been murdered by Jews who,
it was believed, killed Christian children in the period before
Passover so that they could use their blood to make bread
during the festival. Jewish homes were attacked, the synagogue
was wrecked and the situation was brought under control only

when a battalion of infantry was drafted in. And just as rumours spread rapidly in China, winning instant credence, so too did they in Europe. For example, in Britain in 1908 reports that 66,000 trained German soldiers were living secretly in the heart of London ready to seize the capital caused such concern that the government was forced to deny the stories in Parliament.

One Boxer story to gain such ready and easy acceptance was that the foreigners were responsible for the weather. By late 1899 famine was gripping much of northern China because of the drought – some missionaries even claimed to have seen human flesh for sale in the markets. Starving people joined the Boxers because they at least had food, much of it looted from the Chinese Christians. They were also seduced by Boxer posters promising that 'when the foreigners are wiped out, rain will fall and visitations will disappear.' American missionary Charles Price wrote from his mission station in Shansi that 'clouds were constantly being driven away by fierce winds, which led to the story – thoroughly believed by all the people – that we went into our upper rooms and drove the clouds back by fanning with all our might.'[15]

Boxers claimed that the missionaries did their fanning in the nude and that they and their converts were simultaneously poisoning the wells. The water would rot the victim's intestines and the only cure was a 'divine prescription'[16] concocted out of dried black plums and licorice root, among other things. People wasted precious water by drawing it from the wells and pouring it on the roads 'under the impression that they were [thus] removing the poison.'[17] Mission stations were attacked, churches destroyed and native converts murdered in a frenzy of panic fuelled by rumours that were now falling 'like snow in winter.'

The Boxers attacked all manifestations of foreign influence. In particular they hated and feared the railways the foreigners had built and not just for the economic hardship they had brought the ordinary people. They believed that the 'iron centipedes' or 'fire carts' were desecrating the land and disturbing the graves of their ancestors. According to William Bainbridge, the second secretary at the American Legation, the Boxers said that 'the ponderous locomotives and rumbling trains pressed heavily the head of the Dragon and that his beneficent exhalations were smothered and no clouds could form in the heavens.'[18]

Boxers believed that railway engineers too practised gruesome rites. An incredulous George Morrison received a letter from a missionary in Peking: 'Suppose you have heard of the kidnapping scare which has already lasted over a fortnight . . . Five thousand boys and five thousand girls are needed for immolation on the new railway! . . . Unfortunately it is we foreigners who are supposed to be at the bottom of this atrocious scheme, and all the odium falls on us . . . The railway is the cause of all this ado. The Chinese believe that no great work can be successfully executed without a human sacrifice in some form.'[19]

Telegraph lines were similarly feared. Wind moaning through the high telegraph poles sounded like spirits in torment. Rusty water dripping from the wire looked like the blood of the spirits of the air. Foreign-owned mines, dug deep in search of mineral wealth, were a worse violation, disturbing the beneficial spirits of the Chinese earth. Bloodthirsty manifestos now promised: 'When we have slaughtered them all, we shall tear up the railways, cut down the telegraphs, and then finish off by burning their steamboats.'[20]

As the movement gained strength, the Boxers' slogan had become 'Support the Ching [the Manchus], destroy the foreigner.' The Empress Dowager and the reactionary party at court – particularly the virulently antiforeign Prince Tuan and his brother, Duke Lan – noted this with interest. What might have become an anarchic movement of disaffected, dispossessed peasantry aimed squarely against the Manchu dynasty had found a more attractive target and allied itself with the throne.

The Empress Dowager, who was herself profoundly superstitious, listened intently to accounts of how the Boxers practised ritual exercises to induce their gods to possess them. Her passionate love of theatre made her as susceptible as any of her subjects to tales of how 'the devotee was seized with . . . spasms, catalepsy or epilepsy, and often passed into something resembling a state of trance or hypnotism . . . they seemed to be literally mad men, daring everything and fearing nothing . . . When the trance period had been passed through successfully, the worshipper was held to be quite invulnerable.'[21]

She was also intrigued by tales of the Boxers' female wing – the 'Red Lanterns' – whose name derived from the red lights they carried to help the Boxers burn down missionary buildings. These girls, mostly between twelve and eighteen years of age, also claimed strange magical powers, including the ability to fly. It was rumoured that 'the red lantern girls could pull down high-storeyed houses with thin cotton strings, and could set fire to the house simply by moving a fan.'[22] They were considered the equals of the male Boxers despite the Boxer belief that female impurities rendered Boxer spells useless.

On a more practical level, it did not escape Tzu Hsi that, unlike regular soldiers, the Boxers would not have to be paid. On balance she was inclined to look on them favourably. When the governor of Shantung, Yu Hsien, gave them his tacit blessing in late 1899 and punished officials who had sought to suppress them, she supported him. Although forced by foreign indignation to remove him from Shantung, she made him governor of Shansi, where he was to give full vent to his hatred of Christians.

On the last day of 1899, in Shantung, the Boxers claimed their first missionary victim. An Englishman, the Reverend Sidney Brooks, had been hastening back by wheelbarrow after spending Christmas with his sister to help defend his mission when 'about twelve miles from Ping Yin he was attacked by a band of about thirty armed ruffians who after struggling with him and wounding him on his head and arms with their swords bound him and led him away towards Ping Yin. It was an intensely cold day and snow was falling. In spite of this they took from him all his outer garments and led him about for some hours. He endeavoured to ransom himself with promises of large sums of silver but they were unwilling . . . It is said that by some means he managed to escape and fled in the direction of Ping Yin. He was quickly pursued by three horsemen who cut him down when only a mile from our little church at Ta Kuang Chuang and there by the roadside the last act in this terrible crime was committed. His head was taken from his body and both were thrown into a gully.'[23]

A strange and terrible conflict had begun.

3

THE APPROACHING HOUR

We cannot say we had no warning. – Sir Robert Hart

Their sins are numberless as the hairs of the head . . . The will of heaven is that . . . the foreign devils be decapitated.
– Boxer placard

NEWS OF SIDNEY BROOKS'S gruesome murder reached Peking on 2 January 1900. Just hours earlier the American minister Edwin Conger had written to his government warning them of a hardening in China's attitude towards foreigners. Conger, a bearded Civil War veteran, former congressman and friend of President McKinley, had arrived in Peking with his family in late 1898. However, he was facing those first perplexing months of 1900 alone. His wife, Sarah, a fervently devout Christian Scientist, was visiting friends in Iowa with their daughters.

The Congers were slightly dull, well-meaning, worthy, hospitable people who took their responsibilities seriously. When Mrs Conger was in Peking, Thursdays were her days 'at home'. She enjoyed filling her rooms with the 'medley of foreigners'[1] that came to drink tea and chat. Livelier company was to be found at the residence of Herbert Squiers, the athletic, strong-jawed American first secretary, an ex-cavalry officer, and his wife, Harriet, a granddaughter of John Jacob Astor. These stylish and well-connected New England 'blue noses' had excellent taste and an acquisitive streak to match. During their stay in China they amassed such an extensive collection of antique Chinese porcelain that when they eventually left Peking it filled several railway carriages. Several newspapers unsympathetically described it as 'loot'.

Conger and Squiers discussed the implications of Brooks's death and, further, of two disturbing documents that had lately come into their hands. The first was an Imperial decree ordering Chinese officials in the maritime and Yangtze provinces to be on their guard against 'foreign aggressors' and sanctioning them to declare war without reference to Peking. The second was the indignant and heartfelt complaint of November 1899 about the 'tiger-like' appetites of the foreign powers as they hustled one another to seize China's territories. Again it urged the mandarins to defend their homeland against the 'ruthless hands of the invader.'[2] Conger was uncertain how to react. The United States favoured an independent China open to free trade and thus had no wish to see her acquiesce supinely in her own dismemberment. On the other hand, the United States did not advocate an aggressive, xenophobic China. In the end Conger decided to alert Washington to the documents but, despite Brooks's murder, did not suggest that foreigners in China were in any danger.

Meanwhile, in the spacious British Legation, a five-minute walk away, Sir Claude MacDonald was also considering the turn of events. This tall, lean, loose-limbed Scot had been appointed minister in 1895. He was a professional soldier who had fought in Egypt, and his elevation to head the legation in Peking puzzled many. A young member of his staff, Meyrick Hewlett, believed that Sir Claude owed his good fortune to a quarrel with a senior officer in Egypt: 'He was got out of the way by being given a troublesome matter to settle up in the Cameroons. He reported on the result of his mission to Lord

Salisbury and had left the room and was walking away when [Lord Salisbury] sent for him. He was then bluntly told that he was wanted as Minister to Peking, the post having suddenly fallen vacant.[3] However, it was whispered jokingly around the legation that Sir Claude had been appointed minister to Peking only because he possessed irrefutable evidence that 'Lord Salisbury and Jack the Ripper are the same person'![4] Sir Claude could sometimes appear lugubrious and reserved, but, though perhaps not an intellectual powerhouse, he had considerable charm and remarkable patience and tact.

In the closing days of 1899, Sir Claude had complained to the Chinese government about the grave state of affairs in Shantung. Brooks's murder was proof that it was getting worse. However, as Dr Coltman stated, he took the news of the murder 'very coolly . . . intimating he [Brooks] should not have been travelling in the disturbed state of the country.'[5] Coltman was similarly unfeeling, reminiscing how Brooks had consulted him professionally the previous spring and was 'rather a weakling I imagine.'[6] Yet despite his irritation with missionaries who brought their misfortunes on themselves, MacDonald lodged a formal complaint with the Tsungli Yamen, the 'General Management Office' set up to handle contact with the foreign powers after the war of 1860.

In a society where outward show and ritual form were everything and official buildings were the epitome of grace and beauty, the Tsungli Yamen was the exception. It was 'a dirty, cheerless, barren building'[7] and Minister Conger thought it evidence of the contempt in which the Chinese held the foreigner. It was as inefficient as it was uncomfortable and the foreigners considered it 'the most cumbrous body that ever mismanaged the affairs of a nation.'[8] Clive Bigham, a young British diplomat, bemoaned the difficulties of negotiating with the Tsungli Yamen: 'One goes in a green chair or a blue cart, according to one's rank, with an escort of Chinese outriders . . . curvetting round on skittish Mongol ponies. After a clamorous ride through a filthy street the chair is dumped down in a mean and dirty courtyard.'[9]

Meetings were held in a dismal, draughty room with members of the Yamen flitting in and out and making desultory enquiries after the health of the foreigners. Bigham wrote that 'expectoration, sleep, and private gossip go on freely among the Chinese contingent.'[10] Diplomatic discussions were a disconcerting blend of 'childish folly, abysmal diplomacy, and naked truth,' and whatever the foreigners asked for was politely and obliquely blocked. If a British company wished to construct a railway 'from Peking to the North Pole,' it would be delicately suggested that the feelings of others not invited to participate might be hurt, or that 'the Patagonian Envoy would be angry.'

Responses such as this bore the hallmark of the head of the Tsungli Yamen, Prince Ching, a moderate, level-headed man in his early sixties with some understanding of Western diplomatic conventions. Well aware of the rivalries among the respective ministers, he responded to their requests in a manner that, while oblique and no doubt frustrating, at least acknowledged a degree of legitimacy in their requests and in their involvement in Chinese affairs. His task was being made increasingly difficult, however, by the churlish and mettlesome Prince Tuan and his brother, Duke Lan, who saw no need for such niceties.

These no doubt mutually unsatisfactory meetings constituted the only real channel of communication between the diplomats and the Chinese. As many foreigners noted in their diaries, no Chinaman, whether an official or a private person, would willingly frequent the house of a foreigner, let alone go to the legations. The 'stereotyped contempt'[11] of the mandarin masked a real dislike of, not to say disgust for, the manners and customs of the foreigner. 'They even say we smell unpleasant,'[12] wrote Bigham in evident astonishment.

However, on 4 January the Tsungli Yamen officials issued a suitably contrite decree that promised that Sidney Brooks's murderers would be captured and punished. On the surface this seemed satisfactory, but the diplomats had not grasped that although the Imperial Court was still observing its duty to protect foreigners, it would not necessarily suppress the Boxers.

A subsequent edict of 11 January therefore stunned the diplomatic community. In the name of the emperor it stated: 'Of late in all the Provinces brigandage has daily become more prevalent, and missionary cases have recurred with frequency. Most critics point to seditious societies as the cause . . . But reflection shows that societies are of different kinds. When worthless vagabonds form themselves into bands and sworn confederacies, and relying on their numbers create disturbances, the law can show absolutely no leniency to them. On the other hand, when peaceful and law-abiding people practise their skill in mechanical arts for the preservation of themselves and their families, or when they combine in village communities for the mutual protection of the rural population, this is in accord with the public-spirited principle . . . of "keeping watch and giving mutual help."' It went on: 'Some local authorities, when a case arises, do not observe this distinction, but listening to false and idle rumours regard all alike as seditious societies, and involve all in one indiscriminate slaughter . . . It means not that the people are disorderly but that the administration is bad.'[13]

Arthur Smith called this edict a 'bulwark and charter'[14] for the Boxers and it caused consternation. The German minister Baron von Ketteler, a handsome, blue-eyed ladykiller with an American heiress wife,[15] sent his interpreter to enquire what it meant. Dr Coltman wrote humorously to George Morrison: 'Von Ketteler said unto his trusty manservant . . . "Go thou . . . and confer with the Philistines and ask 'em what in hell their last Edict means."[16] The man duly returned and said: "Verily my chief they say that it only means the Doughty Empress wants to encourage societies for mutual protection and gymnastic exercise and no way intends to harm peaceable Germans."'

Coltman likewise lampooned MacDonald's reaction: 'Then Sir C. and those likeminded said unto each other we will just wait and see if they kill any more of our people and if they do we will get real mad and let 'em know it too. And the Yamen smiled into their capacious sleeves.'[17] Sir Claude did indeed take a relatively relaxed view of the edict. Instead of telegraphing

London, he sent a written dispatch to the Foreign Office, which would take six or seven weeks, rather than a few hours, to arrive. The gist of it was that although others were concerned, he did not intend to remonstrate with the Tsungli Yamen. Nevertheless, on 27 January he joined the American, French, German and Italian legations in sending an identical protest demanding the suppression of the Boxers. They received no reply for a month. The court was preoccupied with something more important than the complaints of foreigners – the Imperial succession. On 24 January, an Imperial decree had announced that the emperor was still suffering from ill health, living 'in constant dread of going wrong,'[18] and unable to beget a son. The decree quoted him as 'imploring' the Empress Dowager to select a 'good and worthy' heir apparent. Shortly afterwards, Pu Chun, the spoiled adolescent son of the obsessively antiforeign Prince Tuan, was chosen. It was an ominous sign.

Over the next few weeks, the foreign ministers made a flurry of demands to the Tsungli Yamen for strong measures against the Boxers. These were blandly received and broadly disregarded. Ministers sent telegrams to their governments in March suggesting that an international naval show of force might have a salutary effect. Britain, America and Italy sent a handful of warships to lie off the mud bar outside the Taku forts at the mouth of the Peiho River. The Germans, with what Sir Claude called their 'characteristic thoroughness',[19] sent a squadron to call at their port of Kiaochow. The Tsungli Yamen gave no sign of noticing any of these demonstrations.

On 16 April 1900, a more 'satisfactory edict' from the Empress Dowager persuaded Sir Claude that he was 'justified in expressing the opinion that the Central Government is at last beginning to give evidence of a genuine desire to suppress this anti-Christian organization.'[20] The British warships *Hermione* and *Brisk* were withdrawn from Taku and the foreign ministers breathed more easily. However, by early May the Imperial Court was debating whether to incorporate the Boxers into an official militia. The diplomats found it impossible to penetrate the labyrinthine intrigues of the Imperial Court. Unknown to themselves they had become trapped in a web of 'evasion and apology',[21] as William Bainbridge later called it.

Two factions were locking horns at court. A group of moderates was urging caution and conciliation. Against them were the reactionary conservatives who had dominated since the collapse of the reform movement in 1898 and who saw the Boxers as a useful tool for ridding China of hated foreign influence. Their figurehead was the violent-tempered Prince Tuan, who had led the purge of the reformers and was married to the Empress Dowager's niece. It had not helped matters that not a single member of the diplomatic corps had congratulated him on the selection of his son as heir apparent.

Prince Tuan's desires and prejudices chimed with the Empress Dowager's own leanings. The burning of her beloved Summer Palace in 1860 still rankled. She was also alive to the advantages of having all the country's ills blamed on 'foreign devils' rather than laid at the door of an inert and corrupt Manchu administration. However, she was too shrewd to be swayed by mere emotion and wishful thinking and listened to the more cautious voices of Li Hung-chang, Yuan Shih-kai (now the new governor of Shantung) and Jung Lu, commander of the Chinese forces in and around Peking and, according to rumour, her childhood friend and former lover. For the moment, the moderates prevailed. Yuan Shih-kai even went so far as to denounce the Boxers as a predatory and heretical sect.

The diplomatic community relaxed and went back to their usual pastime of keeping a jealous eye on one another's activities. An amused Lenox Simpson described how the German military attaché, 'a gentleman who wears bracelets, is somewhat effeminate, and plays vile tennis and worse billiards,' was resentful of Britain for raising a Chinese regiment in Weihaiwei under British officers to go 'chasing malcontents' in Shantung, which was regarded as Germany's preserve. He paints a jaundiced but probably accurate picture of the 'Legations bitterly disliking one another . . . squabbling and cantankerous, rather absurd and petty.' However, such bickering was dangerous – it distracted the diplomats from the coming storm, which would soon swamp them all.[22]

As it was, remarkably few real shadows fell over legation life in the early summer of 1900. There were balls and fancy-dress parties. A photograph shows a group of student interpreters, thin, clean-cut, cheerful young men, arrayed in a range of costumes from Mad Hatter to Gooseberry Fool. The little community vigorously pursued a round of amateur dramatics, picnics, dinners, receptions, pony-back paper chases and excursions to the Great Wall or the Ming Tombs. It was a pleasant life. In March young Walter Townsend of the British Consular Service had written delightedly in his diary about the establishment of a new golf club to which Herbert Squiers had donated a trophy cup. In May he was writing that the streets of Peking were beginning to smell a bit but that the legation was 'simply delightful' with fresh green trees and lilac and yellow China roses. Tennis, too, was now 'in full swing'.[23] Clive Bigham observed approvingly that it was perfectly possible to pass a summer in Peking 'and never leave the precincts of civilization.'

As the weather grew warmer, people discussed the rival merits of going to cottages and bungalows at Peitaho on the seashore and removing to the Western Hills to escape the 'long, damp, sizzling summer'. The British had just built a large and comfortable residence for their minister in the hills, while the Americans and Russians leased temples from Buddhist priests. Some of these were very beautiful, with pavilions scattered through acres of lush grounds and clear lakes filled with fish or brimming with lotus flowers. They converted with ease into airy and attractive summer homes that could be reached on pony- and donkey-back and offered a fine view of Peking. As Sarah Conger described it, 'The outlook towards the city is grand and stretches over a vast plain dotted with many cemetery groves and fertile fields.'[24]

The increasingly disturbing reports coming in from remote missions did little to dampen the mood. Yet the missionaries were the best sources of intelligence and, according to Clive Bigham, perhaps 'the only foreigners . . . really at all in touch with Chinese native feeling.'[25] They painted a frightening picture of escalating attacks on Christian converts and, as Luella Miner wrote, sounded a long unheeded note of warning. She herself was acute enough to see that the rising had become more than local and anti-Christian; it was now 'general and anti-foreign'.[26]

The missionaries had been sounding the alarm before the beginning of the year. By 1900 both Catholics and Protestants had penetrated deep into the interior of northern China. Often working in isolated missions far from Peking and Tientsin, they were indeed well placed to see the coming catastrophe. In distant Fenchofu, in the province of Shansi, Iowa-born Charles and Eva Price were wondering anxiously how they could protect themselves, their children and their converts in the event of trouble. So too were British Archibald Glover and his heavily pregnant wife, Flora, at their station in Luan, also in Shansi. For some, both Catholic and Protestant, these fears would prove only too well founded. For others, there would eventually be miraculous escapes. But for the present there was little people could do but wait, hope and pray that someone would pay attention to their concerns.

In early 1900 the British Methodist missionary Frederick Brown had been moved to write to the *New York Christian Advocate* that his district around Tientsin was being overrun with Boxers and that all the preachers were in grave danger. He believed that riot and bloodshed were all too likely. On 30 January, Charles Scott, the bishop of North China and chaplain to the British Legation, had cautioned, 'Things had never before been in quite such a dangerous state. The Boxers were openly preaching destruction to foreigners in the city.'[27] A few days earlier he had lunched with Edmund Backhouse and spoken of Brooks's murder 'as if it was only the prelude to other murders that are speedily to follow.'[28]

However, the diplomats failed to appreciate the true significance of these reports. Indeed, many were wary of the missionaries, holding them responsible for provoking unrest by their high-handed methods. They were also inclined to think they were crying wolf. A colleague of Luella Miner complained that 'the Ministers have not believed us who have gone in and out among the people . . . When our helpers were killed, they would say "Did you see them killed? We want facts not rumours."'[29] A British missionary lamented: 'We should like to see a more able man at the head of British affairs here.'[30]

Neither did the ministers see how the net was beginning to close around them in the capital. Thousands of Boxers were now spilling into the metropolitan province of Chihli from Shantung. Chihli was a natural focus, being one of the most heavily 'missionized' provinces in China with a Christian population of over 100,000, while its largest cities, Peking and Tientsin, both had sizeable foreign populations.

The 250 or so foreign missionaries in Peking were also becoming conscious of their vulnerability. Although less isolated than their colleagues in the countryside, they were scattered across the city, often at some distance from the Legation Quarter and each other, and were soft targets for the disaffected.

Bishop Favier, Catholic Vicar-Apostolic of Peking, took stock of the situation but was not reassured. This elderly but burly and strongly built Frenchman – 'a splendid specimen of the Church Militant'[31] with a genial open face and 'fine eyes full of energy,'[32] as one admiring French officer described him – had lived in China for many years and was a renowned China expert. He was worried because everything he saw and heard reminded him of the events preceding the dreadful massacre of French nuns in Tientsin thirty years earlier: 'The same placards, the same threats, the same warnings, the same blindness.'[33] His Chinese converts were warning him daily that they were all scheduled to be slaughtered.

The bishop was all too aware that his Catholics were dispersed between three main centres in the city. The Tung Tang or East Cathedral was situated on the east side of the Imperial City. The Nan Tang or South Cathedral was just inside the southwest gate of the Tartar City. The large fortresslike Peitang or North Cathedral complex – church, dispensary, schools and orphanage, all ringed by houses of Chinese Catholic converts – lay within the Imperial City to the northwest. Bishop Favier tried to reassure his converts, his European priests and the nuns, such as the tiny Sister Vincenza from Naples, who was wondering how she would provide for the young Chinese orphans in her charge if trouble flared.

The Protestants were similarly dispersed across Peking. The American Presbyterians occupied a large site to the north. The American Board Mission lay in the east, while the American Episcopal Methodist Mission was in the southeast. The London Mission had two compounds – one in the east and the other in the west – while the Anglican Mission lay just north of the Nan Tang.

Nevertheless, the missionaries tried to remain calm and ensure 'business as usual'. Dr Lillie Saville of the London Mission turned out for 'the regulation tennis' despite the rising tension, mainly 'to help our Chinese Christians keep calm'. She had recently dispatched an order for strawberries to Luella Miner and her colleagues at the American Mission in Tungchow, 'who had made strawberry-growing quite an industry.' 'We each filled up the order-book for the whole summer,' she noted, 'but the thought in each one's mind was "shall we be able to stay here all the summer to receive them?"'[34] One of her colleagues believed 'the Empress Dowager is using the Boxers to further her own cruel ends, and the officials know it and will do nothing unless they are forced.'[35]

The man in charge of the Anglican Mission was the Reverend Roland Allen. It was a modest operation consisting of a church, the bishop's house, deaconesses' and clergy houses, and, in a separate compound, a hospital and some small houses for the converts. Dr Gilbert Reid lived just a stone's throw away with his wife and child. Originally a member of the American Presbyterian Mission, Reid was now devoting his time to 'trying to interest the higher classes of China in the science and religion of the West.'[36] The Reverend Allen worried that their little community was quite cut off from the legations and the other foreigners in the east of the city. The only direct route lay past the Chienmen, the great gate, which in times of civil disorder attracted huge crowds. If anything went wrong he knew they would be caught like rats in a trap. Missionary Mrs Courtenay Fenn wrote to her brother in late May that 'we live from moment to moment in constant dread of an outbreak – I try not to be nervous and go right on doing everything as usual to convince myself there is no special danger, but it can't be done. My ears have grown so preternaturally acute the last few days that I hear every unusual sound on the streets, and my heart stands still when a shout or anything unusual reaches me. It is an awful state to live in.'[37]

English-language newspapers had also been warning vociferously of the danger, their reports often based on letters from missionaries. On 14 February, an editorial in the *North China Herald* stated unequivocally: 'It is morally certain the opening spring will witness a rising such as foreigners in China have never seen before. The whole country from the Yellow River to the Great Wall will be a blaze of insurrection which . . . will drive every foreigner out of Pekin and Tientsin.' On 10 May, the 'native correspondent' of the *North China Daily News* insisted that dust was being thrown in the foreigners' eyes and that the Boxers stood in high favour at court and had received official sanction from the lips of the Empress Dowager herself. He warned that a scheme was afoot to crush the foreign devils and that 'all Chinese of the upper class know this, and those who count foreigners among their friends have warned them, but have to my own knowledge been rather laughed at for their pains than thanked for feeling anxiety on their Western friends' behalf.'

It was bad luck that George Morrison, correspondent for the London *Times* and the most respected and influential foreign commentator in Peking, was on leave during the bewildering early weeks of 1900. Handsome, athletic and incisively intelligent, he occupied a unique place in the foreign community. He had chosen not to live in the legation area, opting instead for 'a Chinese house, which I have converted into a European one. I am alone with my books on China, cut off by dirty streets from the rest of the foreign community.'[38] Here he contemplated the follies of his fellow foreigners and the vagaries of the Chinese Court and kept a peppery diary full of cynical asides. A harsh judge of character with a wide network of contacts in the foreign community, he chronicled remorselessly and in detail the weaknesses, affairs and diseases, particularly the sexually transmitted ones, of his fellow westerners.[39] He had not been initially impressed by Sir Claude MacDonald's appointment as minister, writing to a colleague at *The Times* in March 1899 that he had a poor view of MacDonald's judgement and firmness and that 'his chief defect was a weak memory.[40] Surely the F.O. now recognize their folly in selecting an ill-read, half educated infantry major, without brains, memory or judgement.'

Morrison prided himself on being truthful in his reporting, although, as he noted, *'Le vrai n'est pas toujours bon à dire'* – 'it is not always good to speak the truth.' Morrison liked to show off his French but he had not mastered Chinese and often relied for translation and intelligence on the unreliable Edmund Backhouse, whose patron he had become by early 1899. Backhouse was described by contemporaries as a man of independent means studying Chinese. These 'independent means' consisted of a modest allowance paid by his long-suffering family after he had become bankrupt. He shared a house with an eccentric Englishman called Peachey in a village outside Peking. Peachey had resigned from the Consular Service in February 1900 after admitting an affair with a married woman. Despite his foibles, Backhouse was a marvellous linguist. Morrison does not seem to have paid him for his services but Backhouse was no doubt flattered by his interest. In turn, Morrison was titillated by Backhouse's insights and gossip.

Morrison was determined to keep his finger on the pulse both of Chinese Court politics and the rivalries and intrigues among the foreigners and usually succeeded. Asked why *The Times*'s correspondent in Peking had been able to publish important information several days before the Foreign Office knew of it, Lord Curzon famously replied: 'I hesitate to say what the functions of the modern journalist may be; but I imagine they do not exclude the intelligent anticipation of events before they occur.'[41] The same should have been equally true of diplomats and politicians, as Curzon very well knew.

Morrison was well suited for the rigours to come. He had qualified as a doctor in Edinburgh after his earlier studies at Melbourne University ended abruptly when he recommended an excessive dose of medicine as a cure for syphilis in an exam. A self-confessed nomad, he had, at age twenty, walked 2,043 miles in 123 days, alone and unarmed, from the extreme north of Australia to Melbourne along the route that had defeated Burke and Wills a generation earlier. At twenty-one he led an expedition into the then largely unknown New Guinea. Wounded by native spears, he survived for nine months with a barbed spearhead in his body until a somewhat astonished professor in Edinburgh removed it. Morrison was appointed *Times* correspondent first in Indo-China and subsequently in Peking, where he arrived only after a journey during which he was attacked by brigands and caught a dose of bubonic plague.

He had already visited China in 1893 and 1894, sometimes in the garb of a missionary in Chinese dress with pigtail and slippers. While concealed in a London Mission chapel, he had been fortunate enough to see the emperor Kuang Hsu and his entourage pass by on their return from the Summer Palace – one of the very few occasions on which a foreigner had gazed on the Son of Heaven. During an epic journey through China, he witnessed horrific examples of famine and plague, infanticide and slavery. He wrote of girls 'carried like poultry in baskets to the capital'[42] to be sold as slaves. He recorded horrific punishments meted out to Chinese malefactors – a woman done to death in a cage for adultery who took three days to die and a murderer who had red-hot nails driven through his wrists.

Morrison's period of leave had deprived him of the opportunity to exercise his powers of 'intelligent anticipation'. On his return to Peking in April 1900 he 'found "Boxers" everywhere in evidence.' In his diary he noted two small but sinister details – knives had doubled in value and cutlers were doing a roaring trade. However, he confidently attributed the tension to the drought: 'If rains come, the Boxers will soon disappear.'[43] Morrison was hamstrung as much by his attitude as by his recent absence. He found it hard to credit that the Chinese could organize themselves to resist the foreigners, believing that 'there is not an ounce of patriotism in the whole lot of them.'

By late April, Boxer placards were being posted in the city exhorting the people to rise. Roland Allen saw one dated 29 April that declared: 'Disturbances are to be dreaded from the foreign devils; everywhere they are starting missions, erecting telegraphs and building railways; they do not believe in the sacred doctrine, and they speak evil of the gods. Their sins are numberless as the hairs of the head . . . The will of heaven is that the telegraph wires be first cut, then the railways torn up, and then shall the foreign devils be decapitated. In that day shall the hour of their calamities come.'

Even the normally cheerful and optimistic Sarah Conger, who had returned in April to be greeted by the crackle of fireworks and her servants all dressed in their best, confided in her diary: 'The Boxer work grows darker and darker. It comes nearer and nearer and is now within Peking.' By 1 May, Herbert Hoover thought the dangers so great that he recalled his geological expeditions from the interior. It was a frustrating thing to have to do since huge deposits of anthracite were being discovered, 'greater than all the other anthracite fields in the world put together.'[44] He and his wife, Lou, decided it was their duty to stay on in Tientsin through the coming trouble to protect their Chinese staff rather than leave China as they had the opportunity to do.

Bertram Lenox Simpson later claimed to have read the warning signals as May advanced, noting how the weather became closer and heavier. Some rain fell at last but it failed to have the tranquillizing effect predicted by so many. Hot acrid dust blown from the Gobi clotted the air. 'The Peking dust, distinguished among all the dusts of the earth for its blackness, its disagreeable insistence in sticking to one's clothes, one's hair, one's very eyebrows, until a grey-brown coating is visible to every eye . . . has become damnable beyond words, and there can be no health possibly in us. The Peking dust rises . . . in clouds and obscures the very sun at times,'[45] he wrote.

Meanwhile, Morrison's Chinese houseboy was regaling him with tales of how 8 million spirit soldiers would soon be descending from heaven to exterminate the foreigners. Such warnings did not distract him from some lurid preoccupations of his own. His diary of 14 May breaks off from a discussion of political events to speculate on the spread of syphilis among the foreign community and whether 'the syphilitic Simpson'[46] had yet infected his mistress, Lily Bredon.

However, the time for frivolous speculation ended as news of terrible Boxer atrocities came flooding in. In mid-May, reports reached the French Legation that some sixty Chinese Catholic men, women and children had been slaughtered at Kaolo, a village some ninety miles from Peking. The bodies had been thrown down a well and the whole village destroyed. Hard on the heels of the Kaolo massacre came news that Boxers had attacked a London Mission chapel only forty miles from Peking and killed the Chinese preacher. Sir Claude telegraphed London and called on the Tsungli Yamen to complain about official apathy. He was told the usual story that an edict had been issued the previous day ordering the suppression of the Boxers.

Yet the foreign ministers still seemed unmoved by the full gravity of the situation and it puzzled some of their contemporaries. The Reverend Allen attributed it to 'the callousness produced by long residence in a hostile country. Threats had been so often uttered without fulfilment . . . that it seemed impossible for them to understand that the present crisis was more dangerous than many other crises.'

*   *   *

Sir Robert Hart, the elderly inspector general of the Imperial
Maritime Customs of China, later wrote with hindsight: 'We
cannot say we had no warning.'[47] However, he too failed to read
the danger signs accurately, despite living for many years in
China. Born into a strict Wesleyan family in County Armagh in
Ireland in 1835, he entered the Customs Service in May 1859 to
begin an extraordinary career that was to bring him control over
a third of China's foreign revenue. He alone was responsible to
the Chinese government for collecting the maritime customs
dues on their behalf and for every aspect of the service, hiring,
rewarding and discharging all the staff, Chinese and foreign. It
earned him unprecedented honours from Tzu Hsi, who called
him 'Our Hart', as well as recognition from the British government. Sometimes he was criticized for being too pro-Chinese –
The Times wondered whether he was not too inclined to view
the world 'through Chinese spectacles'.[48] Equally, there were
those in China who wondered why such a powerful instrument
of control as the Customs Service should have been put in the
hands of a foreigner.

Hart learned Chinese by the time-honoured method of
acquiring a concubine – a young girl called Ayaou. She bore him
three children, Anna, Herbert and Arthur, whom he had
educated in England as his 'wards'. Ayaou died and in 1866
Hart married the daughter of his family doctor in Ulster, Hester
Jane Bredon. Lily Bredon was her sister-in-law. Ten years later
Hester returned to England with her children and their relationship, which remained amicable, continued by correspondence.

Hart was not averse to telling stories about the old times to
pretty and admiring young women such as Polly Condit Smith
and giving them photographs of himself with such great men as
General Gordon.[49] According to Morrison, Hart had a passion
for young girls, which he perhaps felt able to pursue in Hester's
absence. One of his other abiding interests was his band – 'I.G.'s
Own', made up of Chinese, Portuguese and Filipinos – which
gave weekly concerts in the gardens of the Customs compound
and was a famous feature of Peking's social life. It was rumoured

that musical members of the Customs Service enjoyed the swiftest advancement.

Hart admired the Chinese, whom he considered to be intelligent and cultivated. He also believed he knew them. He of all people was in a position to know what was happening. He had wider connections and greater insight and knowledge than the diplomats. He was far more influential than the missionaries. He knew that the Chinese themselves foresaw cataclysmic events. Nineteen hundred was a year in which the intercalary month – when an additional day must be added to harmonize the calendar with the solar year – fell in the eighth month, which to the Chinese always spelled misfortune. He also knew that the Boxers' professions of supernatural powers, which seemed so absurd to the foreigner, were being taken seriously in the Imperial Court. 'Though professing to know nothing beyond the domain of sense,' he wrote, 'the Chinaman is really an extravagant believer in the supernatural, and so he readily credits the Boxer with all the powers he claims.'[50] He later admitted that he and those others who believed the Boxer movement could become serious 'put off the time of action to September: our calculations were wrong.'[51] Certainly when the storm came it took him by surprise.

Bishop Favier was more clear-sighted. On 19 May, in a forcefully worded letter to the French Legation, he urged the French minister, Stephen Pichon, to send for troops. His language was unequivocal: 'I am well-informed and I do not speak idly. This religious persecution is only a façade; the ultimate aim is the extermination of all Europeans . . . The Boxers' accomplices await them in Peking; they mean to attack the churches first, then the legations. For us, in our Cathedral, the date of the attack has actually been fixed.' He asked for marines *pour protéger nos personnes et nos biens* – 'to protect our persons and our possessions.'[52]

His greatest worry was that nobody would listen.

4

RATS IN A TRAP

We fight by order of the Emperor and for the salvation of the Dynasty. – Boxer Proclamation

Thank God you've come. Now we're safe. – Edwin Conger

THE MINISTERS met the next day, 20 May, to discuss Bishop Favier's stark warning. It was an anxious debate. Did circumstances really justify swift, decisive action or would their respective governments suspect them of panicking? Sir Claude MacDonald was frankly sceptical about 'the gloomy anticipations of the French Father.'[1] Just a few days earlier he had told Morrison that he feared the priest was far from cool-headed and that his reports during the reform crisis of 1898 had been 'most sensational and unbalanced.' Morrison agreed, writing emphatically that 'we cannot feel this peril in the air.' Monsieur Pichon, described by Morrison in a dismissive cameo as plump, nervy, in his early forties and an associate of Clemenceau, was, however, worried. Events were 'simmering'[2] in a way that reminded him uncomfortably of the prelude to the Paris Commune. While prepared to concede that Favier was an alarmist, Pichon argued that this did not necessarily mean he was wrong in the present circumstances. However, after an acrimonious debate amply justifying Morrison's view that 'unanimity is not the predominant characteristic of the Diplomatic Body in Peking,'[3] the ministers agreed not to send to Tientsin for guards. Instead they decided to demand, once again, that the Chinese government should suppress the Boxers and to threaten to summon troops to Peking if no action were taken.

It was not. On 23 May, Morrison, writing in his diary in his surprisingly tiny spidery hand, recorded that the Boxers had 'the cognizance and approval of the Government, as shown by them drilling in the grounds of Imperial barracks and royal princes.' The next day he watched a display of Boxer gymnastics accompanied by William Pethick, a longtime American resident in China who, as Li Hung-chang's secretary, was one of *The Times* correspondent's more useful contacts. Morrison described how a Boxer 'pretends to receive a spirit from Heaven and in a trance slashes the air with sword and knife. [He is] impervious not only to the foreign bullet and the foreign sword, but the foreign poison . . . with which the foreigner is infecting the native wells.'

Meanwhile, Sir Claude and Lady MacDonald were preparing for one of the social events of the year – a party in honour of Queen Victoria's eighty-first (and, as it happened, final) birthday. As she went about her preparations, checking place cards at the dinner table, tweaking flower arrangements, Lady MacDonald had no thought that history might be about to repeat itself. She had already lost one husband and two children in the service of the empire. They had all died of cholera in a single day in India, but she had subsequently married Sir Claude and, now in her early forties, once again had two young children to care for.

The party was as elegant and lavish as the occasion demanded. With Sir Robert Hart on one arm and George Morrison on the other, Ethel MacDonald led a party of nearly sixty British guests into the small theatre, cleverly transformed into a dining room. After dinner they were joined by guests from the other legations. Together they danced to the music of Sir Robert Hart's band on the tennis courts in the soft glow of Chinese paper lamps suspended from the trees. Sir Robert watched with tranquil pleasure, pleased that his boys were playing 'really well' on such an important night. He and his fellow Britons received the congratulations of the other foreigners both on Queen Victoria's longevity and on the recent news of the relief by the British of the South African town of Mafeking after 217 days under siege by the Boers. The latter event brought a lump to Morrison's throat. The Australian was an imperialist par excellence. Kipling and Dr Jameson were his heroes and he was convinced it was Britain's destiny and duty to enlarge her empire. However, such lofty patriotic thoughts did not deter him from recording in his diary some further snide references to the sexual peccadilloes of his fellow guests that night, as they laughed and talked and sipped glasses of iced champagne 'flowing with what effervescence it could muster.'

There were some sombre undercurrents. A few guests were discussing the rise of this bizarre sect of Boxers and the possible complicity of the Imperial Court. However, Bertram Lenox Simpson, writing with the benefit of hindsight, castigated the 'blind Ministers Plenipotentiary and Envoys Extraordinary' for their relaxed attitude on that warm May evening: 'As yet, however, the Boxers are only laughed at and are not taken quite seriously. They have killed native Christians, it is true, and it has been proved conclusively now that it was they who murdered Brooks, the English missionary in Shantung. But Englishmen are cheap, since there is a glut in the home market, and their Government merely gets angry with them when they get into trouble and are killed. So many are always getting killed in China.' Lenox Simpson hinted like Morrison that only Monsieur Pichon showed signs of agitation, waving his 'fat hands' as he talked, and departing early.

The French minister was about to be proved right. Yet almost no one present would have believed that in less than a month it would be inviting death to venture on to the tennis court. However, the signs were there. Just as small chupatties travelled mysteriously across India on the eve of the Great Sepoy Mutiny of 1857, foretelling disaster, little black and red cards appeared that night in the servants' quarters, warning that those who served the foreign devils would be exterminated. The foreign devils, travelling sleepily back to their own residences in carts and sedan chairs as dawn streaked the sky, were not to be left in doubt much longer.

The next day Sarah Conger was writing nervously that 'there is much uneasiness among the foreigners; threatening words have come to us.' The atmosphere was becoming more menacing by the hour. Gardeners and washermen employed by foreigners were leaving their work and going into hiding. It was becoming unsafe for Chinese, Christian or not, to work for foreigners. At the same time, terrified Christian refugees were crowding into the city's Catholic cathedrals, some of them badly wounded and burned from vicious attacks by Boxers. On 28 May a horrified Morrison was visited by a man who hobbled, exhausted and almost overcome, into his house. He had escaped from Changsintien, the headquarters of the Belgian construction staff building the railway line intended to link Peking and Hankow but that now ran only as far as Paotingfu. He gasped out to Morrison that the railway lines were being torn up, telegraph lines severed and that the station at Fengtai, where the Peking–Tientsin and Peking–Paotingfu lines joined, was ablaze. He also said that a group of mostly Belgian engineers and their families were besieged in their compound at Changsintien.

This was the first concerted mass action against foreigners. It was also, as Luella Miner noted sombrely, the first overt act of the Boxers in her region. Only the day before she had been writing cheerfully in her diary of the mission's 'fine new church', but now things looked bleak. The men wrecking Fengtai station were mostly from her beloved Tungchow. The city's prosperity had depended on its role as entrepôt for the tribute rice brought by canal from the interior. Now hundreds of men had been thrown out of work by the coming of the railways.

Morrison also received disturbing reports from Chocow of terrorization and massacre, of Christians forced to abjure their faith and burn incense, and of 'the prettier female converts being sold into prostitution.' Rising to the occasion, both as journalist and as man of action, he galloped with two companions across the race course to Fengtai to see for himself. Black smoke was curling ominously into the sky as they approached, and it seemed to Morrison as if 'the whole countryside was afoot, streaming towards the station. The engine sheds were on fire . . . and the villagers from all around were shouting. We could do nothing, though we should have shot a Chinaman who threatened us with a sword and swore to cut our throats. It will always be a regret to me that I did not kill this man.'

Brushing such regrets aside, Morrison continued on alone. He had remembered that his friend Harriet Squiers, her young house guest and relation, Polly Condit Smith, and Harriet's three children, with their French and German governesses, had gone up into the Western Hills beyond Fengtai to escape the heat, smells and dust of the city. Herbert Squiers was prevented by his official duties at the American Legation from joining them more than twice a week. As luck would have it, he had left them on the morning of 27 May, prophesying that the Boxers' activities were nothing more than 'the usual spring riots which yearly seize Peking.'[4] At his request, the Tsungli Yamen had dispatched a guard of Chinese soldiers to the Squierses' mountain villa – a converted Taoist temple – as a precaution, but Polly was not impressed. They were '*such* soldiers! – opera-bouffe mannikins in a Broadway theatre would frighten one with their martial air compared to these ridiculous apologies for soldiers . . . their only weapons being dull-pointed rusty spears!'

The same day, Clara, the German governess, returned from a shopping expedition to Peking bearing tales of armed natives and companies of Chinese drilling in the temple enclosures. Harriet Squiers's forty servants (safety might be neglected but

comfort was seldom left to chance), most of whom were Chinese
Christians, told Harriet and Polly in alarm that 'these people are
all Boxers, most of them flaunting the red sash, [and] are preparing for a general uprising when the time shall be ripe – an uprising that has for its watchword, "Death and destruction to the
foreigner and all his works."'

Polly was a resourceful and sensible young woman whose
companions found her 'ever calm and always sociable.'⁵ A niece
of Chief Justice Field of the US Supreme Court, she had been
enjoying her travels in the Orient and was not given to hyster-
ics. However, the scene she was now witnessing went beyond the
exotic. From the ivy-covered terrace of their temple she and
Harriet watched smoke and flames rising from the burning
depot, locomotive shed and houses. The fire had even destroyed
the Empress Dowager's special railway coach, which, characteristically, she had never used. They heard the booms and crashes
as the Boxers blew up the foreign-built steel bridge over the
Peiho River. Yet they had no means of knowing what was
happening or what it meant and were unhappily conscious of
their vulnerability as a group of unarmed women and children.
Their 'highly picturesque' guard had run away as soon as the
trouble started at Fengtai and their position was critical. 'Not a
foreign man on the place to protect us; a quantity of badly
frightened servants to reassure; three children, their governesses
and ourselves, to make plans for. We did what women always
have to do – we waited.'

However, salvation was at hand in the buccaneering form of
Morrison. Polly, unaware that he had described her in his diary
in his usual forthright way as 'fat and gushing', watched his
arrival with relief: 'We saw down in the valley a dusty figure
ambling along on a dusty Chinese pony, coming from the direction of Fengtai and making direct for our temple.' Morrison
explained to the grateful women that he had realized that their
temple was directly on the rioters' route to Peking and that he
thought it highly likely that they would 'stop *chez nous*' before
marching to Peking. 'In case of such horrible eventuality he

hoped to defend us for a while, and to send to glory as many Chinese as possible before turning up his own toes!' Polly later wrote.

Morrison was considering how the temple might best be defended when an agitated Herbert Squiers arrived, accompanied by a Cossack lent to him by the Russian minister, de Giers. Alone of all the foreign powers and thanks to a treaty signed in 1689, Russia was allowed to keep a small permanent guard in Peking. Morrison, Squiers and the Cossack worked through the night with the help of the Chinese servants to fortify the temple against any attack or incendiaries during the hours of darkness and kept constant watch. Clothes and valuables were packed up ready for flight.

However, the night passed without incident and they were left unmolested. At 6.00 a.m. the party set out nervously for Peking. They and their dust were hardly inconspicuous – their procession of Chinese carts, ponies, mules and donkeys and the forty servants, grimly determined not to be left behind, could be seen for miles. Polly's description sounds like a journey through Red Indian country: 'The three protectors, heavily armed, rode by us, and three or four of the Chinese were armed also, and the carts held such a position in the caravan that in a moment they could be swung round as a defence in case of an attack.' Attack could have come from two sources – marauding groups of Boxers encouraged by the ease with which they had wrecked Fengtai or the Imperial troops from Kansu commanded by the Moslem General Tung Fu-hsiang, who were also in the vicinity and notorious for their hatred of foreigners.

The fifteen-mile journey took nearly five hours. It was nerve-jangling, plodding across country that seemed eerily deserted 'except for the long, lonely lines of coal-carrying dromedaries.' Polly was worried that the country people had gone to some rallying point and were, even now, preparing to attack them. At last, at 10.30 a.m., the odd caravan turned into Legation Street and in through the gates of the American compound, where, as Polly described, 'most painfully but thankfully we untwisted ourselves from the awful position we were forced to take in the cart, and joyously grasped the hands of friends.' These included William Pethick, who had been planning to use his influence as Li Hung-chang's aide to demand a regiment of Chinese soldiers to go and help them.

Meanwhile, the beleaguered Belgian engineers, cut off sixteen miles from Peking at Changsintien, had not been forgotten. Auguste Chamot of the Hôtel de Pékin and his wife, Annie, had hastily organized a rescue party. Together with four Frenchmen and a young Australian called Willie Dupree, they set out heavily armed with carts, spare animals and provisions. They met no resistance and succeeded in plucking a party of some seven children, nine women and about a dozen men from danger in the very nick of time. As they retreated northward towards Peking, the refugees could see their houses and compound going up in smoke. They were shocked and surprised to see the Chinese soldiers, sent by the local officials to defend them, joining in the looting. However, by evening, 'weary, bedraggled, and in a condition of extreme faintness of body and mind,'[6] they too were safe within the legations.

The Belgian engineers and their families had been extremely fortunate. The fate of another party of foreign engineers, at Paotingfu, was very different and news of it reached Peking only in early June. They were attacked at the same time as the general assault on the railway line but were unable to flee by train. Shortly afterwards, the telegraph line was destroyed, leaving them isolated from the outside world. Uncertain what to do and terrified by the rising hostility against them, they decided their only course was to flee and that the safest, shortest route lay eastward to Tientsin by river. A party of some thirty Belgians, French and Italians, including six women and a child, left Paotingfu on 31 May. Helped by a Chinese official who sent a small force of Chinese soldiers with them, they reached the river and set out by boat. As they entered a narrow channel, they were confronted by Boxers. They tried to sail on but ran aground and the Boxers attacked. Struggling to fend them off, they pushed the boat across to the opposite bank of the river where, wet, exhausted and frightened, they tried to decide what to do.

Four of them – a Swiss called Assent, his sister, an Italian and a Turk – had had enough and set out to return to Paotingfu, only to be caught by Boxers and murdered, their bodies mutilated. Meanwhile, the remainder of the group formed themselves into a square, women on the inside for safety, and began a punishing march to Tientsin. Hungry and thirsty, they were forced to dodge through noisome swamps to avoid detection. It was too much for some of the women, one of whom was heavily pregnant, and they had to be carried. Two of the men managed to get through to Tientsin on 3 June to raise the alarm. The survivors, by now in a pitiful state, semi-naked and bleeding, were finally rescued by the Belgian Consul and a doctor and brought safely into the foreign settlement, where they collapsed with nervous prostration.

Meanwhile in Peking the diplomats had been having second thoughts. On hearing of the burning of the railway facilities at Fengtai, a young American missionary observed cynically to the Reverend Allen: 'We are saved. So long as the Boxers only plundered native houses and murdered converts, the Ministers did nothing; now a few yards of [railway] line have been destroyed, and they *must* act.' The ministers met on the evening of 28 May, and Sir Claude argued that there was now no option but to request the foreign fleets lying off the Taku bar to send guards to the legations. There was a very real possibility that the rail link to Tientsin and the coast would be lost and they must act quickly if the guards were to be able to reach Peking by train.

There was no dissent and Monsieur Pichon smugly announced that he had, in fact, already sent for guards. The Russians had done likewise. Sir Claude now hastened to telegraph his own request to Vice-Admiral Sir Edward Seymour, commander of the British naval forces in China, then patrolling with his squadron in Chinese waters. As Seymour later said, the gist of the message was that 'the Boxers were troublesome and a guard was wanted.'[7] Protocol demanded that the Tsungli Yamen should be asked for formal agreement. However, allowing foreign troops to march into the capital was a deeply sensitive issue for the Chinese and, as Sarah Conger noted without surprise, the Tsungli Yamen 'positively refused to grant this request.' Sir Claude, unusually for him, lost his temper, telling the members of the Yamen that they were a 'damned lot of fools'.[8] He told them to inform Prince Ching, the senior member of the Yamen who was at the Summer Palace with the Empress Dowager, that 'the troops are coming tomorrow, and if [there is] any obstruction, they will come in ten times greater force.'[9] In the early hours of 31 May, the Yamen at last gave permission for the troops to come but imposed a limit of thirty guards per legation, which the ministers contemptuously ignored. The first contingents left Tientsin that day for Peking.

The ministers had taken a debatable step. Some of the diplomatic community feared it 'would be a signal for a general attack upon foreigners, and indiscriminate pillage and massacre.'[10] It would inevitably fuel antiforeign feeling and might thus be endangering the very people it was intended to help. However, the Imperial Court was by now so riven by infighting it was unable to control the Boxers even if it wanted to. The court had tried to take measures against them in mid-May and the Boxers' response had been to kill Imperial troops without hesitation. On 22 May, in the aftermath of the massacre of Christians at Kaolo, they had even murdered a Manchu commander, Colonel Yang Futong, without reprisals. Suitably encouraged, the Boxers had gone on to attack the railway a few days later.

Deaconess Jessie Ransome, of the Anglican Mission in Peking, shrewdly observed that the Chinese officials 'seemed entirely unable to cope with the movement, even when they were willing; and the Government would, or could, do nothing but issue edicts, many of which were so dubiously worded that they might have been taken as equally favourable to the "Boxers", or to Christians and foreigners.' An Imperial edict of 30 May lamely suggested that 'the really guilty must be distinguished from those merely led by the excitement of the moment.'[11] Sir Robert Hart's diagnosis was that 'the Court appears to be in a dilemma: if the Boxers are not suppressed, the legations threaten to take action – if the attempt to suppress them is made, this intensely patriotic organization will be converted into an anti-dynastic move- ment!'[12] In the circumstances the ministers realized they could not look to the court for protection with any confidence. Inflaming an already dangerous situation by calling up their troops seemed less of a risk to the ministers than the risks of doing nothing. They also comforted themselves with the thought that the foreign soldier had a formidable reputation among the unmartial Chinese and that the presence of guards would surely be a major deterrent.

Yet many of the foreign community were worried that the guards would arrive too late. The situation had now become so dangerous that, as Polly wrote, 'no women are allowed to leave the compound, but, of course, the diplomats and the military – such as are here – must move about and try to find out what the situation really is. The people who know most about it are the most pessimistic as to what may happen before the marines arrive from Tientsin.' Captain Francis Poole, who had had the ill luck to be posted just a few days earlier to learn Chinese in Peking where his brother Wordsworth was doctor to the British Legation, was worried by the 'truculent and insolent' behaviour of the Imperial troops swaggering through the city streets. Placards appeared in the Legation Quarter giving such helpful practical hints as 'an admirable way to destroy foreign build- ings.'[13] Sir Claude MacDonald telegraphed the Foreign Office in London: 'The situation is one of extreme gravity, people very excited, troops mutinous; without doubt it is now a question of life and property being in danger here.' Foreigners walking the streets were likely to be stoned by angry crowds.

Boxers were parading openly through the streets of Peking. A French diplomat, Baron d'Anthouard, described in his diary how they were distributing 'handbills, and advocating the massacre of foreigners and the destruction of all religious institutions. They no longer take the trouble to hide, and move about carrying their insignia: a red scarf tied around their heads with the inscription "Fu" [Happiness] on the front of it, a kind of red coat of arms on their chest, and red bands around their wrists and ankles. They also carry flags with the inscription, "We fight by order of the Emperor and for the salvation of the Dynasty." Their handbills announce the forthcoming massacre of the "Western devils."'[14] Hart wrote that the foreign community felt like 'rats in a trap'.[15]

The legations at last began to wonder how best to defend themselves against attack. The British compound with its strong, high walls and bounded by the stinking Jade River on one side and the Imperial Carriage Park on the other was in the strongest position. It would be a natural stronghold if the worst happened, which Sir Claude now feared it might. On the night of 30 May he became so alarmed at the antiforeign demonstrations in the streets and the tales of the panic-stricken refugees flooding into the city that he offered sanctuary in the legation to any British residents who so wished. The Reverend Allen sent along all those in the Anglican Mission compound, including the wife of the bishop of North China, Mrs Scott. He remained behind with the calm, resourceful deaconess Jessie Ransome to guard the mission and try to protect their converts. The Belgians and Austrians, uneasily aware that their legations, which were some distance north of Legation Street, were out on a limb and particularly vulnerable to attack, decided to mount a constant sentry guard, night and day.

The social round continued nonetheless, but there was a nervous frisson to the conversation. On 30 May the Chevalier de Melotte, a big, blond, bearlike Belgian diplomat, dropped in to the Squierses' house to give them 'a most vivid description of the difficulties of their tiny garrison.' Sir Robert Hart also called. He remained optimistic yet he also regaled Polly and Harriet with 'quite terrible' tales of earlier massacres of foreigners by the Chinese. Polly enjoyed his visit, during which he also dwelt on some colourful reminiscences of General Gordon, but confided in her diary that he had not reassured them 'in our present dangerous situation.' Captain Poole was angry with him for 'frightening our ladies' and thought him 'an awful old fool'. Nevertheless, Polly did her best to forget her anxieties and attended a dinner party at Hart's house that evening, where she danced until midnight.

The next day everyone's thoughts were on whether and when the guards would arrive. Bertram Lenox Simpson dined with Monsieur and Madame Pichon and other assorted diplomats and the conversational menu was monotonous: 'Boxers for soup, Boxers with the entrees, and Boxers to the end.' Pichon was full of gloom, talking of sudden massacres in Peking and deploring a Chinese government gone mad. His wife was suitably sad and apparently 'sighed constantly'. Lenox Simpson consoled himself for the trying company by eating and drinking copiously. As the evening passed there was still no news and the nervous speculation continued. Was it true that 6,000 Kansu braves had been deployed between the railway terminus at Machiapu, outside the city walls, and the southern gate through which the troops must enter Peking? Would they attack the foreign guards? What would happen if the Tsungli Yamen ordered the city gates closed against them?

However, the situation was yet more nerve-racking for the missionaries and others dispersed all over Peking and living among the Chinese. Dr Gilbert Reid told Morrison that the evening of 30 May was the worst he had ever spent in China. At about 7.00 that evening he warned the Reverend Allen 'that he did not at all like the look of things . . . he said that he had already prepared a place of refuge for Mrs Reid and the baby in the house of a Chinese friend; and he strongly advised me to warn the Christians at the first sound of approaching danger to leave their homes, mingle with the crowd, and gradually drop out into quiet streets and byways and wait for the day. For the deaconess [Jessie Ransome] and myself he advised me to prepare Chinese clothes.' Allen followed his instructions to the letter, helping Jessie Ransome disguise herself as a Manchu woman. Since Manchu women did not bind their feet, westerners stood a better chance of fleeing in this disguise rather than as Chinese women. However, just as Allen was about to struggle into his own disguise, some of his boys came flying in with the welcome news that the foreign guards were marching into Peking. He went to his church and sang a thankful *Te Deum*.

A bevy of diplomats had been nervously pacing the platform at the railway station. When the trains at last steamed into Machiapu, about 350 men from America, Britain, Russia, France, Italy and Japan disembarked. German and Austrian guards were to follow in a few days. The British contingent consisted of three officers and seventy-six men of the Royal Marine Light Infantry and three Royal Navy ratings. There should have been 100 Britons. However, the Russians, unable to muster that number themselves, had objected to this pre-eminence in an unseemly scrimmage at Tientsin railway station and forced the British to scale their contingent down.

But now all went surprisingly well. There was an enormous mob at the station, but no demonstration 'except to hurl and howl curses on the soldiers' ancestors.'[16] The city gates were open still and the Kansu warriors had retired. The various foreign nations competed for the honour of leading the parade to the legations. The Americans, prompt and efficient, won, stepping out under the setting sun in their slouch hats and khaki uniforms. Polly described with pride how 'Captain McCalla, who had come up with our fifty marines, hurried his men at the double-quick to get it, and our troops were the first to march up Legation Street.' It must have been a strange parade. Captain Jack Myers of the US Marine Corps observed 'the dense mass of Chinese which thronged either side of the roadway.'[17] He found it more ominous than any demonstration of hostility.

Among the American marines marching briskly, with bayonets fixed and ready, was a young private, Oscar Upham, who kept one of the frankest and liveliest records of events. He described how their march into the city became almost a run: 'Capt. McCalla . . . gave us double time for about 300 yards. Taking the place with a grandstand rush, we kept up a rapid march until we reached the American Legation.' They were not only first but had 'a good supper' waiting for them.

Oscar Upham's journey had begun a week earlier when, together with Captain Myers and twenty-five other marines, he embarked on the US flagship *Newark* in Nagasaki in Japan. After an irritating delay caused by having to wait for a couple of 'delinquent officers', the *Newark* set sail on what Upham was going to have cause to describe as 'one of the most exciting ventures ever known in the annals of history.'

The *Newark* had anchored two days later off the vast mud bar at Taku. Upham was not impressed with the flat scenery, complaining that the coast was so low it could be seen only on a very clear day. Disembarking in only eight fathoms of water, and leaving all their baggage aboard the *Newark* in case they had to fight, Upham and his brother marines travelled on by tug, sampan, steamer and cargo lighter, fortified by a lunch of canned beef and hardtack. After passing the forts at Taku, which guarded the mouth of the Peiho, they were allowed on deck to admire the scenery. Upham gazed at paddy fields and native villages of adobe brick, plastered over with mud and grass, clustered along the riverbank. He was astonished to see women and mules hitched to the same plough and working side by side. There was a diversion when Private Horton fell overboard while asleep. As he could not swim he was fished out by a Chinese deckhand.

Arriving at last in Tientsin with orders to go up to Peking immediately by train, they joined the crowds milling around at the railway station. There was confusion, noise and commotion as soldiers of different nationalities argued and jostled with one another. According to Upham, the young American marines bulldozed the officials into letting them have a train made up of 'one gondola for baggage, ammunition and guns, and 10 coaches for the troops.'

Many foreigners turned out to watch the various nationalities as eventually they came marching into Peking. Captain Poole noted that the British fighters were naturally the smartest, that the Americans were 'a serviceable-looking lot', but that the French, Russians and Italians were 'very dirty'. The American Arthur Smith was less kind about the British. They looked very young and inexperienced to him and he could 'comprehend something of the reasons for the disasters in the South African campaign.' It was a harsh comment, perhaps, but it was true that none of them had ever seen a shot fired in anger. Sir Robert Hart put it more tactfully, describing the Britons as nice-looking, cheerful and bright but the Americans as stronger, more mature, self-reliant and resourceful! He also commented that the Americans were all dead shots.

Regardless of nationality, all the guards were ill-equipped for what lay ahead. The admirals who had sent them had not anticipated a protracted siege. They had rifles and a few hundred rounds of ammunition per man but there was no reserve ammunition, no heavy weapons and only three machine guns – the British had an elderly and temperamental multibarrelled Nordenfelt .45 that, according to a disgusted Morrison, 'consistently jammed every fourth round';[18] the Austrians had a Maxim; and the Americans had a light Colt 236. The only artillery was a little one-pounder gun that the Italians had brought and for which they had only 120 shells. The Russians had intended to bring a heavy twelve-pounder gun but had inadvertently left it behind at Tientsin railway station, perhaps while bickering about the size of the British force. They did, however, remember to bring the ammunition.

Nevertheless, the diplomats were delighted to see the guards. Edwin Conger greeted his marines with a heartfelt 'Thank God you've come. Now we're safe.'[19] He posted four sentinels to guard the American compound day and night, and the Colt 236 was placed on the front walk. William Bainbridge thanked his lucky stars that the Boxers had not destroyed the railway line to Tientsin. Otherwise he believed they would not have been able to reach Peking and 'every foreigner of Peking would have met a certain and awful death.' Dr Martin, a seventy-year-old former missionary turned academic, agreed with him, believing they had been saved by the skin of their teeth. In another forty-eight hours 'the whole foreign community in Peking must have perished . . . Without that handful of marines defence would have been hopeless.' Sir Robert Hart and Bishop Favier called on Sir Claude MacDonald to express their delight and their certainty that now the guards had arrived 'the Empress Dowager would see the error of her ways.'[20] Sir Robert wrote to a colleague that 'the crisis I think is past as far as Peking is concerned.'[21]

Bertram Lenox Simpson was rather more sceptical. He noted that everyone was very gay, walking about and having drinks and saying 'it was all right now', but he was apparently not seduced by the euphoria: 'I felt convinced that the guards were too few,' he wrote. Mary Bainbridge, wife of the US second secretary, shared his view: 'It seems a very small number among tens of thousands of Chinese soldiers.' She wondered what the days ahead would bring. Although many of the foreigners slept soundly that night, disturbed only by the bamboo rattles of the watchmen as they patrolled the shadowy compounds, their peace of mind was to be short-lived.

5

'SHA! SHA!'

Death stalked before us and death behind. – Mary Bainbridge

ON 3 JUNE, Sir Claude MacDonald sent a note to Vice-Admiral Seymour assuring him that there was now a 'wholesome calm'[1] in Peking and that the legations would be the very last place to be attacked. The remaining German and Austrian guards had arrived safely that day from Tientsin, and Sir Claude believed that the Chinese had been taught a salutary lesson. He had no qualms about sending his two little daughters, Stella and Ivy, to the British Legation's summer residence in the Western Hills in the care of his sister-in-law Miss Armstrong and an escort of marines.

The apparent tranquillity in Peking was deceptive. Out in the country the harrying of Christians was becoming more violent and systematic. A distressed Sarah Conger wrote in her diary that 'telegrams for help keep coming'. She was very anxious for the safety of the missionaries but could understand their dilemma. 'It seems advisable for them to flee to more promising places of safety, but they are not willing to leave their missions to be burned and their converts to be murdered.' Reports began to filter in of the murder of two British missionaries, Harry Norman and Charles Robinson, just fifty miles south of Peking. There was also alarming news that stations were again being burned and that the railway line to Tientsin was being systematically ripped up by the Boxers. At a hastily arranged meeting of ministers, Monsieur Pichon sensibly pointed out that the Boxers' obvious next step would be to cut the telegraph lines. Once that happened, the foreign community in Peking would be entirely isolated. It was a frightening prospect and the diplomats telegraphed their governments to request that the naval forces lying off Taku should send aid if the situation deteriorated.

The mood of the Chinese officials was becoming increasingly insolent. On 4 June, Sir Claude called at the Tsungli Yamen to protest the murder of the two missionaries only to be met by snores from one of the four members present. On 5 June, a further meeting with the normally helpful and courteous Prince Ching forced Sir Claude to conclude that the Tsungli Yamen was powerless to influence the events now unfolding. His scepticism was reinforced by an Imperial edict that exonerated the Boxers from any responsibility for current troubles and pointed the finger of blame squarely at the Christians. That day the little MacDonald girls were brought back to the city. Not long afterwards the elegant summer residence, only recently completed at a cost of £10,000, was looted and destroyed and the gatekeeper's wife and children were murdered.

The atmosphere in Peking was now one of foreboding. Polly Condit Smith described how 'everyone feels that this is the time to leave Peking – everyone, at least, who is not bound to remain to protect interests they have in charge.' Sarah Conger was planning to send her two daughters, Laura and Mary, on the first train to Tientsin. Polly too was making preparations. She and her maid began packing her trunks so she could leave the next day, assuming that the railway line was still open. However, a note from Sir Robert Hart advised her not to attempt the journey. His agents had warned him that any trains carrying foreigners would be attacked and stoned – 'Things must get better soon or very much worse,' he concluded helpfully. However, it all proved academic. There were to be no more trains to Tientsin. The last foreigners to get out of Peking – a group of missionaries – left on 4 June thanks to a Chinese guard who told them frankly, 'I cannot promise to get you to Tientsin, but will do my best. We may land you over the burning bridges among the Boxers, or have to bring you back.'[2] The men took their place by the carriage windows, armed with revolvers and rifles. Some of the women also carried revolvers. They arrived safely.

Polly was becoming a little apprehensive. It was all too obvious that 'this United States Legation is such a wretched little irregular place to defend – it could so easily be fired.' She described how everyone was 'walking about gesticulating or standing on scorching hot flagstones . . . arguing with one another as to how soon the *coup d'état* will take place, but all agreeing on one point – that a cable should be sent immediately to the State Department in Washington before telegraphic communication is lost; that nothing but a tremendous armed force can free the Americans in Peking from a surely approaching massacre.'

Alarm now followed alarm, escalating the tension. William Pethick, with his long experience of China, was urging Edwin Conger to warn the US government of the seriousness of the situation, 'but all to no avail. The white dazzling star of optimism is blinding him to facts, and with the British Minister to stand with him in his position, he says that the Boxer movement is only a few fanatics, and the mobs and incendiaries are but slight demonstrations of the yearly spring riots!'[3] Robert Coltman was doing his best to send 'some strong cables about affairs here' to the *Chicago Record* but Polly feared that the US papers were so saturated with the sensational and the false that no one would believe him.

The ministers seemed at a loss to know what to do. Should they demand an audience with the Empress Dowager or should they await instructions from their governments? The missionaries, converging on Peking with their flocks of terrified converts, were rather clearer. Thirty Americans, as unimpressed with Edwin Conger's response to events as Pethick and Coltman, decided to wire President McKinley that the situation was 'practically hopeless'.[4] Their telegram also complained fulsomely about the 'double-faced' Imperial edicts. They wondered whether the Imperial Post Office would transmit such forthright language. However, there was no need for worry. The Post Office merely insisted that the expression 'double-faced' was two words, not one, and charged the missionaries accordingly.

On 9 June something happened that in Sir Claude MacDonald's words 'brought home more vividly to the minds of all Europeans in Peking a sense of the perilous position in which they stood.' A mob of Boxers burned down the grandstand at the Peking Race Course not far outside the southern city gates. The news caused huge excitement and some young student interpreters galloped out to take a look. Confronted by an angry crowd, one of them took out a revolver and shot a Chinese 'point-blank in the stomach.'[5] This was the first Chinaman to be killed by a foreigner. Sir Claude MacDonald was fully aware of the foolishness and danger of what had happened. Deaconess Jessie Ransome, who had been forced to abandon the Anglican Mission for the British Legation, noted that 'now Sir Claude has forbidden anyone to ride out of the city at all.'

The ministers met yet again and debated whether to ask the naval commanders to send a relief force to Peking. Sir Claude confessed that he had in fact already telegraphed Vice-Admiral Seymour and told him that unless he sent reinforcements quickly it might be too late. The others balked at what seemed an extreme measure. However, further disturbing news arrived. The emperor and the Empress Dowager had returned to the Forbidden City from the Summer Palace. That in itself would have been welcomed. However, what sent a shiver down the collective diplomatic spine was the report that General Tung Fu-hsiang and his Kansu warriors had escorted the Empress Dowager, and were even now in the city.

As Lenox Simpson wrote: 'A fresh wave of excitement broke

over the city and produced almost a panic. The main body of Tung Fu-hsiang's savage Kansu braves – that is, his whole army – re-entered the capital and rapidly encamped on the open places in front of the Temples of Heaven and Agriculture.' Sir Claude acted at once. He sent a further telegram to Vice-Admiral Seymour advising him that the situation was becoming more dangerous by the hour and asking that troops should be landed and all arrangements made for an advance on Peking at once. The other ministers did likewise and were only just in time. Shortly after a telegram reached the legations on 10 June confirming that forces under Vice-Admiral Seymour were on their way, the telegraph line to Tientsin was cut. All that was left was an unreliable line running north to Russian territory via Kiatka. As Polly wrote, 'We have no more communication with the outside world; our world is this dangerous Peking.'

On 11 June, a long procession of carts rattled out to Machiapu railway station – the 'fire-cart stopping place,'[6] as the Chinese called it – to await the relief force. The convoy had to pass through the belligerent and volatile Kansu troops, who were clearly spoiling for a fight. Their colours of black and blue velvet splashed with blood-red characters looked sinister to the distracted foreigners. The hours passed and no trains came, adding to the nervous tension. As they waited, Herbert Squiers and the other diplomats pondered some disturbing news. The previous day four members of the antiforeign faction at court had been appointed to the Tsungli Yamen in the place of more moderate officials. It seemed particularly ominous that Prince Ching had been replaced as president by the reactionary Prince Tuan. Sir Robert Hart had responded to the news with his usual optimism, reminding his colleagues that other antiforeign members of the Yamen had 'turned out well under the load of responsibility and in the light of fuller knowledge; they began with an honest hatred and ended with an honest appreciation. So I think Prince Tuan's appointment will . . . work well.'[7] Others were less sanguine.

As time went by and nothing happened, the foreigners decided wisely to return to the legations. However, later that afternoon the chancellor of the Japanese Legation, Mr Sugiyama, neatly dressed in tailcoat and bowler hat, returned to the station unarmed and by cart. Just beyond the city gate he was set on by Kansu troops, dragged out of his cart, 'disembowelled and cut to pieces.'[8] According to Morrison, his heart was sent to a gratified General Tung Fu-hsiang as a gift. No attempt was made to recover his body and children were seen poking at it with sticks.

Even the charitable sinophile Sir Robert Hart had no words to excuse or explain what had happened. As Commandant Darcy of the French Legation guard eloquently put it, 'Un silence impressionnant enveloppe le quartier des Légations . . . Chacun sent qu'un danger le menace, mais nul ne veut y croire' – 'A meaningful silence falls on the Legations . . . Everyone senses the danger that threatens them but no one wants to believe it.'[9] Fear mingled with bewilderment. The remaining telegraph line via Kiatka was finally cut. Sarah Conger wrote feelingly: 'We should like to know where our troops are and what the outer world is doing. It seems that day by day we are narrowed into closer quarters; little by little connection with the world beyond Peking has been cut off. Now we stand isolated; both telegraph lines are gone; the railroad is gone. No Legation mail pouch . . .' Two members of the Tsungli Yamen called on her husband to ask him to stop foreign troops entering the city. 'They said it would be much easier for Prince Ching.' However, Conger replied that since the government could no longer protect the foreigners they must protect themselves.

The normally teeming streets of the Legation Quarter were gradually emptying as servants and shopkeepers vanished. The diplomats' minds turned again to the best means of defending the legations. Over at the Peitang Cathedral, Bishop Favier, who had had no illusions from the start, was struggling to accommodate the several thousand Catholic converts now cramming into the compound for sanctuary, while others sought safety in

the Tung Tang and the Nan Tang. He was glad of the force of
some forty French and Italian marines, detached from the main
legation forces, that had been sent to protect the Peitang. It was,
however, woefully small, and the two commanding officers were
very young.

The French were led by a twenty-three-year-old Breton, Paul
Henry; the Italian officer, Olivieri, was only twenty-two. Aware
that many lives might depend on them, the two young men
hurriedly set about directing the defences of the huge
compound, grateful for the citadel-like structure of the cathedral
itself, with its high, thick walls. At one point Henry's commanding officer, Commandant Darcy, sent a message recalling him to
the legations, but it never arrived. Favier later wrote in his diary:
'God permitted that this order . . . never reached us, otherwise
we should all have been lost.' Even so, he was now mentally
preparing himself to join the 'martyrs' murdered in Tientsin in
1870.

A detachment of US Marines, including the observant young
Oscar Upham, had been sent to guard the large Methodist
Mission about half a mile from the American Legation. It was
run by a devoted missionary and former engineer, Frank
Gamewell, who estimated that he now had some 1,500 people
within his walls. Upham described the 700-yard-long compound
approvingly: 'a very nice place . . . inclosed [sic] by a wall 12 feet
high and containing 7 dwelling houses, a fine church, one school
and a hospital.' He and his comrades were comfortably billeted
in Gamewell's house. However, they were nervous times, with
false alarms and rumours of attack. He watched pathetic
streams of refugees flooding in all the time: 'The missionaries are
coming in from outside districks [sic]; some with only such articles of clothing as they could carry in their arms, as they had to
flee for their lives. The situation is getting more serious as the
Boxers are gathering and getting more bold every hour; as the
Chinese soldiers sent out to guard Foreign property are assisting
the Boxers to loot the places.'

Luella Miner and her colleagues were among those to reach

the mission in safety. Their last few days in Tungchow had been fraught with anxiety, not only for themselves and their converts, but also for their missionary friends in the Boxer stronghold of Paotingfu. The few letters that had reached Luella from Paotingfu had been 'pathetic in the brave facing of imminent danger.' Preparing now for the inevitable, the Tungchow missionaries had reviewed their firearms to discover they had just one rifle, two shotguns and a few revolvers. They enquired about boats to Tientsin but there were none to hire. In case of emergency they agreed to make their final stand at the tower on which their new college telescope was mounted, knowing that the Chinese believed it to be 'a terrible cannon' that, if it went off, would destroy 'half of Tungchow'.[10]

Luella still found the thought of deserting their community almost impossible to contemplate. However, there was to be no choice. On 7 June she wrote in her diary that 'the blow has fallen.' The local official who had so far protected them had told them they must leave, confessing 'his utter helplessness . . . fairly wringing his hands and crying in his great agitation.' He was in grave danger himself – his nickname in the city was 'head of the second-grade barbarians.'

Luella wrote of her despair at 'this compulsory desertion' and their powerlessness to protect their Christians. Some of them had already scattered and even as she was packing news came in of whole families cut down as they fled. The missionaries left as 'daylight was just beginning to streak the east' in carts brought out by a friend they had wired in Peking. Luella looked up at the stars and 'it seemed as if they were the only fixtures left.' Beside her were all her worldly possessions – a trunk, a telescope, a bandbox, two pairs of blankets and a pillow.

The Tungchow missionaries helped Frank Gamewell to fortify the Methodist Mission, building sturdy brick walls, stretching barbed wire across the courtyards and digging ditches. The converts worked side by side with them, even tiny children helping by carrying bricks, their faces solemn with the effort of concentration. Gamewell planned to make any final stand in the church and was working to make it both secure and habitable. Frames and glass were removed from the windows and the spaces filled in with brick and cunningly loopholed. Oscar Upham thought that it looked more like a fort than a house of worship.

Gamewell's capable wife, Mary, boiled water, which she stored in barrel-like jars, and laid in supplies of boiled eggs, Chinese biscuits and cases of condensed milk. As she worked she recalled 'parts taken by women in the fights of pioneer days' and offered her services to Captain Hall, who was in command of the US Marine detachment. His tart reply was 'rather stunning': 'The most helpful thing a woman can do in a fight is to keep out of the way.' He nevertheless admired her as a 'sweet motherly type' and thought her husband 'a splendid executive, forceful and capable, but always a leader – never a driver.' Some of the other missionary women were now carrying guns, but Hall 'put a damper' on 'their martial spirit' by remarking that 'the place for women is under the seats in the chapel.'[11]

Meanwhile the foreign community was puzzling over the nonappearance of the relief force. Rumours were rife but there was no firm news. On 12 June the ministers decided to send yet another message to the Tsungli Yamen, if only to keep channels of communication open. The Japanese were invited to join in but their response, stripped of diplomatic niceties, was unequivocal: 'Impossible. The Chinese have murdered our Third Secretary of Legation, and Japan can have no more communication with China – except war.'[12] That night, foreigners in Peking noted that the sky was luridly bright as fires blazed across the city. The sign of a red or bleeding hand appeared mysteriously on the doors of Christian households.

On 13 June, a Boxer appeared in Legation Street. He was seated casually on the shaft of a Peking cart, his hair bound with red cloth. There were 'red ribbons round his wrists and ankles, and a flaming red girdle [around his waist] tightening his loose white tunic.'[13] He was sharpening a big carving knife on his boot and gazing insolently around him. According to a member of the Customs Service, De Courcy, 'The impudence of the whole proceeding was too much for "the fiery Teuton,"'[14] Baron von Ketteler. The German minister was so incensed that he rushed into the street and set about the Boxer with a stick, beating him about the head. The Boxer managed to duck down an alleyway but von Ketteler discovered a young boy hiding in the cart. He thrashed him soundly and had him taken prisoner into the German Legation. It was perhaps not a sensible thing to have done.

Later that afternoon thousands of Boxers erupted into the city. Jessie Ransome described how 'we suddenly saw a great column of smoke to the east, and then, in about half an hour, a volley of rifle-shots in Legation Street . . . The Boxers were streaming into the city by the Ha Ta Men, the gate to the east of us.' They were slashing and stabbing with swords and spears. Morrison's diary captures the drama: '13 June – Attack of Boxers. Cries of Boxer incantations. Passing the French Legation I found all on guard. "The Boxers are coming." Then rush home . . . Kept watch all night . . . Awful cries in the west part of the city all through the night. The roar of the murdered. Rapine and massacre.' The Boxers had prepared blacklists and were searching through the city 'hunting down all who had been connected with the foreigners, cutting them down, hacking them to pieces, or carrying them off for more terrible torture in a Boxer camp.'[15]

Lenox Simpson described scenes of desperate panic: 'Never have I seen such fast galloping and driving in the Peking Streets; never would I have believed that small-footed women, of whom there are a goodly number even in the large-footed Manchu city, could get so nimbly over the ground. Everybody was panic-stricken and distraught, and we could do nothing but look on. They went on running, running, running.' It was like watching a herd of terrified deer fleeing before a predator. Then, once again, the streets grew quiet although the Boxers' fearsome cries of 'Sha! Sha!' – 'Kill! Kill!' – could be heard receding into the distance. That night William Bainbridge watched 'the burning of all the American missions in Peking except the Methodist where our marines stood guard.' Soon many parts of the city were on fire.

Peking became a nightmare world where 'hundreds of torches, dancing like will-o'-the-wisps in front of our straining eyes,'[16] seemed to taunt the foreigners. In his *Decadence Mandchoue* Edmund Backhouse mourned the destruction of Peking's gay quarter, which he claimed was incinerated when fire spread from a foreign drugstore. The East Cathedral, the Tung Tang, and the South Cathedral, the Nan Tang, were attacked and set alight. The Tung Tang 'shot flames into the sky'[17] amid a deafening roar. Those converts not burned alive were cut to pieces by Boxers' knives. The Chamots went into action again. Together with a young Frenchman, the husband and wife galloped through the burning streets and managed to rescue a priest and some nuns. A party of American marines managed to save 300 converts.

The rescuers came across some appalling sights. Even the stoical Morrison was shocked by scenes reminiscent of paintings by Hieronymus Bosch: 'Women and children hacked to pieces, men trussed like fowls, with noses and ears cut off and eyes gouged out.'[18] Lancelot Giles, a young British student interpreter who accompanied him, wrote shudderingly: 'Many were found roasted alive, and so massacred and cut up as to be unrecognizable. I will spare you the sickening details.' Lenox Simpson found that 'the stench of human blood in the hot June air was almost intolerable, and the sights more than we could bear. Men, women and children lay indiscriminately heaped together, some hacked to pieces, others with their throats cut from ear to ear, some still moving, others quite motionless.'

Boxers were discovered systematically torturing their victims in temples. 'Some had already been put to death and their bodies were still warm and bleeding. All were shockingly mutilated. Their fiendish murderers were at their incantations burning incense before their gods, offering Christians in sacrifice to their angered deities.'[19] Luella Miner found it hard to contemplate what was happening. It made the massacre of St Bartholomew pale into insignificance and yet, she wrote helplessly, 'this is the last year of the nineteenth century.'

However, hundreds were brought to safety. Polly Condit Smith watched some of these survivors creeping in. 'Half starved, covered with soot and ashes from the fires, women carrying on their breasts horribly sick and diseased babies, and in one case a woman held a dead baby. One man of about fifty years old carried on his shoulders his old mother . . . A great many of these people were terribly wounded – great spear-thrusts that made jagged wounds, scalp-cuts and gashes on the throat where the victim had been left for dead.' She confessed that 'such a lot of poor, wretched people I hope never to see again.'

She was warm in her praise of Morrison, who had managed to secure the converts a refuge in a beautiful, capacious palace and compound – the Fu – belonging to Prince Su, a wealthy courtier. Aided by Professor Huberty James of the Peking University, who acted as interpreter, Morrison used some muscular diplomacy. He told the prince that 'it would not only be kind, but wise, for him to present his palace and park to his distressed fellow-citizens, who were being massacred.' He also told him that unless he voluntarily gave it up 'we would take it.' Prince Su suavely replied that 'nothing would give him greater pleasure' and departed leaving 'all of his treasure and half of his harem,' according to Polly. She watched the refugees pouring in, the lucky ones bringing their pots, pans, beds and bundles of rice.

The Austrian compound, isolated on the northeastern rim of the Legation Quarter, had come under attack on 13 June. The Austrians, whom young Lancelot Giles thought 'rather fond of firing', let rip with their Maxim machine gun but to little effect. Captain Poole was similarly unimpressed: 'The Austrian picket opened fire with their machine gun at what they said was Boxers but they killed none and after that the French, Russians and

Italians squibbed at shadows etc. We shall have a lot of trouble with these irresponsible jumpy folk.' The general view was that the Austrians had aimed too high to hit anything other than the telegraph lines. However, the Austrians' failure to kill any Boxers seemed further proof to the Chinese that the Boxers' claims of invulnerability were true.

On 16 June, Boxers attacked the richest trading quarter of the Chinese City, setting fire to all shops that sold foreign goods. Over 4,000 stores – goldsmiths, jewellers and furriers; fan, silk, lantern and curio shops – were incinerated as the flames swept northward. It was a terrifying spectacle as 'a lurid light growing ever brighter and brighter turned the dark night into an unnatural day.'[20] The fire engulfed the magnificent city gate the Chienmen. Its great rafters of Burmese teak seemed to the watching foreigners to burn with barbaric splendour despite 'the efforts of several Chinese fire-engines with all their paraphernalia of gongs, and banners, and horns.'[21] The Legation Quarter itself was saved only by the barrier of the city walls.

At the beginning of the troubles, barricades had hastily been erected across Legation Street. Russians and Americans defended the west barricade, French and Italians the east. Everyone was on full alert. Even Sir Robert Hart had several Colt revolvers strapped to his thin body. The main Legation Quarter was not yet seriously threatened, however, despite further provocative acts by von Ketteler. On 17 June, his men fired on some of Tung Fu-hsiang's Moslem braves, causing Sir Claude MacDonald to send a polite but firm warning: 'When our own troops arrive we may with safety assume a different tone, but it is hardly wise now.'[22] Earlier in the day Morrison noted that the baron had been enjoying himself taking pot shots at Boxers: 'Ketteler and his merry men have just shot 7 Boxers from the top of the wall. 50 or 100 were drilling at a distance of 200 yards . . . The stalking was excellently done.' Young Meyrick Hewlett, though, was frightened by the passion unleashed by such thoughtless acts: 'I shall never forget the scenes that ensued – thousands and thousands of voices yelling

"Sha! Sha!" ("Kill! Kill!") for well over an hour . . . No one who has ever heard this sound could ever forget it.'

The confusion of those three days of bloodshed from 13 to 16 June had been compounded by the behaviour of the Tsungli Yamen. The officials continued to send reassuring messages, promising that all would yet be well. However, the Imperial Court was still pursuing its schizophrenic policies, 'decreeing and counter-decreeing night and day.'[23] On 16 June, the Empress Dowager summoned an Imperial council to discuss what was to be done about the Boxers. The usual arguments took place, with the moderates advocating firm measures against the Boxers, whom they saw as dangerous anarchists, and Prince Tuan's faction arguing passionately in their defence. The lame conclusion was that the Boxers should be 'pacified'.[24]

The next day, 17 June, the council met again but with rather different results. A document was produced purporting to come from the governments of the foreign powers. It was in effect an ultimatum making a series of outrageous demands. The foreign ministers were to be given responsibility for all military matters and all raising of revenues while the emperor was to be restored to the throne. It was undoubtedly a forgery, probably produced by Prince Tuan to give him leverage over the moderates. It certainly had the desired effect. According to an eyewitness, a furious Empress Dowager ceased wavering at last. She issued an Imperial edict calling on the provincial governors to send troops to Peking and, to the dismay of such moderate advisers as Prince Ching, began preparing for hostilities. The news that reached her just two days later, that the foreign powers were demanding the surrender of the Taku forts, only confirmed her views. It was tantamount to a declaration of war and the foreigners must be told to quit Peking.

The diplomats were stunned. Edwin Conger's hasty letter to Frank Gamewell told the tale: 'The Chinese government has notified us that the Admirals at Ta Ku have notified the Viceroy that they will take possession of all the Ta Ku forts tomorrow.

This they consider a declaration of war by all the Powers and hence tender Ministers their passports, and ask us to leave Peking in twenty-four hours . . . If we had a thousand men here and any knowledge of where other troops were, we might refuse to go, but under the circumstances there is only one thing to do.'[25]

The Chinese government's ultimatum had arrived in neat red envelopes, one for each minister. The polite, precise wording made it clear that the deadline for the ministers' removal would expire at 4.00 p.m. the next day. The astonishing contents prompted an immediate meeting in the Spanish Legation, where attempts at discussion were punctuated by unwanted pyrotechnics from a nearby firework shop that had caught fire. This did little to steady the diplomats' nerves as they tried to make sense of events. They had been cut off from the outside world for over a week. They had no knowledge of what was happening in Tientsin, or why the foreign powers thought it necessary to seize the Taku forts. Neither could they be sure of the whereabouts of the relief force that had supposedly set out to save them.

Von Ketteler was convinced that if they tried to leave Peking they would be murdered. Pichon and Conger argued that there was no alternative but to go. Sir Claude was undecided. The invitation to depart bore a sinister resemblance to events preceding the infamous massacre of British men, women and children at Cawnpore during the 1857 Sepoy Mutiny.[26] As Meyrick Hewlett wrote, 'recollections of what happened in the Indian Mutiny' caused Sir Claude 'to suspect the sincerity of Oriental promises.' Sir Robert Hart sent Sir Claude MacDonald a note that probably only compounded the dilemma: 'I am not at all in favour of *surrender* but, when I think of the women and children, I wonder and wonder which course would ensure their safety most entirely.'[27]

The ministers were 'moving about from one Legation to another, arguing, talking – always talking. The strong men felt we must not leave Peking until our own foreign soldiers arrived to escort us, but the weak men felt in despair as to which course to vote for,' wrote Polly. She believed the weak would prevail, adding that it looked very much as if they were all to start out to their deaths the following morning. Legation staff began procuring carts and soon, as Polly wrote, 'we women were packing the tiny amount of hand luggage we were to be allowed to take with us, wondering whether to fill the small bag with a warm coat, to protect us on this indefinite journey to the coast, or to take six fresh blouses.'

Morrison was disgusted and took the floor representing 'the vast crowd of intelligent individuals – engineers, bankers, trades-people and missionaries – who one and all were in favour of waiting.' He told the ministers that if they voted to leave Peking 'the death of every man, woman, and child in this huge unprotected convoy will be on your heads, and your names will go through history and be known for ever as the wickedest, weakest and most pusillanimous cowards who ever lived.' Robert Coltman agreed with him, raging against 'the intensely dense ministers'. Captain Poole was worried how the military men could possibly protect 'all these women and children' during a long and perilous journey to Tientsin. He too feared 'a repetition of . . . the massacre at Cawnpore.' After six hours of agonized argument, an answer was finally sent just before midnight. The ministers told the Tsungli Yamen that they accepted the demand to leave but that twenty-four hours was too short a time to make the necessary preparations. It also requested details of how they were to travel and to be protected and sought an interview with Prince Ching and Prince Tuan at 9.00 the next morning.

The ministers reconvened early the next day at the French Legation but by 9.30 a.m. there was still no news. What were they to do? It seemed undignified to descend in a body on the Tsungli Yamen. The only proper course of action was to wait. A reply must surely come. However, according to a letter Sir Claude later wrote to the Foreign Office, Baron von Ketteler at this point lost his temper and announced his intention of going to the Yamen and staying there all night if necessary. Monsieur

Pichon assiduously warned him of the personal danger. Alarmed
at the idea of the Germans seizing the initiative, the Russian
minister de Giers proposed that the entire diplomatic body
should set out with an armed escort. Von Ketteler pooh-poohed
the idea of an escort, pointing out that only yesterday he had
sent his secretary, Heinrich Cordes, to the Yamen and that he
had returned quite unharmed. In that case, why not send him
again? de Giers suggested. Von Ketteler agreed – or appeared to.

However, a little while later two imposing sedan chairs
proceeded out of the German Legation. Their green and red
hoods denoted that their occupants were people of consequence.
So did the liveried outriders trotting on either side. The streets
were unusually quiet – the usual jostling noisy crowds were
gone. There were no top-heavy wheelbarrows pushed by straining men or dragged by mules and donkeys; no passenger and
freight carts with furiously shouting drivers; no slow-moving
camel trains or prancing mules with jingling bells and elegant
riders.

Von Ketteler probably did not notice. Having changed his
mind and decided to accompany Cordes after all, he had
equipped himself with a fine cigar and a good book. He anticipated hours of tedium at the Tsungli Yamen and was determined
not to be bored. To Lenox Simpson he looked as relaxed as a
man setting out on a picnic. However, half an hour later he was
dead. Mary Gamewell was sadly packing up her possessions in
the Methodist Mission when her husband rushed in with the
news that 'Mr Cordes, the German interpreter, desperately
wounded, had just been brought through our barricades by some
of our students; that he had told that Baron von Ketteler . . . had
been shot in the street by an officer of the Chinese imperial
army; that he himself had been fired upon and had barely
escaped; and having told his tale, exhausted by lack of blood, he
sank into unconsciousness.' According to his account later
published in *The Times*, Cordes 'saw a banner soldier, apparently a Manchu, in full uniform with a mandarin's hat with a
button and blue feather, step forwards, present his rifle within a

yard of the chair window, level it at the Minister's head and fire.'[28]

Curiously enough, a full five days earlier the *North China Daily News* had reported the killing of a foreign minister. Several days later the story had appeared in several European papers, telling the same tale but with one embellishment. They stated that it was the German minister who had been murdered.[29] As Arthur Smith observed, 'It is not often that a crime of this extraordinary character is telegraphed around the world four days in advance of its occurrence.' Perhaps there was an element of pre-planning. According to one theory, von Ketteler had been singled out for death because of his savage beating and capture of the Boxer boy in Legation Street. According to another, he was a marked man because the German Legation possessed incriminating documents about a senior Chinese official. According to yet a third, there had been a plot to murder all the ministers that day and the shooting of von Ketteler was a premature mistake that spoiled the plan.

Whatever the case, the death of von Ketteler had one immediate effect: any talk of leaving the legations ceased forthwith. It would clearly be suicide to attempt it. To Sir Claude MacDonald it was proof that 'the Empress Dowager had made up her mind to throw in her lot with the antiforeign party.' Barricades were immediately strengthened and outlying pickets withdrawn within the legation lines.

The Gamewells received a hastily written message from Edwin Conger. It said, 'Come at once within the Legation lines and *bring your Chinese with you*.' Hugely relieved that they were not expected to abandon their converts, the Gamewells and the seventy or so other American missionaries began grabbing what possessions they could. One lady was so distracted she seized a hot-water bottle. Before long a procession had formed up and was snaking its way out of the mission under the protection of American marines. The missionary women and children came first, followed by German guards bearing the wounded Cordes on a stretcher. He had been shot through the thighs and was to have the distinction of being the first patient in the siege hospital. Seven hundred Christian converts, including more than a hundred schoolgirls, brought up the rear. Captain Hall, directing the evacuation, described it as the most pathetic yet sublime sight he had ever seen. He was deeply moved by 'the absolute faith and trust of all the converts, aged and infirm, stalwart and husky, and the small children some of them barely more than tots, in their leaders to protect them from injury or harm.'

It was an eerie walk. Mary Gamewell described the pall of silence hanging heavy over deserted streets as they walked the half-mile to the legations. 'A great hush seemed to have settled upon the city, as if in awe of the enormity of the crime committed, or holding its breath for an expected explosion.' The brooding stillness oppressed her and it was a relief when they reached the barricade that had been set up across Legation Street. Here the missionaries were separated from their flock. The converts were halted and then directed into the Fu. Edwin Conger, watching the great company of Chinese pass by, exclaimed with tears in his eyes, 'We are bringing them here to starve!' He knew that the Fu was already filled with Catholic converts. However, the situation was even more critical over at the Peitang, where more than 3,000 refugees were now huddling with just the few dozen French and Italian marines sent to defend them. The cathedral had already been under attack for some days. A somewhat despairing note from Monsieur Pichon reached Bishop Favier making it clear he could expect no further help.

Meanwhile the bemused Gamewells and their missionary comrades passed into the broad shady walks of the American Legation. The hospitable Harriet Squiers was waiting to serve all seventy of them an impromptu lunch of crackers, sardines, scrambled eggs and tea. She also opened her storeroom and invited the missionary women to take whatever they needed, including crates of milk and cream. However, the American compound was far too close to the city walls for safety. Word came that they were to proceed at once to the greater protection of the British Legation. As the largest compound with the most solid buildings, it was the natural refuge and rallying point. Despite the danger, Dr Ament quickly slipped back to the Methodist compound to retrieve his beloved bicycle. The Gamewells, however, set out for the British Legation. On the way they were joined by Morrison, who said approvingly, 'I am glad you have brought your Chinese with you.' He told another missionary that if the converts had been abandoned he would have been 'ashamed to call himself a white man.'[30]

There were some 4,000 people from eighteen nations within the legation lines. The foreign community consisted of 473 civilians and just over 400 military personnel. Precise estimates of the number of Chinese converts vary but there were at least 3,000, probably more.[31] Nearly all the foreign women, children and nonfighting men were crowded into the British Legation compound, which normally housed about sixty. They had to share the limited space with a flock of sheep, a cow and a number of ponies and mules. The Gamewells tried to find somewhere to lay their heads. It was not easy. Their party had been among the last to arrive and everywhere seemed full to overflowing with trunks of clothes, tins of supplies, mattresses and bedding. They were allocated some space on the floor of the recently decorated legation chapel and tried to settle in, though every aisle and vestibule seemed choked and overflowing.

It was the most cosmopolitan garrison imaginable. Lenox Simpson wrote spitefully of 'perspiring missionaries of all denominations and creeds' and how the overcrowding was putting everyone in 'a very grunting frame of mind.' Yet some people were well provided for – Commandant Darcy excused the stack of trunks brought by some ladies with Gallic gallantry: *'La coquetterie ne perd jamais ses droits'* – 'Coquetry never loses its prerogatives.'[32] Others, like a party of nuns, had nothing.

As the deadline approached, there were frantic efforts to gather in supplies of food from the surrounding shops. Monsieur Chamot, the hotel-keeper, and Fargo Squiers, the son of the American secretary, who seemed to think the whole affair a huge joke, drove furiously to and fro, bringing in stores of all kinds. As the final minutes ticked away and the sun glinted on the yellow-tiled coping of the Imperial City, a small group of men gathered on the well-kept lawn, watches in hand. The sense of keen anticipation reminded the Reverend Allen of the university rowing eights on the River Thames at Oxford, a strange comparison perhaps. At 4.00 p.m. sharp, heavy firing was heard from the east. Overhead a bullet severed a leaf from a tree, which spiralled gracefully to the ground.

The siege had begun, but the question in everyone's mind was how long it would last and where Vice-Admiral Seymour's relief force was. It would have disturbed them to know that the rescuers they were so anxiously awaiting were in grave need of rescue themselves.

II

'Death and Destruction to the Foreigner!'

20 June – 21 July 1900

6

A FAILED RESCUE

These were not fanatical 'braves', or the trained soldiers of the Empress, but the quiet peace-loving peasantry – the countryside in arms against the foreigner. – Clive Bigham

V ICE-ADMIRAL SIR EDWARD SEYMOUR would have been wounded to know that, due to his failure to arrive in Peking, the next seventeen days would earn him the nickname of 'Admiral Seen-no-more'.[1] He had first become aware that something unusual was afoot when he received Sir Claude's telegram of 28 May asking for guards to be sent to Peking as a precaution against 'troublesome' Boxers. When further alarming reports reached him on 31 May, he decided to sail up the Chinese coast and join the other foreign men-of-war from Russia, France, Germany, America, Austria, Italy and Japan anchored off Taku. As Seymour later wrote, he was 'fortunately' the senior admiral on the station, so it was his place to initiate proceedings. He invited the other commanding officers on board his flagship and urged that they work in concert. They agreed that if necessary an allied naval brigade should be landed to advance on Peking.

The sixty-year-old Seymour was confident that he was the proper person to command such an expedition by virtue of seniority and experience. He had a good China pedigree, having served as a young midshipman under his uncle Admiral Sir Michael Seymour in the China campaign of 1860. More importantly, he knew that if he took command it would avoid British men having to serve under foreign command – as great a concern for Britain then as it is for the United States today. He sent a telegram to the Admiralty in London setting out his proposals. However, events moved on before it could reply. Seymour had sent his chief of staff, Captain John Jellicoe, to Tientsin for information. On 9 June, Jellicoe 'found that a telegram had just arrived stating that the [British] Minister had just wired that unless Peking was relieved it would be too late . . . I at once told [HMS] *Algerine* to flash off to the flagship "Serious news, prepare landing parties."'[2]

Seymour lost no time. By 1.00 a.m. on 10 June he had ordered the landing of a British force. He himself went in on the *Fame*, a new thirty-knot destroyer that drew only eight feet of water. Its commander was a lively and ambitious young officer, Lieutenant Roger Keyes, who had been busily ferrying sailors sent to reinforce Tientsin. Despite a dark night and a falling tide, Keyes managed to scrape across the Taku bar and manoeuvre through the swarm of gunboats, torpedo-boats, tugs, lighters and junks to the landing place for the rail terminus at Tongku, five miles up the Peiho River. Here Seymour caught a train for Tientsin. The fact that he was acting without formal authority from London did not concern him. His comforting philosophy was that 'in such cases, whether success or failure attends you, England nearly always approves an officer who has evidently done his best. I never could understand why anyone minds taking responsibility. You have only to do what seems proper, and if it turns out badly it is the fault of Nature for not having made you cleverer.'

Seymour had informed the other commanding officers of his intentions and their contingents followed quickly. Captain Lieutenant Paul Schlieper of the German navy described how when the order to dispatch a landing party reached his ship the *Hansa*, 'A lively time followed on deck and every other part of the ship, and one constantly caught the exclamation "This means Peking and fighting the Boxers." How everything was finally got through all right I cannot tell to this day.'

Arriving in Tientsin at around 7.00 a.m., Seymour commandeered some trains by threatening the station officials with force. There was a general scrum as the station began to fill with various detachments. The expedition was to consist of over 2,100 men, accommodated in five trains with over 100 coaches. The British were the largest force by far with over 900. Seymour chose a young consular official, Campbell, to be his Chinese interpreter. He also appointed Clive Bigham, the young diplomat who was so appreciative of the comforts of the British Legation, to his staff as intelligence officer. Seymour knew that he would need Bigham's knowledge of European languages in leading a multinational force. Clive Bigham decided to take along his servant Chao Yin-ho, an experienced and resourceful man who had previously served in both the British and Chinese navies.

As a former Grenadier Guards officer, Bigham was delighted to have the chance of seeing action. He ran a critical and initially patronizing eye over the other forces, which consisted of a German corps of some 500, together with Russian, French, American, Japanese, Italian and Austrian troops. The events of the next few days would convince him that the Americans were 'the best practical and intelligent fighters it is possible to imagine.' He was warm in his praise of their commanding officer, Captain McCalla of the USS *Newark*, an American Civil War veteran who had delighted Polly Condit Smith by leading the relief force into Peking on 31 May. Bigham was also impressed by the Germans under their leader, Captain von Usedom.

Seymour got away first. By around 9.00 his train was moving off up the Peking line, cheered by the foreign residents of Tientsin, although, as Schlieper noted, 'the station swarmed with Chinese who took careful note of our business and urgency generally with a cynical smile or some contemptuous remark.' It is unclear how Schlieper, who could not speak Chinese, knew the remarks were contemptuous, but he was probably correct.

Unlike the summoning of the legation guards in May, this expedition did not have any sanction from the Chinese authorities and it triggered a rapid and aggressive response. Within hours of Seymour's departure, the telegraph line between Peking and Tientsin had been cut and Prince Tuan had been appointed president of the Tsungli Yamen in place of the moderate Prince Ching. The optimistic Seymour, however, expected only a short train journey, an easy march into Peking, and a swift resumption of diplomacy. Clive Bigham shared his view: 'Little did we think that we should never get to Peking, and that when we struggled back to Tientsin with a seventh of our force killed and wounded, the station, the settlement, and the many signs of civilization that we now saw and took pride in would be burnt and desolated ruins, riddled with shot and shell and disfigured by rotting corpses.'

Seymour was gambling that the railway line to Peking was still open. He also believed he had little option. Sir Claude's message had left him in no doubt that a massacre of the foreigners was imminent. The train was the quickest, indeed the only way to cover the eighty miles to Peking in time. He was later to be criticized for rushing off without due care and attention. However, he may well have recalled the odium heaped on Colonel Sir Charles Wilson fifteen years earlier for delaying a fatal forty-eight hours before vainly setting out to save General Gordon, besieged at Khartoum by the Mahdi. Also, as was so often the case during that hot summer of 1900, Seymour did not have all the facts. Schlieper wrote: 'If it had been known beforehand that our little force would have to encounter the whole of the regular army, to fight against horse, foot and artillery, armed with every modern weapon, it would have been great folly to embark upon it; but this was not foreseen, and just as little was it supposed that the opposition of the Boxers would in a moment assume such large proportions.'

At first all went well. By 9.30 Seymour's train was puffing across the hot dusty plain. At Yangtsun, fifteen miles above Tientsin, they came to a fine iron railway bridge spanning the Peiho.

The Empress Dowager Tzu Hsi, 'Old Buddha' as she was
sometimes known, walking in the snow in the Forbidden City.
One foreign admirer called her 'the only man in China'.

Sir Claude MacDonald,
the taciturn British Minister
to Peking who took charge
of the defence of the
Legations.

Edwin Conger, the earnest
American Minister to Peking.

Herbert Squiers, the wealthy and well-connected First Secretary of the American Legation, an ex-cavalry officer who played a key role in the defence of the Legations.

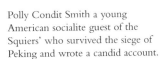

Polly Condit Smith a young American socialite guest of the Squiers' who survived the siege of Peking and wrote a candid account.

Sir Robert Hart the respected Inspector
General of the Imperial Maritime Customs
of China who later admitted: 'We cannot
say we had no warning'.

Vice-Admiral Sir Edward Seymour leader
of the abortive allied relief expedition to
Peking, nicknamed 'Admiral Seen-no-more'
by the besieged

George Morrison, the plain-spoken Peking correspondent of *The Times* with his Chinese household.

Moslem Kansu braves in the army of the virulently anti-foreign
General Tung Fu-hsiang. They were amongst the most professional
and consequently the most feared of the Imperial forces.

The massive walls surrounding Peking which struck visitors with awe.

The magnificent Chienmen, one of the gates leading into the Tartar City.

Fire burning near the Chienmen.

The first British Chinese regiment raised at Weihaiwei who took
part in the relief of Tientsin. Some foreigners predicted wrongly
that they would not fight against their countrymen.

Russian troops at the railway station at Tientsin which they defended
bravely despite the exposed position.

Camped next to it were some 4,000 Imperial Chinese troops under General Nieh. Nieh was in the difficult position of trying to reconcile conflicting orders from Peking. At one moment he was being told to suppress the Boxers and had obligingly sliced off seventy Boxer heads and sent them to the local viceroy in baskets. At the next he was being ordered not to fire on them. For now the two forces exchanged what Seymour described as 'friendly greetings' as the foreigners crossed the river without incident.

The train chugged on across the dull flat landscape dotted with eerie kraal-shaped Chinese graves, but before long Seymour encountered the first signs of Boxer sabotage. Ties and rails near Lofa station, nearly halfway to Peking, had been torn up and a railway bridge damaged. The Boxers had lit huge fires beneath it to warp the rails and destroy the wooden sleepers. Seymour halted for the night and put the hundred Chinese labourers he had brought for the purpose to work on repairs. Schlieper's train then caught up and he described approvingly how Seymour allotted the senior German officers 'a covered carriage ranking as a first-class' for use as sleeping quarters. An open carriage to the rear of an engine served as a club. 'It formed an interesting study in itself, for club life here was certainly most original. At first we observed the distinctions of rank and meaning as on board ship, but later on, when first the bread and then the preserved meat began to give out, everything was thrown into the common stock and we all messed together. The cellar was managed separately, and each man's account entered to him, but how this was done when, say the alarm sounded and our good steward had to rush for his rifle . . . I will not venture precisely to say.'

Schlieper confronted a grimmer reality as they steamed slowly into Lofa early the next morning. 'Near the ruins of a burned down passenger shed, the bodies of four Chinese railway officials were lying, horribly mutilated. It was a sudden glimpse of war in her darkest colours, an unmistakable indication of the way in which our prospective enemies did their work. Men's faces grew pale and the blood froze in their veins . . . The bodies had been cut to pieces, the hands and feet hacked off, and in one case the heart had been torn out. Such would be our fate if we were found wounded.'

The allies' first encounter with these 'prospective enemies' came as they approached the station of Langfang and the Boxers attacked. According to a fascinated Schlieper, they advanced 'with wild gestures swinging their spears, lances or swords about their heads . . . We often saw Boxers spring up into the air, execute a sort of war dance, and then drop to the ground . . . but when we got nearer and could see them plainly, they proved only to have been shamming to make us believe they had been killed and so avert our fire.' Bigham was struck by their courage and dash but also by something more fundamental: 'They came on us in a ragged line, advancing at the double . . . Not more than a couple of hundred, armed with swords, spears, gingalls [a giant smooth-bored two-man blunderbuss usually fired from a wooden tripod], and rifles, many of them being quite boys. To anyone who had been some little time in China it was an almost incredible sight, for there was no sign of fear or hesitation, and these were not fanatical "braves", or the trained soldiers of the Empress, but the quiet peace-loving peasantry – the countryside in arms against the foreigner.'

Progress from now on was agonizingly slow. Seymour was constantly faced with repairing torn-up rails and broken bridges. It was equally problematic to get water for the engines because the Boxers had destroyed the station water tanks and watering the engines by bucket was 'a most tedious process'. The men also needed water for themselves. Hot dry dust blown from the Gobi hung in the air and clogged their mouths and nostrils. The discovery of a clean well by a reconnaissance party prompted a great exodus as men scrambled for a drink of fresh water. Seymour halted his convoy at Langfang, where the station had been destroyed, and sent men ahead to survey the track. A messenger arrived on 12 June from the American Legation in Peking. He told them that news of the allied advance was causing a tumult in the city and advised them of the best way to force an entry into Peking. He also warned of concentrations of

Imperial troops south of the city. However, it was becoming apparent to Seymour that he would not be able to get his trains beyond Langfang quickly, if at all. The party he had sent to reconnoitre reported that the line was very badly damaged.

The allied force held on to Langfang station for five days while trying to repair the line and fighting off Boxer attacks. The young British Lieutenant Fownes-Luttrell found them unnerving: 'They often stopped a few yards off and went through their gesticulations for rendering themselves immune from bullet wounds. Many were shot while kowtowing towards the trains and remained dead in that position.' He worried whether it was fair play 'bowling them over like so many rabbits' but decided that 'it has to be done, they are doing such a lot of fearful damage to the country.'[3]

Commander Mori of the Imperial Japanese Navy was curious to inspect the bodies of the Boxer dead: 'They were young and old . . . their costumes were various, and they had red bands tied round their heads and hanging down behind, as well as red aprons . . . Their shoes also were tied with red.'[4]

On 14 June, the situation deteriorated further when vital contact with Tientsin was lost. The supply train, which had been plying backwards and forwards, failed to get beyond Yangtsun because heavy concentrations of Boxers were now holding the bridge and doing their best to destroy it. Of General Nieh's camp at Yangtsun there was no sign. On the same day five Italian pickets who, somewhat unwisely, had been playing cards, 'fell into the power of the cruel brutes who literally cut them to pieces.' All their shocked comrades found were their dismembered bodies, and the deaths had a profound psychological effect. A young British sailor wrote glumly that 'one thing is certain, you know what to expect if you are captured by them.'[5] They were the expedition's first fatalities and were buried that night. An English naval chaplain prayed as the bodies were lowered into makeshift graves in front of a parade of the whole force. Schlieper wrote: 'It was a very affecting scene – many must have asked themselves the question "Shall I too soon be laid to rest?" Some men turned faint and had to be led away.'

Seymour still hoped he might break through to Peking. He sent a note by courier to Sir Claude MacDonald saying that he hoped to enter the city in a few days. The postscript ended in hopeful tones: 'All will yet be well.'[6] However, on 16 June, Seymour sent Schlieper and his company down the track to try to restore communication with Tientsin. They reached Lofa without incident but further on found 'havoc in front of us'. Schlieper reported to Seymour that the track would require extensive repairs. He set his men to work but requested reinforcements. He also reported the discovery of a partly decomposed body stripped of its clothes. It was presumed to be the body of a Chinese messenger carrying allied dispatches for Tientsin who had been captured and murdered.

Seymour now inspected the track himself and realized the predicament: 'We were now isolated, with no transport or means to advance, and cut off from our base behind.' He believed the only sensible course was to attempt to repair the line backwards and retreat towards Tientsin. He hoped there was an outside chance that when he reached Yangtsun he might be able to take the relief force up towards Peking by river, the route of the allied expedition in 1860, but he must have realized the possibility was remote. He could hardly sail up the Peiho with no communication or supply lines before or behind him. He was, however, to be criticized for not attempting to push on to Peking, only thirty miles away, by foot from Langfang. Sir Robert Hart complained that 'had [his force] left the train and marched straight across the country to the Capital it could have been with us on the 13th or 14th and so changed history.'[7] Clive Bigham, who had the advantage of actually being with Seymour, took a different view: 'There was no road, we were absolutely without transport, and directly in front of us lay . . . the camps of the Peking Field Force . . . and in front of the south gate of the Chinese city lay, we knew, most of General Tung-fu-hsiang's Kansu soldiery.' Captain McCalla agreed that 'the expedition could have gone no further than it had.'[8]

*   *   *

Preparations were now made for the withdrawal. The German commander, Captain von Usedom, was left with orders to hold Langfang and protect the allies' rear while mighty exertions were made to repair the bent rails and girders and burnt crossties to enable the trains to be moved back to the bridge at Yangtsun. By now the bridge itself was so damaged that it was impassable. According to Schlieper, 'the havoc was so complete that the cooperation of regular troops, already suspected, had to be accepted as a certainty. We might wait a long time now for our return to Tientsin.' The station at Yangtsun and the water tower had also been rendered useless and 'the situation was obviously desperate.' Even a 'splendid supper' of broth and fricasseed fowl, concocted from a clutch of looted chickens, failed to raise Schlieper's spirits.

Seymour, 'very nervous and unstrung', according to Schlieper, summoned a council of war in his dimly lit railway carriage. They agreed that the trains would have to be abandoned and some other means of transport found. Not only was the track impassable but there was a further factor in the equation. At Langfang, von Usedom had come under ferocious attack from some 5,000 Imperial troops – Kansu braves commanded by General Tung Fu-hsiang. He managed to rejoin the main force at Yangtsun with half a dozen dead and over fifty wounded on the evening of 18 June. His report confirmed that Imperial troops were indeed making common cause with the Boxers and convinced Seymour that a retreat to Tientsin was the only possible course of action.

Admiral Seymour took comfort that he was at least near the river and commandeered the only four Chinese junks he could find to transport wounded men and essential equipment. In the early hours of 19 June, the allies abandoned their trains and began to march back to Tientsin down the left bank of the Peiho, escorting the captured junks loaded with groaning, crying, sick and wounded men wedged in among guns, ammunition, provisions and baggage. Only absolute necessities were taken and everything else was flung into the river: 'All our

trophies of war . . . the large standards, the curious weapons, all
the plunder with which our carriages had been hung, all had to
be sacrificed.' The officers' dress uniforms – a curious thing to
have packed for a rushed rescue mission – were buried in the
hope that they might be retrieved in more auspicious times.
Looking back, the sailors could see Boxers pouring in from all
sides and swarming over the deserted trains, which they later set
on fire. Schlieper was reminded of Napoleon's retreat from
Moscow – 'In the foreground troops of differing nationalities, in
the background a sea of flames.'

They began a punishing journey in tremendous heat. Exhausted
men could slake their thirst only by drinking the dubious dark
brown waters of the Peiho. They had only some thirty miles to
cover, but the junks kept grounding in the shallow waters and it
was 'the most toilsome and disheartening work imaginable.'[9]
The Boxers held many of the mud villages along the riverbank
and the allies had to keep halting to deploy the guns. As
Schlieper wrote: 'When one village was cleared a still hotter fire
was sure to be opened on us from the next. It was a tough bit of
work.' It was quite a blooding for some of Seymour's inexperienced young officers. One young midshipman, who manned a
Nordenfelt machine gun mounted on a railway wagon, wrote: 'I
find that being in action is not quite like the description given in
books. I don't think I felt any fear but there was a curious sensation at first which gradually wore off . . . I saw several men
killed and they all fell over quite quietly, no jumping in the air
or anything of that sort.'[10] At the same time, the convoy was
being harassed on the flank by Imperial troops with light guns
and the provisions were running out. The whole force was put
on half-rations although, as Seymour later cheerily observed, 'it
is astonishing how little food you can do with for a short time.'
    The fact that there had been no opportunity to unpack suitable
clothing before setting out added to their discomfort. The
German contingent was marching in thick blue clothing,
designed for operations in the North Sea in winter, which

contrasted oddly with their sun helmets. It was not, as Schlieper observed, an occasion for dandies and drawing-room loungers. And from time to time there came the depressing sound of the Chinese guns pounding the foreign settlement at Tientsin.

The journey also brought home to Seymour the absolute terror felt by the ordinary Chinese at the sight of the foreigners: 'We had got one or two more junks to hold the wounded, and I sent some men on board to examine and prepare them; no sooner had they reached the decks than, as if in a pantomime, the closed hatches flew open, and out popped some women and children and leaped over the side into the river, preferring drowning to falling into the hands of the "foreign devils".' Some of his men jumped after them and fished them out, but Seymour found it a puzzling and disturbing episode.

On 20 June, the day the siege of Peking began, Seymour made only eight miles' progress, fighting the entire way. The day had begun with the burial of two English sailors who had died during the night from their wounds. Schlieper wrote: 'Breakfast had no flavour, a funeral so soon after rising does not induce the right frame of mind for it.' For the first time Seymour's men noticed that he seemed 'a little despondent'.[11] On the following day came the worst battle so far at the large village of Peitsang. The allies took the village but at a heavy cost. Schlieper's left shin was broken by a rifle shot and Captain Jellicoe was seriously wounded. He had been hit in the chest but thought at first that his left arm had gone. He was also coughing up a lot of blood. A doctor bandaged him up and gave him morphine but told him frankly that 'he thought he was finished.'[12] The captain made his will on a piece of paper and gave it to his coxswain. A grim-faced Seymour asked the senior German officer, Captain von Usedom, to act as his chief of staff and, if he, Seymour, were killed, to take over the command of the expedition.

Seymour's priority now was to get his 200 or so wounded men to safety. He decided that as soon as they had been loaded on to the newly acquired junks he would push on through the

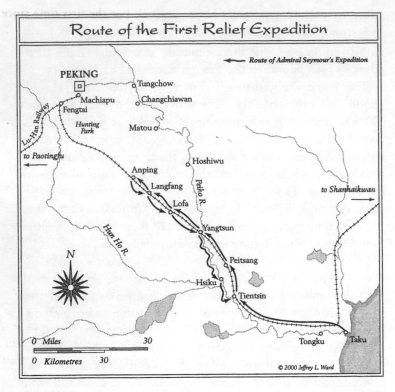

Route of the First Relief Expedition

night. He was worried that his force might be surrounded and wiped out. He knew that the Chinese gave no quarter and the spectre of an 'international holocaust' drove him forwards. On 22 June, the convoy moved off at 1.15 a.m. and before daylight marines had taken the first village to resist. However, as the dawn came up a strange sight met the eyes of the exhausted men. They were abreast of a fortified position with a long embrasured parapet on the opposite bank of the Peiho. Some uniformed soldiers came out and asked who they were. Seymour's men replied that they were 'a friendly force on our way to Tientsin.'[13] The almost immediate response was a 'roar of musketry, and the whole line of parapet flashed into a sheet of flame.'[14]

The allied expedition had stumbled on something they had not known existed – the great Hsiku arsenal. For the first time since Seymour had left Tientsin twelve days earlier, providence had smiled. Seymour later wrote that the attack from the ramparts probably saved the expedition. They now set their minds to capturing the arsenal. Had they continued on towards Tientsin, hauling their junks of wounded through the narrow and intricate watercourse above the city and with forts on either side, Seymour was certain they would have met with 'complete disaster'.

Nevertheless, the arsenal did not seem like their salvation at the time. To Bigham it was 'a sort of death-trap and for an instant all was confusion.' Seymour launched the attack on the arsenal at once. He sent British marines to cross the river upstream using a bridge of junks and to attack the northeast side of Hsiku. At the same time he dispatched a party of Germans to cross by raft to the southwest. Working together they succeeded in capturing the arsenal after an hour of fierce fighting.

Hsiku turned out to be a massive rectangle enclosing some thirty to forty acres. It contained a temple, barracks and a huge stone arsenal stuffed with Krupp field guns, rifles and 7 million rounds of ammunition, some of it similar to the allies' own equipment. In addition to this military bonanza were fifteen tons of rice and ample stocks of medical supplies. The allies had long ago run out of bandages and had been improvising with the bindings from officers' and marines' helmets.

However, almost at once General Nieh's forces launched an all-out assault to try to retake the arsenal and were repulsed only with great difficulty. Then, at 3.00 the next morning, 23 June, the Imperial troops attacked again, this time in concert with Boxer forces. Some managed to scramble over the walls in the darkness and the allies lost a number of men in the bitter fighting. Seymour decided that given the obvious strength of the forces between him and Tientsin and his large number of wounded it was impossible to move on.

That day Polly Condit Smith was writing in her diary that she feared it might be very difficult for the legations to hold out until the troops come. 'Until the troops come! What a wail that is! and it is heard at all times, and all people take their turn in asking somebody else, "When will they come?"' Monsieur Pichon was muttering disconsolately to Lenox Simpson, 'Il a disparu complètement – entièrement; c'est la fin' – 'He [Seymour] has completely, entirely vanished; it is the end.'

There might just have been more sympathy for 'Admiral Seen-no-more' had they known of his predicament. As one young midshipman wrote: 'It is quite impossible to describe the nastiness of life in the arsenal: quarter rations, rice and sand-storms, rice puddings absolutely brown from the dirty water they were cooked in. The bones of a mule boiled into soup were greatly relished.'[15] Bigham described 'every morning hurried burials with bullets flying over the common grave; every day renewed fears for our friends in Peking and Tientsin; every night the same forlorn expectation of a returning messenger who never came.' He noted sorrowfully that the rum had run out long ago and that they had finished most of the ration beef and biscuit. They were now surviving on the rice they had found in the arsenal supplemented by the occasional troop horse of the Imperial cavalry. Schlieper, lying in the courtyard while sheds were cleared for the wounded, was grateful for the luxury of hot cocoa and cakes brought to him by the young British consular official, Campbell, who was acting as interpreter. However, he found it a harrowing wait. They were 'days of torture . . . dragged through amidst the groans of wounded and the cries of dying men, the piping of bullets whizzing close by us, and the noise of shells and shrapnel falling on the roof.'

Seymour deployed his forces as best he could and dug in. Firing was heard from the southeast. This meant that the European settlement in Tientsin was under attack but also that it was holding out. It was essential to communicate with the settlement and, after several unsuccessful attempts to get messages through, Clive Bigham's Chinese servant, Chao Yin-ho, was entrusted with the task. He set out on 24 June 'with a cipher message from the Admiral to the Consul which he was to eat if caught. He swam the river in the early morning and went alone on his perilous way.'[16] The eight-mile journey to the foreign settlement was indeed perilous. Chao was first stopped and interrogated by Boxers. He was then caught and questioned roughly by Imperial troops, who tied him to a tree. However, his coolness and quick wits saved him. He managed to swallow the message and convince his tormentors that his journey was innocent and that he should be released. By evening he was able to reach the native city.

At first Chao thought he was too late. On enquiring of other Chinese what had happened to the 'foreign devils' he was told that nearly all were dead or had fled. Nevertheless he set out for the settlement, keeping to the shadows and managing to reach a deserted zone of houses. Almost immediately he came across a French outpost, which fired on him mistaking him for a Boxer. By semaphoring desperately with his arms he at last managed to explain that he had brought a message and was escorted to the British Consulate. Here he told his tale.

Preparations were immediately put in hand to send a rescue party to bring in Seymour's men. The settlement itself had been reinforced a few days earlier by an international force sent up from Taku. Even so, the defenders of Tientsin knew that they would be left short-handed by the need to send out a relief column. Nevertheless, as Captain Bayly, the acerbic naval officer left in command of the British forces by Seymour, acknowledged, 'Rules won't always do.'[17]

Meanwhile, a dust storm had been raging at the Hsiku arsenal and spirits were low. But 'at last came the end, when we had almost given up hope,' wrote a thankful Bigham. On the morning of 25 June 'the welcome cap and lance of a Cossack was decried to the south, then a European bugle was heard, and finally on the opposite shore appeared the welcome relieving force.' It consisted of some 1,800 men, including 900 Russians lately arrived from Port Arthur and 500 British seamen led by Commander David Beatty and Commander Christopher

Cradock, a veteran of previous land campaigns in the Sudanese desert, under the overall command of the Russian colonel Sherinsky. They had marched out by night under the railway embankment guided by Clive Bigham's loyal and brave servant after a guide provided by the British Consulate had led them hopelessly astray.

The force came under fire as they crossed a bridge. According to a Royal Navy officer, 'it was necessary for the force to pass along a narrow bend in single file. A few Chinese snipers had discovered this, so that the spot was rather a "Windy corner". The Germans in extraordinary khaki uniform and yellow straw hats, were holding us all up . . . Cradock and Beatty arrived, both mounted, and were furious at the delay. Failing to goad the Germans into activity, they dismounted and led their horses up an incline . . . On reaching the top, they mounted again under a shower of whistling bullets and walked their horses down the other side. This was too much for us, and we became braver and scrambled over the Germans, carrying some of them with us. Beatty had no fear, or better still, nobody ever knew if he had any.'[18]

The relieving force reached Hsiku at about 10.30 a.m., after spotting the white flag flying from the battlements. They had brought food and, happily, cigarettes. A young British midshipman wrote that he had had 'a cigarette which was simply lovely, we having been reduced to smoking Chinese tea in our pipes.'[19] Commander Mori wrote of the troops' cries of delight and how they 'joined hands in congratulation.'[20]

Sherinsky was anxious to return as soon as possible and Seymour agreed to start early the next morning. Work began immediately on preparing litters for the wounded, who would all have to be carried since the river running through the native city was not open to the allies. There was no way of removing the guns from the arsenal, so they were wrecked. The thousands of ammunition boxes were stacked in great piles in the courtyard and surrounded with gunpowder. The party moved out of the arsenal in the small hours of 26 June. It was dank and cold and the sky was filled with a dull red glare from burning houses in Tientsin. As soon as the march began, there was a mighty explosion as Lieutenant Lowther Crofton of the Royal Navy blew up the ammunition, sending huge tongues of flame leaping into the night sky. The conflagration lasted for more than a day and consumed an estimated £3,000,000 worth of munitions.

The six-hour march through stubble fields and ravines, along railway embankments and across bridges, was uneventful and the column gradually snaked its way round by the deserted railway into the suburbs that stretched outside Tientsin. The houses were burnt and pillaged, the station destroyed, 'and everywhere blackened ruins and corpses – the smoking desolation of war.'[21] At 9.00 in the morning they re-entered the foreign settlement. Mrs Scott, wife of Bishop Scott, watched them come in: 'I never shall forget to my dying day, the long string of dusty, travelworn soldiers . . . officers almost unrecognizable with a fortnight's beard and layers of dust, but so glad to get back and have a handshake; while the men were met by kind ladies with pails of tea which the poor fellows drank as if they had never drunk before – some bursting into tears – like children. The saddest part was the long line of stretchers with poor motionless figures inside which turned into the hospital gate.'[22] Captain McCalla, who had been shot through the left instep and the hip a few days earlier, was propped up on a donkey. According to a comrade a bullet had also 'gone through his scabbard and another through the brim of his hat. He was grit clear to the core.'[23]

Seymour's men had been away for seventeen days and had seen action on fourteen of them. Sixty-two men had been lost and 228 wounded. There was no news from Peking. However, Seymour's battered force now learned of the taking of the Taku forts and the desperate struggle to defend the foreign settlement of Tientsin, which was by no means over. As Seymour said, 'I found the European settlements in a complete state of siege.'

7

CITY OF MUD AND FIRE

It was in the centre that the melodrama and comedy were played – the rim was nearly all tragedy. – Herbert Hoover

THE PEOPLE OF TIENTSIN had the unenviable reputation of being among the most 'quarrelsome and obstreperous'[1] in China. The arrival of thousands of Boxers in the early months of 1900 had compounded this natural truculence. Local malcontents, petty criminals and boatmen thrown out of their jobs by the Peking–Tientsin railway mingled with young peasants flocking in to escape the drought-ravaged countryside. By early June they were swaggering openly through the Chinese City, which they now controlled and which abutted the foreign settlement. Boxer placards plastered over the city's mud walls whipped up anti-foreign feeling and preyed on people's superstitions. One placard concluded with an instruction reminiscent of a chain letter: 'Those who see this sheet and distribute six copies will deliver a whole family from calamity. If ten sheets are circulated they will save an entire district. If any see this hand-bill and fail to disseminate it they will certainly be beheaded.'[2]

The Boxers instructed the population how to do their hair,

what to wear, what to eat and when to burn incense. They even led them in singing a curious little rhyme: 'When women don't dress their locks, we can chop off the foreigners' blocks; when women don't bind their kickers, we can kill all the foreigners with snickers.'[3] The Tientsin correspondent of the *North China Herald* wrote angrily that 'the public mind [native] here is almost inconceivably excited. No rubbish is too preposterous for belief – the Boxers can fly, they can spit fire; even the most sober-minded, sensible Chinese are persuaded that they [the Boxers] are immune to steel and lead. The infection is running to craziness.'[4]

It was now highly dangerous for any foreigner to be seen in the Chinese City. Within hours of Seymour's departure, reinforcements were being rushed up from Taku to protect the foreign settlement. On 11 June, Commander Beatty of the Royal Navy had landed with some 150 sailors and marines and two Maxim machine guns. Two days later, as he was anxiously inspecting the British concession's defences, some 1,600 Russians arrived just in time to beat off a Boxer attack on the railway station. According to Anna Drew, wife of Edward Bangs Drew, the American local commissioner for customs and one of Sir Robert Hart's employees, they were 'great strong dirty fellows, looking as if they had grown into their heavy clothes and big rough boots.' Their arrival brought the size of the defence force up to about 2,400. It was tiny compared with the 30,000 Boxers and 15,000 Imperial troops reputedly camped in and around Tientsin.

On 15 June the Boxers rose. They burned down all the mission stations in the Chinese City including Notre Dame des Victoires, the Catholic cathedral built to commemorate the massacre of the French nuns in the city in 1870. They rampaged through the streets, attacking the homes of Chinese Christians, massacring the occupants, and destroying any foreign goods they could find. There were hysterical scenes as people claimed to see female Boxers, the Red Lanterns, ascending high into the air and circling round the churches in sheets of flame. Foreigners in the adjoining settlement watched in horror as the whole sky lit up with a lurid glare and wondered when the Boxers would turn their attention to them.

The first attack came at 2.00 a.m. on 16 June. Beatty watched as Boxers 'came in great strength, setting fire to all the Houses and outlying Villages they could . . . They came on quite heedless of the Volleys we opened on them, never replying because the poor beggars had no arms to reply with, and coming up to within 300 and 400 yards armed with swords, spears and torches. So there we squatted, knocking them over as they came along.' In the meantime there was panic and confusion in the settlement. The 'gallant Tientsin Volunteers', composed of excitable and inexperienced young civilians, galloped through the streets yelling and shouting 'The Boxers are on you!' and sounding their bugles. Beatty, who set great store by discipline, noted crossly that this was strictly against orders. They also rang the church bells, which was the signal for all the women and children to flee to the Municipal Hall. 'Out of the Houses they poured in a dreadful state of excitement, anxiety and terror, some with nothing on but nightshirts and pyjamas . . . It was difficult to reassure and persuade them to return to their Houses.'[5]

Anna Drew was amused despite the circumstances. She watched a German family set out for the safety of their consulate 'in a great funk – and it was amusing to see the father heading the procession as they walked down the street. There was the mother – a pretty young governess, two sturdy little children with huge sun-hats looking very abused in the middle of the night – an amah [Chinese nanny] and baby and several servants, all with arms full of bundles, and all very serious.'

Meanwhile the admirals lying in their ships off the Taku bar were becoming increasingly anxious. There had been no news from Peking since the cutting of the telegraph line on 10 June; the foreign settlement in Tientsin was clearly in danger and Seymour's relief force was seen no more. His last message to get through had been on 14 June. Everything suggested that the

Chinese indeed intended to block the way to Tientsin. They were reportedly reinforcing the garrisons of their strong, well-armed forts at the mouth of the Peiho River, priming the torpedo tubes in their ships, and laying mines in the river. The situation had every appearance of a trap. Once the Peiho was closed, the naval squadrons would be powerless to help either their trapped comrades in the interior or the civilians of Tientsin and Peking.

The admirals met on the morning of 16 June on board the Russian flagship. With the notable exception of Admiral Kempff of the United States, who had no authority from Washington to take part in hostile action, they agreed to issue an ultimatum. The Chinese must surrender the Taku forts by 2.00 the next morning or the allies would attack. A Russian officer was sent to deliver the message accompanied by a former Irish missionary, Mr Johnstone. They approached the Taku forts nervously and were taken to the Chinese commander. His firm but courteous response to what must have seemed an outrageous request was that 'he would be glad to surrender the Forts, but that he was there to obey orders.' The messengers left at once. As they safely regained their boat, the relieved Russian officer confided to Mr Johnstone that 'he thought their heads would be taken off as the only reply,' and when Johnstone's hat had blown off into the water, he had taken it as 'a very sinister omen'.[6]

Monsieur Matignon, an army doctor attached to the French Legation in Peking, later described how the French consul general in Tientsin, a decisive individual, now took it on himself to telephone the local viceroy to advise him to surrender the forts with a good grace or face the consequences. Matignon wondered whether future historians would be struck by the strangeness of a declaration of war by telephone.

The allied commanders knew that their action was indeed tantamount to declaring war on China. They also knew that taking the forts would not be easy. There were four forts – two on each side of the river – and they had only recently been rebuilt and reinforced by German engineers. The walls and parapets were of mud mixed with chopped straw – a combination impervious to shell fire. The forts were reputedly garrisoned by around 3,000 men, and the armaments included some heavy, quick-firing Krupp guns. Any approach from the seaward side would be extremely hazardous. Not only would the allies have to fight their way under fire across oozing mud flats studded with sharpened stakes, but the Chinese navy had four new German-built destroyers equipped with rapid-fire guns bobbing at anchor beneath the forts. The prospects on the landward side were equally dismal. The allies would have to negotiate a large plain intersected by small canals and irrigation works, while immediately behind the forts lay the Boxer-infested townships of Tongku and Taku.

Another difficulty was that the allies could take only shallow draught vessels over the Taku mud bar and hence within range of the forts. A quick survey revealed that, excluding the USS *Monocacy*, which was not permitted to take part, only nine ships fitted the bill: the three British Royal Navy ships HMS *Algerine*, an elderly unarmoured sloop and two modern thirty-knot destroyers – Lieutenant Keyes's *Fame*, which had taken Admiral Seymour across the bar, and the *Whiting*; the German *Iltis*; the Russian *Gilyak*, *Bobr* and *Koreytz*; the French *Lion*; and the Japanese *Atago*. Another handicap was the extreme narrowness of the river, only some 200 yards wide, and the impossibility of escape should the attack fail. Nevertheless, soon 'all became bustle and activity on the ships outside the bar. Officers and men vied with one another in the work of getting everything ready to equip the storming party, and everyone was strapping up blankets, filling water-bottles, buckling on bandoliers, cutlasses, revolvers and all the other man-killing paraphernalia.'[7] Bad jokes disguised nervousness. 'A brawny bluejacket looked at the small package [his wound dressing] containing gauze, lint and bandage, and asked, "'ere, Bill, what's this for?" "Why, to tie up the Chinamen, of course." "Well, this won't be big enough when I've finished with 'em; give me another dozen."'[8]

*   *   *

Some 900 men were loaded into the nine ships and in the closing hours of 16 June the little vessels lined up to face the forts on the northern bank. The prearranged hour for the bombardment was 2.00 a.m. However, at 12.50 the Chinese opened fire: 'A shell shrieked over the *Algerine* in unpleasant proximity to her topmasts'[9] and began a six-hour battle. Seven of the nine allied ships fired back. The Russian gunboat *Gilyak*, 'a pretty little ship which impressed the observer with a power she was far from possessing,'[10] unwisely turned on her searchlight – a modern innovation of which she was very proud. She instantly became the focus of the enemy gunners and was nearly sunk. Lieutenant Keyes had previously carried out a personal reconnaissance of the forts, wondering whether it would be best to try and storm up the sides in tennis shoes or hobnailed boots. Now he steered the *Fame* and the *Whiting* on a bold mission to capture the Chinese destroyers. In the confusion the two British ships managed to slip upstream until they were abreast of the four Chinese vessels. As Keyes later recalled: 'The shells were literally shrieking around us; several fell just short and splashed muddy water right over us; several pitched just over; we really had a charmed existence.' Each British destroyer then cast off a whaler crewed by a dozen men and an officer.

As they bumped alongside the Chinese destroyers, Keyes's men sprang from the whalers and from the bows of the *Whiting* and the *Fame*. Within minutes they had taken all four without a single allied casualty. Keyes gave strict orders to his men not to fire at the Chinese escaping up the riverbank. He later wrote that this was 'a mistake which no foreigner would have made (but one is rather squeamish about these things).' The escaped men immediately began sniping at them. However, the British sailors were jubilant. As they towed their prizes past the American ship *Monocacy* one of her officers called out, 'Well done! Just like you British – bagging all the most valuable prizes!'[11] They would have been amused to know that the parsimonious British Admiralty subsequently refused to pay any prize money on the grounds that China and Great Britain were not officially at war.

Meanwhile, at about 3.00 a.m., landing parties began to advance towards the forts, struggling through the mud. Again the Chinese put up only a lukewarm defence. The first fort on the north bank was taken at bayonet point. The British and the Japanese were the first to scale the mud parapet; indeed, they raced each other. The senior British officer Commander Cradock was 'frantic at the idea of the Japanese getting in first; they were very keen and in better condition than anyone else.'[12] The Chinese yellow dragons were torn down from the flagstaffs and the white ensign of the Royal Navy was hoisted, followed by the red sun of Japan. However, the danger was not over. A British midshipman described how 'my Lieutenant and myself were standing in the square cheering our flag going up, with our men taking cover in a passage, when two Chinese nipped out of a gateway about twenty yards away and came for us with fixed bayonets, firing their magazines as they marched, from the hip. My Lieutenant had emptied his revolver and was drawing his sword to defend himself when I chipped in and "bagged the brace".'[13] Some of the killing was less discriminating. Another midshipman, who 'had the great good luck to see active service and the bad luck to have been shot through the leg by one of my own men . . . an idiot of a stoker,' described in *The Times* how the Russians and the Japanese then 'ran amok and slaughtered everyone they saw.'[14]

As men now raced towards the second fort on the north bank, an allied shell hit its magazine. The resultant explosion choked the air with dust and smoke. The Chinese struggled to fire their remaining guns but soon gave up and fled. There was barely any need to attack the two forts on the south bank. Here too allied shells had fortuitously pierced a huge magazine, knocking out most of the guns and ending any attempt at defence. A Chinese commander was seen galloping away on a white horse. An account in the *Shanghai Mercury* painted a grim picture of the scene he was leaving behind. 'The forts were a mass of ruins, rivers of blood, with headless and armless bodies everywhere, which the blue-jackets were gathering together and cremating in heaps.'[15]

By 8.00 a.m. many of the storming parties were back on board ship having breakfast. Others, detailed to garrison the forts, squatted among the ruins and the bodies to eat tinned beef, salmon and ship's biscuit and to reflect on their own good fortune at still being alive.

All in all it had been a brave action assisted by a liberal helping of luck. With only nine little ships, the allies had secured the route into northern China at relatively modest cost. However, the consequences were to be vigorously debated and many – including some of the people the admirals had intended to help – argued it should not have happened at all. Herbert Hoover believed that 'it was this act of aggression which marked the downfall of the moderate party in Peking, unmasked the gigantic plot of the powerful party behind the Boxers, and turned the Government over definitely into their hands . . . no more favourable moment could have been chosen by our Admirals to precipitate a general massacre.' Some of the besieged community in Peking echoed his sentiments. Sir Claude MacDonald thought it a little unfortunate that he should have been sending his earnest assurances to the Empress Dowager that Britain wished to maintain 'the friendliest relations' at the very time she learned that British and other foreign naval forces 'were battering down the fortified seagates of her Capital.' As he wrote, this was hardly calculated to put the 'old Buddha' in a good temper.

In Tientsin's foreign settlement, people heard the booming of the guns. Lou Hoover recorded that 'about 8 o'clock we received word by telephone from Taku, that the forts had been taken.' They waited apprehensively, wondering what would happen next. 'All the forenoon at Tientsin there was an ominous silence, nothing doing on either side, each waiting for the other to play the next card, neither knowing the result of the attack at Taku, and yet both sides knowing that now we were committed to a war, if not with China itself, with Northern China and the Manchu Dynasty.' Then, at about 3.00 p.m., the Chinese artillery opened fire and shells began whizzing about their

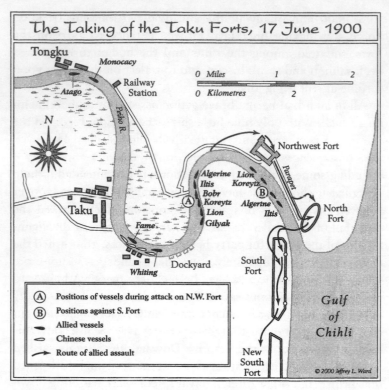

The Taking of the Taku Forts, 17 June 1900

Tongku

Monocacy

Railway Station

Atago

Peiho R.

0 Miles 1 2

0 Kilometres 2

N

Northwest Fort

Algerine Lion

Iltis Koreytz

Bobr

Koreytz Algertne

Lion Iltis

Gilyak

Taku

Parapet

North Fort

Fame

South Fort

Dockyard

Whiting

Gulf of Chihli

Ⓐ Positions of vessels during attack on N.W. Fort

Ⓑ Positions against S. Fort

━ Allied vessels

◡ Chinese vessels

➜ Route of allied assault

New South Fort

© 2000 Jeffrey L. Ward

heads. Anna Drew, who had spent the morning 'bracing up the gardeners who had been rather lax of late,' was lying on a comfortable sofa reading a book 'when – sss – sss – sss – boom!, a long hissing sound, followed by a loud explosion – seemingly directly over our house' brought her instantly to her feet. The alarm bell on the Municipal Hall began to ring. Foreign residents spilled into the streets, dragging their children after them. Rifle bullets, ricocheting off the walls of the brick compounds, sent them dashing for cover.

On the face of it, the situation looked hopeless. Six hundred foreigners were trapped in an area a mile long and about a quarter of a mile wide bounded by the river on one side and a flat plain on the other. As Lou Hoover wrote, 'it was not chosen for defence.' Originally the foreign settlement had been sited some two miles southeast of the 'noxious' walled Chinese City – far enough away to escape the smells, but close enough for trade. However, the two were now linked by an untidy maze of narrow alleys and single-storeyed Chinese houses – a perfect concealment for snipers. The whole was enclosed by a mud wall about fifteen feet high and wide enough for four men to walk abreast.

Midshipman Dix wrote: 'The prospect was hardly brilliant; inside the settlement was a mixed force of 2,400 men, with nine field guns, and a few machine guns; outside were 15,000 Imperial troops, with immense numbers of quick-firing guns. Their ammunition was of the best, and practically unlimited, and they had the dreaded Boxers at their back.'[16] The foreigners learned only later that there was not complete harmony between the Boxers and the regular Chinese soldiers garrisoned at Tientsin. 'The comfort-loving Chinese soldier was not at all pleased with his compulsory assignment to distasteful work, and freely accused the Boxers of causing the row . . . Numbers of incidents are related to us where tragic dialogues took place . . . when a body of soldiers would get hold of an isolated and smaller body of Boxers:

> "Are you real, genuine Boxers?"
> "Yes!"
> "Well then stand up and let us see if you are genuine or not,' and forthwith a little rifle practice would take place on the false Boxer."[17]

There was no time for fruitless and depressing reflection. The Russian Colonel Wogack was the most senior foreign officer in Tientsin and the Americans, Japanese, Germans, French and Italians agreed to serve under his command. The exception was the British, who remained under the command of the floridfaced Captain Bayly of HMS *Aurora*, the man whom Vice-Admiral Seymour had left in charge. The Russians were deployed in the most hazardous and exposed position. It was their job to hold the railway station on the opposite side of the river from the settlement despite the proximity of Chinese graves, houses, embankments and ditches, which provided excellent cover for snipers. The Russians, together with the French, also held the river in front of the French concession and the north end of the settlement as far as the Taku road. Then came the Americans, occupying what Lou Hoover sympathetically called 'a trying stretch', with the British along the entire east side of the settlement. The Austrians, Germans, Japanese and Italians defended the mud wall down to the river and a portion of the riverbank.

A hurried council of war decided that the civilians should do sentry, police, ambulance and engineering duty. Herbert Hoover and his men were the only engineers in Tientsin, and Wogack asked them to instruct the Chinese Christians, who had fled into the settlement, in building barricades. They hunted frantically for material and were delighted to find godowns (warehouses) stacked with sacks of sugar, peanuts, rice and grain. Hoover wrote: 'Soon we . . . had a thousand terrified Christian Chinese carrying and piling up walls of sacked grain and sugar along the exposed sides of the town and at cross streets.'[18] By the next morning Hoover reported that the settlement was in a rather better state.

Within hours there was a fierce assault. Even the calm and practical Hoover feared it might be the end: 'With the smoke of many burning buildings pouring over the settlement, with the civilians erecting barricades across the streets for the final rush, the terrific bombardment, the constant sound of rifle-fire in the distance, and the knowledge – if not the sight – of the scores of wounded brought in from the lines – it all seemed bad – very bad. It was really the climax of terror, of the black fear, as it was of the fighting. And this was the "black fear", not that the siege would be successful and we should be compelled to lower our flag and surrender to an honourable enemy – but that, if every man fought to his utmost strength and was beaten, there were without – *Chinamen* – mobs of Chinamen, at their very worst – barbarians who knew no quarter.'

Women, children and other noncombatants huddled in the bombproof catacombs beneath Gordon Hall – the robust stone municipal hall of Victorian high-gothic design opposite the elegant Astor Hotel. Mrs Scott described with surprising levity how, in the thick of the fighting, her husband the bishop had to conduct a funeral service for two allied casualties. 'It was very comical for such a lover of peace as he is to have to go out under fire and be told by a marine guard to dodge behind the hearse when they were in a very exposed place, and then double!'[19] As she also wrote: 'We have all of us had our squeaks. My nearest one I think was in the hospital where I was giving breakfast to the wounded and a shell came slick through a ward full of beds covering everyone with glass splinters but hurting no one. I just managed not to spill the cup of tea I was handing.'

The Chinese made a determined assault on the railway station. Beatty took some British sailors across the bridge of boats from the settlement to reinforce its Russian defenders, but he and his men were soon pinned down. First they tried sheltering among the Russian artillery horses but then found that 'the safest place . . . was along and under the station platforms. Time after time the Chinese advanced under the cover of their artillery fire, the whole place being alive with shells and fragments of shell . . . Anyone rising to fire at the advancing Chinese was immediately struck down. The only chance we had was to let them come on and as they got closer and became more exposed let them have it in volleys when they invariably fell back.'

Beatty noted how the Russian defenders 'worked their guns like men, scorning to build up protection with the bales of goods that were there and which we utilized for our riflemen.' This seemed 'exceeding stupid', but he could not but admire their stoical courage. He was later less impressed with the Germans, whose incessant demands were an 'infernal nuisance'. Time after time they would send messages to say that they were being heavily attacked, and unless reinforcements came would have to abandon their position. According to Beatty they were invariably false alarms and he gave the Germans a piece of his mind, making it clear that they could expect no reinforcements from him.

However, the sailors and marines managed at last to beat off the attack and the foreign population dug in for the seemingly inevitable siege. Most civilians moved into a small area in the heart of the settlement. This was enclosed by a defensive ring manned by allied troops. Herbert Hoover wrote: 'It was in the centre that the melodrama and comedy were played – the rim was nearly all tragedy.' The Hoovers' rented house was on the very edge of the settlement and right in the firing line. On the first night of the bombardment, together with several other American families, they moved in with Edward Drew, whose house in the centre of the settlement was shielded by godowns.

The Drew children – including their daughters, described by Morrison as 'very dark but attractive' – had been sent to Japan for safety a few days earlier, where they joined Captain McCalla's wife and daughters. Anna Drew had been preparing their rooms and busily hanging fresh curtains ready to receive some of the foreign community from Peking. Now she put them to another purpose as Tientsin residents sought sanctuary. Lou Hoover cycled over, accompanied by bundles of food and bedding in a rickshaw. It was arranged that the women would sleep on the floor of one large room, the men in another.

Many of the Drews' Chinese servants had run away or been sent to safety. The exceptions were a 'very antiquated and devoted' gateman and 'a devoted old coolie.' The old man was so frail that Anna Drew gave him cherry brandy to keep his strength up. She also took a nip or two herself, finding she had completely lost her appetite. He took over the cooking, learning to deal with 'jellies, jams, California tinned fruits, quite a lot of tins of California crackers, tinned meats and vegetables,' which the Hoovers had collected for a trip they had been planning to Mongolia. Rice and sugar were easily obtainable from the bags in the barricades. Two of the Hoovers' servants – their 'Number 2 boy' and their 'rickshaw coolie' – came with them, as did some of the other refugees' staff. So, as Anna Drew noted, 'we got on very well for servants.' Every morning they swept up the spent bullets that lay strewn on the ground 'like fallen leaves'.

The servants of the Drew household were well protected. However, Hoover was concerned for the welfare of the three to four thousand Chinese Christians within the settlement. In particular he was worried by the behaviour of 'a number of foreign civilians already in near hysteria mood.'[21] They insisted they were being fired on from within the settlement. On one occasion some Chinese were arrested on suspicion of being snipers and spies. According to Hoover's own account, he rushed to the scene and confronted Captain Bayly, whom he found conducting a 'drumhead trial' by torchlight. Various 'hysterical wharfrats' were testifying to things that could never have taken place. Hoover tried to intervene but Bayly told him to get out. Hearing that some Chinese had already been executed, he cycled as fast as he could to Colonel Wogack's headquarters and asked him to intervene. Wogack whistled up a Russian platoon and returned instantly with Hoover. He ordered a furious Bayly to stop the trial and to hand the Chinese over to Hoover, who led them back to their compound.

Captain Bayly's account is rather different. He later claimed that he was irritated by wild accusations flying around the foreign community, noting that 'accusations of treachery, double dealing, relations with the enemy etc, were common, and in one case, the Consul was asked to get me to execute one person! The charge was absurd on the face of it . . . Indeed, the accused has always rendered service and given useful information . . . and was far less likely than some others to have held any communication with the enemy.' However, he added, perhaps in a swipe at Hoover, that 'too much "touch" with the Chinese was undoubtedly kept up, and too great faith in them held to, for too long a time, by certain people in Tientsin, who had been mixed up with them for years, in business or in various schemes and projects.'[22]

The missionary Frederick Brown acknowledged that 'the

work of the native Christians was of the greatest possible service in saving the settlement.' The women and girls sewed grey caps to cover the British bluejackets' straw hats, which made such excellent targets for the enemy. The men built barricades; carried ammunition, provisions and water; and dug graves, even though 'most of them were not accustomed to this kind of labour, and did their work under heavy fire.'[23] Luella Miner later described how an immensely wealthy Chinese of progressive views had fled for his life from Tungchow to Tientsin, where foreign soldiers 'doubtless ignorant of his identity, impressed him as a water-carrier!'

Despite Hoover's efforts, life remained precarious for the Chinese in the foreign settlement. There was always a fear that spies would infiltrate it and, according to Mrs Drew, 'a great feeling of distrust of all the Chinese.' In one ugly incident a company of sailors was taken by the British Consul to surround a Chinese mansion whose occupants were suspected, quite unfairly, of sending messages to the enemy by carrier pigeon. Any Chinaman on the streets unescorted by a European was liable to be shot. One of Edward Drew's Chinese clerks thought it wise to dress his little boys in some European clothes Anna Drew had given him, hoping that the trousers, stockings, shoes and 'little crimson sweater' would be some protection.

Lou Hoover volunteered to work in the hospital, which was set up in the elegant Tientsin Club. According to her husband, who now saw little of her, she became adept at cycling close to the walls of buildings to avoid stray bullets and shells, although one day a bullet punctured her tyre. It was gruelling, at times dispiriting, work. Some days as many as 200 wounded were brought in from the barricades, but everything – bandages, bedding, dressings, disinfectants – was in pathetically short supply. Lou improvised and commandeered what she could. She also organized some Chinese women to milk the settlement's herd of cows, describing herself as 'Chief Cow-boy and Dairy Maid.' The cows had been saved thanks to the resourcefulness of one of Hoover's mining staff, Wilfred Newberry, at the beginning of the siege. Spotting the settlement's dairy herd peacefully grazing about a mile away, he had leaped on a pony and brought it safely back while under enemy fire.

Lou Hoover adapted to the privations of siege life just as she had adapted to China. She and her husband had set sail for China on their wedding day. Herbert Hoover's remit was to prospect for coal and mineral deposits and together they had explored far into Manchuria and Mongolia. They rode shaggy Manchurian ponies, their equipment following behind in carts or on pack mules, with guards riding ahead on the lookout for bandits. At night they lodged in bare native inns, the servants spreading out the bedding and lighting charcoal fires to heat the Chinese brick beds or 'kangs'. The Hoovers slept on plaited mattresses laid over the kangs, rising at dawn to begin their travels afresh. Amused by how the village children milled about hoping for their first glimpse of a white woman, Lou found it all exciting and stimulating. Now, in addition to her hospital duties, she kept watch at night on the Drews' house and grounds. She had a small rifle that she was proficient in using and used to walk quietly around the garden and the stables in the darkness checking that all was as it should be.

Meanwhile her husband was cycling around the three-mile defensive perimeter, braving streets that were 'canals of moving lead.'[24] He checked the barricades, went on foraging raids with his young staff, or crept out with them at night to work the small pumping plant just outside the town. This enabled them to purify the polluted river water, which they brought back in municipal street-sprinkling carts. It was dangerous work. As soon as the Chinese heard the plant beginning to chug they opened fire. Nevertheless there was a macabre humour about these nocturnal expeditions. As Hoover later recalled, 'the British Tommies who formed our nightly guard, being aware of the corpses floating in the nearby canal, painted large signs on the sides of the water carts "Boxeril", being reminiscent of a British beef extract, "Bovril".'[25] He appreciated the irony and preferred this to the doom-laden Cassandras, particularly 'one dreadful person who periodically wanted to know if I intended to shoot my wife first if they closed in on us'.[26]

As the bombardment continued, the civilian community settled into a routine. Frederick Brown wrote that most of the women 'bore the trouble well' but that 'a few were hysterical and one or two nearly died of heart failure.'[27] Mrs Scott, who had taken refuge in a cellar under Gordon Hall, thought that most people were behaving 'splendidly' but found it 'horridly trying to be thrown all day and night with a most promiscuous collection of humanity with no privacy and no order, magnitudes of children who are not quiet exactly, and every imaginable rumour flying round.'[28] This 'promiscuous collection' included a circus company stranded in Tientsin who drank themselves silly every night on looted champagne – strange company indeed for a British bishop's wife.

Mrs Scott was not the only one to be shocked by the motley crew. The highly respectable von Hanneker household went to the hall one evening intending to remain, as their house was considered unsafe, but they returned after two or three hours, preferring 'to die decently at home if necessary, rather than remain in such a place under such dreadful conditions.'[29] Many friendships broke under the strain. Herbert Hoover later wrote: 'No one will again dare to organize a dinner party in Tientsin without consulting an inmate of Gordon Hall, for how could Mrs E. ever sit at meat again with Mrs F., who slapped Mrs E.'s Peking pug?'

Everyone realized that the situation was becoming more critical with each passing day. On 22 June, Beatty, injured and faint from loss of blood following an abortive attempt to seize an enemy gun, had a narrow escape when a shell burst through his bedroom, setting his bed on fire. Others fighting on the barricades were not so lucky. Beatty was horrified by the many 'unfortunate victims that were killed or mutilated beyond recognition.' While thankful that no women and children had been hit, he observed acidly that 'the civilian men were able to place themselves in a place of safety.'

The commanding officers took stock and it was not a reassuring picture. Contact with Taku had been lost on 17 June; casualties were high and the settlement surrounded. The only reason they had not been overrun was that the Chinese had not attacked simultaneously on all fronts. A Russian warned that if fighting continued with the same intensity over the next four days, the Russians' ammunition would be exhausted and they suggested that Tientsin be evacuated during the night. The women, children, sick and wounded would be escorted by the Germans, Austrians, Italians, French and Japanese, while the Russians and British would hold Tientsin and form the rear guard. Beatty was appalled, calling it 'the maddest, wildest, damndest, rottenest scheme that could emanate from the brain of any man.' It would mean abandoning Seymour to certain destruction. According to his journal, Beatty nudged Captain Bayly and said, 'Sit on his head.' Bayly did not want much nudging. 'He got up with a face like a peony, and swore lustily, which flattened the whole thing out. The Russian plan received no support and so fell flat.'[30]

Help was closer at hand than they realized. On 19 June, a young English civilian, James Watts, had volunteered to set out with three Cossacks in an attempt to get through to Taku. He was a first-class rider, 'possibly the finest rider in the east,'[31] but it was a dangerous journey. They galloped through hostile villages, keeping low in the saddle. Watts was recognized in one hamlet 'and his name was shouted out, coupled with the most awful threats by the erstwhile servants and grooms who had all become Boxers.'[32] As they neared the coast, a welcome sea mist shrouded them from view and they got through safely. The message they carried from Captain Bayly read: 'Hard pressed, heavy fighting; losses, 150 killed and wounded; Chinese Imperial Artillery shelling the Settlement; women and children all in cellars; fires all over the Settlement; everyone worn out with incessant fighting.'[33]

The story had a familiar ring – yet another relief expedition was required. In fact, a force of Russian infantry and American marines was already attempting to get through to Tientsin. Only the previous day they had been pinned down near the outskirts of the city. According to an American gunnery sergeant: 'We fell into a trap . . . we laid on our faces with the bullets coming like hail not knowing what to do . . . we fell and got up, staggered, crawled – but got out. I never saw such a tired party in my life and yours truly was on the hog!'[34] However, Bayly's message made it clear that a more substantial effort was required.

With barely 1,000 men at Taku and with the forts to garrison, it was a major task for the admirals to provide a force. However, once again luck was on the allies' side. Two further ships arrived – HMS *Terrible* from Hong Kong carrying 300 men of the Royal Welch Fusiliers and some Royal Engineers and a Russian troopship from Port Arthur carrying an even larger force. On 23 June, an international relief column of some 2,000 men set out. The British contingent included soldiers of the First Chinese Regiment from Weihaiwei, raised just eighteen months earlier in a neighbouring province. Straw-hatted and clad in black-sashed khaki, they were described by one journalist as 'examples of how Great Britain makes "men of mud", as Kipling puts it.'[35] They were wondering what kind of reception they would get in Tientsin. According to one of their British officers, Captain Barnes, 'we even heard that there were some who were opposed to our entry into their sacred Settlement at all' because of their 'feeling against the Chinese race as a whole.'[36] Nevertheless they were cheered lustily when, at last, the bedraggled force marched into the foreign settlement. Beatty watched them come limping in 'without much law and order, deadbeat,' but he was mightily relieved, writing that 'a great weight was lifted off our minds.'[37]

Their arrival removed Hoover's 'black fear' of massacre and facilitated the rescue of Seymour's column three days later. Some individuals now grew more confident. Mr von Bergen of the Customs Service appeared for the first time since the siege began. Anna Drew tartly observed that he must have fared quite well judging by all the empty tins and bottles found in the post office cellar where he had taken refuge, but that he 'looked rather miserable in spite of his excellent food.' He slept on a divan on the Drews' veranda.

As Lou described to a college friend, after the initial euphoria the relief was something of a damp squib: 'A good many hundred civilians and a couple of thousand troops sat still and repelled faint-hearted charges while 10,000 or 15,000 Chinese troops and 20,000 Boxers plunked shells of all sizes into us for exactly one week without a sound or a word from the outside reaching us. Then the first relief cut their way into us . . . enough to get in but not to do anything more than we could when they got there.' Yet the settlement could lick its collective wounds and reflect on events. Uppermost in everyone's minds was what would happen next and what was going on in Peking.

8

BEHIND THE TARTAR WALL

I never believed even dying people could look that way.
– Polly Condit Smith

ON 21 JUNE, the foreigners in Peking awoke to their first full day of siege life. It was a disagreeable and disorienting experience. One female missionary wrote with feeling that she had not dared disrobe in case she was forced to flee and that the night had been 'warm, the babies were cross and the rest is better imagined than told!'[1] Some male civilians had been unable to find a billet and had slept under trees, on benches or anywhere that offered protection. Lenox Simpson had snatched just three hours' sleep. He surveyed the scenes around him with a weary, jaundiced eye concluding that 'few people would believe the extraordinary condition to which twelve hours of chaos can reduce a large number of civilized people who have been forced into an unnatural life.' The prospect of any breakfast looked slim and he was contemplating stealing some food when Monsieur Chamot of the Hôtel de Pékin came to his rescue with a cup of coffee. Inside the hotel Simpson found the exhausted Russian commander Baron von Rahden. He was fast asleep, mouth wide open and sword and revolver lying on the table amid the debris of a meal he had been too tired too finish.

Lenox Simpson's next call was the British Legation, where everything was in confusion. He found it astonishing that so little had been done to organize the defences since the arrival of the relief force on 31 May. A few days earlier a British officer, Captain Halliday, had suggested building barricades out of dry-goods boxes filled with earth but had merely been laughed at. It had taken the death of von Ketteler to focus minds and persuade the commanding officers to agree on a defence plan. Inevitably it was somewhat haphazard. Sir Claude MacDonald later recalled how 'a barricade, a portion of which, I recollect, consisted of Her Majesty's Office of Works' best garden roller, was hurriedly commenced in front of the main gate.'

By contrast, the opening hours of the siege had brought genuine panic. Indeed, even before the real attacks began, the Austrians abandoned their isolated legation and fell back on the French barricades, leaving the northeast sector of the legation area in enemy hands. The Customs staff, whose buildings were close by, were forced to flee with them. Sir Robert Hart had to watch the Customs compound, which he had tried to defend, according to Juliet Bredon, with fortifications 'reminiscent of the Siege of Troy',[2] go up in smoke. Lenox Simpson believed that 'the iron had entered his soul' at the sight. The work of decades – all the voluminous records, correspondence and archives – was a pile of ash. Only his extensive diary was rescued, something that in later life Hart was to regard with mixed emotions. The dazed old man moved into a house in the British Legation with his staff. 'Poor old Sir Robert!' wrote Lancelot Giles. 'This is poor thanks for the good work he has done China during the last thirty odd years!'

The previous evening had seen another shock. The kindly and trusting Professor Huberty James, who had worked so hard with Morrison to find sanctuary for the Chinese converts, was seen to walk calmly out of the Fu and up to the north bridge over the canal. He had every appearance of a man who wanted to parley.

However, Imperial troops fired on him immediately and his body was dragged away. No one knew whether he had been killed outright or whether, as was widely rumoured, he had been tortured to death. Edmund Backhouse later claimed that he was decapitated outside the eastern gate of the Imperial City on the express orders of the Empress Dowager and his fearfully grimacing head displayed in a cage.

The loss of Professor James seemed all the more terrible because the foreign community still confidently expected imminent relief. They were puzzled by the delay but did not yet suspect that Vice-Admiral Seymour might not come at all. A letter from Captain McCalla, dated 14 June, that had managed to get through to the American Legation, irritated Morrison exceedingly. He later wrote in *The Times* that 'it was written from a point only 35 miles from Peking. It was a casual chatty letter which gave no indication that in the opinion of the writer there was any need for hurry.'[3] In his diary he scribbled, 'the Relief party *farce*. Crawling to our Rescue!'

As 21 June unfolded, people strove to adapt to their new circumstances. According to Lenox Simpson: 'Orders and counter-orders came from every side; the place was choked with women, missionaries, pulling children, and whole hosts of lamb-faced converts . . . Heaven only knew how the matter would end.' Fortunately the energetic American missionaries took the initiative, proposing a number of committees to take charge of key aspects of siege life. The ministers readily agreed and members were appointed. There was a committee for 'General Comfort' under Mr Tewkesbury. Others included the Health and Sanitation Committee, which Dr Coltman helped supervise; the Water Committee, which measured the depth of the legation's five sweet-water wells; the Fuel Committee, responsible for foraging for coal and kindling; and the Labour Committee, which conscientiously listed and classified the available Chinese workforce.

There were good stocks of cereals and grains – wheat, maize and especially rice. When committee members ransacked the

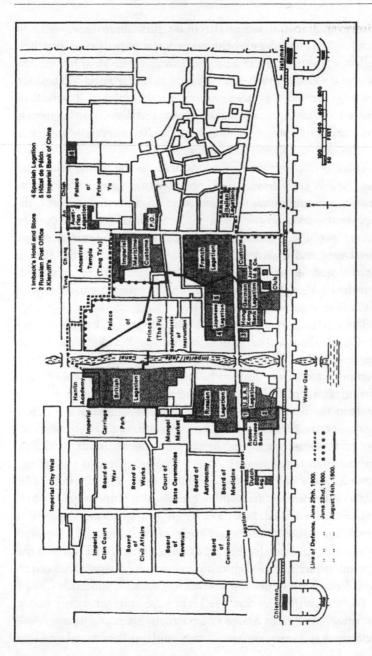

The Legation Quarters in 1900.

Chinese grainshops within the lines, they discovered an additional 8,000 bushels of wheat and several tons of rice, although the latter was mostly the musty yellow grain disliked by foreigners. Polly Condit Smith was amused that the Food Committee had two articles 'in tremendous quantities' – all kinds of tobacco, including long black cigars and Egyptian cigarettes, and dozens of cases of wines, which, she observed, 'will be a great help to the Continentals here.'

There was also plenty of meat, because the spring races had been held in early May. Soon speed was no longer what meant most in a racing pony; as Miss Condit Smith quipped, 'the all-important question now is not if Cochon will win more cups in future, but if his steaks will be tender.' The committee also found cats and dogs tied up and left to starve by the fleeing shopkeepers. Missionary Ada Mateer was deeply shocked, considering this abandonment of innocent animals to be typical of Chinese wickedness.

The Fortifications Committee was the most vital of all, and Sir Claude had no hesitation in putting Frank Gamewell in charge. He had already shown his talents in defending the Methodist Mission – skills to be expected of a star pupil of engineering at Cornell University and the son of the man who invented the first burglar-alarm system. He immediately began organizing the digging of bombproof shelters and the construction of barricades made of bricks surmounted with sandbags. The besieged foreigners of Peking seldom agreed on anything. However, no one had anything but praise for Gamewell as he sped around the defences on his bicycle, often under galling fire. Arthur Smith called him 'a limited omnipresence'.[4] William Bainbridge wrote admiringly: 'For a man of peace he displayed a surprising aptitude for the art of war.' As he cycled around the legation at night, shells whizzing overhead, he would call out to the ladies, 'It's all right – it's never as bad as it sounds.'[5]

The committees worked well from the start with only minor sparring. Even Lenox Simpson gave them his grudging approval, deciding that Americans were 'the people of the future' and that their missionaries, despite being sometimes 'odorous and unpleasant to look upon,' would hustle the British Legation into shape. One feature of the committees on which, as a true man of his time, he did not comment was that not a single woman served on them.

Nevertheless, many women found ways of contributing, particularly in the hospital. This was set up in the chancery under the direction of Dr Poole and the capable and cheerful German Dr Velde – a short, thick-set, fair-haired man with 'stumpy little hands and a keen blue eye.'[6] The matron, Miss Lambert, was a trained nurse attached to the Anglican Mission, and her many helpers included Jessie Ransome and several female doctors who agreed to act as nurses. According to Jessie, 'The great difficulty was the suddenness with which we found ourselves confronted with the necessity for a hospital at all. Up to the very day on which our first patient was brought in, it seemed probable that Admiral Seymour's party would arrive to relieve the situation.' She was grateful that there was a good supply of drugs – no one died of septic poisoning during the siege.

There was, however, very little basic equipment – for example, just four iron bedsteads and seven camp beds. Conditions soon became cramped. A missionary helper described how 'one room was given up to the officers and civilians and cots were furnished for those unless the number of officers was in excess of the number of cots, when they slept on the floor as did most of the men.' Sarah Conger and her daughters quickly got to work making sheets and pillowcases out of bales of calico while many donated their own mosquito nets to the sick and wounded. However, there were never enough nets to keep the armies of insects at bay. When people complained about the plague of flies, which 'made all miserable', Dr Poole quietly remarked: 'They always follow an army.'[7]

The missionary women living in the chapel began to organize themselves, allocating floor space and converting a little room 'used for witnessing marriage contracts' into a makeshift bathroom. 'A sheet was hung across the middle behind which one could take a sponge bath,' wrote Sarah Goodrich. She also noted that 'here was kept the dustpan and other implements . . . and on the wall hung a notice sternly warning ladies not to borrow that dustpan.'[8] Those who forgot faced having their rations docked.

On 22 June, just two days into the siege, it appeared that such arrangements might be in vain. At 9.00 a.m., the Italian, Austrian, French, German, Japanese, Russian and American detachments suddenly abandoned their positions and stampeded into the British Legation 'all jabbering in a mass.'[9] Three-quarters of the defences were now undefended, including the Fu, whose Chinese population might be massacred at any moment. For a few tense moments the besieged were, in Mary Gamewell's words, 'face to face with what seemed the end.' The man universally blamed for the fiasco was the choleric captain von Thomann of the Austrian cruiser *Zenta*. Von Thomann had been in Peking on a sightseeing trip when the Boxer troubles began. As the senior officer, he insisted on taking overall charge of the legations' defences, untroubled by his inexperience of land operations. According to Morrison, the panic was initiated when 'an irresponsible American'[10] told von Thomann that the American Legation had been abandoned. The Austrian then lost his head. Without waiting to verify the facts, he instantly ordered all forces east of Canal Street – running north–south through the Legation Quarter – to retreat to the British Legation.

There was tremendous anger when it was realized what had happened. Captain Poole wrote crossly in his diary: 'What impossible people foreigners are.' The troops were immediately ordered back to their positions but were too late to save the Italian Legation, already in flames. The Chinese had also occupied an allied barricade in Customs Street. However, it was the legations' great good fortune that the Chinese had not pressed home their advantage. Whether this was due to surprise, carelessness or inertia is unclear. Certainly the foreign ministers could hardly believe it themselves.

Von Thomann was immediately relieved of his command and Sir Claude MacDonald, as the most senior minister with forces in Peking, took over. He was of course an ex-soldier, but had little experience of the guerrilla tactics favoured by the Chinese. Lenox Simpson saw parallels between the way they scuttled from position to position, making maximum use of cover, and the tactics of the Boers, currently giving the British such problems in South Africa. Another difficulty was that MacDonald had no direct control over the other nations' soldiers. He had to deliver his orders or suggestions in writing through the respective minister. It was an absurd arrangement but he accepted it, impressing Meyrick Hewlett whom he appointed his secretary during the siege with his tact, cheerfulness and a sense of what posts were in truth most threatened.

One of Sir Claude's first acts was to dispatch the Italian guards, who now had no legation of their own to defend, to help the Japanese in the Fu. Lying across the canal from the British Legation, the Fu was one of the keys to the defence – if it fell the French, German and Japanese legations would be cut off and the British Legation would be hardly tenable. Sir Claude then took stock of the overall position. The legations' defence force of just over 400 – 20 officers and 389 men of eight nationalities – was pitifully small in the circumstances. However, it was supplemented by two bands of armed volunteers. The first, numbering some 75 men, was quite professional. Its members included civilians with military experience such as Nigel Oliphant of the Chinese Imperial Bank, who had served with the Scots Greys, and soldiers such as Captain Poole of the East Yorkshire Regiment and Captain Labrousse of the French Infanterie de Marine, both of whom had had the ill luck to be in Peking when the trouble broke out.

The second group of 50 men was rather more amateur, although Morrison admired their buccaneering spirit. They did garrison duties in the British Legation and were known as the 'Carving Knife Brigade', from their habit of lashing cutlery to a variety of weapons from elephant rifles to a *fusil de chasse* (hunting rifle). 'They were formidable alike to friend and foe,'[11] according to Morrison, who added that the most experienced was a man who had once witnessed the trooping of the colour in St James's Park! They had an unfortunate habit of carrying their rifles horizontally over the shoulder so that as they swung round the bayonet blade almost grazed the throat of the man behind. Their ranks included six 'fighting parsons'.[12]

All of them, professionals and amateurs alike, were short of ammunition. Because each nationality used a different type of rifle, they could not even pool their supplies. Sir Claude knew they must be very sparing. A British marine who lost his head and fired off sixty rounds for no reason had his rifle confiscated. Chinese prisoners were frequently bayoneted to death by the French simply to save cartridges. There was also a shortage of ammunition for the legations' only piece of artillery, the Italian one-pounder, and for the three machine guns – the American Colt, the Austrian Maxim and the unreliable British Nordenfelt.

The lines of defence had already shrunk alarmingly. By the second day there were just seven legations to defend – the out-lying Belgian and Dutch legations had been abandoned to shorten the defence lines; the Austrians had retreated from their compound; and the Italian Legation had just been needlessly lost. The area now to be defended was roughly a parallelogram. It ran some 700 yards east–west from the Russian and American legations at the western end of Legation Street to the French Legation at the eastern end, and some 750 yards north–south from the Fu and the British Legation to the north to the Tartar Wall in the south. Sandwiched in between lay the German, Japanese and Spanish legations, the Hôtel de Pékin, and various shops, banks, and houses.

All the legations, except the British, were on Legation Street. The Germans and Americans on the south side of the street were overshadowed by the massive Tartar Wall. Sir Claude knew that the foreign quarter could survive only by holding the stretches of wall directly behind those legations. If they were surrendered, the Chinese would be able to lob shells right into the heart of the foreign enclave. Sir Claude also worried that the British Legation was open to attack from the north, where the ancient Hanlin Academy adjoined it. It was vulnerable too from the west and south because of the proximity of the Imperial Carriage Park and the smaller Mongol Market, where the nomadic tribes brought their ponies, cattle and sheep for sale.

Meanwhile, the civilians were trying to adjust to the strangeness of siege life. Mary Gamewell decided to abandon the overcrowded floor of the British Legation chapel and to find a room elsewhere. She and some other missionary ladies discovered one but soon realized why it had been left unoccupied: 'We spread a bed on the floor, with the veranda full of people in front and the sinister hiss and sput-spat of rifle shot in the rear: we lay down in the darkness as we were. We listened to the rifle fire and felt the darkness and the wakefulness of the silent crowd. We wondered what the night would bring forth. Was death really near? Would the relief column come with the morning? If not, how near and what the end? The rifle fire thickened, the shots snapped and hissed more constantly and seemingly at closer range.' Hearing of their plight, Lady MacDonald offered shelter in the ballroom. The grateful Mary spent the remaining nights of the siege there, making do with 'a piece of mattress, which someone kindly gave me, and a laundry bag in which were shoes and other odd ends of personal belongings served as my pillow.'

Her compatriots Polly Condit Smith and the Squiers family were living in comparative comfort in two rooms in the bungalow of Wordsworth Poole, the British Legation doctor. Poole himself had moved out into the makeshift hospital, taking his bed with him. Polly slept in the larger of the rooms with Harriet Squiers and her maid. In the daytime it was the family's living and dining room. They would roll up the big double mattress and use it as a seat, together with the trunks and two silver chests they had managed to bring with them. At one stage the room was decorated with five pigtails cut from the heads of dead Chinamen and presented to Polly by a Belgian diplomat. However, thinking

them in poor taste and likely to upset the servants, she wisely
disposed of them. The increasingly nervous French and German
governesses were billeted at the ends of the hallways.

Polly reflected a little gleefully that a degree of politics had
entered into the accommodation arrangements. The suspicion
and rivalry that dominated Russo-British relations explained
why the Russian minister, de Giers, had to make do with the
British second secretary's house, which was 'in bad repair, and
. . . anything but commodious.'[13] It accommodated the fifty-one
members of his staff and family, as well as the Dutch minister,
who slept in a cupboard.

The Squierses' adolescent son, Fargo, was a source of both
pride and anxiety to the household. He commandeered a
Chinese cart, forced two coolies to accompany him and raided
the abandoned Imbeck's store next to the US Legation. 'Imagine
our surprise,' wrote Polly, 'when . . . a Chinese cart, driven by
Fargo Squiers, a boy of fifteen years old, came thundering into
the British compound with the upper part of the cart riddled
with bullets.' One coolie was killed and the other wounded, but
Fargo was unscathed. In tribute to his courage, Fargo was
allowed to keep the food instead of handing it over to the Food
Committee. 'What a terrible price might have been paid for
these stores!' Polly wrote. The fate of the two unfortunate
coolies did not apparently strike her as a terrible price and she
exulted in the windfall since the Squierses' own supplies had
been seriously depleted by gifts to the missionaries.

Polly was now knuckling down to such tasks as sewing sandbags out of curtains and the rolls of sumptuous silks and satins
hastily commandeered from shops within the legation defences.
Thousands of sandbags were needed as quickly as possible.
Some men donated pairs of trousers that converted nicely by the
simple process of tying up the legs and filling them. There were
furious arguments about what size the bags should be. One
sentry complained that they were too small and refused to risk
his neck behind anything so inadequate. When the ladies
stitched bigger bags they were told that they were now too large

and broke easily. The ubiquitous and diplomatic Dr Gamewell solved the problem, calculating the optimum measurements and ordering the women to stick to them whatever anyone else might say, before hastening on his way again.

Polly and Harriet Squiers helped to cook rice and corned beef for the American marines. A Chinese had been contracted to feed them on their arrival in Peking but this convenient arrangement had ended with the outbreak of the siege. Since then Herbert Squiers had taken on responsibility for catering for fifty men and two officers. Polly and Harriet also visited the small hospital. A dying Cossack was lying on the floor, shot through the lungs, and there was nothing Polly could do for him except to brush the flies away. She found it a sad and frightening experience. Blood had trickled down his chest to form a pool around him. His face was olive green – 'the colour one sees in unskilfully painted pictures of death – so livid, I never believed even dying people could look that way.'

Frequent visits from George Morrison put Polly and Harriet in a more cheerful frame of mind. His own house just beyond the Fu had been destroyed, but he had managed to save his books with the help of an eccentric Norwegian missionary called Nestergaard who had acquired many nicknames, including 'Nearest to God'. The volumes were now piled around Morrison, making the pavilion he shared with employees of the Hong Kong and Shanghai Bank somewhat cramped. Polly thought him 'as dirty, happy and healthy a hero as one could find anywhere.' Whether he still thought her 'fat and gushing' is less clear.

Morrison worried about the Chinese living in the Fu. Although they were being ably defended by the small Japanese force under Colonel Shiba, the retreat on the first day had shown how vulnerable they were. Morrison had earnest discussions with Frank Gamewell about how best to protect them and helped to strengthen the barricades himself. He also went out on sorties to flush the Chinese out of the adjacent alleyways.

Like everyone else, he was hungry for news and frustrated by the lack of it. The Bell Tower in the British Legation grounds soon became the place where people congregated, hoping for information. 'On the boards which were set there were posted notices of all kinds, scraps of news, rumours of the relief force . . . translations of edicts.' There were even notes about articles lost and found and 'any of the thousand and one things which interest or amuse a besieged people.'[14] This 'intellectual market', as one of the besieged called it, was also one of the safest places to be. It was hit only once throughout the entire siege and no one was wounded there.

Meanwhile, the work of fortification went on under Gamewell's determined eye. The Chinese converts were proving an invaluable source of labour. Indeed, many of the besieged foreigners believed the legations would have been untenable without them. Their movements were controlled because of the risk of infiltration by enemy spies or snipers. Arthur Smith and Dr Martin were appointed gatekeepers to keep watch because, as Mary Gamewell explained, 'With the going and coming of large numbers of Chinese, who lived in Prince Su's palace over the way and worked in the British Legation it was necessary to watch the gates closely to prevent any emissary of the enemy from entering . . . No one was allowed through the gates unless he were vouched for by some leader on the spot or could show a pass.'

Early in the siege both foreigners and Chinese in the legations came face to face with a very real hazard – fire. Luella Miner was to be haunted by the memory of how 'again and again the alarm of fire sounded, as Boxer Torches found adjoining buildings.' The British Legation was surrounded on three sides by highly flammable Chinese buildings. It was all too easy for the enemy to twist rags dipped in kerosene around the end of long bamboo poles and ignite anything they could reach. On 22 June, they set fire to some buildings west of the legation and to Luella, busily stitching sandbags, it seemed as if all Peking must be ablaze. The fire was eventually extinguished but only with great difficulty and amid scenes of panic and confusion. The first British casualty, Private Scadding, was shot dead as he stood watch and a

British diplomat lost his house, the smouldering contents spilling out on to the street. People stumbled hither and thither in the smoke trying to find leather fire buckets and coax the elderly fire engines to work. No one knew who had been appointed to the Fire Committee and in the confusion 'orders were given by anyone with a loud voice and an impression that he knew what ought to be done.'[15] All the while, the Chinese fired down on them from the rooftops of the adjacent Mongol Market.

The besieged decided to demolish the few remaining buildings adjoining that part of the legation to create a *cordon sanitaire*. The demolition was hard work but Mr Bailie, the Scottish Professor of English at the Imperial University, relished it. Physically very strong, he was apparently 'pining for violent manual labour or bloodshed.'[16] Arthur Smith must have been thinking of men like Bailie and Gamewell when he noted 'a marked and an impressive contrast between the conduct of the representatives of the Anglo-Saxons, and that of many of the Continentals, who for the most part sat at ease on their shady verandas, chatting, smoking cigarettes, and sipping wine, apparently trusting for their salvation to fate; while their more energetic comrades threw off their coats, plunging into the whirl of work.'

The following day the Chinese, fairly predictably, tried to burn the foreigners out again. However, no one had anticipated that they would set fire to the Hanlin Academy, immediately to the north of the British Legation. The Hanlin was a unique place of learning – the Chinese equivalent of Oxford and Cambridge, Harvard and Yale, Heidelberg and the Sorbonne all rolled into one. Its exquisitely painted pavilions housed one of the most ancient libraries of the world. Thousand upon thousand of silk-covered volumes, illumined by hand and written by masters of the Chinese brush, filled the groaning shelves. Yet in some places, buildings of the Hanlin were just feet away from the British Legation wall. The temptation was too much. On the morning of 23 June, Chinese were spotted moving through the four-acre compound throwing torches soaked in petrol on to the bone-dry rafters while soldiers took up position.

Recognizing the potential danger, the commander of the British forces, Captain Strouts, had several times suggested to Sir Claude that some of the Hanlin be pulled down. The idea, however, was dismissed. It was too great an act of vandalism, especially when it seemed inconceivable that the enemy would strike there. Sir Claude would agree only that a gap be made through the adjoining wall in case allied troops needed to gain quick access. Now that time had come. The Hanlin's ornate halls and courtyards burned frighteningly quickly, the leaping flames fanned by a stiff northerly breeze. Soon an enormous column of fire was bearing down on the legation. Sarah Goodrich described how 'Chinese soldiers . . . were keeping up a steady rifle fire' from nearby buildings 'hoping thus to prevent us putting it out!'[17]

Sir Claude sent a party of marines through the hole in the wall into the Hanlin and they organized a long line of fire fighters. Polly Condit Smith was one of them. She later wrote that if she lived to be a thousand she would never see 'a queerer collection of people working together to extinguish a fire, and with the object to save themselves from a massacre – coolies, missionaries, soldiers and Ministers Plenipotentiary working and straining every muscle for the same object . . . I was in that line of men and women passing buckets, and so was the wife of the French Minister, and many other well-known women.' She reflected that Peking had probably never seen such unanimity among its foreign residents. The fire fighters worked frantically 'like New York firemen' to pull down the burning halls and prevent the fire from spreading.

Just at the moment of greatest danger, the wind shifted from the north to the northwest, leaving the main library, containing the choicest volumes, still standing. In particular it housed the only surviving copy of the fabulous *Yung Lo Ta Tien*, an encyclopedia completed in 1408 by 2,000 Ming scholars and comprising about 12,000 volumes bound in yellow silk. However, the fire flared up again between 4.00 and 5.00 that afternoon. Miss Andrews, a missionary, wrote: 'Evidently kerosene had been put on the trees to spread the flames.'[18] This time the library itself caught alight. There seemed no prospect of saving it and the contents were unceremoniously tumbled into the yard. Some were even flung into the lotus ponds to prevent them catching fire en masse.

Scholars among the foreign community were close to tears as they picked amongst the debris. Morrison was furious and blamed the Chinese, writing that 'the combustible books, the most valuable in the Empire, were thrown in a great heap into the pond round the summer house . . . a heap of debris, timber in ashes, sprinkled with torn leaves, marked the site of the great library of the Middle Kingdom . . . what can we think of a nation that sacrifices its most sacred edifice, the pride and glory of its country and learned men for hundreds of years, in order to be revenged upon foreigners? It was a glorious blaze. The desecration was appalling.'[19] Some books and manuscripts were salvaged and Sir Claude offered them to the Tsungli Yamen. There was no reply. Others found their way into private hands. Lancelot Giles secured a volume of the *Yung Lo Ta Tien* 'merely as a specimen', and appropriated other interesting curios, including essays by Imperial examination candidates. In 1913, Edmund Backhouse was to present the Bodleian Library in Oxford with six volumes of the *Yung Lo*. Marines helped themselves to some of the beautifully carved wooden blocks used to preserve very ancient works. They made excellent shutters for their loopholes.

By evening the fire was still burning – a vast red glow against the deep blue of the Chinese evening sky. Reverend Allen found it both beautiful and grotesque. 'One great tree still stood stretching its bare leafless arms to heaven. It was very dry and burnt like tinder, with no flame but a pure translucent glow, as if it had been cut out of a living ruby.' The ornamental pools were choked with debris. Wooden printing blocks, manuscripts and books, some still smouldering, lay scattered and trampled. Later, when they had been left to rot, the order was given to heap earth on the sodden stinking mass to stop them infecting the neighbourhood.

The thirsty, soot-covered fire fighters straggled back to their quarters. A parched Dr Poole croaked to Polly that the only thing that could quench his thirst was the big loving cup he kept in a small closet in his house. She obligingly filled it with Apollinaris mineral water and he added four fingers of Scotch, draining it to the very last drop. That night as Polly looked down towards the Hanlin, the isolated buildings still burning under the watchful eyes of the sentries reminded her of the flames to be seen burning at night in the oil districts of Pennsylvania.[20]

Many other fires were also started that day around the besieged quarter. The Russo Chinese Bank containing $80,000 in cash was burned down and the officials abandoned their houses for the safety of the British Legation. The young US Marine Oscar Upham, who had been obliged to leave his bedding on board ship during the rush to Peking in late May, was delighted when the officials 'gave our boys permission to . . . make use of anything we thought we would need'. However, the offer was not without hazards. Oscar had just helped himself to a fine blanket when a three-inch shrapnel shell burst through the roof directly over his head, struck the wall four feet away and exploded, tearing down half the wall and covering him with dust and plaster. He got out 'double-quick' with nothing more serious than a bad headache.

Civilians too were becoming used to close shaves. Robert Coltman's wife had been rocking her baby son – the youngest of her six children – and talking to Polly Condit Smith when a bullet buried itself in the crib's headpiece. The women grabbed the baby and flew to a room on the other side of the house, where they were joined by Sarah Conger. According to Polly, who clearly had little time for the ideas of this devout Christian Scientist, she earnestly assured them that 'it was ourselves, and not the times, which were troublous and out of tune.' There was an appearance of warlike hostilities, Sarah argued, but it was in their own brains. She even maintained that no 'real' bullet had struck the baby's crib. 'I can honestly say that we were more surprised by her extraordinary statement than we were by the very material bullet which had driven us from the room,' wrote Polly. Dr Martin took a different view, finding Sarah's approach comforting: 'I wished many a time that, like her, I could look on all those events as nothing more than a horrid nightmare, merely conjured up by a distempered imagination.' He also noted that Laura Conger, who had been a bundle of nerves at the start of the siege, throwing herself into her father's arms at any loud noise, was growing stronger by the day. Indeed, by the end of the siege she was 'to have obtained a complete cure.'

Although Seymour's force was still eagerly awaited, many women had taken steps to ensure they would never fall into the hands of the Chinese. Dr Martin was intrigued to notice a handsome young lady sitting for her portrait, while a lady artist, Miss Payen, 'with untrembling hand, transferred her pleasing features to canvas. I wondered at the composure of both. Nor was my astonishment diminished when, in the evening, I overheard that same young lady saying to Captain Myers: "Now, remember, should they overpower us, your first duty will be to shoot me."' Another woman was given a revolver by her husband with the injunction to shoot her daughters first and then herself, if he were not there to do it for her. Such conversations were to become a famous feature of the siege folklore. However, Luella Miner vigorously refuted the idea that any such arrangements were made, in her hearing at least.

The next day, 24 June, was the first Sunday under siege. Asked whether he intended to stop work, Gamewell replied that he did not. The most divine thing he could do that day was to stretch every nerve to protect the women and children of the legations. It was indeed a day that needed all his skill and ingenuity. There were more incendiary attacks. The Chinese also mounted a three-inch Krupp gun on the charred Chien Men, the gate opposite the Forbidden City, sending shells crashing into the legations. One shell fell into the British Legation, badly frightening

Monsieur Pichon. He had left his own legation at the very start of the fighting and, according to Lancelot Giles, 'especially showed himself a poltroon, as indeed he has all through the siege' – an unsympathetic comment, perhaps, about a man who, more than most, was entitled to say 'I told you so.' The Fu's wall was breached and Chinese soldiers swarmed in. The Japanese kept their nerve, shooting them down like rabbits from behind their loopholed barricades, but they were vastly outnumbered. Colonel Shiba sent an urgent request for reinforcements and the Chinese converts were temporarily evacuated. No safe place could be found and so they were quickly moved back.

A detachment of Germans and Americans made a dash along the Tartar Wall behind their legations, scattering the enemy before them almost as far as the Chienmen to relieve the pressure on their positions. The Americans, under the command of Captain Myers and with the help of the Chinese converts, managed to build a breastwork across the width of the wall while the Germans built a similar fortification on their stretch of it. These two positions were some 500 yards apart and became a critical part of the defence. So long as they could be held, the enemy forces were denied free access to the Tartar Wall, from whence they could have directed a punishing fire into the heart of the defences. They were, however, highly dangerous positions, as Oscar Upham discovered. Because they were just yards from Chinese barricades, it was possible to relieve them only at night. There were to be accusations that the marines on the wall spent much of their time drunk. Some of them certainly confided to Luella Miner that 'they were never in such a tight place as this before, that the war in the Philippines was child's play in comparison.'

The besieged were becoming weary as well as frightened, longing for a good bath and a clean bed. On 24 June, pony meat appeared for the first time on the menu and people debated whether it tasted better minced, curried or in rissoles and how long it should be cooked. One of Luella Miner's colleagues enquired where their dinner was only to be told 'the horse is not yet curried.' Luella tried to swallow the 'French beef', as it was nicknamed, but could not. The rather epicurean Lenox Simpson thanked his lucky stars that there was plenty of Monopole champagne to wash it down with. The besieged were also tormented by the stench of the rapidly putrefying corpses of the Chinese soldiers and Boxers who had been shot. Their bodies often lay in the high-summer heat within feet of the legations' defences. 'The number of corpses that accumulate is astounding,' wrote Polly, who was clearly acclimatizing to her surroundings. The missionary superintending the gangs of coolies who threw any dead bodies they could reach over the wall remarked that he should be dubbed 'Major-General of the Corpses'.

On 25 June came one of many curious, indeed seemingly inexplicable, events of the siege. The day had begun with the execution of two Boxer prisoners whose bodies were duly tossed over the wall. Sir Claude MacDonald was suffering from dysentery and most people were feeling despondent. Captain Poole wrote bleakly: 'I've had no time to analyze my feelings – on my legs all day and night, marines all exhausted and are incessantly on duty, no proper sleep night or day – I wonder how long it can last. Men try and put courage into the women . . . Everybody's eyes bloodshot from want of sleep.' There was fierce fighting all day during which Edwin Conger told Sir Claude MacDonald that the American position on the wall must be abandoned. The British minister as strenuously dissuaded him from such a rash step, sending British marines to help. Overall the situation was looking very grim.

Then suddenly everything stopped and the nightmare took on the quality of a fairy tale. In the words of Lenox Simpson, 'The sun . . . was sinking down slowly towards the west, flooding the pink walls of the Imperial City with a golden light and softening the black outline of the sombre Tartar Wall that towers so high above us, when all round our battered lines the dropping rifle-fire drooped more and more until single shots alone punctuated the silence . . . All of us listened attentively, and presently on all sides the fierce music of the long Chinese trumpets blared out uproariously – blare, blare, sobbing on a high note tremulously, and then, boom, boom, suddenly dropping to a thrilling basso profondissimo.'

The firing ceased immediately and the sudden unexpected silence seemed eerie. The foreign troops watched suspiciously as the Chinese left their barricades and sauntered away. A huge white placard bearing a message in Chinese characters appeared on the north bridge, where Huberty James had been taken. Using field glasses and helped by the Chinese scholars among them, the foreigners deciphered the message. It was an Imperial edict and announced that, in accordance with Imperial orders to protect the ministers, firing would stop at once. It also promised that a dispatch would be delivered at the Imperial Canal Bridge. The bewildered foreigners immediately scrawled on a piece of card that they had understood the message. They gave the card to a nervous Chinese man who tottered towards the bridge, official hat on his head and white handkerchief in his hand. However, the strain was too much for him. The Chinese troops shouted out *'lai liao, lai liao'* – 'he has come, he has come.' Their tone was jocular rather than bellicose but he dropped the reply and bolted back to the legations.

The foreigners excitedly discussed this new development. What did the cease-fire mean? Some believed it was all hoax and humbug. Others were convinced that Seymour's arrival must be imminent. Every day there had been reports of rockets and flares in the sky to the west or claims of carrier pigeons fluttering in with messages. They all proved false. However, it was tempting to believe that the relief force must be at the very gates of Peking. Some even felt secure enough to venture on sightseeing trips behind enemy lines, climbing over their barricades and gazing about them in the setting sun. Lenox Simpson was one of them and he described a scene of raw, savage beauty. 'Just outside the Palace gates were crowds of Manchu and Chinese soldiery – infantry, cavalry and gunners grouped all together in one vast mass of colour. Never in my life have I seen such a wonderful panorama – such a brilliant blaze in such rude and barbaric surroundings. There were jackets and tunics of every colour; trouserings of blood-red embroidered with black dragons; great two-handed swords in some hands; men armed with bows and arrows mixing with Tung Fu-hsiang's Kansu horsemen, who had the most modern carbines slung across their backs. There were blue banners, yellow banners embroidered with black, white and red flags, both triangular and square, all presented in a jumble to our wondering eyes. The Kansu soldiery of Tung Fu-hsiang's command were easy to pick out from amongst the milder-looking Peking Banner troops . . . but of Boxers there was not a sign.' It had almost been worth five days of siege to see such a sight.

Not everyone was seduced by this strange cease-fire and the defenders wisely used the time to reinforce their barricades, pile up sandbags in particularly dangerous places, fashion more loopholes and bring in fresh supplies of food. They noticed that the Chinese too were busily strengthening their positions. As the shadows lengthened over the city there was no sign of the promised dispatch from the Imperial Court. Then, at midnight, firing resumed as fiercely as before. Many of the besieged had gone to bed early hoping to catch up on some sleep. Mary Bainbridge woke in terror to 'the heaviest firing we had ever heard.' It seemed to break over her head like a series of thunderclaps.

As their frightening small world closed around them again the besieged debated how long they could hold out. The consensus was another eight or ten days at most. Mrs Coltman decided to stop worrying how to get washing done for her six children. 'If the troops come within ten days, my children can wear what they are wearing; if Peking is not relieved within that time, we will all be dead.'[21] However, there was also a new realism and determination to fight back. It was not enough merely to wait to be saved. Many would have agreed with the little boy who wrote in a letter he had no hope of sending: 'We are trying and trying in every way to save our lives.'[22]

9

THE DRIFTING HORROR

With tears have we announced in our ancestral shrines the outbreak of war. – Imperial edict, 21 June 1900

THE UNCERTAINTY WAS perhaps hardest to bear and the foreigners exhausted themselves with questions. Luella Miner wrote sadly: 'We are as isolated here as if we were on a desert island. Our latest news of the outside world – even of the other parts of China . . . is two weeks old . . . Is the whole of China in turmoil? Are our Christians everywhere being slaughtered?' Had the allies carried out their threat to seize the Taku forts, she wondered? Where was Seymour? Had the foreign settlements in Tientsin been overrun? And were the Powers now formally at war with China?

As far as China was concerned they were. An Imperial edict issued on 21 June told the citizens of the Celestial Empire that 'with tears have we announced in our ancestral shrines the outbreak of war.' The edict described the Boxers in caressing tones as 'patriotic soldiers'. They were to be incorporated into the militia and rewarded for their loyalty with silver and grain. On 23 June, a rather more sinister decree stated that 'the work now undertaken [in Peking] by Tung Fu-hsiang should be completed as soon as possible, so that troops can be spared and sent to Tientsin for defence.'[1] The word used for 'work' – 'shih' – was intentionally vague and a euphemism for a swift massacre of the foreigners. Imperial troops were to carry out the annihilation, while Boxers were withdrawn behind the lines.

The foreigners knew nothing of this. They did not even know the fate of Bishop Favier and his beleaguered community in the nearby Peitang Cathedral, although the firing of field guns from that direction encouraged them to believe that the cathedral was still holding out. The brief cease-fire had, however, made one thing clear: the attack on the legations was no longer the maverick work of a disorganized rabble of antiforeign peasants whom the court was unable to curb. It had become a centrally controlled assault by Imperial troops that the court could turn on and off like a tap.

On 29 June, what were to be the last communications from Peking for a long time reached an increasingly worried outside world. A Chinese courier managed to slip through to Tientsin with two messages. The first, from Sir Robert Hart, was written in a style quite different from his usual measured tones. It said bluntly: 'Foreign community besieged in the legations. Situation desperate. MAKE HASTE!' The second, from a missionary, told the shocking tale of von Ketteler's murder, giving added weight to Sir Robert's plea. However, the naval commanders were in no position to respond. Seymour's mauled force had only just been rescued and the foreign settlements in Tientsin were still being bombarded. Furthermore, the Chinese City of Tientsin had to be taken before a major relief exercise could be mounted.

Mercifully unaware of this, the besieged were acclimatizing to a life that, just days earlier, would have seemed unthinkable. Their ears were attuned to the whistle and crack of rifle bullets. Sarah Conger described how 'the balls are continually whizzing by. When a general attack is made, the bell in the tower rings rapidly to tell all the men to be ready to do their best. This was exciting at first, but night after night of this firing, horn-blowing, yelling . . . has hardened us to it.' Jessie Ransome, fast at work in the hospital, was conscious of the same phenomenon: 'It is curious how we get used to going about with bullets whizzing about our heads.' Death was becoming commonplace and people reacted casually to dangers that were not merely prospective but 'actual and grimly disgusting.'[2] Some even found the days monotonous. A grim humour began to flourish. The first child to be born since the troubles began – a baby boy – was called 'Siege' in the hope that he might eventually be raised.

Sometimes survival seemed highly doubtful. There were now five Imperial armies in the region of Peking and attacks on the legations were fierce, with storms of bullets flying over their defences. The besieged estimated that on one night alone Chinese riflemen fired 200,000 bullets. Yet no one could understand why the Chinese aimed so high. Casualties would have been far higher had they paid more attention to their aim. One theory was that the Chinese intended to keep up a barrage of noise to wear the foreigners down. Morrison suggested they wanted to frighten away the devils they believed were protecting the legations, just as they set off firecrackers to drive away evil spirits at festivals. In fact, the Chinese often exploded firecrackers to enhance the sound of their firing and increase its psychological impact.

The besieged redoubled the digging of bombproof shelters, but these were little more than damp, dark shallow cellars roofed with boards and covered with a few feet of thin earth. They were certainly not shellproof. Lancelot Giles called them 'awful death-traps' and decided nothing would induce him to climb into one. Polly Condit Smith shared his view. In fact, she saw no point in taking any special precautions, as she told Sarah Conger. 'Mrs Conger came back to our room,' Polly wrote, 'and her manner was more than tragic when she saw me lying on my mattress on the floor, not even beginning to dress for what I suppose half of the women in the compound believed to be the beginning of the final fight. She said: "Do you wish to be found undressed when the end comes?" It flashed through my mind that it made very little difference whether I was massacred in a pink silk dressing-gown . . . or whether I was in a golf skirt and shirt waist that I was in the habit of wearing during the day hours of this charming picnic. So I told her that . . . I was going to stay in bed unless something terrible happened, when I should don my dressing-gown and, with a pink bow of ribbon at my throat, await my massacre. This way of looking, or I should rather say of speaking, did not appeal to the Minister's wife, but I must say that at such terrible moments during the siege it is a great comfort to be frivolous.'[3]

Polly's compatriot Baroness von Ketteler was still in a state of shock. Mary Gamewell sometimes saw her grief-stricken figure standing at her window in the grey light of dawn: 'One day she caught her black robes about her and stepped towards me. We clasped hands. She is an American, and she looked only a girl . . . "I am so alone," she said.' Born Maud Ledyard, daughter of the president of the Michigan Central Railroad, she now mourned that neither title nor position nor wealth could help her. One day a bullet whistled past her ear as she and Polly were sitting on a bench on the tennis court. Polly immediately dropped to the ground and tried to pull the baroness after her but she refused. Polly was forced to find a young student to help her and between them they dragged the despairing widow back to the British Legation. Polly believed that 'in her agony of mind . . . a bullet to end her suffering would have been truly welcomed.'

Meanwhile the casualties were mounting. By 3 July, thirty-eight legation guards had been killed and fifty-five had been wounded. A quarter of the officers were dead or lying in the little makeshift hospital. Conditions there were becoming increasingly grim. Every window had been at least partially bricked up as protection against stray bullets. The stench in the heat and dust of a Peking summer was terrible. So were the thickly swarming flies attracted by bleeding wounds. There was no space to prepare the dead properly for burial, just 'a hideous little room at the back,'[4] and no coffins. The corpses were simply sewn into shrouds of coarse white cloth, booted feet protruding.

The doctors struggled to keep pace with the number of operations, cursing the lack of X-ray equipment that would have helped them locate bullets and splinters of shrapnel in the bodies of the wounded.[5] As Polly wrote, 'an apparatus for applying X-rays would have saved the lives of many.' Nigel Oliphant, who had been shot in the left leg, complained that 'the worst was when the doctor was feeling with his finger for the bullet.' Several ministers' wives helped Miss Lambert's overworked nurses. Madame de Giers's energy, compassion and graceful good looks were appreciated, but Dr Poole, as forthright as his brother the captain, found Madame Pichon 'a great nuisance'.

Baroness von Ketteler won the doctor's gratitude by donating one of the hospital's very few thermometers. Jessie Ransome was so worried by the lack of these that whenever a patient bit or dropped one she confessed she 'felt inclined to shake him'. Wound dressings were also in short supply so powdered peat and fine sawdust were made up into little bags for use instead. Neither were there enough hospital gowns and substitutes had to be fashioned from brilliant Chinese silks and satins, giving an air of spurious gaiety to the bleak surroundings. Dysentery was becoming a major problem and Polly helped Harriet Squiers to boil gallons of the thick, nutritious but tasteless rice-water used to treat it.

Bad as things were becoming for the foreigners, conditions were far worse among the converts. By 1 July, Nigel Oliphant was recording that the Chinese Christians were 'dying like sheep from smallpox,' adding that 'we do not reckon Chinese converts in our casualty lists' and that he could not therefore be more precise. Morrison went to inspect the Fu, where the Chinese refugees were crowded 'like bugs in a rug', and was appalled. His doctor's sensibilities were outraged by conditions that were 'stinking and insanitary . . . children ill with scarlet fever and small-pox, with diptheria [sic] and dysentery.' A committee was set up to try to improve the sanitary arrangements.

Sandbags were being produced at an ever more furious rate and transported to wherever the need was greatest in rickshaws drawn by young Chinese boys. Several hundred thousand bags were now piled around the defences, butterfly confections of Liberty satin curtains, linen monogrammed sheets from Paris, soft velvets, luscious Chinese satin brocades of sky blue, blood red and Imperial yellow. It was a very democratic activity. Mary Gamewell and Luella Miner were both amused to see Sarah Conger standing in a deep, dusty trench holding bags open while a Greek orthodox priest with long flowing hair shovelled in earth using a porcelain kettle. It could also cause dissent. Mary Bainbridge was busily sewing bags for the American marines then in desperate straits on the Tartar Wall when a lady claiming to be 'a Faith cure and a fanatic on religion' suggested that she lay aside her work to pray. Mrs Bainbridge rapped that she was more than capable of sewing and praying at the same time.

Sir Claude was trying to bring greater order to the defences now that relief no longer appeared imminent. His account tells of ceaseless and relentless assaults on the barricades and how he sent exhausted troops hither and thither to try to plug the gaps. In the event of a general attack, Sir Claude ordered any man with a gun 'of any description' to rally at the Bell Tower. However, such occasions were rare. The Chinese seemed to prefer to attack at random, now here, now there.

On 30 June, Imperial troops had opened fire on the Fu with a Krupp gun. The commander of the Italian guards assisting the Japanese, Lieutenant Paolini, led a brave sortie to take it. However, all ended in disaster when, as Captain Poole alleged with characteristic bluntness, Paolini 'appeared to have lost his head and taken the wrong turnings.' Using a faulty map, he certainly led his small party into an alleyway where they became caught in crossfire and Paolini was hit. The only escape was through a small gap in the wall into the Fu. As the men struggled to get through some were shot, including young volunteer Walter Townsend, who, 'feeling he would never be so near the enemy again, somewhat rashly stayed to take a shot at the Chinese barricade.'[6] Their comrades yanked them through as the Chinese tried to grab at them, spurred on by the Imperial government's offer of a reward for every foreign head.

The greatest worry remained the Tartar Wall. On 1 July, Chinese soldiers were spotted creeping up the ramp on to its broad top. They surprised the German guard, who immediately retired 'before the Chinese had fired a single shot, and without having had a man even wounded,' as Nigel Oliphant wrote angrily. Captain Poole raged against 'those confounded Germans'. Their precipitate flight left the American barricade, several hundred yards away, dangerously exposed to the rear. The result was that the Americans too withdrew, tearing pell-mell down the ramp. Sir Claude called a rapid council of war, very much in the style of the Boer commandos, 'with everybody talking at once,' or so Lenox Simpson thought. A mixed force of Russians, British and Americans was dispatched to storm up the wall and reoccupy the American position. Luckily the Chinese had failed to press their advantage and the action was successful. However, the German position had been lost for good, which would have been a disaster had it not been held by Prince Ching's men who, as Sir Claude wrote gratefully, 'gave little trouble.'

Nevertheless, the pressure on the American barricade was now severe. A pencilled note to Edwin Conger from the American marines' commanding officer, twenty-eight-year-old Captain Jack Myers, was despairing: 'It is slow *sure* death to remain here . . . The men all feel that they are in a trap and simply await the hour of execution.'[7] Myers had spent nearly a week up on the wall and was mentally and physically exhausted – Morrison believed he was being worked to death. The stress was at least partially due to the deadly accuracy of the Chinese sharpshooters, which was very different from the random firing elsewhere. Oscar Upham described, in his usual cheerful way, how a Russian was killed because he insisted on smoking and blowing the smoke straight out through his loophole. 'We told him to knock it off. One of the Chinese sharpshooters spotted him and put a slug through his head . . . I saw the blood spurting . . . Those Chinks have got it down pat; they can put five shots out of six through a loophole three inches square and don't need a field glass to do it either.' No one could afford to relax for a moment.

On 3 July, Myers was ordered to lead a sortie to capture a crucial position on the wall held by the enemy and hence to relieve the pressure on the American barricade. Morrison later explained in *The Times* why this was imperative. An 'error committed in the construction of the American barricade . . . left the width of the bastion outside instead of within the Legation lines. The two barricades faced each other at a distance of the width of the bastion . . . Then the Chinese, working with great cleverness, always keeping under shelter, pushed forwards a covering wall across the bastion, until it curved round and reached the left-hand corner of the American breastwork. Here they began erecting a small fort, the centre of which was 25 ft. from the nearest American picket. The position was intolerable.'[8] William Bainbridge described the situation rather more fancifully but in language typical of the time: 'Brick by brick that fateful tower rose while its savage builders discussed with diabolical laughter the expected slaughter of the foreigners on the morrow.'

The assault team, consisting of some sixty Americans, Russians and British, gathered at 3.00 a.m. under the Bell Tower. They were nervous, and the sudden apparition of the Norwegian missionary Nestergaard, who had been showing increasing signs of dementia, did not help the situation. Crow-like in his long black cassock, top hat askew, he howled that people had been abusing his good name. He called on King Oscar and the entire Norwegian royal family for justice. He was hastily gagged, bundled away and locked up in the stables, where he raged against the world's wickedness, occasionally cuffed into silence by an unsympathetic Scottish doctor.

Meanwhile, Captain Myers addressed his men. Nigel Oliphant, who was taking part as a volunteer, found his speech interesting 'because it was so utterly unlike what a British officer would have said under similar circumstances. He began by saying that we were about to embark on a desperate enterprise, that he himself had advised against it, but that orders had been given, and we must do it or lose every man in the attempt. He then explained what we had to do – viz. line up on the wall and rush the covering wall . . . then follow up that covering wall till we got to the back of the Chinese barricade. He ended up by saying that . . . if there was anyone whose heart was not in the business he had better say so and clear out. One man said he had a sore arm and went down – not one of ours, I am glad to say.' The British marines were apparently so disgusted by the tone of Myers's address that they showed no desire to be first over the barricade. Conversely, the American accounts of Myers's speech were all very complimentary.

At Myers's word 'go' the men scrambled over the barricade, dropped ten feet on the other side, and charged, the Americans 'yelling like Indians.'[9] They seized the bastion and the barricade behind it, killing some sixty Chinese in the process. Three allied men were killed and six wounded, including poor Myers, who tripped on a spear in the dark and was put out of action for the remainder of the siege with a thigh wound. It was one of the most significant and decisive actions of the siege, turning a precarious hold on the wall into a tenable position. It was held for the rest of the siege and nicknamed 'Fort Myers'. A missionary called it 'a struggle which more than any other was the pivot of our destiny.' The success certainly cheered the besieged, whose spirits had been flagging. An admiring Luella Miner drew a detailed diagram of the action in her diary. Sarah Conger wrote that the night of the assault had been 'the most anxious and trying period' of her husband's life.

The action seemed a fitting prelude to the Americans' Independence Day celebrations. A relieved Edwin Conger visited Mary Gamewell, bearing a framed copy of the Declaration of Independence that had been hanging in his office in the American Legation. She was amused to see that a bullet had torn away 'that portion wherein the revolutionary fathers had expressed themselves in somewhat disparaging terms concerning King George.' Harriet Squiers gave a party for some of the smaller American children, while some of the missionaries gathered to sing 'America' and 'The Star-Spangled Banner.' Luella Miner caught herself blinking back tears. Up on the Tartar Wall the American marines celebrated with a well-earned drink.

Meanwhile, Colonel Shiba was struggling to defend that other crucial portion of the defences, the Fu. By late June nearly a third of the buildings had been abandoned and the Japanese had been forced back to a second line of defence. Nevertheless he was deploying his small force with such efficiency and coolness that the universally held view was that the Japanese were 'the pluckiest beggars we have got.'[10]

The defenders were not helped by the rains that broke in the last days of June, bringing terrific storms. Oscar Upham described nightmare scenes on the Tartar Wall with torrents of rain, a fierce driving wind, and blinding lightning that seemed to excite the enemy: 'The Chinks seemed to go wild with delight and poured in a ton or two of lead at us.' Arthur Smith concluded that the Chinese regarded thunder and lightning 'as a signal of the approval of the whole Chinese Pantheon [of gods].'

Temperatures were reaching 110° F in the shade so that the air felt as humid as a Turkish bath but 'without the clean smell.'[11] Black flies swarmed over every surface and the stench of dead bodies was becoming overpowering. Morrison called Peking 'a city of the dead,' while Mary Gamewell described how 'the odour of decaying flesh filled the air. The drifting horror made night more hideous, and roused from sleep even those who slept the sleep of exhaustion.' Men smoked cigars from morning till night to overcome the stench, and many women, Italians and Russians in particular, threw social niceties to the wind and chain-smoked cigarettes.

As the heat mounted, so, apparently, did the inactivity of the ministers. None of them except Sir Claude appeared to feel that they had any very active role to play in the defences. As Polly wrote: 'The only strong men in the compound who have no special work to do are Ministers Plenipotentiary.' She ran an amused eye over the diplomats. 'The Marquis Salvago [the Italian minister] sits chatting with his wife, a very beautiful woman, on a *chaise longue* most of his time. M. Pichon, the French Minister, nervously and ceaselessly walks about, telling everyone who chats with him: "*La situation est excessivement grave; nous allons tous mourir ce soir.*" ['The situation is exceedingly grave; we are all going to die tonight.'] M. de Giers, the Russian Minister, walks eternally between his Legation and the British compound, and looks every inch a Minister. Poor Señor Cologan, the Spanish Minister . . . is very ill. M. Knobel, the Dutch Minister, offered his services as a sentry . . . but stated at the same time that he did not know how to shoot, and was very shortsighted. Mr Conger, the American Minister, walks about.' She does not mention the Japanese minister, Baron Nishi, whom Morrison described as bearing 'a curious resemblance to an anthropoid ape.' Nishi apparently believed his duty as a minister 'to consist in keeping his mouth shut which is wise and his ears shut which is unwise.' Whatever the case, he was cut off from events. The only language, other than his own, he could speak was Russian, and Russia and Japan were not good friends.

Although Polly was unimpressed by her own minister Edwin Conger, writing meaningfully that, for the Americans at least, Herbert Squiers, her host, was '*the* man in Peking,' she had real sympathy for Sir Claude as commander-in-chief. He was sincerely trying to do his best; 'his path is a thorny one, however; most of the legations are so jealous of this compound being the centre and last stronghold *par excellence*, that they are outrageously inconsiderate of all orders issued.' One incident in particular must have irritated Sir Claude. In early July von Below of the German Legation, who had earlier been a tower of strength, became convinced that the end was nigh. He sat down at a piano and hammered out Wagner's 'Ride of the Valkyries,' determined, as Polly wrote, to die 'in a storm of music.'

Sir Claude's own account paints a revealing picture of daily idiocies and frustrations. 'The Russian Minister asks, twice, that the British should remove a sandbag barricade which is blocking his withdrawal route to the British Legation . . . Sir Claude replied that he is being heavily attacked from the north and can spare no men for this duty. "Indeed I may have to call upon you and Mr Conger for help to repulse this attack – so please have some men ready." . . . Mr Conger's comment is: "We are having the heaviest attack we have ever had here and every man is engaged." . . . At 2.30 p.m. Sir Claude writes again: "It is absolutely essential that the Fu should be held at all hazards. I hope therefore you will order over as many men as possible." . . . The Russian Minister complies: "I am sending you my last ten men, but I must have them back as soon as you no longer need them."'[12] Lenox Simpson decided that the position within the legations could best be described as one of 'armed neutrality'. Sir Claude would no doubt have agreed.

However absurd, the problems facing Sir Claude required tact and patience. At one stage the Chinese turned their Krupp guns on the large Union Jack over the British Legation gateway. Three shells struck the gateway itself. Others whizzed on to explode on the tennis court, endangering the women and children sheltering there. The ever-practical missionaries suggested that the flag was provocative and should be hauled down or moved somewhere less conspicuous. However, MacDonald's chief of staff, Captain Strouts, was adamant that moving the flag would only encourage the enemy and lead to 'possible mutiny on the part of the British Royal Marine Guards.'[13] Luckily the Chinese became bored with their target practise. They turned their attention elsewhere, ignoring the flag for the remainder of the siege, so that Sir Claude was spared that particular thorny decision.

One of Sir Claude's greatest frustrations was lack of real news from the outside world. The many false alarms and reports heightened the defenders' feeling of impotence. Morrison had just been telling the Reverend Allen that 'we should probably only meet with one siege in a lifetime, and that it was just as well to have a good one whilst we were about it,'[14] when he saw rockets streaking through the sky to the southeast and leaped excitedly to his feet. They turned out to be fireworks let off by the Japanese. On another occasion Sir Claude MacDonald went to check on reported sightings of signal lights. He told Monsieur Pichon 'quite categorically'[15] that they were the very lights used at Ladysmith and brought to China by HMS *Terrible*. When this pronouncement proved false it only added to the Frenchman's gloomy scepticism. Monsieur Pichon had already been experiencing difficulty both in persuading Commandant Darcy to accept his orders on where to deploy French troops and in defending his wine cellars – the best in the legations – from pilfering by French civilians whom his wife abused as *'pires que les Boxeurs'* – 'worse than the Boxers.'[16]

Various attempts to lower Chinese converts over the Tartar Wall or to smuggle them out through the canal sluice gate with messages failed. However, on 4 July a young boy from Shantung, well known to some of the American missionaries, volunteered to try to get through. MacDonald gave him a letter to Mr Carles, the British Consul in Tientsin, sewed up in a piece of oilcloth. The whole package measured no more than an inch long and half an inch wide. Instead of putting it in his shoe or sewing it into his clothes – hiding places well known to the Boxers – he concealed it in a rice bowl so that 'when the charitable filled up his bowl of rice, they helped to conceal the urgent cry for help sent out by the besieged.'[17] He was to be the first messenger to reach Tientsin since late June, slipping through the allied sentries into the foreign settlement on 21 July after an eventful journey.

Meanwhile the Russian financial agent Pokolitov, whose current duties consisted of tending the legation cow, offered $10,000 to any courier who could reach Seymour's forces and bring back word of his whereabouts. No one would accept and Morrison explained the reason in some disgust: 'Liu, the Frenchman, said he would go if the father – the eczema-cheeked padre who eats and smokes all day – would permit him to deny that he was a Christian if seized and questioned. He was forbidden; a Protestant might do it, a Catholic could not.'[18]

By now casualties were mounting ever more alarmingly. On 1 July, *'[une] journée de tristesse poignante'* – 'a day of poignant sadness,'[19] as the French commanding officer Darcy sadly recalled – young Wagner, the son of a former French Consul General in Shanghai, was shot dead during an attack on the French Legation. He had been one of Sir Robert Hart's most promising protégés and his death depressed the foreign community. On 5 July another popular young man, David Oliphant of the British Consular Service, brother of Nigel Oliphant, was mortally wounded while cutting down a tree in the Hanlin. Captain Poole had given the order to withdraw but Oliphant ignored it. Poole rushed back to find him lying on his back, with a sailor – Henry Swannell of HMS *Orlando* – sitting beside him, and shot dropping everywhere. Too small to carry Oliphant, Swannell was attempting to shield him by 'placing himself between Oliphant and the direction from which the Chinese were firing.'[20] Oliphant was carried to the hospital on a door in terrible agony but died three hours later, the victim of 'his desire to make himself useful.'[21] He was buried during a thunderstorm. The same day Dr Gilbert Reid was shot in the leg. On 8 July, the Austrian captain von Thomann, who had been so ignominiously removed from command, was killed when a shell-burst took him 'full in the chest' in the French Legation, some said after exposing himself recklessly to danger.

Funerals often took place at night, when it was cooler and the enemy's fire slackened. Sometimes three or four bodies were buried in one grave. Lenox Simpson described one grotesque but typical scene with bearers struggling under the weight of a heavy man whose body burst through his winding sheet: 'His feet shot out as if he were making a last effort to escape from the pitiless grasp of Mother Earth extending her arms towards him in the form of a narrow trench.'

By the early days of July, much of the shelling was directed against the French Legation. There the Austrian chargé d'affaires Herr von Rosthorn and his wife were helping in the defence, having fallen out with the MacDonalds and decamped from the British Legation. Monsieur Pichon had watched them attempt to set fire to an enemy barricade by throwing bales of petrol-soaked straw at it during which efforts Madame von Rosthorn's face, hands and arms were scorched. Monsieur Pichon, himself still declaring that all was lost, decided to burn his papers in a ditch in the British Legation grounds. Morrison jestingly offered $5,000 for a sight of them first. An unsympathetic compatriot said of Pichon, *'Il ne fait que pisser dans les caleçons'* – 'He does nothing but piss in his pants.'[22] His spirits were certainly not improved by an English newspaper photographer who told him he was convinced that the Chinese were mining underneath his house and that he was determined to get a good picture of the explosion. He asked Pichon, as the probable chief subject of the photo, whether he would prefer to be photographed 'going up wholesale, or as you are coming down retail?'[23] Pichon's response can only be guessed.

A conversation with a Chinese prisoner reported by Paul Pelliot, an archaeologist and member of the French volunteer corps, confirmed fears of mines. Pelliot wrote: 'We killed two prisoners with rifle shots and with bayonets. One said little of significance . . . the other revealed without being asked the existence of a mine being dug in the East.'[24] The defenders began to dig trenches to frustrate the miners' progress.

The Hôtel de Pékin was also suffering sustained attack. It had been hit at least ninety times and set on fire on several occasions. Nevertheless the resilient Chamots refused to leave. They were busy organizing the baking of 300 loaves of brown bread a day. When a shell burst into the bakery and killed one of the Chinese bakers, Madame Chamot kept the others to their work by brandishing a rifle. Monsieur Chamot's Chinese servants delivered meals for the hotel guests all over the legation area, calmly dodging 'a shower of stray bullets.' Asked whether he did not think this dangerous, one servant is reported to have replied simply and perhaps ironically that 'the meals of the foreigner are very important.'[25]

The Chinese were now aiming four- and eight-pounder guns at the British Legation. One shot pierced both walls of the dining room, passing behind a portrait of Queen Victoria and nicking the frame. The besieged knew that a similar incident had occurred earlier in the year during the siege of Ladysmith by the Boers shortly before it was raised, and they took it as a good omen. Nevertheless, the elegantly laid table was damaged, with cut glass and china sent flying, suggesting that while Lady MacDonald might be under siege she had not abandoned her standards. However, with the exception of the elegant Italian minister, the Marquese di Salvago Ragi, her guests had apparently given up dressing for dinner.

As the first week in July drew to its close, the defenders were dismayed to find their ammunition running low. Only fourteen shells were left for the small but useful Italian one-pounder, which was being trundled between the British stables, the Tartar Wall, the Fu, the Hanlin and the main gate. In desperation, a munitions technician from HMS *Orlando* began melting down pewter vessels, teapots, vases, incense burners, candlesticks – in fact anything he could find – to make conical shot, which he fitted into old copper shell casings. The defenders even resorted to filling fireworks with nails and scrap iron.

So far the Chinese had only brought some ten guns into action, most of which were antiquated. They had many bigger and better guns they might yet deploy and the besieged wondered why they had not already done so. They also reflected that the situation would be worse if the Chinese were better gunners. Early in the siege Polly had decided that all the foreign-drilled troops must be at Tientsin and that the Peking gunners were 'utterly incompetent'. Nevertheless, with each passing day, the Chinese guns were pounding away at the defences, slowly reducing them to rubble. In some places the Chinese were able to fire on the outer walls of the Fu at point-blank range.

They were also pushing their barricades ever forwards, advancing, dismantling and rebuilding with relentless energy and determination as well as mining beneath the legations' defences. The besieged were in danger of being overrun or blown up without the guns or the ammunition to hold back the tide. However, on 7 July they had a stroke of luck. Chinese converts discovered the rusty old muzzle of a gun lying neglected in a foundry. Some people believed that it dated from the Anglo-French expedition of 1860, but it was probably just a common Chinese iron cannon. Far more interesting to the besieged than its origins was the fact that it was still serviceable. A resourceful American gunner, Sergeant Mitchell, scraped off the rust and mounted the muzzle on a spare set of wheels belonging to the Italian gun. The shells brought by the Russians for the gun they had abandoned on the railway platform at Tientsin, and which they had flung down a well, were retrieved and found to be quite a good fit.

The new gun had no sights and was too inaccurate for long-range shots. It also had terrific recoil and produced clouds of sooty black smoke so that its whereabouts were hard to keep secret. Nevertheless, it dealt very efficiently with nearby barricades and it certainly surprised the Chinese. As William Bainbridge wrote: 'This unexpected addition to our equipment must have led to much speculation among the ignorant Chinese soldiery as to the warlike resources of the foreign devil who could thus apparently construct a cannon out of his inner consciousness.' Edmund Backhouse later claimed that the Empress Dowager told him it had made a most exasperating noise and kept her awake during her siesta time.[26] The besieged regarded their new weapon with pride and affection, lavishing a range of nicknames on her from 'The International' because of her multinational provenance to 'Old Betsey', 'Puffing Betsey', 'Boxer Bill', and even 'The Empress Dowager'.

As the foreigners in Peking became more innovative in their quest for survival, they wondered how their colleagues in Tientsin were faring. In fact, the Chinese City in Tientsin was still in the grip of the Boxers, who were continuing to terrorize Chinese Christians and anyone unlucky enough to have connections with foreigners.

Many were trying to flee and Chinese travellers recorded such macabre scenes as 'a female corpse without its head, still clutching the dead body of a child . . . a dreadful sight to behold.'[27] The river had become choked with mutilated bodies, many with missing limbs. In early July, James Ricalton, a photographer sent to China to make a visual record of the Boxer rising, was travelling by barge in an attempt to get through to Tientsin, but his words are more graphic than any picture: 'Many mud villages were passed . . . from most of which the inhabitants had fled back into the country. We were constantly passing dead bodies floating down, and on either bank of the river, at every turn, hungry dogs from the deserted villages could be seen tearing at the swollen corpses left on the banks by the ebb tide. It was forty miles of country laid waste, deserted homes, burned villages, along a river polluted and malodorous with human putrefaction.'[28]

Ricalton reached Tientsin on 5 July to be stunned by the air of desolation. He noted housetops bristling with fortifications, storehouses turned into barricades, bales of wool, bags of peanuts, sacks of licorice-root and rice thrown up into breastworks. Smoke was curling from smouldering ruins and three of the four hotels had been destroyed. So many dead bodies were floating in the river that several times a day gangs of coolies were sent to free them with bamboo poles and float them downstream.

The bombardment of the foreign settlements continued and the sniping was constant. The reinforcements that reached Tientsin on 23 June had, as Lou Hoover feared, been too few to lift the siege. If anything, the Chinese shelling was even fiercer. Mrs James Jones, an American, wrote that the Chinese gunners were so proficient that 'general admiration would have been expressed if only they had been shelling somebody else.'[29] They were firing three- and four-inch quick-firing guns from within the Chinese City and using smokeless powder, which made them hard to locate and attack. Casualties from shell and rifle fire were never fewer than twenty a day, sometimes rising to double that number.

The besieged foreigners of Tientsin heard rumours of a rift between the Imperial troops under General Nieh and the Boxers. Nieh himself was killed on 9 July. According to reports, he had deliberately exposed himself to danger because of the impossible position in which the Imperial Court had placed him. However, just as in Peking, the besieged had no way of knowing what was really happening and attacks had acquired the banality of the routine. According to Herbert Hoover: 'As a rule they begin about 3 a.m., and keep it up more or less steadily, with an especially hot hour at some time [in this period], until time for a 7 o'clock or 7.30 breakfast. It then begins about 9 a.m. and keeps it up in a desultory manner all morning, with a very hot hour from 11 to 12. Tiffin is always eaten in peace. There is usually, but not always, an hour or two between 3 and 6. They seldom begin operations at other times, but they are always ready to answer us at a moment's notice if we begin, and give us shell for shell straight through – with a striking likeness to the woman of tradition in insisting on having a few last words.'

Vice-Admiral Seymour was no longer in supreme command and tension among the allies in Tientsin was leading to some unfortunate incidents. In one such occurrence, recorded by Herbert Hoover, a group of British Indian Army Sikhs were left in an exposed position by some retreating French sentries. 'Not knowing what it meant for other than traitors to run under attack without orders,' the Sikhs set about 'exterminating the squad of Frenchmen, which only the most frantic commands of the English officers prevented.'

By the beginning of July, the arrival of a stream of reinforcements had brought the total allied force around Tientsin to over 10,000, with as many more at the Taku bar. Some of them were hardly crack troops. Mrs Drew watched the arrival of a French regiment from Indo-China in faded blue uniforms looking as if they were 'full of fever and quinine.' Roger Keyes called them 'simply the scum of the French army.'[30] However, the additional forces and the capture of two Chinese arsenals outside Tientsin meant that the foreign settlement was in a stronger position both to defend itself and, soon, to attack the Chinese City. Many, like Roger Keyes, were anxious to be off to Peking as soon as possible. He noted that there were more allied troops in and around Tientsin than there were British troops in India during the Mutiny. He could not understand why they allowed themselves to be penned up by a few thousand Chinese and prevented from marching to the relief of the legations. However, the commanders were all too conscious that one attempt to get through to Peking had already failed. The first priorities must be to subdue and secure the Chinese City of Tientsin and then to amass a very substantial force before advancing to Peking. It would be some weeks before this could be achieved.

In Peking, the realization that relief was still a long way off was dawning. On 9 July, a Christian messenger sent into the city in disguise to gather information returned with some disturbing news. It was posted on the Bell Tower in all its brutal simplicity. After stating that the emperor and the Empress Dowager were still in Peking, it announced: 'Nothing known of the approach of foreign troops.'[31] It was a terrible moment.

However, the incredulous people surging around the tower would have been even more distressed to know that the wider world believed they were already dead. On 5 July, Queen Victoria had received a shocking message through Reuters, a forerunner of the more graphic reports that would appear in mid-July: 'All the foreigners, including 400 soldiers, women and children, who held out at British Legation, till ammunition and food exhausted, reported killed.' Although she knew it might not be true she was nevertheless 'quite miserable, horror-struck.'[32]

The same day an alarmed British government warned the Chinese envoy to London that the Chinese government would be held 'personally guilty if the members of the European Legations and other foreigners in Peking suffer injury.'[33] But for the moment it could only wait and hope that such warnings were not too late.

10

THE DARKEST NIGHT

The night is darkest before the dawn. – Sir Claude MacDonald

'JULY 13TH – AND A FRIDAY,' wrote Sir Claude with feeling. He thought it 'the most harassing day' of the entire siege. Meyrick Hewlett wrote that many believed 'the end had come.'[1] As dawn rose the Fu was shelled heavily by four Krupp guns. The Japanese and Italian defenders, dodging a hail of shells and shrapnel in the thin grey light, could see the guns just 150 yards away. As the attack grew yet more furious and burning buildings collapsed around them, Colonel Shiba ordered a retreat. He had originally planned nine lines of defence and now fell back to the last but one. No one blamed him. Even the acerbic Captain Poole wrote, 'I put Colonel Shiba . . . on a golden pedestal for endurance and perseverance.'

At 4.00 p.m., the Chinese attacked on all sides. The Jubilee Bell rang out and as men came running Sir Claude dispatched them to the most vulnerable parts of the defences. He was about to send ten Russian marines to the Fu when he received a welcome message from Shiba that he was holding his own again. At that very moment the German second secretary von Bergen appeared, gasping that the German Legation was under great pressure. The Russians were sent there instead, arriving just in time. The Imperial troops were about to charge, shouting, yelling and brandishing their banners. The Russians joined the German forces under Lieutenant von Soden and counter-attacked with fixed bayonets, driving them off.

In the early evening a tremendous blast seared the twilight and people sitting on the British Legation veranda felt the earth shake. Two mines had exploded in the French Legation – one beneath the second secretary's house and the other close to the minister's house. Both buildings were completely destroyed, rather as the British photographer had predicted to Pichon. The minister was not among the casualties, either 'wholesale' or 'retail'. However, two French sailors were killed, their bodies crushed beneath the ruins. Only a foot was found. The Austrian chargé d'affaires, von Rosthorn, had a miraculous escape. The first explosion buried him deep in the rubble, but 'the second explosion vomited him forth free and unhurt,' according to Sir Robert Hart. The Chinese themselves suffered the greatest losses because they misjudged the force of the blast. Oscar Upham recorded with satisfaction that 'the Chinks . . . gathered around to see how it was going to work. They saw to their sorrow, and spent the rest of the night hauling off their own dead and wounded.' According to a spy sent out into the city, Chinese carts the next day collected some thirty bodies from around the crater formed by the explosion. The besieged speculated that the Chinese were using dead bodies as material for their barricades. The cloying stench of decaying flesh seemed to get everywhere in the hot, humid, and confined legations.

The defenders of the French Legation compound now too fell back to a new line of defence, having lost about two-thirds of their original area. Monsieur Pichon had promised to spend the next day – 14 July, Bastille Day – with the French marines in the French Legation, but nothing was now left of the building except *'des ruines calcinées'* – 'ruins burned to cinders,'[2] while Chinese banners fluttered where the tricolour should have been.

Many predicted it would not be long before the French were forced to fall back again on the adjacent and 'almost impregnable'³ Hôtel de Pékin.

Meanwhile there had been a skirmish in the Hanlin. Captain Poole led a small party through the wall into the Hanlin grounds to occupy a ruined temple in the vulnerable west corner by the Imperial Carriage Park. He set up two sentry posts that were so close to the Chinese sandbag entrenchments on the Carriage Park wall that 'amenities in the shape of bricks, stones, and watermelon rinds were freely exchanged between the besiegers and the besieged, and our sentries could hear the enemy quarrelling over their rice rations and discussing matters generally.'⁴

It was a small success. However, looking back over a traumatic day, Sir Claude knew that much more had been lost than gained. The lines of defence in the French Legation and the Fu had shrunk alarmingly, while five men had been killed and ten wounded. He must have wondered how much longer they could go on. Yet there was no other option. One thing all the besieged agreed on was that there was no question of surrender. Diary after diary bemoans the cruelty and barbarity of the besiegers and the fact that there could be no honourable surrender, only massacre. And if it was to be massacre they preferred to go down fighting, preferably shooting their women and children first. Polly Condit Smith had been given a small pistol loaded with several cartridges by a Belgian diplomat – 'in case you need it, mademoiselle.'

During those dangerous and uncertain days, the legation's extensive library held a macabre attraction. As Polly wrote: 'Occasionally some inquisitive soul will go to it and try to find, compared with other sieges and massacres, what place this one will have in history.' The consensus was that 'the nearest similar harrowing siege seems to be that of Lucknow, where a heterogeneous multitude, closed up in the Residency, were holding out against fearful odds in expectation of relief by Havelock's Highlanders, resolved to die of starvation rather than surrender.'

The besieged read Tennyson's tremulous poem about Lucknow. Such lines as:

Heat like the mouth of a hell or a deluge of cataract skies,
Stench of old offal decaying, and infinite torment of flies [5]

must have struck home. However, in Polly's view there was an essential difference between the two situations, though the British might not have agreed. In India the King of Delhi had been trying to regain his throne, whereas the Empress Dowager 'has no such excuse in making war on practically all the nations of the civilized world.'

People were particularly intrigued by one old pamphlet. Written by General Gordon at the request of the Chinese government, it advised the Chinese how to wage war against foreigners. It recommended that they should never show themselves in open attack but should gradually wear out the enemy by constant firing at night. Nigel Oliphant wrote dryly: 'It would be very interesting to know if it is in pursuance of this advice that the Chinese favour us with their erratic and annoying fusillades.' Unfortunately, the demented Norwegian Nestergaard escaped through the legation lines to advise the Chinese on their tactics in person. He was taken to Jung Lu's headquarters where the Chinese examined his papers, which must have puzzled them since they included a letter to the Russian minister in which Nestergaard apologized for indecently exposing himself to his wife. Luckily for him, however, the Chinese respected the insane, believing them to be possessed by sacred spirits. They gave him a good dinner, and he showed his gratitude by volunteering a great deal of useful information about the state of the legations' defences and advising the Chinese not to aim so high. They sent him back unharmed to the legations, where the effect of his advice became quickly apparent – the Chinese began shooting lower. The general opinion was that the tiresome Norwegian should be shot, but Sir Claude simply had him locked up again.

Nestergaard's exploits were an irritant but some moments of

pure farce lightened the mood. Sergeant Mitchell, who had brought 'Old Betsey' to life, climbed on a Chinese barricade and wrested a black flag from a Chinese soldier by 'pounding him with sandbags until he let go.'[6] Having gained possession, he 'put his thumb on his nose and wiggled his fingers saucily at the Chinese.'[7] The Chinese were so astonished that they forgot to fire until after he had dived for cover.

Despite such antics, the defenders were all too aware of the fragility of their situation. The Tartar Wall was still a source of anxiety. The plain-spoken Captain Newt Hall had replaced the wounded Myers as commander of the American Marines who were still holding out there. Captain Poole dismissed Hall as 'a funkstick' who was not to be trusted, while Morrison considered he had no control over his men, who got blind drunk and 'insult[ed] their NCO commanding with impunity.' They were nearly all suffering from diarrhoea, which did not help tempers. Hall was also at odds with Conger and Squiers, and the traditional animosity between the army and the marines was perhaps a little to blame. They wanted him to move the American barricade closer to the Chinese position but Hall disagreed. He reconnoitred the proposed new position and decided to leave his barricade where it was.

On 14 July, there was excitement when an elderly Chinese messenger, sent out on 10 July by missionaries, returned. He had been captured by Boxers and badly beaten in a temple before being taken to Jung Lu's headquarters in the Imperial City. Here he had been well treated and after three days was given a message purporting to come from Prince Ching 'and others' and allowed to return. The message blamed the attacks on the legations squarely on the aggressive actions of the foreign soldiers and congratulated the ministers for still being alive. It also advised them to leave the legations with their families and staff and place themselves under the protection of the Tsungli Yamen. It promised them safe conduct but stipulated that not a single armed soldier could accompany them.

The message was greeted with astonishment, ridicule and contempt. Oliphant thought it must be a practical joke while Jessie Ransome, pausing in her back-breaking work in the hospital, decided: 'The Chinese idea of our intelligence must indeed be small!' A prisoner captured by the French two days earlier had said that there was tension between Prince Tuan, the Boxers' patron, and Prince Ching. Some people hoped this might be a genuine olive branch from the latter. However, Sir Claude replied frostily that the ministers' persons were sacrosanct, that the legations would continue to defend themselves and that the foreigners had no intention of going to the Yamen. Should anything happen to them there would be severe reprisals and if the Chinese government wished to negotiate 'it should send a responsible official with a white flag.'[8] The poor old messenger was sent out again.

While awaiting the Chinese government's next move, the foreign community was shaken by the death of one of the most popular British student interpreters, Henry Warren, who was hit in the face by a shell splinter while doing duty with the Japanese in the Fu. Polly, who had often danced with him, watched him carried past, 'his face almost entirely shot off.' The doctors struggled to save him but a splinter of bone from his jaw slipped down his throat. The doctors performed a tracheotomy but to no avail. Lancelot Giles wrote that he had lost his best friend in Peking. A German officer was unsympathetic, complaining to a French customs official that many of the defenders, especially the English *avec leur flegme* – 'with their bravado'[9] – took stupid risks. He pointed out that Warren had enjoyed teasing the Chinese by waving a flag at them from the barricades.

However, poor Warren's death was the precursor to another serious loss. A little while later Colonel Shiba reported that all his men – sailors and volunteers – were exhausted. They had been on duty since the beginning of the siege on 20 June and had not even changed their clothes. Neither had they ever had more than three or four consecutive hours of sleep at a time. Shiba asked that first one half, and then the other half, of his men be taken off duty for a full twenty-four hours to give them a chance to recuperate. He also asked that they be replaced by British volunteers and marines. Sir Claude could not but agree. The performance of the Japanese had been truly astonishing and the surprise had been that they had kept going for so long.

The following morning, 16 July, Captain Strouts, accompanied by Morrison, took the relief party over to the Fu. However, on the way back the two men were caught in a shower of bullets. Morrison described what happened: 'I . . . felt a cut in my right thigh. At the same moment, "My God," said Strouts, and he fell over into the arms of Shiba, who was on his left.' Shiba ran for a surgeon while Morrison tried to apply a tourniquet but it was no good. The thighbone was shattered and Strouts's body was 'soaking in blood.' Both Morrison and Strouts were carried by stretcher to the hospital, under such heavy fire that a bullet passed through Shiba's coat. It was immediately obvious that nothing could be done for Strouts, who had a severed artery in his thigh. He died three hours later, Morrison still by his side. 'He said nothing,' Morrison later wrote, 'but by and by gave a few sobs of pain then his breath came quietly and then he sank away into death.' He was buried that evening in the same grave as young Warren, whose funeral Strouts had helped to arrange, little suspecting it would also be his own. Their bodies were wrapped in a Union Jack and flowers strewn over them. There was no military salute to save ammunition and to avoid attracting Chinese fire. The loss of two such vital young men struck several onlookers as a defining moment in the siege. Captain Wray replaced Strouts as commander of the British marines, but Captain Poole thought him 'an excitable irresponsible chap who has not the confidence of his men.' Perhaps for this reason Sir Claude chose Herbert Squiers to take over Strouts's role as his chief of staff.

Sir Claude reflected bitterly that 'the end, to those who knew, was clearly in sight, for a very simple problem in "possibilities and probabilities" showed that if our losses continued at the same daily rate, by the end of July, or even before then, there would be nobody left to oppose the entry of Tung-fu Hsiang's bloodthirsty ruffians, but women and children and 120 grievously wounded men.' However, as he also noted, 'the night is darkest before the dawn.' While he was still standing by the graveside, the old messenger he had sent out was spotted approaching from the North Bridge, carrying a white flag of truce. Sir Claude later wrote: 'Whether to accelerate his movements or because the troops in that quarter belonging to the antiforeign leaders objected to the peaceful purport of the letter he carried, two shells were fired over his head, the fragments from which tore through the trees of the little cemetery in which we were standing.' The message he bore was, again, from 'Prince Ching and others.' It begged the foreigners to refrain from attacking the Chinese and promised that the Chinese government would 'continue to exert all its efforts to keep order and give protection.'[10] As one of Sir Claude's staff went towards the messenger, waving his handkerchief, he was fired at – 'an amusing comment on this pacific note.'[11]

The old man was also carrying another message – a telegram in cipher for Edwin Conger, from the State Department in Washington, which read simply albeit rather unhelpfully, 'Communicate tidings bearer.' There was no date and it was unclear who had sent it. Neither was it obvious who the 'bearer' was. Arthur Smith called it 'densely mysterious'. However, it was the first communication received from the outside world since the middle of June, and there was no doubt that it was genuine. Only Conger and the State Department possessed the cipher in which it had been written. Conger asked for details of when it had been received and who had sent it, but meanwhile responded in code: 'For one month we have been besieged in British Legation under continued shot and shell from Chinese soldiers. Quick relief only can prevent general massacre.' He learned the next day that the cable was dated 11 July and had been transmitted by the Chinese envoy to Washington, Wu Ting-fang, on behalf of the secretary of state.

Ironically, the State Department believed Conger's response to be a forgery. While passing through Washington a year later, Sir Claude MacDonald was told by State Department officials that 'as they had quite made up their minds that we had all been massacred, the reply telegram was supposed to have been sent by the Chinese Government, who had possessed themselves of the cipher.'

By the middle of July 1900 the outside world indeed had reason to believe that the diplomats were dead. A wave of reports in the media appeared to confirm the earlier stories of massacre that had so distressed Queen Victoria. On 16 July the *Daily Mail* carried the shocking story from its 'Special Correspondent' in Shanghai under the headline 'The Pekin Massacre. All White Men, Women and Children Put to the Sword. Death Not Dishonour.'

Following this lead, *The Times* on 17 July told its horrified but doubtless avid readers how 'the Europeans fought with calm courage to the end against overwhelming hordes of fanatical barbarians thirsting for their blood. While their ammunition lasted they defied Chinese rifle and artillery fire and beat back wave after wave of their assailants. When the last cartridge had gone their hour had come. They met it like men. Standing to their battered defences they stayed the onrush of the Chinese, until, borne down by sheer weight of numbers, they perished at their posts. They have died as we would have had them die, fighting to the last for the helpless women and children who were to be butchered over their dead bodies . . . Of the ladies, it is enough to say that in this awful hour they showed themselves worthy of their husbands. Their agony was long and cruel, but they have borne it nobly, and it is done. All that remains for us is to mourn them and to avenge them.'[12]

The Times also published obituaries of Morrison, MacDonald and Hart.[13] Sir Claude's included the comment: 'How the British Minister and his colleagues, together, it must be added, with Sir Robert Hart and all the leading members of the foreign community in Peking, failed altogether to see any signs of the coming storm, is a mystery which will probably now remain for ever unsolved.' However, Morrison's was so radiantly flattering, referring to 'our devoted Correspondent at Peking,' that a young Australian friend later suggested he ask the newspaper to double his salary. A memorial service for the Europeans massacred in Peking was planned for 23 July while messages of condolence flew around the world and the Powers considered what to do next. However, persistent doubts about the truth of the *Daily Mail* story, reinforced by Conger's cipher message, which if not immediately regarded as authentic at least gave food for thought, set alarm bells ringing. The service was cancelled at the last minute and in early August messages from other ministers began to come through proving that the story had been entirely fictitious.

All the newspapers that had taken the *Daily Mail*'s lead were outraged and embarrassed. Under the headline 'The Lies from China,' the *New York Times* told its readers that 'for the past months the minds of men in all parts of the civilized world have been shocked and depressed by the stories of massacre and torture in Peking . . . As early as June 30 it was reported . . . that the public execution of foreigners had been going on in Peking for some ten days, and that the priests had been engaged in administering extreme unction to the dying, while the heads of the murdered marine guards at the embassies were borne about the streets on spears . . . Then came reports of the poisoning of the women at the moment of the final attack on the British Legation, of the suicide of Sir Robert Hart, the Chief of Customs in China, of the plunging of the Russian Minister and his wife in boiling oil, of the dismemberment and mutilation of the victims of the mob, of the compulsory suicide of the Emperor and the Dowager Empress at the command of Prince Tuan . . . The definite statements of the correspondents, especially in Shanghai, practically destroyed doubt that all these had been slaughtered in circumstances of the most revolting cruelty . . . Now it turns out that almost every statement sent out from China . . . was essentially false.'[14]

An indignant Morrison some months later exposed the identity and disreputable background of the *Daily Mail*'s 'Special Correspondent' who had sent the misleading dispatch from Shanghai. He was an American fraudster called Sutterlee who had a track record of dubious business dealings in the East, including arms smuggling to the Philippine rebels. Morrison concluded, rather smugly perhaps, that 'the *Daily Mail* did not exercise a very wise choice in the appointment of their Correspondent.'[15]

Happily unaware of all this confusion, Sir Claude had replied to the message from Prince Ching by suggesting that a cease-fire might be a good way for the Chinese to demonstrate their goodwill. Prince Ching agreed, responding with an assurance that 'now that there is mutual agreement that there is to be no more fighting there may be peace and quiet.' On 17 July a truce began. The psychological effect of being in touch with the outside world again, however unreliably and distortedly, was almost more important than the cease-fire. Mary Gamewell wrote joyously that 'the heartbeat of the great, living, throbbing world was now felt by the beleaguered garrison, and it braced itself for the days of holding on that must elapse before the allies should arrive at the gates of Peking.'

III

War and Watermelons

21 July – 14 August 1900

11
A TRUCE AND A TRIUMPH

Our little world is tired; we have all had enough.
– Bertram Lenox Simpson

THE BREAK IN THE FIGHTING had come just in time. The defenders were exhausted, run down and suffering from stress. Some civilian men had gone to pieces, using minor ailments as an excuse to shirk work, while those women who had collapsed 'simply spent their hours, day and night, behind the nearest closed door, and await each fresh attack to indulge in new hysterical scenes.' The Squierses' French governess, upset by the amount of curry powder in her food, seized Polly's hands and sobbed that someone was trying to poison her. She had just one request – that she be immediately returned to France. Lenox Simpson summed it up: 'Our little world is tired; we have all had enough.'

Their physical condition was not helped by a poor diet. Occasional raiding parties to the Mongol Market yielded some useful pickings. People also braved the decomposing corpses lying in front of Kierulff's store on Legation Street to pick hopefully through the debris. However, for most the diet was a monotonous one of horse, pony or mule and rice, which gave many people digestive problems and made them feel 'out of sorts'.[1] A few were still faring quite well. The Squierses' larder had been bolstered by Fargo's exploits in the early stages of the siege and their 'splendid stores'[2] were the best in the compound. An invitation to join the Squierses' mess for a meal was always gratefully accepted. Nigel Oliphant described the breakfast he ate there as 'the best meal I have had since the siege began,' while Frank Gamewell would gladly grab a cup of coffee before cycling off on his rounds.

The Squierses were certainly nothing if not generous. They invited missionaries in for tiffin, while friends who were 'sadly in need of food'[3] came to breakfast and dinner. Harriet Squiers still had sufficient supplies of tinned beef for her to be able to refuse the daily allocation of horsemeat to her household. They ate the beef with plenty of tomato catsup, which, as Polly observed, 'tastes very good in this hot weather.' They also had a good stock of jams, tinned fruits, tinned vegetables, sardines, tinned mackerel, Liebig's extract, coffee, tinned butter, white flour, some Stilton cheese and some 'wonderfully preserved' dried fruits from California.

Dinner at the Squierses' was usually accompanied by a magnum or two of champagne, which Polly thought 'a blessed help' given that the men were so tired and the women's nerves were so much on edge. In the topsy-turvy world of the siege, champagne and wine – of which there were large supplies – had become cheaper than soda water. Lenox Simpson believed that 'had it not been for the Monopole, of which there are great stores in the hotel and the club – a thousand cases in all . . . I should have collapsed.' Arthur Smith wrote that there were so many empty glass bottles as a result of 'the great consumption of wine' that they were a positive danger. If hit by a shell, glass splinters would fly everywhere. However, alcohol was clearly a useful stimulant. Captain Poole confessed that taking 'a pull' helped him get by without much sleep or rest.

Polly compared the relative luxury of the Squierses' table with the monotony of the Customs' mess where the diet was invariably rice, jam and tea for breakfast; rice and horse for tiffin; and rice, horse and jam for dinner. Sir Robert Hart had declined Lady MacDonald's invitation to eat at her table, preferring to share the spartan conditions of his staff. However, he was delighted to come to a special dinner at the Squierses'. Their enterprising cook had slipped through the defences into the Mongol Market and procured a dozen tiny chickens. Polly made an ironical note of the meal:

MENU	Remarks
Celery bouillon	Liebig's extract, celery
Anchovy on toast	Anchovy paste
Broiled chicken	Procured at risk of cook's life
Green peas, fried potatoes	Tinned peas and two potatoes
Bean salad	Tinned beans
Black coffee	Plenty of coffee

In the hospital kitchen the missionary women took special care over meals for the wounded. Jessie Ransome thought it 'truly astonishing what excellent breakfasts, dinners and suppers were produced daily from very little else than horseflesh and rice.' The patients' appetites were tempted with roasts, stews, rissoles, pies, patties and curries, 'always served most beautifully hot and looking most appetizing.' There were 'wonderful' blancmanges, fritters, pancakes, rice puddings, all made without eggs or milk. Their diet was further enlivened by gifts of tinned meat, fish and fruit from private larders. Sometimes there was a little 'game' on the menu 'in the shape of a magpie or a few sparrows, which were daintily cooked and served, and no questions asked.' An egg was a great treat. One convalescent became skilled at listening for the telltale clucking of a hen and would then 'dart off on his crutches to secure the prize.' It was sometimes difficult cooking for so many nationalities with such widely differing tastes, but Jessie concluded the Japanese were by far her happiest customers, 'always hungry and always pleased.'

She also found that the Japanese made the best patients. The Russians were usually 'stolid and silent'; the French and Italians tended to 'make the most of their wounds'; the British and Americans were usually 'in too great a hurry to make out that they were well enough to return to duty'; but the Japanese were always 'brave and cheery'. When the Reverend Allen discovered that a Japanese soldier whose knee had been smashed by a shell had managed to reverse his position in bed to move his head out of the sun, he told him not to move himself without asking for help. The poor man, who had misunderstood every word, painstakingly shuffled back to his original position. Allen found him ten minutes later 'with his head in the blazing sun, and a smile of conscious virtue on his face.'

Jessie and her fellow missionaries exercised considerable ingenuity with their own food as well as the hospital patients'. A particular specialty was griddle cakes made from leftover rice and millet porridge mixed with a little white flour then cooked in horse- or mulemeat drippings, each cake 'the size of a tea-plate – very light, very brown, very beautiful, in fact the most popular article of diet that graced our tables.'[4] A lady from the Customs mess saw them and requested the recipe. Mary Gamewell traded it for advice on how best to cook horse. The lady told her to cut it into steaks, simmer it for three hours, then brown it in fat and add spice.

The missionaries were too numerous to be able to eat together and so were fed by denomination. As Mary Gamewell described: 'We had everyday a Congregational breakfast, a Presbyterian breakfast and a Methodist breakfast, and dinner and supper were served in the same order.' They pasted paper fringes on the edge of a punka, which was kept in motion by a servant at mealtimes to keep the swarms of flies off the food. Each denomination's servants, who were given exactly the same to eat as the mission-aries, took their turn at pulling while another denomination ate. The system collapsed one day while the Congregationalists were eating. Mary asked one of her servants why no one was pulling the punka. After much obfuscation the truth emerged. The servants of the Congregationalists had fallen out with the servants of the other denominations over some trifle. The upshot was that 'while Presbyterians will pull the punka for Methodists, and Methodists will pull the punka for Presbyterians,' neither of them would do so for the Congregationalists. Mary appealed to them to remember the common peril and 'the punka swung again.'

The missionaries were quite pleased to wait on one another at table. According to Mrs Ewing: 'The waiters eat after all the rest are through, and I like that, for we know how much there is left and can have a second helping without fear of robbing others. I ate all I wanted to on those days . . . I generally do get enough but I have such a greedy feeling all the time.'[5]

They were all increasingly concerned about the Chinese in the Fu. They were under constant attack and effectively cut off from the rest of the besieged because it was so dangerous to venture into the streets. In mid-July Lenox Simpson went to see the conditions for himself: 'The feeding of our native Christians, an army of nearly two thousand, is still progressing, but babies are dying rapidly, and nothing further can be done. There is only just so much rice, and the men who are doing the heavy coolie work on the fortifications must be fed better than the rest, or else no food at all would be needed . . . The native children, with hunger gnawing savagely at their stomachs, wander about stripping the trees of their leaves.' He described 'terrible water-swollen stomachs' and 'pitiful sticks of legs.' 'To the babies we give all the scraps of food we can gather up after our own rough food is eaten, and to see the little disappointed faces when there is nothing is sadder than to watch the wounded being carried in . . . Thus enclosed in our brick-bound lines, each of us is spinning out his fate. The Europeans still have as much food as they need; the Chinese are half starving.'

In spite of the extra rations, many of the converts disliked working on the fortifications within the British Legation. They told a Chinese Methodist serving as a labour supervisor that 'the work at the British legation is crushing and they don't feed you enough. And if you do not carry out their orders to the letter, they flog you . . . Therefore, we don't want to go there.'[6] They much preferred working for the non-Christian Japanese, for whom 'we are ready to risk our lives.'[7] Colonel Shiba had raised a force of Christian volunteers, drilling them and arming them with rifles captured from the enemy.

While the attacks went on, there was little the missionaries could do for their converts. They had their own safety to worry about. The chapel where many of the women were sleeping was not particularly secure. One night a bullet flew in over the heads of a Congregational party, struck the wall over a Methodist bed and dropped, spent, into a corner upon a Presbyterian – 'A non-sectarian missile surely!' wrote Mary Gamewell. On the days when the firing was worst and the women were ordered to keep under cover, the children were piled on the tables while the cleaning and mopping of the floor went on. On one occasion a child exclaimed in discouraged tones, 'Oh, dear! When we are inside we are in the way, and when we are outside we get shot.'[8]

The insects were also worse than ever – mosquitoes, fleas, cockroaches, and clouds of sticky aggressive black flies swarmed on the mosquito nets and made it almost impossible to sleep. Oliphant called them 'literally a curse'. An enterprising individual invented some bug powder that proved very effective but made everyone sneeze.

The American missionaries found some relaxation in gathering in the evenings outside the chapel door to sing hymns and songs. The British Reverend Allen enjoyed sitting in the dim twilight listening to the strains of 'Hail, Columbia!', 'Marching through Georgia', 'De Ring-tailed Coon', or 'Nearer, My God, to Thee' to an accompaniment of rifle shots. It made him wonder what the Chinese thought of it and 'why it did not serve to stir in them a burning desire to put an end to that concert.' Certainly when Madame Pokolitov, a former St Petersburg diva, sang operatic arias it elicited a storm of rifle fire. According to Lenox Simpson, she sang the Jewel Song from *Faust* 'so ringingly that the Chinese snipers must have heard it, for immediately they opened a heavy "fire", which grew to a perfect tornado, and sent the listeners flying in terror. Perhaps the enemy thought it was a new war-cry, which meant their sudden damnation!'

As the siege went on, a particular concern for the missionaries – if Lenox Simpson is to be believed – was how to protect the large number of 'buxom Chinese schoolgirls' from the guards – particularly from the Russians, whose barricades were close to the girls' lodgings. After a number of unfortunate incidents, a notice was posted on the Bell Tower forbidding anyone to approach the 'delectable' building. It puzzled the Russian commander Baron von Rahden: 'Taking off his cap, and assuming a very polite air of doubt and perplexity, he enquired of the lady missionary committee which oversees the welfare of these girls: *"Pardon, mes dames,"* he said purposely in French, *"cette affiche est-ce seulement pour les civils ou aussi pour les militaires?"'* – 'Excuse me, ladies, does this apply only to civilians or also to the military?'

With the Chinese girls declared off-limits, Russian patrols apparently went further afield. Again according to Lenox Simpson, one young man tiptoed into the wrong room to be confronted by the wife of a minister. She calmly called out into the gloom: *'Monsieur désire quelque chose? Je serai charmée de donner à Monsieur ce qu'il voudra s'il veut bien rester à la porte.'* – 'Is there something the gentleman desires? I would be delighted to give it to him if he would be good enough to remain by the door.' The horrified young man had the presence of mind to reply, *'Merci, Madame, merci mille fois! Je cherchais seulement de la Vaseline pour mon fusil!'* – 'Thank you a thousand times, madam! I was merely seeking some Vaseline for my rifle!' This ambiguous phrase apparently became 'immortal among the besieged.' According to Morrison, Lenox Simpson himself was still indulging in nocturnal trysts with Lily Bredon, while clandestine liaisons flourished in the heightened atmosphere of the siege. The British Legation gardens were a favourite meeting place after dark. One missionary wrote mildly that 'more than one romance is at present interesting those who love to watch and report such matters.'[9]

The stresses and strains of siege life also had a more prosaic effect: the community became better organized. In the very early days it was apparently 'unfashionable to appear with a clean shirt.' However, this pragmatic affectation faded with the opening of a 'model laundry'.[10] Several men virtually fought for the privilege of supervising it and the victor was Mr Brazier, a commissioner of Customs. The distinguished Mr Brazier held court in the outhouses by the British Legation's north stables. In the cool of the morning, residents could be seen wending their way to the washhouse with their little bundles of clothes, which Mr Brazier duly checked and handed over to the washermen. As the Reverend Allen wrote: 'The washing was a little rough, since no clothes could be starched or ironed, but they were made clean, and the general success of the works was so great that the officers who marched in on the day of the relief declared that we all looked as if we were met for a garden party.' Sometimes demand was so great that in the interests of self-preservation Mr Brazier would post a bulletin informing his customers that 'no washing will be received today.'[11]

While people adjusted to the dangers and inconveniences of life in those hot July days, the absence of real news became increasingly hard to bear. On 12 July, Nigel Oliphant was lying in the hospital with an injured leg, reflecting that he was in the very room where his brother, David, had died, when a friend came to tell him of rumours that the foreign troops had taken and burned Tientsin. Oliphant's immediate reaction was that the rumours were, 'of course, just Chinese yarns, and are utterly unworthy of credence.' However, as with von Ketteler's death, events were being prefigured. As Oliphant lay fretting in bed, the allies were indeed laying plans to capture the walled Chinese City of Tientsin. By mid-July, sufficient reinforcements had arrived from the coast to relieve the pressure on the foreign settlements in Tientsin, although they were still being attacked with 'a heavy but indiscriminate rifle fire'[12] and there was still fierce hand-to-hand fighting around the railway station.

Among the forces pouring in through Taku were the men of the US Ninth Infantry, who had sailed from the Philippines to China. During their voyage they added a perceptive new verse to an old song, which looked beyond the conflict with the Chinese to wider rivalries:

> The Ninth is on the 'Logan' to China for to go
> Where we may mix up, in an Oriental row
> Against Japanese and Germans we may have to make
>   a stand
> When it comes to dividing up, this Ancient China land.[13]

Recognizing that the situation was now more military than naval, Vice-Admiral Seymour had returned to his squadron on 11 July, leaving Captain Bayly as senior British naval officer in Tientsin. Bayly was deeply irritated by the selfish, commercial attitude of the foreign business community, who were anxious about attacking the Chinese City. 'Various merchants solemnly protested to the British Consul, urging him to represent to me that any bombardment of [the] City would do an immense injury to their trade, as numerous undelivered cargoes of goods (paid for, I understand) were in canal and river, alongside banks.'[14] After the rescue of Seymour's column, he had managed to find the admiral a house that was 'most kindly "placed at his disposal" by the then tenant, but nevertheless the *owner* subsequently sent in a heavy bill for rent!'[15]

Brigadier-General Dorward was in overall command of the British forces but there was no supreme allied commander. This caused delays as the national commanding officers argued and consulted among themselves. However, they finally agreed that the Chinese City of Tientsin must be taken before there could be any talk of marching to Peking. The assault was to begin in the early hours of 13 July and the plan was a simple one – to take the city

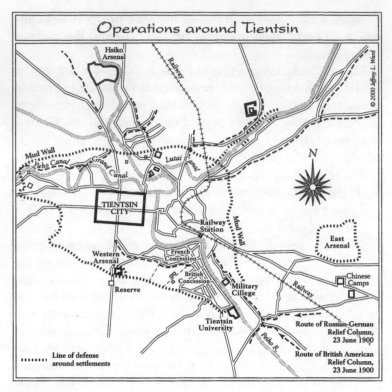

Operations around Tientsin

by storm. They knew they would be outnumbered. An allied force of some 6,000 men would face a Chinese force of around 30,000 Imperial troops and Boxers. The British, Americans, Japanese and French were to advance on the south gate in three columns while the Russians, with German support, were to circle around to the northeast and enter through the east gate.

The terrain was far from ideal. The only way to approach each gate was along a causeway that traversed a flat marshy plain intersected by canals, irrigation channels and lagoons. Herbert Hoover, who knew the lay of the land, was asked to act as guide and accepted with alacrity. He had been losing patience with all the endless talk and had come to view the attack as 'one of those affairs, like the millennium, that one rather expects will take place sometime.' He wrote a very honest account of a frightening experience. 'We came under sharp fire from the Chinese located on its old walls. We were out in the open plains with little cover except Chinese graves. I was completely scared, especially when some of the Marines next to me were hit. I was unarmed and I could scarcely make my feet move forwards.' He asked the officer he was with for a rifle and 'at once I experienced a curious psychological change for I was no longer scared, although I never fired a shot. I can recommend that men carry weapons when they go into battle – it is a great comfort.'[16] He was relieved of his duties as the dawn light came up, and returned to his wife, Lou, who, though many women and children had been evacuated to Taku, had stayed behind to continue nursing the sick.

Hoover would have been distressed to see what happened next. The attack was badly coordinated and ill-tempered, with poor communications between the various contingents. The main force became pinned down under fire from the city walls, suffering heavy losses and making little headway. Lieutenant Harry Rotherham of the Royal Welch Fusiliers described how 'the whole of the city wall was lined with Chinese firing through loop-holes and they just fired all day as hard as they could. They also attacked our left flank and we were told off to keep them back, so we were under fire all day from the front and the left flank as well. I never want anything quite so warm again.'[17] Commander Beatty, who blamed his fellow Briton Brigadier Dorward for some of the mess, wrote that the British 'were lying out in the open without any cover in a stupid place, as the bullets kept falling all round.'[18] The American Ninth Infantry, new to modern rifle- and shellfire, became caught in a very exposed position and their colonel was mortally wounded. Beatty rushed a company of British bluejackets to help them. Eventually the troops were pulled back and the advance was halted until dark. There was no news of how the Russian advance on the eastern gate was faring.

Meanwhile there had been great excitement in the foreign settlement with 'sightseers' and 'ink slingers', as Bayly disgustedly called them, crowding on to the roof of the German club for the view. However, the first Chinese shell that landed nearby 'cleared them out, and a good job too, as they asked silly questions.'[19]

It was the Japanese who turned failure into success. At 3.00 a.m. they blew open the south gate. According to young Lieutenant Herbert Hirschinger of the US Marines, 'The Japanese had been trying to accomplish it for some time, but the Chinks would cut the fuse.' In the end a Japanese officer volunteered to light a short fuse. 'The gate was blown in . . . but the officer went up with the gate. This only goes to show the mettle of which the little fellows are made.'[20] The Japanese burst into the city followed by the Second Battalion, the Royal Welsh Fusiliers, and Beatty's men. Later that morning the Russians entered through the east gate. According to the French doctor Matignon, his compatriots, who had also been heavily engaged, were irritated to see that, although the Japanese had done the hard work, the Union Jack was flying side by side with the Rising Sun over the south gate. At the foot of the gate they discovered *'trois ou quatre soldats anglais . . . flegmatiquement, fument leur pipe'* – 'three or four English soldiers . . . calmly smoking their pipes.'[21]

Many of the Imperial soldiers and Boxers had already slipped away, so there was little real fighting left to do. It was the civilian population that bore the brunt of the disgraceful looting and killing. A Chinese eyewitness described the panic: 'People rushed about in all directions in dread of what was to come next. When someone shouted that the North gate was open and that it was possible to leave by it, the whole city converged on the North Gate. In an instant the press of the crowd was such that one couldn't move . . . The foreigners and Christians . . . fired repeatedly on it [the crowd], each volley resulting in the deaths of several tens of people . . . The greater the numbers of people killed, the greater became the numbers of those fighting to escape . . . Dead from bullets, dead from artillery shells, dead from swords, dead from trampling. It was horrible . . . The corpses were piled several feet high. After three days of cleaning up, following the foreigners' entry into the city, the streets still were not clean.'[22]

James Ricalton, hurrying hither and thither with his camera, saw 'a holocaust of human life, lines of homeless, weeping human beings – their homes in ashes, without food, friendless, and, in many cases, their kindred left charred in the ruins of homes.'[23] He described how 'doors were smashed; shops were entered and plundered; men and women were fleeing, carrying their precious heirlooms – their jewels, their silks, their embroidery, their money. These much-prized valuables were snatched from them, and they dared not protest.'[24] American Marine Harold Kinman saw streets 'wet and slippery with blood,'[25] while a British sailor described 'shocking sights'[26] with brains strewn over the streets and dead Chinamen pinned to the wall by Japanese sword bayonets. The reports consistently blamed the Russians and the Japanese for the bloodshed. However, all nationalities took part in the looting and the city was denuded of everything the Boxers and Imperial troops – no mean looters themselves – had left. Soldiers of all nationalities smashed exquisite pieces of porcelain and jade and tossed rare furs aside in a frenzied search for silver ingots until measures were taken to stop them. Kinman wrote gleefully to his sister that 'the city was full of silver and jewellery. I got $500.00 silver, all I could pack and a silver watch . . . I also got a lot of other trinkets.'[27]

On 15 July, pickets were posted at the approaches to the British concession with orders to allow no one to retain plunder except French citizens whose authorities had not agreed the general plan to suppress looting. As a result, many Britons pretended to be French, doing bad music-hall impressions. Midshipman Dix wrote that they 'jabbered away in French, shrugged their shoulders, lifted their hands, and twirled their mustachios.' They were detected by a small but officious midshipman, giving the lie to 'people who say that the British Naval Officer's greatest failing is his want of knowledge in foreign tongues!' Dix thought that the British troops were anyway 'comparatively unsuccessful as looters' but that the

British civilians 'supplied all deficiencies and made most successful hauls.' They knew which houses and shops to go to and had
servants to carry away their booty.[28]

The allies had lost some 750 killed, wounded or missing in the
battle for the Chinese City. American officers who fought there
later told Sarah Conger that America had not 'seen such a fearful battle since the Civil War.' However, Tientsin had now been
secured as a base from which the allies could move on to Peking.

Reflecting on the whole episode of Tientsin, Herbert Hoover
concluded that the foreigners had had a remarkable escape and
that their experiences bore comparison with the 'dramatic and
much news-commented sieges of Kimberley, Mafeking and
Ladysmith,' which had just been relieved in South Africa. 'The
total loss of defenders in all three of these put together did not
equal our white losses at Tientsin, to say nothing of the losses
among the Chinese refugees. But their publicity arrangements
were better.'[29] The Hoovers were also struck by the novel international character of the siege of Tientsin. Lou wrote to a college
friend that 'never have so many flags been in action together
since our history began. Russian, Japanese, French, German,
Austrian, Italian, English and American! And such a motley
array of troops – artillery, cavalry, infantry, marines, sailors –
Cossacks, Sikhs, Siamese, a couple of English *Chinese* regiments
on *our* side – and a lot of our own darkies, who strike terror to
the hearts of some.'[30]

Meanwhile, eighty miles away, the foreigners in Peking were
wondering whether their ordeal had truly come to an end or
whether they were merely being duped.

12

THE HALF-ARMISTICE

No sensation is lacking among us. – Luella Miner

THE TRUCE OF 17 JULY seemed a little surreal to the besieged of the Peking Legations, who felt as if they had been plunged into 'a state of amazed suspense.'[1] The sudden silence was disconcerting rather than comforting, so that some found it difficult to sleep. The Chinese began replacing their brilliant-coloured war banners with white flags, and hundreds of heads could be seen cautiously peeping over the barricades. Then they began to climb up on to their barricades, waving white cloths and shouting. Warily, the defenders scrambled on to their own fortifications and gazed at the desolate landscape around them. The ground beyond the defensive perimeter was littered with human bones – all that remained of corpses devoured by gaunt wolflike pariah dogs. Once familiar buildings had been reduced to heaps of rubble and ashes.

As their confidence grew, the Chinese soldiers began to surge towards the defenders' positions and there was some bizarre fraternization. At one of the French barricades, the ever-hospitable hotelier Monsieur Chamot found himself offering cups of tea to yesterday's attackers. One of Sir Robert Hart's former bandsmen appeared with his ear partially severed. In some embarrassment he explained that he was now a regimental bugler in the Imperial army and that his officer had struck him with his sword 'because he did not blow his horn loud enough to suit him.'[2] He had come to the legations because he knew 'that foreign surgeons were good and humane men.' He hinted that the Chinese were very discontented and sick of fighting the foreigners. He related how foreign troops had won a big victory between Taku and Tientsin and that Tung Fu-hsiang's troops and many Boxers had gone to oppose them.

Meanwhile Paul Pelliot, the young French volunteer who had cultivated a reputation as a bit of a daredevil, announced that he was going to call on the Chinese and hopped over the barricades. Nobody expected to see him alive again and people wondered how long it would be before his severed head appeared in a cage. He confounded the pessimists by reappearing a few hours later, having enjoyed a good meal at Jung Lu's headquarters and with his pockets bulging with melons and peaches. Three mandarins had tried to pump him about conditions within the legations and whether there was any prospect the foreigners would agree to leave. He responded cheerfully that they were 'having a charming time'[3] and only needed some ice and fruit to make them perfectly happy, even in the great summer heat. Jung Lu himself bade him farewell 'with the significant words that his own personal troops, on whom he could rely, would attempt to protect the Legations, but . . . that it was very difficult to do so as everyone was fearful of their own heads and dare not show too much concern for the foreigner.'[4] Lenox Simpson thought this proof positive that 'this extraordinary armistice is the result of a whole series of events which we cannot even imagine.'

Nevertheless, the besieged soon began to make an informed guess. The obvious explanation was that the allies had defeated the Chinese forces – as Sir Robert Hart's bandsman had admitted – and that a relief force was near. This was partially correct. The fall of Tientsin had confirmed the views of the moderate faction at court that the Chinese government was embracing a path of self-destruction. These views were shared by the majority of viceroys and governors in the southern and eastern provinces, who never allowed the fighting to spread to their areas. Since early June they had been counselling caution and the suppression of the Boxers. Most of them had ignored the edict of 21 June declaring war, while their response to the empress's request for troops had been desultory. On 14 July – the day that Tientsin fell – they wrote a memorial to the court urging the protection and compensation of the foreigners because any other course would put China beyond the pale of international law. They also proposed that a letter regretting the death of von Ketteler be sent to the kaiser. In yet a further memorial on 16 July, they explained respectfully but firmly why an Imperial edict ordering the cessation of payments due on foreign loans was unwise.[5]

This passive resistance, coupled with furious representations from the capitals of the foreign powers about the consequences should the reports of massacre prove true, had caused the Empress Dowager to think again. On 17 July, the day the truce began, the Imperial Court issued an edict declaring that 'all foreign Ministers ought to be really protected'[6] and sent letters to America, France and Germany asking them to help China out of its current difficulties. A further edict talked of 'deep grief' at von Ketteler's murder and asserted that while the taking of the Taku forts had left China no option but to go to war, 'the Government is not willing lightly to break off the friendly relations which have existed.'[7] It blamed vagabonds for robbing, burning and killing, and producing a state of chaos. However, the Empress Dowager was still uncertain which way to jump. Luella Miner was more accurate than she realized when she wrote in her diary that 'the Empress Dowager has got into too deep water and has now no fixed policy.'

The besieged in Peking knew little of this, gleaning only scraps of information from Chinese soldiers. However, on 18 July there came intelligence from an unimpeachable source. A messenger sent by Colonel Shiba to Tientsin returned and confirmed that Tientsin was indeed in allied hands. The messenger also reported that a combined relief force of some 11,000 Japanese, Russians, British, Americans and French would march to the relief of Peking on about 20 July. This was the first hard news to reach the legations and it was joyfully received. 'At last we have a message from the outside world,' wrote Luella Miner gratefully. Some were disappointed that the force was not already on the march, yet they would have been more disturbed had they known the whole picture – the messenger had also brought disquieting details of the heavy allied losses and of the 'absolute absence' of transport. However, these remarks were carefully omitted from the notice posted on the Bell Tower, which, according to Sir Claude, 'was made as cheerful as possible' in the interests of morale.

Sir Claude took advantage of the lull to go up on to the Tartar Wall to inspect the defences. With him went Herbert Squiers, his new chief of staff. As he was a former cavalry officer, his military experience was useful. Even more valuable, however, were his energy and resourcefulness, which had become increasingly apparent as the siege wore on. A 'hustler' was what Luella Miner approvingly called him. She hoped his diplomatic skills would smooth the animosities between the various nationalities. She felt that the British and Americans were almost one people despite the frequent exchange of such insults as 'damned Yankees' and 'damned limejuicers'. However, she worried about the Russians' strong animosity towards the British; the sullen uncooperative behaviour of the Germans, still smarting over the murder of von Ketteler; and the strongly pro-British, anti-Russian sentiments of the Japanese. The British captain, Gordon Casserly, shared Luella's view of the camaraderie between the British and Americans, who, he wrote, united in calling all the other European contingents 'dagoes'. They did, however, distinguish among them, so that 'the terms "Froggie Dago", "Sauerkraut Dago", "Macaroni Dago", and "Vodki Dago" left little doubt in the hearer's mind as to which nationality was meant.'[8]

For the moment, however, MacDonald and Squiers were more concerned about the intentions of the Chinese than internal rivalries. As they strolled along the Tartar Wall, a Chinese officer commanding some Kansu braves at a barricade sixty yards away shouted a request for permission to bury his dead. They had been killed on the night of 3 July during the raid led by Captain Myers but their bodies were still lying at the foot of the barricade and were in an advanced state of decomposition. Sir Claude's interpreter explained what the officer wanted and he at once gave permission. He and Squiers watched as six of Tung Fu-hsiang's men dressed in scarlet and black climbed down with spades and large pieces of matting on which they carried away the rotting corpses.

Oscar Upham, who had had to cope with the ghastly smell, was mightily relieved: 'It's about time as they have been lying there under our noses for near three weeks. As they lower them off the wall in straw matting we can see heads and limbs fall out and flatten when they hit the ground. We are very thankful to them for removing their dead as the stench has been something awful, for a dead chinaman has a peculiar oder [sic] all his own . . . I think all of the flies in Peking were here.'

Sir Claude invited the officer to come and talk with him. Reluctant at first, he was eventually persuaded to come and sit side by side with Sir Claude on top of the defenders' barricade. They smoked the British minister's cigars and chatted amicably through an interpreter. The officer was curious to know the identity of the men wearing the big slouch hats. Sir Claude explained that they were American marines, whereupon he shook his head and complained that every time they fired a shot he lost a man and his troops were afraid of them. He said that although he belonged to the Kansu troops, he was under the immediate command of Jung Lu, who wished the fighting to stop. Sir Claude 'remarked that the fighting was none of our doing' and that the legations were only defending themselves.

The officer listened thoughtfully, then suggested that Sir Claude should write to Jung Lu explaining his views. And so the strange encounter ended.

Walking back along the wall, Sir Claude realized exactly what the legations had been facing: 'I could see the enemy's positions stretching away to the north until they disappeared in the direction of the Imperial City. There were barricades in the streets below the wall; a large temple was loopholed and . . . full of men; more men were amongst the ruins west of the Russian Legation and a species of mound which commanded this Legation and the Mongol Market was gay with the uniforms of hundreds of Imperial infantry. Following the line west of the Mongol Market, the tops of the houses carried nests of these bright-coated soldiery; altogether from my position I saw some 1,500 to 2,000 men, and many more must have been hidden behind the walls and ruined houses.'

Immediately on his return to the legation, Sir Claude wrote to Jung Lu proposing some rules of conduct. He promised that the foreigners would fire only if they were attacked. However, Chinese soldiers seen building barricades or any armed soldiers who left their barricades would be shot. Unarmed persons could approach the legation defences in safety provided there were no more than two at a time. The dispatch was delivered to the Kansu officer, who duly delivered it to Jung Lu. The next day one of Jung Lu's men was seen on the wall carrying a flag of truce. Some of the defenders recognized him as a former policeman on the Peking–Tientsin railway. He climbed down to the German defences and gave Sir Claude a letter accepting his proposals.

However, the defenders noticed one disturbing fact. The new goodwill was not universal. The 'friendly' soldiers were the men of Prince Ching and Jung Lu who had been fighting to the south and east of the legations' defences. Tung Fu-hsiang's troops to the north and west were still 'decidedly treacherous and unfriendly.' Sir Claude's cigar-smoking officer was the only one who made any attempt at contact. Furthermore, heavy firing could still be heard coming from the direction of the Peitang, some two miles away. On a clear day the besieged could make out the cathedral and they wondered what was happening. Sarah Conger wrote: 'It must be very hard for the people there. They can hear nothing from here or elsewhere, and cannot know the situation.' On 18 July, Monsieur Pichon demanded to be allowed to communicate with Bishop Favier but received no answer from the Tsungli Yamen. Despite the terms of the agreement, the Chinese were busily strengthening their positions; Mrs Bainbridge noted that the Chinese went 'right on with their work and consequently our boys turned the gun on them and blew the barricade down, killing a few Chinese.' However, the defenders also flagrantly ignored this aspect of the truce, reinforcing walls and digging deep trenches to frustrate Chinese attempts at mining.

As the days passed, it became clear that the word 'truce' was perhaps a misnomer. Polly Condit Smith was more accurate when she called it a 'half-armistice', It was still dangerous to appear at certain points in the defences and some 100 to 200 shots were being fired into the legations each day. The Chinese were also heard mining close to the Hanlin. By 29 July, Oscar Upham was writing: 'The war is on again in earnest. The Chinese started it by picking off some of our coolies. We retaliated by picking a few of them off their roost. This brought on a general engagement. We feel better, having something to do.'

Yet these ominous developments did not prevent a degree of tomfoolery. The Chinese soldiers east of the Fu developed a novel way of communicating with the Japanese. 'One day a large dog trotted into the Japanese barricade with a note tied round its neck; this was from the Chinese general commanding in that quarter pointing out the futility of further defence and recommending unconditional surrender. A reply, declining the suggestion in somewhat forcible terms, was tied on the dog's neck, with which it trotted back, this was repeated several times, the dog seeming to enjoy the fun, the advisability of surrender being urged with greater insistence each time, the answers varied only in the strength of their language.'[9]

Chinese soldiers approached the besieged with offers of fruit, vegetables and chickens. The vigorous bartering sometimes led to arguments. A Chinese soldier held out a watermelon on the end of a pole and a marine tried to grab it. When the man 'would not give it up without immediate payment, the marine thumped his head and then knocked him over.'[10] Both sides rushed for their rifles and it was only the false promise that the marine would be beaten and the offer of a dollar to the injured man that calmed tempers. There was also plenty of scope for confusion. According to Arthur Smith, 'yesterday a Japanese shot a Chinese who was getting over his barricade, a Chinese in retaliation shot a Chinese Christian, when the Japanese returned the fire; the Chinese then wounded an Italian, on which a British marine killed the man who shot *him*!' On another occasion, Jessie Ransome wrote that 'the French have distinguished themselves this morning by shooting a nice peaceful Chinaman who was coming to sell us eggs.'

Despite the truce's oddities, many of the besieged were feeling more cheerful. Nigel Oliphant, still in the hospital, was amused by the transformation in some people. 'One who last week used to go about with a graveyard face and openly argued that we were all bound to be massacred before help arrived, now wears a beaming countenance and tells cheerful lies to the effect that he never for a moment doubted that we should all get through this business.' Captain Poole thought that everyone was looking rested and more cheery. His complaint was now that the siege had become 'monotonous'. A newborn litter of kittens provided some distraction for the British marines guarding the main gate. They put coloured ribbons around their necks and watched the tiny creatures sleeping serenely in the loopholes.

The further antics of Nestergaard – or 'Nasty Guy', as Oscar Upham called him – also provided some diversion. He escaped yet again only to return after several days, whining about his ill-treatment by the Chinese. They had probably had enough of this 'intellectually aberrant'[11] Norwegian during his first visit. A weary Sir Claude asked him whether he had given the Chinese any information. He replied that they had asked him questions and he had had to answer. Oscar Upham wrote with some regret that 'there was strong talk of shooting him but they put him in double irons in the brig with a Chinese prisoner instead for safe keeping.' However, British marines had orders to shoot if they saw him trying to leave the legation again.

The timid Edmund Backhouse was sufficiently encouraged by the truce to put in an appearance. According to Lancelot Giles, he claimed to have strained some muscle early in the siege and to have been laid up ever since. However, Backhouse was now 'just about able to crawl'[12] and spent his time reading Goodrich's pocket Chinese–English dictionary from cover to cover. The far more adventurous Polly Condit Smith took advantage of the lull to go on a sight-seeing trip to a barricade in the Hanlin with Herbert Squiers and Baron von Rahden. Peeping through a loophole, she was both fascinated and appalled: 'What I saw was what I might see in looking through the wicket-gate of a horror chamber at the Eden-Musée in New York. A group of gorgeously apparelled Boxers with their insignia were pitilessly caught by death in a mad dash at this barricade and there they were, stiff and stark, nearly all in the furious attitudes of assault! Even the standard-bearer was stiffly and conscientiously gripping his gay-coloured pennant . . . The sentry tells us that this hideous, almost theatrically posed, death-group has been thus for a couple of days.' She could now understand the 'all-pervading charnel-house smells,' which almost made people faint.

Her tour also showed her the damage of the past month. The Chinese houses in the Legation Quarter were sacked and charred. The Hôtel de Pékin, flags still flying defiantly from its upper windows, was battered almost beyond recognition, although it was now one of the most strongly fortified positions in the entire Legation area. Monsieur Chamot was determined not to be driven from it; he had taken the precaution of countermining the main drain under Legation Street and was fully prepared to set off an explosion with acetylene. The surviving legations, pock-marked by shells, seemed like oases amid the destruction. Yet as

Polly looked towards the Forbidden City, it seemed to rise up 'a song of green and gold, the fairyland palaces of the wicked old ogress, the Empress Dowager, these ideal gold-topped pavilions, palaces, and pagodas, rising out of a veritable sea of green,' quivering and shimmering in the warm summer sunlight.

The Japanese exploited the freedom and opportunities of the truce to start a small market for eggs, which Chinese soldiers brought them hidden in their capacious sleeves. The Food Supply Committee distributed them to the hospital and to the women and children. However, according to Lenox Simpson, some were put to less meritorious use: 'Everyone professes tremendous rage because a certain lady with blue-black hair is supposed to have used a whole dozen in the washing of her hair.' He dismissed her as 'one of those who have not been seen or heard of since the rifles began to speak. There are lots of that sort, all well-nourished and timorous.'

The Japanese were also able to buy rifles and ammunition from the Chinese soldiers for $15 apiece. The Reverend Allen wrote that this would have been incredible anywhere but China. Arthur Smith, the acknowledged China expert, mentally shrugged his shoulders and said he no longer claimed to understand anything about the Chinese. Polly was also amused and puzzled by the schizophrenic behaviour. 'A letter comes today to Sir Robert Hart from the Yamen which is most polite and gushing. They regret most sincerely that his house and compound have been burned, and state at the same time that the Customs affairs have been turned almost upside down in consequence of lack of orders during the past six weeks from the Inspector-General.' Sir Robert's day, otherwise notable only for heat, flies and the 'ever-present stench of putrid flesh,'[13] was enlivened by a further message. This bemoaned the fact that Nanking was 'in great confusion' and that the customs dues were not flowing as they should into the treasury. It suggested that the authorities would be grateful for Sir Robert's advice on what to do. 'The effrontery of this is something sublime. Oriental diplomacy is certainly entertaining,' wrote Luella Miner.

The Yamen twice sent gifts of fruit, vegetables, flour and ice to the besieged in the name of the emperor. Some people argued that it was morally wrong to accept gifts from the enemy and the ministers were lectured by 'a deputation of ladies against the acceptance of such treacherous bounty.'[14] Others worried that the food might be poisoned and the flour was first tested on a dog and then put aside for emergencies. Mary Bainbridge's more prosaic objection to the gift was that melons might be very well 'after a substantial meal of fried chicken, mashed potatoes and all sorts of good things, but when one has been living for six weeks on rice and horsemeat three times a day with shot and shell booming all around you, mellons [sic] are not very palatable.' Most people, however, were delighted. 'Men formed melon clubs, and had solemn meetings in the morning for the discussion of these delicacies with true Epicurean precaution. The luscious gourd was allowed its proper season to cool in the well; then, brought forth with care, it was duly scooped and seasoned with claret. It was a most superb performance and quite unworthy of the tragic style of a serious and protracted siege. But men did not then want a dramatic famine, they wanted fruit.'[15]

Meanwhile the diplomats were maintaining a frequent and confusing correspondence with the Chinese government. As William Bainbridge put it: 'The war of bullets was suspended but an equally sharp conflict of wits followed.' A man of his time, he added that it was a case of 'western caution pitted against oriental treachery and deceit.' A constant stream of letters arrived for the ministers, many under the signature of 'Prince Ching and others'. However, it was unclear who the letters were really from and what authority they had. A recurring theme was that the foreigners must depart – either to the protection of the Tsungli Yamen or to Tientsin. It was also dulcetly suggested that because the Chinese converts might be a bother to the foreigners they should be sent home, since the city was quiet. The advice was ignored. Luella wrote that 'we have not advised the lamb to trust itself to the wolf yet.' A Chinese request that the allies give up their position on the Tartar Wall was similarly disregarded and the ministers continued to play for time.

The Chinese government was also acting as a conduit between the ministers and their governments, ferrying messages back and forth. On 27 July, the ministers learned that their respective governments were asking about their welfare. A British marine suggested that 'Not massacred yet'[16] would be an appropriate answer. At the end of July, Pichon received 'a very nice telegram from France, saying: "You are unanimously voted to have the Legion of Honour. Your mother sends her love and greeting, and 15,000 Frenchmen are on their way to your support."'[17]

However, none of this counted for very much. It was sometimes hard to know when messages had been sent and, indeed, whether they were genuine. The besieged were still on tenterhooks for news of the relief force, which was supposed to have set out on 20 July. But as Nigel Oliphant wrote: 'Altogether the news is so contradictory and confused that it is hard to know what to think.' A Chinese soldier was bribed to bring the foreigners a bundle of back issues of the *Peking Gazette* – the official Chinese government journal – which had been published throughout the siege. They made interesting reading and convinced the foreigners of the court's complicity in the attacks on the legations. 'We see by edicts and other official matter that the Government has been in sympathy with the Boxer movement, and that the Empress Dowager seems to have "mothered" it,' wrote a disillusioned Sarah Conger. Luella Miner hoped that the 'wilfully blind' foreign ministers would at last acknowledge that the missionaries had been right to warn them of the Boxer threat and the government's duplicity.

If the issues of the *Gazette* fuelled people's anger and resentment, they gave little clue about what might happen next. A Chinese spy employed by Colonel Shiba exacerbated the confusion. His encouraging, elaborate, but entirely fictitious reports of the progress of the relief force put the besieged on an emotional roller coaster for a week. Luella was half amused, half angry. 'The soldier-spy came as usual to give his information and collect his dollars, but having marched our foreign troops too rapidly, so that we ought to be able to hear their cannonading from the city wall, he was obliged to have them retreat.'

On 28 July, a messenger arrived with a letter from Mr Carles, the British Consul in Tientsin. This messenger was the fifteen-year-old Shantung boy who had slipped out of the legations three weeks earlier with a message from Sir Claude concealed in his rice bowl. This 'smart lad', as Sir Robert Hart called him, had managed to avoid detection despite some close shaves. People crowded excitedly around the Bell Tower to read Carles's message but it was disappointingly vague. It ran: 'Your letter 4 July. There are now 24,000 troops landed, and 19,000 here. General Gaselee expected Ta-ku tomorrow. Russian troops are at Peitsang. Tientsin city is under foreign government and "Boxer" power here is exploded. There are plenty of troops on the way if you can keep yourselves in food. Almost all the ladies have left Tientsin.'[18] The Reverend Allen wrote crossly: 'That was a nice sort of letter to send in answer to people who had said that they were hard pressed, and had been expecting relief for six weeks!' To Monsieur Pichon it appeared more and more likely that the delay would inevitably result in *notre sacrifice*.[19]

According to Morrison, men moved out of the hearing of the women to give full vent to their feelings about the letter's contents.[20] What particularly angered them was that it said nothing about when the relief force would arrive. Neither was it clear whether the troops who were 'on the way' were travelling to Tientsin from Europe or to Peking from Tientsin – or, as Luella Miner tartly put it, 'from Ethiopia to the North Pole.' Mary Gamewell was later told, when safely in Tientsin, that when that letter was written, Mr Carles 'had lost hope because of the delays of the military in Tientsin. He thought the besieged would be dead before help could arrive, and out of a heart burdened with such conviction he wrote as he did.'

*   *   *

On 1 August, 'a real Tientsin letter' arrived.[21] Dated 26 July and addressed to the Japanese minister, Baron Nishi, it said that the departure of troops was delayed by transport difficulties but predicted that the advance should start in two or three days. This exposed the lies of the spy employed by the Japanese, who, rather strangely, continued to retain his services 'on the understanding that he will tell the truth in future.'[22] On the same day, however, Sir Robert Hart received a cablegram from London confirming that Edwin Conger's note, reporting that the legations were still holding out, had got through. The besieged could at least take some comfort that the wider world now had 'authentic information as to the real state of affairs in Peking.'[23]

Nevertheless, it was clear that relief might still be some way off. Every household was ordered to send in a list of its stores of tea, sugar, white rice and other 'luxuries'.[24] Until now every household had lived on what it had gathered at the onset of the siege with only such staples as flour and meat supplied from the general store. Now the moment had come to pool the stores and begin strict rationing. Lenox Simpson was sceptical, believing that few people would be honest and predicting 'very unpleasant scenes' if the siege went on another month. Some 600 pounds of white rice, 11,500 of 'yellow' or old rice, and 34,000 pounds of wheat were left. Hasty calculations showed that the public stores could provide 1,000 people with a pound of wheat and a third of a pound of rice each day for five weeks. Only thirty ponies remained. At a rate of three every two days, these would last just twenty days.

Nigel Oliphant noted that 'cigars and tobacco are running out, which is more serious to some of us than want of food.' He was in the minority; most people were very anxious about the risk of starvation. By late July even Polly was writing that she and the Squierses were living 'quite sparingly and are hungry most of the time.' This posed all kinds of temptations. She confessed that while she was walking with the Dutch minister Knobel, he spied, roosting in some branches, some fat hens belonging to a woman in the legation. 'He whispered to me, "If you will watch, I will get a chicken. There will be no noise, and tomorrow we will have a real dinner and eat that chicken." It flashed through my mind that at home, if clever darkies could not steal chickens without making a racket, I did not see how Knobel, who has probably never in his life come nearer to one than to pay his steward's bills, could expect to be successful. However . . . a rustle, a slight squawk, and my Minister friend was by me again, with a squirming bundle under his coat.'

Such antics were a welcome diversion from some very real worries. Polly fretted that the children were suffering badly from the heat and the poor diet. She found the collection of perambulators huddled together in the shadiest part of the compound with their limp, languid babies one of the most poignant sights of the 'half-armistice'. Three babies in the British Legation had already died since the siege began and many were sick. 'All look like faded flowers,' wrote a worried Jessie Ransome. Lady MacDonald was particularly moved by the death of one child whom she had tried to help, finding it better accommodation and food. The mother, a Mrs Inglis, wrote: 'I shall never forget the morning that baby died when Lady MacDonald came with tears in her eyes and said, "I know what it means to lose a child for I lost two."'[25] In the Fu many Chinese children had died, including seventy Catholics. Luella attributed the high Catholic mortality rate to lack of care about sanitary conditions compared with her own Protestant converts, and poor care by the priests.

In fact, the condition of all the several thousand converts in the Fu – young and old, Protestant and Catholic – was becoming desperate. Lenox Simpson wrote on 24 July that 'the miserable natives imprisoned by our warfare are in a terrible state of starvation. Their bones are cracking through their skin; their eyes have an insane look; yet nothing is being done for them. They are afraid to attempt escape even in this quiet, as the Water Gate is watched on the outside night and day by Chinese sharpshooters . . . Tortured by the sight of these starving wretches, who moan and mutter night and day, the posts nearby shoot

down dogs and crows and drag them there. They say everything
is devoured raw with cannibal-like cries.' He was prone to exaggeration, but other accounts bear out the converts' hunger.

Some attempts were made to relieve the suffering. The
Chamots ground grain for the converts in their mill and they
were also given the entrails and heads of the ponies killed for the
foreigners. When two ponies were found to be infected with a
parasitic worm, the meat was sent to the Fu since, according to
Arthur Smith, 'the Chinese are never deterred by any trifles of
this nature' and another pony was substituted for the foreigners.
Yet, although many of the besieged seem to have been genuinely
concerned for the converts, there was apparently no attempt to
distribute the legations' food stocks more equally.

The converts' treatment worried Morrison but as a result of
his wound – a somewhat ignominious shot in the buttock for
which he later put in a compensation claim of £2,625 – he was
unable to visit the Fu. Instead he was lying fretfully on a
mattress stuffed with straw from some of the many cases of
wine, fending off clouds of sticky black flies and wondering
what on earth was going on. On 2 August, no fewer than six
letters arrived from Tientsin, brought by a messenger who had
ingeniously sewn them between two straw hats. People surged to
the Bell Tower, where 'a joyful Babel of voices filled the air.'[26]
Five of the messages were addressed to Americans and, unlike
messages sent to Sir Claude, the contents were disclosed at once
and in full. A persistent complaint against Sir Claude was that
in his desire to keep everything 'as cheerful as possible' he hung
on to information for too long and then released only edited
versions. One of the letters was from the American consul at
Tientsin, Mr Ragsdale, and it was rather in the Carles mould.
He said he had had a bad dream about the besieged the night
before, that he had lost all hope of seeing them again, but that
now the prospects looked brighter. He then dwelt at length on
his own experiences in Tientsin. Polly thought it typical of the
emotional but uninformative and irrelevant messages they were
receiving. 'The writers are pleased that we are not dead, then

give us some trifling details about themselves in Tientsin and long, rambling accounts of what wonders they have gone through.'

Yet this contact with the outside world was still immensely cheering. Mary Bainbridge, who was sick and had forsaken her horsemeat diet for cornstarch mixed with sugar and water, began to perk up. A group of American missionaries sat on the steps of the Bell Tower and sang everything from 'America' to 'The Star-Spangled Banner.' Then, having exhausted their own national repertoire, they joined the British in singing 'God Save the Queen' and the Germans in 'Watch on the Rhine.' Not to be outdone, the Russians called on the majestic Madame Pokolitov, 'who rendered grandly Russia's grand national hymn'[27] amid a storm of clapping. There was further excitement for the Russians when one of their soldiers nearly died of strychnine poisoning, having looted a bottle of the poison from a store and downed the lot in the belief that it was alcohol. To everyone's amazement, he recovered. Lancelot Giles wrote admiringly: 'It takes more than strychnine to kill a Russian.'

The US Marines were clearly also enjoying some relaxation. Oscar Upham heard that one of his comrades, Private Hobbs, was ill. He went to visit him and 'found a very sick man there all covered up with blankets. The boys told me that he had been coughing up large worms and a few snakes. I don't remember what else, but from the collection of empty bottles lying, I concluded that they had a glorious old time.' Captain Hall apparently concluded the same and informed Hobbs that 'he might sojourn on the wall for 48 hours until he got better.' Another American marine who got drunk and began shooting from the wall was thrown in a cell to cool off.

However, it had already been clear for some days that the so-called truce was dissolving. The Chinese were industriously constructing a barricade across the north bridge, which crossed the canal under the walls of the Imperial City. Sharpshooters had taken up position in the ruins across the canal ready to snipe at any foreigner who tried to fire on the barricade. 'Old Betsey'

was wheeled out and flung a few shots at it, but the gunner,
Mitchell, was wounded and the Chinese swiftly repaired the
damage to their new fortification. The situation brought out the
schoolboy in Sir Claude. He had been a musketry instructor
while in the Highland Light Infantry and could not resist taking
a pot shot. He borrowed a marine's rifle, took aim through a
loophole, and 'at the third shot carried away a large brick which
was being placed on the top of the barricade by visible hands
belonging to invisible workers. With the brick went, I think,
portions of a human hand.' As he handed the rifle back, a bullet
flicked viciously through his loophole, causing the marine to
comment, 'Nearly had you that time, Sir!'[28]

By the next morning the foreigners saw that the Chinese had
built a robust barricade six feet high along the entire length of
the bridge. When they complained, the reply was that they 'must
not be alarmed as the troops of Tung Fu-hsiang were only
engaged in mending the road'![29] However, it meant that the road
along the canal was now highly dangerous. The defenders retaliated by building a barricade over the south bridge to secure
communications between the British and other legations.
Meanwhile, an ever more ludicrous correspondence was continuing between the ministers and the Tsungli Yamen, which was
still assuring them they only had their best interests at heart and
asking them to leave the legations. The ministers, who had no
intention of going anywhere, asked permission to send cipher
dispatches to their governments in a bid to gain time.

Time was not on their side. By 4 August, there was still no sign
of the relief force and the spasmodic truce was over. Full-scale
bombardment had resumed and Captain Hall was reporting
'heavy firing by the enemy on all sides.' The women and children were again forced to keep indoors in stifling conditions. It
was obvious that the pendulum had once again swung against
the foreigners at the Imperial Court.

The reason was the arrival in Peking on 26 July of Li Peng-
heng, former governor of Shantung and favourite of the Empress

Dowager. His deep, almost pathological, hatred of foreigners and all their works immediately strengthened the hand of the pro-Boxer faction, while his philosophy that 'only when one can fight can one negotiate for peace'[30] seems to have appealed strongly to the Empress Dowager. He was allowed the rare honour of riding within the Forbidden City and was appointed Deputy Commander of the Northern Armies. Just two days after his arrival, two moderate and liberal-thinking courtiers were executed as traitors for criticizing the Boxers and advocating peace. One was a former minister to St Petersburg and president of the Imperial University, the other a member of the Tsungli Yamen. Three more officials were killed a few days later in a continuing ideological purge. It was effectively a reign of terror. The numbers of Boxers in Peking increased sharply and the moderates were cowed. A nervous Prince Ching wrote to the southern viceroys that he agreed the Boxers should be suppressed but that 'the responsibility is too great for my humble abilities, and as the power is exercised by the Court, I really dare not make any request.'[31]

If the besieged in Peking were confused at this latest twist in their fate, the picture seemed equally bewildering in Tientsin. First there had been the shock of the *Daily Mail* report of wholesale massacre in Peking. Then, once that had been debunked, there had been a confusing series of messages from the legations. No one knew what condition the legations were in or how long they could reasonably hold out. An earnest desire not to repeat the fiasco of Seymour's expedition added to the uncertainty, leading to squabbling and procrastination. Arthur Smith later wrote bitterly that 'diplomatically next to nothing was done beyond exchanging notes and ascertaining by slow processes of conference, proposition, and explanation, iterated and reiterated, what the Powers respectively were *not* prepared to do.'

One bone of contention was the size of the relief force required. After his debacle, Vice-Admiral Seymour had advised the British Admiralty that 'quite 40,000 troops'[32] would be needed. Now figures from 60,000 to 80,000 were being bandied about. Admiral Kempff, the US naval commander, told Washington that 60,000 men would be needed for the campaign itself and another 20,000 to guard the lines of communication. The Japanese foreign minister estimated that the task would require at least 70,000 men. The logistics of mounting an international relief effort on such a scale were awesome. How could it be done, and quickly?

Another consideration was that many of the Powers could not muster large numbers of troops. They were all, with the exception of Japan and Germany, at present heavily engaged on other fronts – America was battling in the Philippines, Britain was still fighting the Boers, the Russians were engaged on the Manchurian border, and the French were embroiled in Indo-China. Japan was the only ally with available troops within easy reach of North China. Lord Salisbury recognized this. He appealed to Japan to send more men, offering to bear the financial burden. Without delay, Japan agreed to increase its force at Tientsin to 20,000 men.

The Russians were anxiously monitoring the moves of their rivals, the Japanese and the British. Conversely, when Russia alluded to the 'ulterior military measures which the Powers may have to undertake in China,'[33] an alarmed British government demanded an explanation. Across the world, politicians debated what would happen after Peking were taken. If the Chinese government disintegrated, the nations with the largest contingents would be best placed to reap the spoils.

This tense political atmosphere made the selection of a Supreme Commander extremely sensitive. All nations accepted that they must together appoint a chief military officer of the entire allied operation in northern China. But who should it be? And what nation should he come from? It was an unprecedented situation.

Anxious for Germany to be seen as a leader in world politics, the kaiser pressed his country's claim on the strength of von Ketteler's murder. He was also privately convinced that, whatever the reports to the contrary, the foreigners were already dead. He thought a campaign of severe and righteous retribution, rather than of swift rescue, was what was required, and that an avenging Germany must lead the way.

The kaiser's nominee was Field Marshal Count von Waldersee, who eventually won by default. As von Waldersee later wrote, 'a Japanese Supreme Command, no less than an American, was out of the question from the start' (this presumably because Japan and the United States were newcomers to the world scene, or because 'only a European' could do the job). The French, he continued, 'had not made any effort to get the Supreme Command,' leaving only Russia and Britain as Germany's rivals. But, von Waldersee smugly concluded, 'neither would concede it to the other, and, moreover, no one favoured England, as the reputation of the English Generalship had suffered a set-back in the Boer War.'[34]

The kaiser eventually persuaded the tsar to back the German nominee and coaxed the Japanese into seconding the nomination. But the British prime minister, Lord Salisbury, was worried, writing in a letter to Queen Victoria that, while unity of command would be of great military value, it was an entirely new experiment to put entire troops of English soldiers under foreign command. The British, however, at last capitulated, as did the Americans. So too did the French, though not without reservations – von Waldersee had played a prominent part in the Franco-Prussian War, which had ended in 1870 with France's ignominious defeat by Germany. Von Waldersee was appointed, and was set to depart for China on 18 August.

Meanwhile, the kaiser reviewed the advance contingent of the German expeditionary forces at Bremerhaven on 27 July and made a memorable, indeed notorious, speech. Aware of the kaiser's penchant for spontaneous, bellicose oratory, his aides had attempted to manage the media. Members of the press were invited on board the kaiser's luxurious steam-powered yacht *Hohenzollern*, where the prepared text of the kaiser's speech was dictated to them. Happy to have their copy so early, they rushed to catch the next train to Berlin. One thoughtful newspaperman, however, spotted a kind of pulpit standing on the quayside and decided to wait. The kaiser duly climbed into it and delivered his speech. Predictably, he did not stick to his prepared text but burst into vitriol, which the journalist reported to a startled world. 'You must know, my men, that you are about to meet a crafty, well-armed foe! Meet him and beat him! Give no quarter! Take no prisoners! Kill him when he falls into your hands! Even as, a thousand years ago, the Huns under their King Attila made such a name for themselves as still resounds in terror through legend and fable, so may the name of Germany resound through Chinese history . . . that never again will a Chinese dare to so much as look askance at a German.' When the terms of the kaiser's speech reached Peking, they 'caused a good deal of astonishment.'[35]

Despite the practical and political difficulties, preparations at Tientsin had, in the meantime, finally been gaining momentum. Towards the end of July some 25,000 men were at Taku and Tientsin and many more were on their way. Britain was calling up troops from her Indian army while the Americans were drafting forces in from the Philippines. A British naval lieutenant recalled the arrival of men from the seventh Rajputs and the first Bengal Lancers: 'They caused a great impression by their soldierly bearing, and were eyed with curiosity by the other European soldiers. After them came the Sikhs . . . Madras pioneers, and Baluchis, all of whom impressed the onlooker as preferable allies rather than antagonists.'[36]

The appearance of the American troops also struck onlookers. One British officer thought that 'the men of the American Army were equalled in physique only by the Australian Contingent and our Royal Horse Artillery.' He noted that their 'free-and-easy ideas on the subject of discipline' shocked some of their Continental colleagues, causing one German officer to exclaim, '*That* an army? Why, with the Berlin Fire Brigade I could conquer the whole of America!' The British officer found this remark amusing, and 'so typically German!'[37]

Tientsin was soon awash with foreign troops waiting for

something to do. Russian officers filled their hours toasting one another extravagantly on the veranda of the Astor Hotel. British officers sprawled about, 'an eyeglass [monocle] often stuck over the eye, which did not always add to their otherwise intelligent appearance.'[38] All kinds of equipment began pouring in. Some of it, like the goat's-hair socks and lambswool drawers ordered up by the British, seemed curious kit for a hot-weather campaign, but the quartermasters were leaving nothing to chance. It might be a protracted campaign, and the North China winters were cold. The French and British ordered balloons for aerial reconnaissance but these arrived too late to be of any use. Doctors began vaccinating their men against the hazard of smallpox.

The various nationalities competed to secure means of transporting their equipment for the forthcoming campaign. The British gleefully seized a shipyard containing eighty new junks, which they considered 'an extraordinary capture, considering the way in which other nations usually forestalled us in matters of this sort.' British troops were also ordered to commandeer junks on the river but found this distressing, 'consisting, as it did, of turning whole families out on to the banks, from what had been their sole living place; but the orders were to get junks, and empty ones are not found floating about in war-time, even in China.' The British boarded one seemingly empty junk and found it 'tenanted by eight corpses of people who had met violent deaths and was therefore allowed to go on floating. Sights like this, and others more horrible, were only too common.'[39]

Despite such preparations, and despite careful reconnaissance by the Japanese patrols to assess the strength of the enemy in the hinterland, there was still no firm date for the relief force to march out. Internal rivalries still preoccupied the respective forces – the Russians and the Japanese were bickering furiously over which of their commanders was the more senior. In the end the Japanese avoided a crisis by a diplomatic compromise: their chief of staff, Yamaguchi, would deputize for the Japanese commander at all meetings where the Russian commander,

General Lineivitch, might be present and there was risk that the seniority issue might be raised.

It was only with the arrival in Tientsin on 27 July of the British commander-in-chief, General Gaselee, that any real sense of urgency began to prevail. At an allied council of war, Gaselee argued for quick action. He met resistance from the Russians and the French, who wanted to delay. They used the pretext that they were anxious about what would happen if rains broke out during August. Some even argued for delaying the advance until fall. 'The rainy season will set in in a few days,' they said, 'and the whole place will be under water.'[40] Both Russians and French had the concealed motive of wishing to win more time to build up the strength of their contingents and thus their influence.

But a determined Gaselee firmly but courteously made it clear that the British would go alone if necessary. He found allies in two American officers, Major General Adna Chaffee and Colonel Dagget of the Fourteenth US Infantry. The United States government had reacted sharply to the receipt on 20 July of Edwin Conger's telegram asking for relief. As the US secretary of war wrote, 'This dispatch . . . presented a situation which plainly called for the urgency of a relief expedition rather than for perfection of preparation; it was made the basis of urgent pressure for an immediate movement upon Peking, without waiting for the accumulation of the large force previously proposed.'[41]

Gaselee's chief of staff, General Barrow, lauded the Americans' 'ready-for-action' attitude, calling Daggett 'an elderly, sober man whose appearance gives one confidence' (even if, he added ungraciously, 'he wastes time by talking in a slow deliberate manner which bores me stiff').[42] The objections of the remaining Powers, which had no wish to see the British and Americans steal the march, dissolved, and to his relief Gaselee no longer had to worry about 'the vacillation of the foreigners.'[43] His men, too, were relieved. The general view in the British camp was that Gaselee was 'too good-natured to cope with foreigners.'[44]

*   *   *

It was agreed that on 5 August an international relief force would march to the relief of the Peking legations. There was great commotion in Tientsin as cars, ponies, mules, donkeys and rickshaws were commandeered in all directions. Twenty-six-year-old Lieutenant Steel, who was on leave from his post as aide-de-camp to Lord Curzon, then viceroy of India, and was to go as Gaselee's orderly officer, worked away assembling kit, organizing boats, and 'getting Union Jacks made'.[45] Then he took fifteen British officers to visit the Americans for a cheery concert, which concluded with 'Auld Lang Syne'. It was a 'very good business' and put them in a cheerful frame of mind for the difficulties ahead.

The relief force was ready to depart a day early. At dawn on 4 August the advance column began to move out of the settlement, raising clouds of dust and rattling the heavy gun carriages over the rickety wooden bridges. One US Marine officer, Smedley D. Butler, recalled an exotic sight: 'French Zouaves in red and blue, blond Germans in pointy helmets, Italian Bersaglieri with tossing plumes, Bengal cavalry on Arabian stallions, turbaned Sikhs, Japanese, Russians, English.'[46] Their ranks included the young American marine Harold Kinman, who had written proudly to his sister that 'we are going to fight the greatest battle at Pekin that has been fought for one hundred years.'[47]

13

HORSEMEAT AND HOPE

Thank God they are coming. – Mary Bainbridge

THE RELIEF FORCES were in better heart than the besieged. After the end of the truce many were again sceptical about the prospect of deliverance. They also felt oppressed by the sheer problems of day-today existence. In the hospital, supplies were nearly out while casualties were mounting. Caring for the sick and wounded was made yet more harrowing by a British marine who, according to Lenox Simpson, had become 'hopelessly mad'. He had shot and bayoneted a man early in the siege, driving the bayonet in up to the hilt in the man's chest and then discharging the entire contents of his magazine. Now, badly traumatized, he lay thrashing about, shrieking hour after hour, 'How it splashes! How it splashes!'

The state of the Chinese converts had deteriorated still further. Morrison went out for the first time since being wounded to see for himself. Carried in a chair by four coolies, he witnessed the pitiful conditions in the Fu, where many Chinese were barely clinging to life. The several hundred able-bodied male converts used in the fortification work were still receiving extra horsemeat and rice, but most of the others were existing on a mixture of chaff, sorghum seeds, wheat and the leaves of plants and trees made into 'a most revolting sort of cake'[1] and on the stray dogs and cats that were shot for them.[2] Seven or eight Chinese children were dying every day. Luella Miner sadly recorded in her diary the death of the last remaining child of one of her flock from Tungchow, predicting that 'many of our Chinese mothers will go out from this place with empty arms.'

Polly Condit Smith was haunted by the sight of a Western baby who had died from lack of food: 'It lay in its little coffin looking so white and tired.' She noticed how all the mothers with ailing children seemed fascinated by the pitiful funerals and always attended them. Polly was feeding a 'good, busy old hen' that laid an egg every day. She distributed them to the mothers of three babies so that each received an egg every third day, but 'the horror of it all is that these agonized mothers know, and I know, that, could I give the egg to them each day, instead of every third day, their babies could probably live; but as I can't, I have to divide them, and I cry with the pity of it.'

There was no question of the foreign adults starving as yet, although Captain Poole thought that the 'women look very peaky' and everyone had got thin. Polly noticed how after-dinner conversation revolved around the quantities and contents of the tins people possessed rather than more elegant or intellectual topics. She felt sorry for Lady MacDonald 'with that enormous mess to keep going. The complaints that people actually have the impertinence to make at her table, loud enough for her to hear, got so bad that one day she rose from her chair and said: "I give you the best I have; I can do nothing better; and, what is more, let me remind you that what is good enough for the British Minister to eat is more than good enough for anybody here."'

People had begun to hate the monotony of their diet of horse and rice, particularly since the white rice had run out and people were forced to eat the yellow, uncleaned rice, which was much like chewing sand. A special dish, such as a suet pudding made from mule fat, was a cause for celebration, while the killing of a cow caused 'great joy'[3] to those who managed to get some of it. According to Arthur Smith, 'One of the legation ladies sent for the cow's liver, only to find it had been calmly appropriated by the marines. An attaché of the British Legation sent up for a part of the cow's kidney as a great luxury but it had already been distributed. The sympathetic superintendent of the meat apportionment, however, not wishing to disappoint him, sent the man the kidney of a horse . . . afterwards meeting him, he enquired how he liked it. He had enjoyed it greatly, and remarked that while eating it he had forgotten that he was in China!' Luella Miner was greatly cheered by a supper of 'beef soup and meat with rich gravy.' 'Never did Thanksgiving dinner taste so good!' she wrote, hoping that no one had counted the number of slices of bread she had taken to mop up the gravy. A request to the Tsungli Yamen to supply food for both the converts and the foreigners received no response. Arthur Smith, who had once believed he understood China, shrugged his shoulders and exclaimed helplessly to Luella: 'War and watermelons!'[4]

This summed up the paradox of their existence. At one moment the Tsungli Yamen might well send them fruit. At the next it might be plotting to murder them. The situation was as confused as it had ever been. Despite the resumption of hostilities, messengers from the Tsungli Yamen continued to come and go with clockwork regularity. They brought condolences on the death of King Umberto of Italy, who had been assassinated by anarchists,[5] and, several days later, delivered 'a charming dispatch'[6] on the death of the Duke of Edinburgh. Just as Sir Claude was composing a response in best diplomatic style, a two-inch shell flew into his bedroom and blew out both his windows into the flowerbeds outside. The irony amused him. Sir Claude replied that he was grateful for the news and the sympathy but politely pointed out that it still remained true that he could not put his head out of his own legation without the danger of being shot!

The conciliatory messages continued. The Yamen sent word

that it was 'decapitating wholesale'[7] the soldiery who had been firing on the legations and talked of truces and peace. It also told the besieged that Li Hung-chang had been appointed to begin peace negotiations and would soon be telegraphing the foreign governments with proposals. When asked why the legations were still being attacked, however, it could offer only 'some frivolous explanation.'[8] Luella Miner thought it inexplicable, but suggested acidly that it might be 'to celebrate the appointment of a peace-commissioner.'

On 12 August, Prince Ching sent word that members of the Yamen intended to call on the ministers the next day. Mary Bainbridge wrote vengefully that if they did indeed attempt to visit 'I would lock them up as soon as they entered the gates and treat them exactly as they have been doing by us, then seize the Old lady and give her a dose of her own medicine.' Arthur Smith thought the ministers should reply that 'they would be obliged to meet him [Prince Ching] elsewhere, as bullets were flying so thickly in the British Legation that it wouldn't be safe for his Excellency to come here!'

The besieged hoped that these overtures meant the relief force was close at hand. Many were becoming more optimistic. They began to argue about designs for a siege medal to commemorate their experience. They also held an auction of looted goods, which achieved high prices as people bid against each other for mementos. Sir Robert Hart tossed a letter over the wall to a messenger. It was addressed to his tailor in London and instructed him to 'send quickly two autumn suits and later two winter ditto with morning and evening dress, warm cape, and four pairs of boots and slippers. I have lost everything but am well.'[9] The note got through.

Just previously, on 10 August, definitive news had at last reached the legations. A message from General Gaselee announced: 'Strong force of Allies advancing. Twice defeated enemy. Keep up your spirits.' A further message from the Japanese general Fukushima was even more cheering: 'Probable date of arrival at

Peking August 13 or 14.' The besieged exulted, 'We are to become reasonably clean and quite ordinary mortals again,' wrote Lenox Simpson. Sarah Conger paid a visit to the American Legation only to find it infested with swarms of fleas, flies and mosquitoes. She decided to begin cleaning the house 'so that we can move at once when our troops come, as the British will need their Legation.' Even Monsieur Pichon brightened, saying to Dr Martin, *'Eh bien, nous sortirons d'ici'* – 'Well, we shall get out of this.'[10]

However, the legations were not out of it yet. The besieged found themselves under increasingly vicious attack. Bullets and shrapnel peppered the air and the defenders were alarmed to see that new and aggressive Imperial troops had appeared, planting their gaudy black and yellow banners just twenty or thirty yards from the legation outposts. The banners flaunted the names of new Chinese generals unknown to them. They had, in fact, been sent to Peking by Yu Hsien, the governor of Shansi, in a last-ditch attempt to overrun the foreigners and were commanded by a bellicose officer who had sworn to take the legations in five days, 'leaving neither fowl nor dog.'[11] His plans proved over-ambitious – he was shot dead on 12 August by a Customs Service volunteer, Mr Bismarck.

That very day Lenox Simpson was writing that 'all thoughts of relief have been pushed into the middle distance – and even beyond – by the urgent business we have now on hand . . . What stupendous quantities of ammunition have been loosed-off on us . . . what tons of lead and nickel! Some of our barricades have been so eaten away by this fire, that there is but little left, and we are forced to lie prone on the ground hour after hour . . . The Chinese guns are also booming again, and shrapnel and segment are tearing down trees and outhouses, bursting through walls, splintering roofs, and wrecking our strongest defences more and more.' The young British volunteer Walter Townsend wrote wistfully: 'The glorious 12th! I wish we were chivying the festive grouse, instead of being potted at all round like rats in a hole.'[12] The casualty list passed two hundred. Polly Condit Smith could hear 'the shrill cries of "Sha! Sha! Sha!"' and the constant blow-ing of trumpets. During the rare lulls they could hear guns pounding the Peitang to the north. That evening Captain Labrousse of the French marines was shot dead as he strolled with comrades behind the French Legation position. He had just remarked that 'the end of the siege being so near, it was neces-sary to be extra careful as regards exposing oneself.'[13]

When the allied relief force had marched out from Tientsin on 4 August, they had left their comrades to a more peaceful exis-tence. Some, sharing Walter Townsend's passion for shooting game, were even planning to hunt autumn snipe in the marshes. A British naval officer wrote of 'how enjoyable it was to be killing, or even frightening, something a little less imposing when in the bag than human beings.'[14]

However, the commanders of the allied relief force knew that they faced a far from relaxing time. Military intelligence was negligible, but it was rumoured that some 70,000 Imperial troops and anything from 50,000 to 100,000 Boxers lay between them and the capital. The allied force consisted of between 18,000 and 20,000 men, although precise estimates vary. Roughly half were Japanese, with some 3,000 Russians, 3,000 British, 2,200 Americans and 800 French. In addition there were several hundred Germans, Austrians and Italians. Between them they could muster some seventy guns. The British artillery included four of HMS *Terrible*'s long-range naval twelve-pounders, which had seen land action at the relief of Ladysmith five months earlier. Captain Barnes of the British Chinese Regiment was detailed to escort these heavy guns and was struck by the polyglot character of 'our good old "International Battery" . . . The guns were worked by natives of India, of the Hong-Kong and Singapore Asiatic Artillery, offi-cered by Englishmen, and the escort was found – and, more often than not, the haulage power – by Chinese, of the 1st Chinese Regiment, also officered by British officers. Verily a unique unit, and typical of the resourcefulness of our race.'[15]

The elderly Californian poet Joaquin Miller, sent to report on China for the Hearst papers, had longed to accompany this extraordinary caravan. He had hired a rickshaw to take him, but Lou Hoover, after failing to convince him of the danger, wisely bribed his rickshaw boy to desert him. The 'picturesque old gentleman'[16] remained quietly and safely behind in Tientsin.

The allies' great weakness was a lack of suitable cavalry. The only properly equipped unit was Bengal Lancers supplemented by a few Cossacks. There was a Japanese cavalry regiment, but its horses were of poor quality and quickly succumbed to the heat – only 60 out of 400 animals would complete the march to Peking. The Sixth US Cavalry had disembarked at Taku before the relief departed, but their horses were still too weak from the voyage to join the march.

The allied commanders decided to follow the same route as the 1860 expedition, along the winding banks of the Peiho River. The French, Russians, Germans, Austrians and Italians marched along the east bank until flooding forced them to retrace their steps and cross over. The British, Americans and Japanese advanced along the west side. The British Methodist missionary the Reverend Frederick Brown, who had been on the last train to get through from Peking, was appointed an intelligence officer because of his knowledge of Chinese. Looking back, he saw 'a long, narrow line of khaki-dressed human beings moving slowly; from its winding form, it gave one the idea of a serpent wriggling its way along. At its head were the picturesque uniforms of the Generals and staff, followed by the fine Indian soldiers, mounted on their beautiful horses. Then came the gallant Welsh [*sic*] Fusiliers; while the well-set, business-like United States Infantrymen marched next . . . Then came the Japanese general, with his soldiers in white clothes; they seemed fitted to run in where the others were too big to pass.'

Ponies and mules carried the immediate supplies, but other equipment was pushed and pulled up the shallow Peiho in a six-mile-long procession of junks and sampans. Roger Keyes was riding along on a small Chinese pony he had purchased, complete with saddle, for $50, and whose antics earned him the name of 'the Torpedo'. Keyes had persuaded his commanding officer to allow him to accompany General Gaselee as naval staff officer. Ever practical, the young British naval lieutenant had visited the Americans' 'excellent military store' stocked with equipment brought from the Philippines and had bought himself a capacious mosquito net that could be suspended from four bamboo canes stuck into the ground. According to Keyes, the only man better equipped was the regimental doctor of the Seventh Rajputs, who slept in his hospital dhoolie – a litter designed to carry a man at full length and fitted with a water-proof roof and curtains.

The first battle came on 5 August at Peitsang, a few miles north of the Hsiku arsenal, where some 20,000 Chinese were rumoured to be waiting. After a wet and uncomfortable night lying out on muddy ground, the Japanese advanced with their customary determination supported by British guns and infantry. Keyes, employed as a 'galloper' or mounted messenger, dashed hither and thither on the Torpedo and had a good view of the fighting. He described how the Chinese fled 'when the Japanese went forwards with a yell in their final rush,' apparently terrified of being bayoneted.

Next day the allies fought again, this time attacking heavily entrenched positions at Yangtsun, where the British and Americans led the assault. The town fell by evening. Lieutenant Richard Steel, General Gaselee's orderly officer, wrote that it was 'absolutely filthy, like every Chinese town, but filled with corpses of Chinese.' Its capture had been neither an efficient nor a clean-cut affair. At the height of the battle Keyes came upon a company of the Fourteenth US Infantry trying to take cover under a railway embankment, 'cursing horribly, and swearing that they were being shelled by our artillery.' A number of men had already been killed or seriously wounded. Keyes believed that Russian guns were to blame. Placing a handkerchief on the

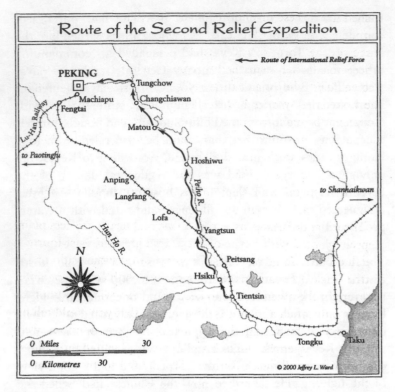

point of his sword, he galloped up the embankment to signal
that they were firing on allied troops. The shelling ceased and
that night the dead Americans were given an impressive and
moving funeral. 'Preceded by the brass band'[17] – America was
the only force among the allies to bring a band on the march to
Peking – 'the killed were brought up to a large grave, where a
touching service was read, and then the bodies were laid to rest
side by side until they could be conveyed, at the expense of the
State, back to America.'

At Yangtsun the allies were intrigued to find the remains of
the trains abandoned by Seymour during his retreat to Tientsin.
'Still standing on the embankment were the boilers and wheels
of the engines used in that fruitless attempt to reach Peking.
How the Boxers must have gloated in their hate when they

rushed upon these inventions of the "foreign devils"! They had
burned the woodwork . . . looted the brasses, nuts and bolts,
and had even torn up and buried the rails and sleepers. But the
wheels and boilers remained there in defiance,' wrote Frederick
Brown. 'The white man's forgings had proved too unyielding for
the Boxers.' A young British naval officer wondered whether
'some portly mandarin is still wearing the Admiral's full-dress
clothes, and his children, perchance, appear on swell occasions
in the Sunday-go-to-meeting garb of British midshipmen.' Yet he
thought it a fair exchange, 'for it is at least as certain that some
. . . midshipmen's female relations are wearing Mrs Mandarin's
best sables!'[18]

The route to Peking lay across a vast and nearly treeless plain,
densely planted with a type of maize that grew 'at least fourteen
feet high.' These giant crops, pressing in on either side of the
rutted tracks of road, made it almost impossible to reconnoiter
or even for the allied troops to keep in contact with one another.
'It was only when a man was close to you that you could tell his
whereabouts by seeing the top of his lance – pennons were
furled – above the high crops,' wrote Lieutenant-Colonel
Vaughan of the Seventh Rajputs. This caused some unfortunate
incidents. A troop of First Bengal Lancers on reconnaissance
fired by mistake on some Russians and were fired on in return.
'Explanations were given, and the Russian commander, on being
informed that one Lancer was wounded, replied, "I also have
one man wounded. It is all right; we are quits."'

On another occasion Keyes was horrified to see 'the banners
of a large body of Tartar cavalry and the pennons of our Bengal
Lancers showing above the standing maize, and within a mile of
one another, apparently unaware of each other's proximity, but
closing fairly rapidly.' He set off on the Torpedo to warn the
Lancers but trying to find them was like searching for a needle
in a haystack. Another officer described how the high maize
made it like fighting blindfold. However, the allies found that
two long bamboo ladders, carried by Japanese coolies, made an
excellent lookout station when lashed together to form a double

stairway. They were also useful for signalling allied positions by raising them in an inverted V above the maize.

Another difficulty was that the raised wagon road running from Tientsin to Peking was very crooked. Colonel Daggett, commanding officer of the Fourteenth US Infantry, grumbled: 'The object is to prevent the passage of evil spirits, for they always fly in straight lines, according to the Chinese lore. Part of the way the armies marched on this road, for it raised the soldiers above the cornfields, where they found refreshing breezes and comparative freedom from dust. But to follow it too closely would increase the distance; so, like the evil spirits, as the Chinamen doubtless thought they were, they descended to the cornfields to cut off angles.'

Yet the worst problem was the intense and relentless heat – one day it rose to 105° F in the shade. British officers thatched the inside of their solar topees with maize leaves, which hung down nearly to their waist belts and made them look like pantomime figures. Men felt they were suffocating and collapsed with heat stroke. The Americans were wearing felt hats, which were 'a very inadequate protection, and they suffered most,' wrote Keyes. One US Marine recalled that it was 'like walking through a blast furnace.'[19] Vaughan remembered how 'at one point we marched through an American detachment; the men were marching slowly along at about two miles an hour with heads bent and eyes half closed, as though sleeping or dead tired, and though utterly knocked up by the heat, yet determined to stick to it and come into camp on their own feet. I don't think they even noticed us as we passed them.'

Daggett wrote bitterly of 'a fierceness in that China sun's rays which none had experienced in the tropics or our Southern States during the Civil War . . . Its prostrating effect was unaccountable, and caused our men to fall by hundreds.' The crops made it worse. 'The dust of ages . . . rose at every footstep. The corn obstructed the breeze, and did not allow it either to blow away the dust or fan the burning faces of the fainting soldiers.' Soon the route was strewn with abandoned kit – haversacks, greatcoats and blankets – and men lay fainting by the roadside. Some turned into the maize fields to build shelters out of the stalks. Fortunately for them, as Keyes noted, the Americans had brought from the Philippines 'a wonderful transport train of great big, lightly built wagons, drawn by the most magnificent mules I have ever seen. These followed a day behind and picked up scores of weary Americans and their jettisoned equipment.'

Before long everyone was finding the heat unbearable – even the British Indian troops, whose suffering moved the compassionate Gaselee. He admitted that he 'had never experienced anything so trying in India, or had seen troops so overcome by heat before.'[20] Lieutenant Steel was rather more graphic: 'The heat was *awful*, the whole road being littered with men fallen out, Americans, Japs and ours. The country is so dense with crops we couldn't see anywhere, and the flies and bad water made life pretty sickening.' He recorded other horrors as well. 'Everywhere one came across dead bodies of Chinese and mules and horses in various degrees of foul composition. I nearly catted [vomited] dozens of times.'[21] Vaughan recorded such macabre sights as the 'head of a Chinaman hanging by the pigtail from a post by the road-side' and corpses lying pale and spectral in the moonlight.

Water was in short supply because the wells were too few for the large number of thirsty animals and men. By the time the rear of the column caught up they had frequently been emptied. However, in the evenings the men bathed in the river. In a letter to a friend, Keyes described the hazards and delights of the 'silvery' Peiho: 'One has often to step aside to let a dead Chinaman or dog pass; but bathing in it is simply delicious after the terrible heat and dust of the march, and we drink it too, without waiting for it to be boiled, after it has been treated with alum to make the mud settle.' Vaughan was less enthusiastic, describing how the water was 'almost like pea soup, and after drying one's self, the towels appeared as if made of khaki-coloured material.' He did not blame the water, however, for the diarrhoea to which many had succumbed, since 'even those who drank nothing but tea and filtered water [were] suffering from it.' He blamed the unripe melons the men were eating.

Yet despite all the problems, this 'heterogeneous army'[22] had marched twenty-five miles and won two victories in as many days. The original plan had been to advance to Yangtsun and there await reinforcements, including the Sixth US Cavalry, but Peking now seemed more easily within their grasp than anyone had foreseen. At a council of war on 7 August it was decided to press on quickly. The Germans, Italians and Austrians, mostly sailors, were in no state to continue and decided to return to Tientsin to equip themselves properly. The French forces were also to turn back. These consisted of ragged, exhausted, diminutive Tonkinese, who, worn out by duty in Indo-China, were uniformly reviled by the other nationalities. Vaughan's comments about their 'puny stature and inferior physique' were typical. 'They were marines, I believe,' he continued, 'and were apparently unable to keep up with the rest of the allies; otherwise it is difficult to account for their absence on every important occasion.' Their transport consisted almost entirely of wheelbarrows and rickshaws and was not well suited for a dash to Peking. Their commander, General Frey, intended to start out afresh and catch up with the relief force before it entered Peking. He also left a small garrison behind at Yangtsun.

Meanwhile, the field was clear for the four major players – Americans, British, Japanese and Russians – who now pushed on with the Japanese leading and the British bringing up the rear. According to some accounts, the Russians insisted on this as a device for separating the two nationalities whose intentions they distrusted the most. The Chinese fled in panic at their approach. One village had been so recently abandoned that allied troops found a teapot full of hot tea. On another occasion Vaughan and his men came across the curious sight of a quantity of Chinese umbrellas abandoned on the road by the Chinese troops: 'As the sun was very hot at the time the men picked them up as they passed, and opening them, held them over their heads, when the column presented the curious sight of a mass of troops moving with umbrellas.' They proved heavy to carry and were quickly jettisoned, though one officer wisely retained a pair and bivouacked under them for the rest of the march.

Daggett recorded how 'the villages were all deserted, except occasionally a Chinese man or woman would be found crouching in some hidden corner, expecting to be killed every moment. And, to the disgrace of humanity . . . some of these innocent, unresisting people were shot down like beasts *but not by Americans*.' The British journalist A. Henry Savage Landor, who was travelling with the relief force, agreed, writing that the majority of the 'American boys' were 'as a rule extremely humane, even at times extravagantly gracious, towards the enemy.'[23] He also claimed that the British soldiers showed greater humanity than their Continental brethren.[24] As the allies advanced, they captured many prisoners. Some were regular Imperial troops while others were wearing the red sashes and ribbons of the Boxers. The Chinese Regiment took charge of those caught by the British and they were usually put to work. However, Savage-Landor was horrified to see a supposed Boxer spy dragged away by French and Japanese troops, who punched and kicked him then shot him in the face. 'The poor devil, who showed amazing tenacity of life, afterwards had all his clothes torn off him, the soldiers being bent on finding the peculiar Boxer charm which all Boxers were supposed to possess.' The man lived for another hour 'with hundreds of soldiers leaning over him to get a glimpse of his agony, and going into roars of laughter as he made ghastly con tortions in his delirium.'[25]

On 8 August, a note from Sir Claude MacDonald reached General Gaselee and General Chaffee, together with a sketch map indicating the best way to approach the legations. It advised the allies to enter Peking by the south gate of the Chinese City, advance up the main street, then turn off towards the sluice gate running under the Tartar Wall. It also told them

that the defenders would mark that portion of the wall with the
American, Russian, and British flags. However, the notes were
written in cipher, the key to which had been left behind at the
British Consulate in Tientsin. Captain Griffin of the First Bengal
Lancers was sent racing back to obtain a translation from the
British consul.

Spurred by this contact with the legations, the army moved
on again, the British sometimes marching by night to escape the
insufferable heat. Frequent rainstorms soaked their clothing and
equipment but the air remained stagnant and humid. Sometimes
the exhausted men barely had the energy to break down some
stalks of maize to make a space to spread their blankets, falling
asleep 'without more of a supper than a drink of cold water.'[26]
On other occasions they made more effort. The Reverend
Frederick Brown was invited to dine one night with the officers
of the Fourteenth US Infantry, which he thought a great honour
because of their heroic reputation. It was not a dinner for
heroes. 'Two empty boxes on end did duty as a table, while a
newspaper was the tablecloth. There was a metal knife, fork and
spoon for each, and each had but one enamelled plate for all the
courses.' Nevertheless, Colonel Scott-Moncrieff of the Royal
Engineers was amazed by the quality of the American provisions: 'Their rations seemed to us to be more luxurious than
ours . . . They gave their men such things as canned peaches and
tomatoes, which we should look upon as certainly not in the
category of soldier rations.'[27]

Notwithstanding the conditions, the allies were making
steady progress, taking a series of towns. At one of these –
Hoshiwu, halfway to Peking – they found that plans had been
made to flood the countryside and drown them. 'We found the
cutting nearly completed, and the workmen's tools and baskets
lying in it, so precipitately had they fled. However, although the
thing didn't come off, the Chinese general informed his government that he had cut the banks of the Peiho, and inundated the
country, drowning 25,000 of the foreigners, at which, he naively
concluded, "they are much disheartened." We read this account

of our being drowned some months later in a Chinese paper, and were much amused,' wrote Vaughan.

At Hoshiwu the allies also discovered a Chinese magazine containing some eighty to one hundred tons of powder and blew it up. An immense column of flame shot into the sky, a penetrating crack rent the air, and Vaughan's horse staggered. Looking back he saw 'a cloud of dark smoke . . . high up in the air like a ball, full of convolutions all in motion. These kept shooting and rolling out while the cloud continued spreading and spreading until it appeared to cover half the sky.' It looked like a great 'mushroom-like growth of dun grey cloud.'[28] Lieutenant Steel was also impressed, writing in his diary with schoolboy glee: 'We were three miles away when the powder exploded, *tremendous.*'

Frederick Brown observed yet another example of the misunderstandings that afflicted this polyglot force. Colonel Scott-Moncrieff, who had laid the fuse, was running away when he noticed a Russian soldier walking directly towards the magazine, not knowing it was about to explode. The colonel tried to explain the position by gesturing. When that failed he resorted to physical force, which the Russian resented. At that moment the flame reached the magazine, the explosion took place, and both were thrown violently to the ground. 'Then, and only then, did the Russian understand the meaning of the conduct of this excited British officer.'[29]

In the early hours of 12 August, the allies arrived before the sealed gates of Luella Miner's beloved walled city of Tungchow. They were now just fourteen miles from Peking. The Imperial troops had simply melted away at their approach. 'As we followed the retreating army, we came across pots, pans, umbrellas and fans, the necessary paraphernalia of a Chinese army, scattered about in all directions . . . It seemed, therefore, that there would be no serious stand till Peking should be reached,' wrote Frederick Brown in evident surprise. The Japanese dynamited the south gate and the allies poured in to find the Chinese garrison gone. There was the usual looting and it was some time before the commanders could bring it under control. A US Marine officer described a desolate scene where 'corpses, with skulls smashed in, lay sprawled across the streets. Brocades and fragments of porcelain spilled out of the broken fronts of shops. The gilded archways were shattered. Carved teakwood furniture was being split up by the Allied soldiers for firewood.'[30]

Journalist George Lynch came across the distressing sight of two Chinese girls who had tried to commit suicide by jumping from a window: 'From their richly embroidered silken tunics and trousers, their elaborate coiffure and their compressed feet, they were evidently ladies.' Their legs were broken and they were lying on the ground in agony. He tried to ease their suffering by giving them water. He observed sadly: 'It was no unusual sight to see an entire family lying dead side by side on the *kang*, where they had suffocated themselves, or to see them suspended from the rafters of their houses, where they had committed suicide by hanging.'[31] General Gaselee tried to reassure the local population by setting up a market for their produce in the ruined compound of Luella Miner's mission and encouraging the terrified local people to return to their homes and trade with the foreigners. When Frederick Brown, somewhat unchristianly, queried this conciliatory behaviour, he replied mildly: 'Well, you know, we do not wish to antagonize the 350 millions of China.'[32]

As Gaselee tried to restore order and calm in Tungchow, Imperial resistance to the allied advance was dissolving completely. Li Ping-heng, who had promised to hurl the foreign devils out of China at the first battle, had retreated up a narrow spur of the river with forty boats of wounded. On 11 August he had written despairingly to the Empress Dowager: 'For the past few days I have seen several tens of thousands of troops jamming all the roads. They fled as soon as they heard of the arrival of the enemy; they did not give battle at all.'[33] The situation was getting out of control and he believed the only solution

The bulletin board by the Bell Tower in the grounds of the
British Legation where the besieged gathered hoping for news.

The American Legation with a barricade to one side.

'The International Gun' also known as 'Old Betsey', a useful piece of artillery imaginatively put together by an American gunner from spare parts of multinational provenance.

The British Legation gatehouse and the elderly, temperamental Nordenfeldt gun which apparently jammed every fourth round.

The ramp leading to the American position on the Tartar wall.

Defenders firing through a window
in Sir Claude MacDonald's house.

View through a loophole towards
the Chinese positions. The accuracy
of the Chinese sharpshooters made
loopholes very dangerous to man.
One defender was killed because a
marksman spotted smoke rising
from a cigarette he was smoking.

The gatehouse of the British Legation showing the barricades
and the noisome canal known as the 'Jade River'.

A group of missionary defenders known as 'The Six Fighting Parsons'.
Many believed that the Legations would have fallen long before the
relief without the efforts of the missionaries and their Chinese converts.

The Fu, the Chinese palace which sheltered several thousands of Chinese Christian converts and was virtually destroyed by the end of the siege.

Destruction in the streets around the foreign Legations in Peking.

The walls of the Chinese city Tientsin after bombardment by allied forces.

The gate through which the allies entered
the Chinese city of Tientsin to take it.

The Gordon Hall, where many foreign civilians sheltered during the siege of the foreign settlement in Tientsin, as it looked in August 1998.

was to execute the 'retreating generals and escaping troops.'[34] The day Tungchow fell he committed suicide.

On 12 August, the allies held a council of war. General Lineivitch argued that the Russians would be too exhausted to take part in an assault on Peking immediately on arrival. The commanders therefore agreed on a three-phase approach. According to one of General Gaselee's staff officers, it was arranged that the allied forces should each send out a strong cavalry reconnaissance on the morning of the thirteenth to halt some three miles short of Peking, that on the fourteenth the main bodies should advance to join them, the general attack on Peking to be on the fifteenth. A determined General Frey had returned from Tientsin with some 400 French troops so there were now five nations to share the struggle and its fruits.

The plan for the final attack was that the allies would advance simultaneously along parallel lines with each contingent aiming for a particular gate in the eastern walls. The Russians were to march farthest north, on the right flank. Then would come the Japanese; next the French; then, south of the Imperial canal, the Americans; and finally the British on the left flank. General Gaselee had volunteered to take this position after talking to Frederick Brown. Contrary to Sir Claude MacDonald's advice, Brown advised him to aim for a gate in the east wall of the Chinese City – the Shawomen. Although this would mean fighting through the Chinese City the Shawomen was relatively weak and was nearer to the legations than the gate suggested by Sir Claude. It was reported that enemy troops were concentrating to the south-southeast of the Chinese City, so Gaselee knew that the British might find themselves in the most exposed position. He decided, however, to bow to the missionary's knowledge and experience. According to Keyes, the Russians were 'very tickled' and the Japanese 'much surprised' at the British choice, but they did not try to dissuade him.

Yet events did not go as planned. During the evening of 13

August, news spread that the Russians had broken the agreement and were making a dash for Peking. Keyes wrote: 'A
message has just come from the Russians that some Cossacks
have pushed on to within a mile and a half of Peking, and the
gates are open. I wonder if it is true; if so we are properly left
behind.'

What precisely happened is unclear. It appears, however, that
Russian scouts sent ahead on the evening of 13 August reported
that the Tungpienmen – the gate by which the Americans were
to enter – was only lightly defended. On the strength of this
intelligence, General Lincivitch sent an advance guard under
General Vassilievski, including artillery, to secure the
approaches to the gate in readiness for an assault by the main
force. Arrived in the shadow of the city walls, Vassilievski saw
an opportunity to do more than hold the approaches. Leading
his men over a bridge across the moat, he surprised the Chinese
soldiers in the outer guardhouse. They raised the alarm but it
was too late. The Russians brought up their guns and blasted a
hole through the iron-clad gate to take possession of the
Tungpienmen before daybreak on 14 August and become the
first allies to enter Peking.[35]

The day before, as promised in Sir Claude MacDonald's
dispatch to General Gaselee, the besieged had hoisted the Union
Jack, the Stars and Stripes, and the Imperial eagle of Russia on
the Tartar Wall as a signal to the advancing allies. Oscar Upham
was given the honour of raising the Russian eagle but was
pleased that 'the American flag was the first foreign flag hoisted
on the Tartar Wall.' The Chinese now launched one last supreme
effort, beginning with 'sharp firing in every direction.'[36] The
members of the Tsungli Yamen excused themselves from calling
on the ministers after all. They said that they were too busy and
complained that the shooting of the senior officer from Shansi
had not been 'a friendly procedure'. Oscar Upham wrote
contemptuously that 'the facts of the matter are they made the
attack and we did the rest.'

However, there was no time to exchange barbed messages

with the Yamen. The Legation Quarter was being assaulted on
all sides and as night drew on the attacks worsened. The
besieged would remember it as one of 'the three terrible nights'[37]
of their experience. Captain Poole wrote: 'Legation full of
danger, up all night, fiercest attack I can remember,' but added,
'let them do their worst.' The terrific thunderstorm that broke
over the city that night intensified the sense of peril. William
Bainbridge recalled how 'the first long roll of thunder seemed
the signal for beginning the most terrible and desperate assault
of the entire siege. The night was intensely dark save for the
sharp flashes of lightning; the wind was driving the rain in
sheets. But the rattle of musketry and roar of cannon drowned
the elemental tumult.'

In the midst of the fighting, yet another messenger from the
Tsungli Yamen arrived with a note expressing the hope that,
'dating from today, neither Chinese nor foreigner would ever
again hear the sound of a rifle.'[38] Sir Claude 'read this sanguine
aspiration to the accompaniment of a violent fusillade from the
Chinese troops, which began shortly after a shell had burst in
my dressing room.' The situation was as dangerous as at any
time since the siege began. In the Fu a desperate Colonel Shiba
was ordering his men to bang pots and pans while the Italians
shouted and whistled and shouted 'bravo' to convince the
Chinese that there were more defenders than there really were.
Frank Gamewell was rushing from position to position trying to
shore up the defences. The Jubilee Bell rang out, signalling a
general attack, and Sir Claude called up the reserves three times,
rushing them to critical parts of the line.

Imperial troops armed with modern Mannlicher carbines
were pouring into the Mongol Market, their officers shouting to
them not to be afraid – they could get through. In the fading
light the horrified defenders saw a 'modern piece of artillery'[39]
being mounted high up on the Imperial City wall. It was a two-
inch, quick-firing Krupp gun, which proceeded to do more
damage in ten minutes than the enemy's smooth-bores had
achieved in five weeks. It was knocked out by the defenders'

Colt machine gun and Maxim. However, Mausers, Mannlichers, jingals, and muskets blasted away. Lenox Simpson wondered whether it was 'the last night of this insane Boxerism, or merely the beginning of a still more terrible series of attacks with massed assaults pushed right home on us.'

The commanders of every post were on full alert. Every sleeping man was awakened and pushed against the barricades. Splinters of brick and stone broke off in clouds from the defences. In several places there was hand-to-hand fighting. The noise was so deafening that Nigel Oliphant, still nursing his painful wound, wrote in his diary: 'We can't hear ourselves speak. I shall probably soon rise and see what is up, though it is very dark, and my leg gives me trouble.'

Then, suddenly, above the clamour of rifle-fire the distant boom of heavy guns was heard coming from the east. There was a sudden lull as both sides paused to listen. Unsure what it meant, Dr Coltman grabbed his double-barreled shotgun and hurried outside. Then he realized 'the relief were outside the city engaging the Chinese troops, and the automatic gun was not ours, but theirs,' and he fell to his knees in prayer. Polly was also deeply moved by 'the dull boom of distant artillery – artillery coming to our rescue! We no longer asked each other, "When will the troops arrive?" we simply stood still, listening to this wonderful music, and goose-flesh ran up and down us.' An emotional Mary Bainbridge wrote of 'faint sounds . . . of, what seemed to us, like Heavenly music, nearer and nearer came the sounds of cannonading and artillery, until every foreigner said in their hearts, "Thank God they are coming." There was no mistake in that sound. All were up listening eagerly, rejoicing deep down in their hearts. "The troops are outside the city and we are saved."'

The news spread from building to building and people poured outside. Sir Claude later recalled how the legation grounds were suddenly alive with men, women, and children shaking hands, dancing, laughing, crying, 'going mad with joy.' Women wept on one another's necks. Señor Cologan, the

Spanish minister and doyen of the diplomatic corps, rushed around like a schoolboy, shouting 'We are saved! We are saved!'[40]

Amid the euphoria people began to wonder which country's troops would be the first to reach them.

14

IN THROUGH THE SLUICE GATE

An ominous silence made us fear the worst . . . and that the flag was only a ruse to lure us on. – General Gaselee

THE SAME QUESTION was also exercising the various contingents of the relief force. At the news of the Russians' apparent duplicity, the Japanese had marched rapidly for Peking, followed by the Americans. Meanwhile, in the British camp, General Gaselee had at first refused to believe that the allied agreement had been broken. It took the dull booming of the guns from the direction of the Tartar City to convince him. By 3:30 on the morning of 14 August, the main British force was moving out to join its advance guard some six miles from Peking. Frederick Brown was riding with them, fortified by a modest cup of cocoa and a cracker. Despite the early hour, some of the officers had opted for a whiskey and soda. It was a difficult journey. The road had been turned to mud by the heavy rain and men and horses slithered to gain a purchase. As dawn rose the high sodden crops obscured the view of the troops, but the British rendezvoused with their advance party at around 7.00 a.m. and after a brief pause pushed on again towards Peking.

The Chinese made no attempt to stop them. 'As we British marched along the soft road to the south, we could see and hear that sharp fighting was proceeding to the north, but not a shot or shell came near us,' wrote Brown. By 1.00 they could see the Chinese City wall looming in the distance but at first many were uncertain what it was. Lieutenant Colonel Vaughan described how 'here was a high castellated wall . . . and the subahdar-major said: "I suppose we ought to occupy and hold the wall of that fort," pointing to it. I replied, "Yes," little knowing that it was the city wall of Pekin that we were in sight of.'

With their target, the Shawomen, before them, General Gaselee ordered up two guns. According to Lieutenant Steel: 'The battery fired some dozen shots, and the Chinese scuttled, and we burst the door open and were inside.' General Gaselee was anxious to signal to the Americans and French directly the gate was captured in case they turned their artillery on it. Roger Keyes had brought both the white ensign of his ship *Fame* and a Union Jack for just such an eventuality. In an episode redolent of *Boy's Own*, he gripped the Union Jack in his teeth and managed to get a foothold in the angle of the wall to the right of the gate where some stones had come out. After some anxious moments he succeeded in climbing thirty feet up the wall. Poking his head over the parapet he was amazed to see 'an encampment all along the wide city wall, with little tents and equipment, and cooking utensils lying about without a soul in sight.' Once on top he tied his Union Jack to a Chinese pike and waved it vigorously backwards and forwards.

Keyes had hoped he might be able to unfasten the gate from the inside but before he could climb down the inner gate was burst open and British troops began streaming through. General Gaselee now sent detachments to seize the Temples of Heaven and Agriculture and ordered an advance westward, parallel with the Tartar Wall. It was eerie. As Lieutenant-Colonel Vaughan described: 'Not a Chinaman was to be seen, but the banging of doors was heard, and many of the rings hanging from the door knobs were shaking as we passed, showing that the doors had only just been shut. At last we entered a long and broad street, and while going up it saw hundreds of Chinamen running down the side streets away from us.'

When they estimated that they were lined up with the sluice gate leading into the legations, the relief force turned north hoping to find the gate ahead of them. There was some desultory shooting from behind houses but, as Keyes wrote, 'we saw no troops and there was no real opposition.' As they neared the Tartar Wall they came under fire from the outer gate of the Hatamen. The Chinese were using smokeless powder and it was unclear where the shots were coming from. Vaughan heard 'a tick-tick, as if some one was tapping the scaffolding poles of which there were a number bunched together by the roadside, with a hammer . . . Suddenly my eye caught a puff of smoke coming from the rampart of the gateway, and heads were seen appearing and disappearing at the embrasures.' As the British got closer to the legations they saw the British, Russian, and American flags on the Tartar Wall directly above the archway over the sluice gate. They were hanging idly in the still, heavy air.

The question was, what did the flags mean? A rumour had spread among the relief force that the legations had fallen, in which case the flags were not what they seemed. In his official

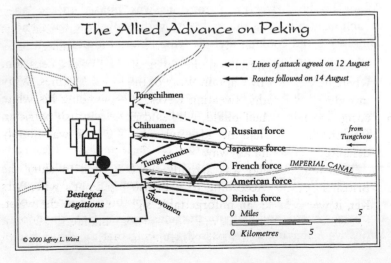

dispatch, General Gaselee wrote that 'the British flag was still flying on the portion of the Tartar wall which we knew the legations had occupied, but an ominous silence made us fear the worst had occurred, and that the flag was only a ruse to lure us on.'[1] Then a marine with a signalling flag appeared on the wall and began to spell out a welcome message in Morse code: 'Come in quickly by the sluice gate.' The relieving force gave a great cheer and before the signal was even finished there was a rush of troops along the street. Lieutenant Steel described how 'we all dashed across the canal, bullets fizzing and spitting all round, a small shell exploding in front of my nose, no harm done.' A fastidious young man, he was apparently rather more alarmed by the discovery that the sewer, the so-called 'Jade River', was 'absolutely *filthy*'.

According to his account, Keyes leapt on his Torpedo and galloped directly for the gate along the canal bed. Some US Marines had run down from the wall and were working furiously to loosen the great perpendicular wooden bars blocking the archway. They were helped by Chinese converts. Being very slight, Keyes managed to squeeze through the bars. Running up the sloping side of the sewer and through a gate, Keyes found himself in the gardens of the American Legation. One of the first people he saw was Edwin Conger, 'who appeared to be quite calm, and did not strike me as being particularly interested,' but who told Keyes the way to the British Legation. Running on, he suddenly found himself on the lawn of the British Legation, where he was met by Captain Wray of the Royal Marines. Wray introduced the filthy, sweating Keyes, still clutching his white ensign, to Lady MacDonald, who said in best British patrician fashion that she had no idea who he was but was simply delighted to see him anyway.

It is unclear who was actually the first man to enter the British Legation. According to a British diplomat's wife, Mrs Ker, it was a Sikh: 'an unforgettable sight, naked to the waist, sweating like a pig, hair tumbling on his shoulders. He kept waving his rifle and shouting "Oorah!" . . . and in a bunch, with officers and men, that old darling, General Gaselee, about twenty-five yards behind.'[2] She concluded that Lieutenant-Colonel Vaughan, 'cousin of the Headmaster of Rugby, *really* was the first man to reach the gate, but sat himself down in a ditch to light his pipe, and so got left.'

Many of the besieged felt dazed by the day's events. Few had slept since hearing the booming of the allied guns in the early hours. As the sun rose, the defenders had stood in excited groups around their barricades. People had made bets among themselves on where the relief columns were and when they would arrive. Some had been convinced they would fight their way in by noon, others that it would take at least twenty-four hours to force the city gates. Shells could be seen dropping thickly to the east and many, including Nigel Oliphant, went up on to the wall to watch. Monsieur Pichon was among the spectators and his soul was so moved by the beauty of the scene that he wrote a lyrical poem praising the azure skies, limpid light, and gilded horizon. The Reverend Allen was staggered that anyone could contemplate scenery at such a momentous time.

Yet for those with more pressing, if more mundane, responsibilities than the French minister, the tides of siege life were flowing as usual. The mills were grinding grain, soap suds were still splashing in Mr Brazier's efficient laundry, a cobbler was vainly trying to reconstruct the tattered remnants of a refugee American's only pair of shoes, the butcher was dividing up two horses for the midday meal – one of them a favourite mount of Sir Claude's, and Frank Gamewell was still flying from place to place superintending the Chinese converts in the work of reinforcing the defences.

The hours ticked by. Sarah Conger was feeling almost ecstatically happy but schooled herself to be patient, writing: 'We are waiting, and have learned how to wait.' Like others she ate her 'hard luncheon of horsemeat,'[3] as Morrison called it, and tried to keep busy. By 1.00 Lenox Simpson could stand it no longer and, receiving permission to lead a scouting party, he called for volunteers and slid over the barricades to the east of the Fu. Cautiously approaching the nearest enemy positions, they found them deserted – the Chinese riflemen were gone. Moving more boldly into the open, they came out on to a brick-littered street. The gruesome and squalid detritus of the past weeks lay all around – skulls picked clean by crows and dogs; 'pathetic wisps of pigtails half-covered with rubbish, broken rifles, rusted swords, heaps of brass cartridges.' Reaching the extreme eastern corner of the legation area, they found a fire still smouldering on the ground and earthenware bowls full of rice.

Moving on, Lenox Simpson caught fleeting glimpses of figures darting through the rubble, many throwing off their tunics and loosening their leggings as they ran. Approaching the pink walls of the Forbidden City, he saw bodies of troops heading north, 'always marching rapidly with hurried looks cast around them,' and troops of cavalry also heading north at a furious gallop. He realized he was witnessing nothing less than a general exodus. Climbing a wall to get a better view, he made out the tiny specks of advancing soldiers and knew it was the relief force.

Shortly before 2.00, a breathless messenger had arrived with news for Sir Claude MacDonald that foreign troops were beneath the Tartar Wall opposite the sluice gate. Oscar Upham, up on the wall itself, had a fine view. 'At 2.15 p.m.,' he later wrote, 'we sighted the English Sikhs in the Southern City opposite our own position on the wall.' To cries of 'The British are coming!' Sir Claude hurried to the gate in time to greet General Gaselee as he and his staff came through. He led them triumphantly to the British Legation, where Indian troops were already gathering on the tennis court. Morrison, hobbling about and anxious to capture the supreme moment of his journalistic career, wrote of the 'indescribable emotion'[4] as Indian troops – the First Regiment of Sikhs and Seventh Rajputs – poured on to the lawn of the British Legation. To the American Dr Martin's emotional eyes, these men with their long spears and high turbans 'appeared the handsomest men on whom my eyes had ever rested.'[5] The Sikhs and Rajputs were followed by the First Bengal Lancers and the Royal Welch Fusiliers. Morrison, after the euphoria of the relief had faded, made the curious comment that the commanding officer of the Welch Fusiliers 'was given the Companionship of the Bath for meritorious service in bringing his troops into Peking without a casualty except for drink.'[6]

Jessie Ransome was just getting dressed after resting on Lady MacDonald's bed when she 'heard a cheer which increased in volume every minute.' Rushing to the window, she was in time to see General Gaselee surrounded by Indian troops riding in and hurried to shake hands with them. She thought the Bengal Lancers looked magnificent and was delighted to see 'a real horse again.' Mary Gamewell had been stitching sandbags when she heard the sound of running feet and voices calling excitedly. Running outside she too saw the Indian troops. 'On they came up through the water gate almost on the run. First the turbaned Sikh warriors led by British officers, then the helmeted British.'

Luella Miner, one of the siege's most diligent diarists, wrote in her neat hand that 'this has been such a wonderful day that I can hardly write about it – the compound is swarming with foreign soldiers and we are overwhelmed with thankfulness.' She was fascinated by the 'black-faced, high-turbaned' Sikhs and touched by the British officer who stopped in passing to kiss 'a pale-faced girlie who looked as if she needed to be saved by a relief army.'

Polly Condit Smith had been debating whether to go across to the American Legation 'and take the cheerful bath which I had been indulging in each day lately . . . I was about to start with bathing paraphernalia and the little maid, when my inner consciousness was struck by something unusual happening out in the compound. I tingled all over, for my instinct had told me the troops had come.' She ran to the tennis court and found everyone else flying in the same direction. She was in time to see the Sikhs come in. 'It was queer to see these great fine-looking Indians in . . . huge picturesque red turbans strutting around the compound, and as they entered right into our midst they all whooped a good English whoop.' She watched a little blond Englishwoman, overcome at being rescued, fling her arms around the first Sikh she could reach, much to his embarrassment. Polly thought it entirely in keeping with the extraordinary events of the siege that 'these Eastern and heathen-looking Sikhs' should personify the relief.

Polly and Harriet Squiers rushed to find a good vantage point in Legation Street and were in time to watch General Gaselee enter, escorted by a squad of Sikhs. Gaselee jumped down from his horse and, 'showing on every inch of him the wear and tear of an eighty-mile midsummer relief march, he took our hands, and with tears in his eyes said, "Thank God, men, here are two women alive," and he most reverently kissed Mrs Squiers on the forehead.' There was still danger. Polly paid for leaving the comparative safety of the British Legation when a ricocheting bullet grazed her ankle and one tipped the top of her ear.

Bolting back into the legations, Lenox Simpson ran to the Hôtel de Pékin and suddenly a pungent smell greeted his nostrils. 'It was the smell of India!' Rajput troops were pouring into the courtyard, faces streaming, asking for water. In the British Legation compound he found a confused mass of marines, sailors, volunteers and diplomats laughing, cheering, clapping, talking, waving handkerchiefs and hugging. He later noted sourly: 'People you had not seen for weeks, who might have, indeed, been dead a hundred times without your being any the wiser, appeared now for the first time from the rooms in which they had been hidden and acted hysterically. They were pleased to rush about and fetch water and begin to tell their experiences.'

According to Nigel Oliphant, there were scenes of 'hysterical enthusiasm,' and for Lancelot Giles it was 'a moment of a lifetime' with 'shakings of hands galore! Women in tears! Sikhs patted on the back! Grimy gunners hugged!' For old China hand Arthur Smith it was a veritable 'riot of joy as is seldom seen in Asia.' He hoped somewhat grandiosely that he was witnessing 'the dawning Twentieth Century victorious against the Middle Ages, a potentially glorious Future vanquishing an inert and lifeless Past. In it was the seed of a New China, and Hope for the Far East.'

Yet more troops came pouring in and the confined space became a confused tangle. Some two hours after the British and having had a much harder fight, General Chaffee and the Fourteenth US Infantry arrived right in the midst of 'this wild welter . . . to add to the joy and the chaos.'[7] Mary Gamewell cheered and waved but was moved by the men's 'pitifully haggard faces'. Chaffee at once went to greet the Congers and Sarah saw tears in his eyes. He told her that hearing the fierce firing during the night he had known they were still alive but 'when the firing ceased for a time, we were sure we were too late, that all was over, that you were massacred. The awful thought of defeat, of failure, came over me.'[8]

The American officers were invited into the British Legation and there was a momentary silence as they entered. Dr Martin, 'with trembling voice, said: "We are glad to see you."' Conversation gradually picked up, but Colonel Daggett noticed that people spoke in low, subdued voices, as if under a spell no one was willing to break. A young woman with a little girl in her arms and another by her side suddenly confessed to Daggett that she and her husband had discussed what to do if the Chinese overcame the defences. They had agreed that if he were present at the time he would shoot his wife and children and then himself. If he were absent the mother was first to shoot the children and then herself. She told Daggett of her absolute terror of being tortured 'in all ways Chinese ingenuity could devise.'

The Americans, led by the Fourteenth US Infantry, had reached the walls of Peking to find that the Russians had been having a difficult time since their initial success in attacking the Tungpienmen in the early hours. Instead of being able to advance triumphantly into the city, they had found themselves pinned down under a devastating fire from the high Tartar

Walls to which the Chinese had retreated. Unable to escape the exposed position, General Vasilievski had been hit in the chest by a Mannlicher bullet as he desperately rallied his men on the lower wall of the Chinese City. Two Cossacks trying to carry him to safety were mortally wounded. The main Russian force had not arrived to reinforce Vasilievski's men until around 10.00 a.m.

The Americans, who had arrived shortly afterwards, proceeded to scale the wall to the south of the Tungpienmen, taking some of the pressure off the Russians. A twenty-year-old bugler, Calvin P. Titus, volunteered to be the first up the wall. He was a small man, just five foot seven, and weighed a mere 120 pounds. His commanding officer, Colonel Daggett, waited for someone else to offer but they did not. Titus duly swarmed up, unarmed, in an act of consummate courage for which he received the Congressional Medal of Honour and an appointment to West Point. Looking around him, he saw huts made of matting against the outer parapet of the wall. He checked that they were all empty, then signalled to Daggett that the coast was clear. Other officers and men followed and by 11.00 a.m. the regiment's flag was unfurled, the first foreign colours to fly on the walls of Peking. By noon there were sufficient American troops on the wall to force the Chinese to retreat from their vantage points around the Tungpienmen, through which American infantry and artillery now poured, shouldering the disorganized Russians to one side.

As the American relief force advanced through the southeast of the Tartar city they became embroiled in dogged street fighting. It took some hours to force their way through to the Tartar Wall, where they saw a US Marine signalling to them to enter the legations. General Chaffee gave the Fourteenth Infantry the honour of being first through the sluice gate in recognition of their gallantry that day and at the battle of Yangtsun. They marched in, flags flying to a storm of applause, to discover they were the runners-up by a mere couple of hours to the more fortunate British. Daggett reflected on the bad luck. The

Americans had done the fighting and 'the British gathered the fruits.' This, however, 'is not in disparagement of the British. They kept their agreement.'

The danger was not over yet and the legations were still under attack. According to Lieutenant Steel, everyone was talking and cheering and waving their hats 'whilst the bullets were flying thick overhead and banging on the roofs all high, no one caring a hang! The Chinese simply went mad when they realized we were in and let off every bally gun they had at random.' The wife of a Belgian engineer was hit – the only foreign woman to be wounded throughout the entire siege. 'It was only a flesh wound, but she happened to be very fat, and we were told no military probe could reach the bullet,' wrote Keyes. A Sikh who had been sent by General Gaselee to mount guard on the front gate was hit by a bullet through a loophole and promptly carried to the siege hospital. People were ordered to take cover but apparently did so with no more urgency than if they were coming in from the rain.

Mary Bainbridge wrote approvingly that the relief force had not been in more than an hour 'before they began work on the Chinese.' A detachment of Sikhs was dispatched to deal with the nuisance of snipers. Meanwhile, in the Fu, Colonel Shiba launched a final attack on the remaining manned Chinese barricades, driving off the attackers. Work began quickly to clear the surrounding streets and seize the larger yamens. The relieving force cleared snipers out of the Mongol Market 'who actually did not know that the relief was in the walls!!' wrote Giles. Captain Poole blasted a hole in the thick wall of the Imperial Carriage Park and occupied it with sixty marines. He was appalled to discover two mines already laid, complete with powder and fuse, and marvelled that they had survived 'this sword of Damocles.' 'If the troops had come one day or one night later, God only knows what the result would have been!'[9] wrote De Courcy of the Customs Service. Nigel Oliphant agreed: 'It gives us defenders a cold shiver to think how all the time these fiends were burrowing under the very places where we ate and slept.'

There had also been action up on the Tartar Wall. At the sight of British troops entering through the sluice gate, the Chinese had lowered the banners on their barricade on the wall and begun to fall back. American and Russian troops rushed forwards to seize the advantage. Private Daniel Daly of the US Marines was the first to reach the enemy's position, which he found deserted, but as Oscar Upham described, they could see hundreds of Chinese ahead of them. The marines surged forwards again towards the towering Chienmen, sweeping the enemy before them. Upham described with relish how one Chinese soldier darted behind a fence 'and was pumping away at us as fast as he could load.' A man from the Fourteenth Infantry pointed him out to Upham, yelling, '"There he is! Shoot him! Shoot!" I asked him why he didn't do a little shooting himself. The man did not reply but kept jumping up and down, yelling, "Shoot him!"' Upham duly obliged, hitting his man at the third shot. As soon as the gate was cleared, a US Marine scaled the ruins of the Chienmen and hoisted an American flag and 'the evening breezes caught and kissed its starry folds,' wrote a lyrical William Bainbridge.

The Reverend Frederick Brown had chosen not to accompany General Gaselee into the legations but to remain for a while outside, hoping to save respectable Chinese citizens from trigger-happy troops. 'Our men could hardly resist the temptation of shooting at every passing Chinaman, not being able to distin-guish between decent civilians and Boxers. I was able to save some lives, by keeping the officers informed as to who were peaceable inhabitants.' However, at last he too entered 'over the ankles in sewage and covered in filth.' He was invited to dine with some missionary friends but before the meal was through changed his mind. The menu of pony soup and brown bread followed by mule steak and musty rice was unappealing. As soon as politeness allowed he excused himself and went in search of army rations of bully beef and biscuit. As he ate his second meal, he reflected that the British had been extraordinarily lucky that day. They had been the last to set out and the first to arrive and had encountered no serious opposition. Their casualties had been minimal.

The British officers were invited to dine at the British Legation. General Barrow, who had already decided that Lady MacDonald was 'a very alert and managing woman,' sat 'next to Sir Claude under the picture of the Queen and enjoyed my champagne, but not the menu of mule flesh and rice.'[10] Colonel Scott-Moncrieff was struck rather more by his surroundings than the food and wondered whether he was dreaming: 'After the rough life of the past few weeks and the exciting events of the past day, I was sitting at a civilized dinner table with clean linen, silver, glass and all the surroundings of refined taste among ladies in evening dress.'[11]

It had been a strange and bewildering day for everyone and in the cool of the evening the relief force took stock of events. Roger Keyes later described how it had been 'just as if we had run into a garden party. The lawn was crowded with ladies, looking very cool, clean and nice – rather an excited garden party, but really like nothing else. Some of the men, who had run in from the barricades armed to the teeth, looked very fierce, but most of them were in flannels, having a quiet afternoon off . . . There were a good many American ladies, who all wanted to shake hands, and all said, "Pleased to meet you."' The relief force had felt shabby by comparison in clothing soaked with sweat and bespattered with mud and sewage from the canal. Colonel Daggett wrote: 'Having just come from such scenes as the scaling of the walls . . . their faces grimy, haggard, shrivelled, the contrast could not have been greater than between the parties now mingling with such affecting emotions.' It felt like arriving in an oasis after a long desert journey. Daggett saw soldiers stretched out in the shade of the legation's beautiful trees and noted the abundance of cool water.

The besieged certainly seemed to be in much better condition than the relief force had anticipated. One young woman wrote:

'They seem to have expected to find us lying gasping on the ground.'[12] Luella Miner explained tartly that the women looked so neat because 'the American woman who will not try to make herself look presentable under any circumstances is considered a disgrace to the sisterhood.' She asserted that any woman wearing a clean shirtwaist or collar had probably been saving it for the relief. It did not imply that the siege had not been both gruelling and dangerous. The Reverend Allen also defended the neat appearance of the besieged, attributing it, sensibly enough, to Mr Brazier's laundry.

Keyes later explained that he had not intended to belittle the defenders by describing the scene of the relief as a garden party. It was simply that the besieged were in a much better state than anyone had dared to hope. Like many of the rescuers, he soon realized that first impressions had been deceptive. A correspondent from the *Daily Graphic* who was struck initially by the contrast between the superficially pristine besieged and their haggard, rough-bearded rescuers, wrote: 'A second glance showed that the besieged were pathetically pale and thin. They looked in fact like a company of invalids.'[13] There was ample physical evidence of their ordeal. Colonel Daggett noticed the hundreds of thousands of bullet-marks on the buildings and the evidence of heavy artillery fire, while the ever fastidious Lieutenant Steel concluded that 'the state of dirt and filth in the Peking legations could hardly be exaggerated, sanitary arrangements practically nil.'

Such reflections reinforced their satisfaction that the British and the Americans had been first into the legations. According to Lenox Simpson, all sorts of excuses and theories were advanced to explain why the Russians, Japanese, and French had lagged behind – that their generals were acting prudently and wisely, that they were securing the gates of the city, even that they were engaged in capturing the Imperial Court. He learned about the prelude to the relief from a group of officers who were drinking champagne at the Hôtel de Pékin and noisily discussing events. 'They said that the Russians had attempted

to steal a march . . . on the night of the 13th, in order to force
the Eastern gates, and reach the Imperial City and the Empress
Dowager before anyone else. That had upset the whole plan of
attack, and there had then simply been a mad rush, everyone
going as hard as possible, and trusting to Providence to pull
them through.'

The Russian troops had eventually entered the legations an
hour or so after the Americans. Meanwhile, the Japanese had
been having a frustrating day. George Lynch, who was with
them, described their brave but futile attempts to blow in a gate
in the Tartar Wall: 'The Japanese engineers went forwards one
by one until twenty minutes passed and expanded into half an
hour. With cheerful and unwavering gallantry these men went
forwards to blow up that gate, across the open space over the
bridge, from which they could be fired on by hundreds of
Chinese. The attempt was absolutely hopeless. It was not that
there was any wavering amongst them after ten had been shot
. . . But it was a task that the bravest man could not accomplish.'
'Working like marionettes', they fired their guns again and
again, but they were of very light caliber – 'little war dogs',
Lynch called them – that 'spat their rather impotent projectile
against that great mass of centuries-old masonry.' He concluded
they might as well have been firing peashooters.

It was not until about 9.00 in the evening that the Japanese
at last succeeded in blasting their way in through the great
wooden doors bossed and studded with iron. Lynch found it a
hauntingly beautiful spectacle, with the deep circular archway of
the gateway forming 'an ebony frame for the ivory moonlight
picture within.' The attacking Japanese had no time for such
thoughts. They ran in, skewering Chinese with their bayonets so
that they 'squirmed and wriggled like a worm,' and finally
entered the legations late that night. They were not the last,
however. The French did not arrive until the next day after a
nightmarish march in which they had blundered across the path
of other allied forces and lost their way.[14]

Rescuers and rescued took stock of what had happened

during the siege. The tally was 66 foreigners killed and 150 wounded. The siege hospital had treated not only the injured but also some forty cases of sickness, two of whom had died. None of the foreign children had been wounded but six babies had perished due to the heat and the lack of suitable food. Characteristically, no record had been kept of Chinese deaths within the defences but the mortality rate among the convert children had clearly been heartbreakingly high.

Jessie Ransome thought the fact that no one had died of septic poisoning a great tribute to the hospital, but she knew her work there had taken its toll. Looking back, she wrote movingly of the 'constant sense of danger' and 'sickening suspense' that had dogged her. The besieged community was so small that she had known many of the sick and wounded personally. As yet another 'mangled heap of pain' was carried in, she had been unable to help wondering who would be next. Yet now that the hospital was about to close – the missionaries' offer to keep it open had been rather ungraciously refused on the grounds that 'the army had its own doctors and field hospital' – her feelings were tinged with something like nostalgia. She was grateful to have been allowed to work there and certain that 'the occupation it gave me was one of my greatest blessings during the siege.'

Polly was also in a thoughtful mood now that the siege was over and she was returning to the real world again – a world in which, as a well-connected socialite, she had many useful contacts. Colonel Churchill, the British military attaché to Tokyo, who had accompanied the Japanese relief force, had sent word to Polly's brother-in-law, the American naval attaché to Japan, that she was safe and well. 'How wonderful to think that, as the troops were marching up to Peking, the engineers were steadily placing the telegraph-wires, so that six hours after we were relieved a message went flying down to the coast with the tidings!' she wrote gratefully. General Chaffee also called. She had lunched with him and his wife in Havana the previous year and thought it delightful to see him again 'here in this wicked old Peking.'

However, like many of the besieged, she felt a curious melancholy. She and the Squierses dined that night at their little eight-sided Chinese table. As they opened all the tins they'd been so carefully hoarding, Polly realized, perhaps for the first time, the truth of the saying 'There is a sadness about the last time of everything.' She felt like a child playing a wild game of make-believe when adults say, 'Come, children, there has been enough of this.' The terrible times were past. Nothing remained now but to try to restore some sort of equilibrium to their lives and come to terms psychologically with their experiences and their own and others' behaviour. They were conscious that only those who were there would truly know what the siege had been like: 'We might all talk until doomsday, but the world will never understand.'

Lenox Simpson too felt a little depressed: 'We were mere puppets, whose rescue would set everything merrily dancing again – marionettes made the sport of mad events. We had merely saved diplomacy from an impossible situation.' He also shared Polly's view that no one would really appreciate what had happened during the past eight weeks, but for different reasons. He noted that an official diary had been kept and was convinced it would be full of diplomatic half-truths. He thought Morrison's lips would be sealed and that 'with an official history and a discreet independent version, no one will ever understand what bungling there has been, and what culpability.' His own highly colourful but in places dubious book *Indiscreet Letters from Peking* was no doubt intended to remedy the deficiency.

Dr Coltman was similarly reflective, and, he felt, a little wiser. For him the past few weeks had been an education in human nature. Siege life had accentuated people's mean and selfish characteristics as well as their qualities of heroism and self-sacrifice. 'People who in time of peace pass for very nice, sociable individuals, with no particularly mean tendencies, when subjected to deprivation in the food-supply, and their nerves became a bit shattered with the sound of whistling bullets, the shrieking of flying shells, or the dull thud followed by the crashing and grinding of solid shot, show up in their true bedrock character, and are meanness to the core.' He had seen new friendships blossom but old relationships dissolve under the pressure of privation. He had seen people beg for a tin of milk or a can of soup 'or some little delicacy or necessity from a friend having abundance of stores. Upon a flat refusal . . . the aforementioned friend realizes the depth of the former friendship and has no wish to continue it.'

Young Oscar Upham, one of the most honest diarists of the siege of Peking, took a more pragmatic view: 'Well the seige [sic] is ended so I think that I will close hoping that we will soon have the extreme pleasure of greeting our shipmates once more, which I suppose will be a great surprise to them. All through the siege we had never held out any hopes of a rescue and never gave it a second thought.' And so, in his neat level writing, he closed this chapter of his life.

However, the events of that hot Peking summer had not yet run their course.

IV
Murder, Rape and Exile

Scenes from the Boxer Summer

15

'TOUR OF INSPECTION'

The Emperor, the Empress Dowager, and indeed, the whole Court, had disappeared – had fled, was gone.
– Bertram Lenox Simpson

THE NEXT DAY, 15 AUGUST, did not augur well for international collaboration. Despite their late arrival and rain-sodden, mud-coated, and sorry condition, the French lost no time in trundling four guns on to the Tartar Wall and beginning to bombard the pink walls of the Imperial City. A group of ladies and diplomats gathered on the wall to watch and applaud. According to A. Henry Savage-Landor, the women 'stopped their ears as each shot was fired, and opened their mouths wide with admiration and yelled with joy when the shells were seen to explode a mile or so off.'[1] The officers courteously handed round their spyglasses to afford their guests a better view.

These proceedings were, however, a serious annoyance to General Chaffee, who was mounting his own attack on the Imperial City. An American officer, red-faced with fury, came galloping up to the French position. According to an amused Lenox Simpson, he demanded to know 'if the commander of these d—— pop-guns knew what he was firing at, and whether he could not see the United States army in full occupation of the bombarded points. He swore and he cursed and he gesticulated, until, finally, cease fire was sounded, and the guns were ordered down.' Monsieur Pichon reacted angrily, vowing that if the French were required to stop then so must everyone else.

US forces had been battering their way through a series of courtyards leading to the south gate of the Imperial City. Their objective was the dwelling place of the Son of Heaven – the Forbidden City itself. Sarah Conger climbed up on to the Tartar Wall to watch the efforts of her compatriots and saw the glistening yellow tiles quake. She thought it a wonderful sight. 'We were in a battle! But we were free and felt no fear with our own American soldiers.' Oscar Upham was also in a cheerful mood as he took part in the attack: 'The weather is fine and everyone is in good spirits. To see them one would think they were in anticipation of going to a circus although we all knew that we had a hard nut to crack before we reached the "Forbidden City".'

However, it was not to be. The Americans were within a hairsbreadth of their goal when a disgruntled General Chaffee commanded them to withdraw. The order was largely the result of French and Russian pressure at a conference of commanders that afternoon, where, after much wrangling, it was agreed that the allies should take a conciliatory approach towards the Manchu government. Colonel Daggett was probably close to the mark when he asked: 'Was it the success of the Americans during those eight hours that caused the conference to reach that conclusion?'[2]

American bitterness was exacerbated by the death of the popular and efficient artillery officer Captain Reilly, who had played a key role during the relief operation but was shot down as he commanded his guns. Oscar Upham described how a bullet entered 'his mouth just as he was giving an order and came out at the back of his head, killing him almost instantly.' He was buried that same day, his coffin draped with the Stars and Stripes. When Edwin Conger attempted to remove the flag as the casket was lowered into the ground, on the grounds that they were scarce, Chaffee thundered that if it was the last American flag in China it should be buried with Reilly. The tough old Indian fighter had his way. Polly Condit Smith thought him 'the personification of justice for the dead and wrath for the living.'

So the attack on the Forbidden City had been halted, but many were curious to know whether the emperor and the Empress Dowager were still within its walls. If there were to be a policy of conciliation, their role would be critical. Ever more colourful and dramatic rumours flew around the legations. 'We don't know if the Empress is here still or not; but it is generally thought she will commit suicide rather than be taken prisoner,' wrote Jessie Ransome. 'It is certainly a puzzle to know how things will be settled by all these foreign nations, or how it will be possible to work harmoniously for much longer.'

A curious Lenox Simpson rode up to the Imperial City in search of news just after the American attack had ceased. He discovered an elderly palace eunuch almost paralyzed with fear huddling by one of the Chinese guardhouses in the outer wall. The trembling eunuch pointed to the guardhouse and through the open door Lenox Simpson could see a confused mass of dead bodies. They had been bayoneted and were lying in a pool of reeking, congealed blood. Above them 'hung a miserable wretch, who had destroyed himself in his agony to escape the terror of cold steel.' His thin body dangling from a beam in the half-light in its long loose clothes looked pathetic and puppet-like. Even the unsqueamish Lenox Simpson found it a chilling sight.

Averting his gaze, he began to question the eunuch about the strength of the forces within the Forbidden City and the where-abouts of the emperor and the Empress Dowager. The eunuch answered willingly enough but then blurted out that it was no use, the foreigners were too late. 'The Emperor, the Empress Dowager, and indeed, the whole Court, had disappeared – had fled, was gone.' He was telling the truth. As Arthur Smith described, the enemy had, as it were, 'folded their tents like the Arabs and silently stole away.'[3]

Many accounts, often fanciful, have been written of the court's dramatic flight and it is impossible to reconstruct exactly what happened. It seems most likely that the decision to fly was taken at the last moment and that the court fled westward under armed escort in the early hours of 15 August. No proper arrangements had been made, and there must have been scenes of chaos in the moonlit courtyards of the Forbidden City. According to the scholar and magistrate Wu Yung, an official who later helped the Empress Dowager during her flight, the elaborate rituals of the court were tossed aside as Tzu Hsi disguised herself in the coarse, dark blue clothes of a Chinese peasant woman. Further indignities followed – the clipping of her long talons and the dressing of her hair like a common Chinese. She told Wu Yung that as she completed her hasty toilette she could hear bullets flying, 'making noises like the crying of cats' – a revealing simile, given her intense dislike of felines. In her haste she ransacked her closets, overturning boxes of blue and yellow silk handkerchiefs as she snatched up handfuls. As she gazed at her bizarre reflection she is said to have murmured, 'Who would have thought it would come to this?' She took with her an ancient and precious bloodstone that she believed 'protected her through all dangers.'[4]

Three wooden carts were found to convey the Imperial party. Tzu Hsi summoned the emperor, whom she had no intention of leaving behind as a bargaining counter for the allies, and demanded that he accompany her, together with her niece the empress and the loutish Heir Apparent. There were emotional scenes as the Imperial concubines – forbidden by decree to accompany the emperor – came to make their adieus. According to some stories, Kuang Hsu's favourite, the Pearl Concubine, begged either that the emperor be allowed to remain or that she be permitted to accompany him. The Empress Dowager, who disliked the Pearl Concubine, apparently lost her temper and shouted to her eunuchs to throw 'this minion' down a well in a corner of the courtyard. In the torchlight poor Kuang Hsu saw his beloved concubine wrapped unceremoniously in a carpet and tossed down the well to drown.

Reginald Johnston was told another version many years later by palace eunuchs. They claimed that Tzu Hsi tricked the Pearl Concubine by saying: 'We will all stay where we are, but we cannot allow ourselves to be taken alive by Western barbarians. There is only one way out for you and me – we must both die. It is easy. You go first – I promise to follow you.'[5] Then at a sign from the Empress Dowager, the eunuchs seized the girl and threw her down the well to drown alone. Princess Der Ling relates yet another version – that the girl was murdered by sadistic eunuchs – 'neuter-minions', as she called them – after the Imperial party had left but with the full knowledge and acquiescence of Tzu Hsi.

Whatever the case, the emperor never saw the Pearl Concubine alive again and was given little time either to grieve or to make his adieus. Tzu Hsi rapped out her orders and the makeshift cavalcade rumbled out of the Forbidden City. One can guess the old lady's feelings as she passed northward through the Gate of the Victory of Virtue and embarked on her long journey. Perhaps she thought back to that other escape forty years earlier, when, as a young concubine, she had accompanied the Imperial Court as it fled the ire of the advancing Anglo-French forces. It was said that she had advised the emperor to remain, arguing that it was the best protection against the depredations of the invaders: 'How, said she, could the barbarians be expected to spare the city if the Sacred Chariot [the emperor] had fled, leaving unprotected the tutelary shrines and the altars of the gods?'[6] On this occasion she had weighed the options but decided on flight. She was, nevertheless, leaving trusted courtiers behind. An Imperial decree of 10 August had ordered General Jung Lu and other grandees to remain in Peking and maintain a caretaker government if the court went into exile.

The journey was a rude brush with the realities of the situation. The roads were clogged with other carts as terrified citizens scrambled to leave the city.[7] There had been no time to prepare food but the Imperial eunuchs had assumed that they could buy provisions along the way. Instead they found that the countryside had been devastated. Even the wells were said to be polluted with piles of floating heads. According to Prince Su, who accompanied the royal party, they were escorted by a force of several thousand soldiers 'of various commands'.[8] Lacking any discipline, they pillaged, murdered and raped along the whole route. He claimed that they even stole the meals prepared for the Imperial table and it took drastic measures, even large-scale executions, to bring this rabble under control.

Tzu Hsi apparently looked like a wrinkled old peasant woman. Even the guards at the Summer Palace, where she paused briefly, failed to recognize her. On 17 August the bedraggled and desperate royal party and their shabby retinue halted outside the small town of Huailai, north of Peking, of which Wu Yung was the local magistrate. According to his account, the first he knew about his illustrious visitors was a note from the magistrate of a neighbouring district instructing him to provide, among other things, 'a table and full feast' for the emperor and the Empress Dowager, 'a table and kettle of food' for the accompanying nobles and officials, and 'much fodder for the horses.' Donning his official robes, including a purple cloth overcoat and oiled silk covering for his tasseled hat to protect him from the heavy rain, he set out to meet the royal party. He was shocked by their appearance, writing that they looked like 'dejected jackals'. The Boxers and disaffected troops had so ravaged the neighbourhood that all he could offer the Empress Dowager was a bowl of millet and green-bean porridge. He was worried that it was too coarse a food for her, but she apparently ate it gratefully, saying, 'In time of distress this is enough. Can I at this time say what is good and what is not good?'

Later she sent word via the chief eunuch that she had a desire to eat eggs. Wu Yung feared that there were none to be had but hunted high and low. He eventually discovered five in a drawer in a kitchen table and set about cooking them himself. His culinary efforts met with approval. The chief eunuch informed him that 'Old Buddha enjoyed the eggs very much. Of the five you sent she ate three, the remaining two she gave to the Lord of Ten Thousand Years [the emperor].' Wu Yung consolidated the favourable impression he had made by furnishing Tzu Hsi with paper lighters for her water pipe. Indeed, he received rather more favour than he bargained for. The grateful Empress Dowager ordered him to travel ahead of her retinue to obtain provisions. She also purloined his cook, who, once more food-stuffs were found, had prepared her delicious dishes of noodles and fried pork strips. Wu Yung had little choice in the matter and wisely responded: 'A cook is a small matter.'

The Imperial caravan then proceeded northwestward to Kalgan and Tatung, on the rim of the Mongolian plateau, before turning south for Taiyuan. The royal progress became grander and less pathetic the further the distance from Peking and the greater the certainty that the allies were not pursuing them. It was easier now for the emperor and the Empress Dowager to sustain the myth that they were making an official 'tour of inspection,' as the decrees grandly called it, rather than a panic-stricken dash from the clutches of a vengeful enemy. Tzu Hsi seems to have enjoyed looking about her at the people and the countryside, frequently halting to inspect interesting temples and monuments along the way. Perhaps it was stimulating and novel after her narrow and confined, albeit pampered, existence. She also apparently enjoyed conversing with Wu Yung, encouraging him to 'Talk as you please.' His candour brought him into conflict with the Imperial councillors, who accused him of stirring up trouble. Wu Yung reflected: 'I should not have told her everything. My purpose had been for her to know the affairs of the people. Things the great officials could not say, we small officials could.' It was a perceptive comment and an insight into how information was filtered and manipulated for the Imperial ear.

Tzu Hsi abandoned her coarse peasant clothes for elegant and luxurious Manchu garb and began to grow her fingernails again. Her aged bones were spared the joltings of the common wooden carts, which were replaced by mule litters and sedan chairs. Members of the Imperial Court caught up, one of them apparently bearing the Imperial seal, which had been forgotten in the precipitate departure. Soon the court was issuing edicts, receiving reports and accounts, and picking up the reins of government again. Respectful officials – provincial governors and viceroys – flocked to pay their respects and bring tribute. The Imperial party caused dismay to some. One poor district magistrate was apparently so shocked at the arrival of such magnificence on his doorstep that, 'crazy with grief and fear, he drank poison and died. When the Imperial party arrived they found an empty city, and supped that night on a few drops of soup.'

The retinue paused for three weeks at Taiyuan, the capital of Shansi, where the Imperial guests were apparently splendidly entertained in the governor's residence, the home of the reactionary Yu Hsien. Fabulous gold and silver tableware fashioned for another royal progress over a hundred years earlier was produced for their use. Some accounts relate that Yu Hsien himself regaled the Empress Dowager with an account of his murder of a group of foreign missionaries on 9 July. Tzu Hsi supposedly visited the courtyard where the executions had taken place and praised Yu Hsien for his splendid behaviour in 'ridding Shansi of the whole brood of foreign devils.'[10] The Heir Apparent is said to have skipped about gleefully waving an executioner's sword used in the killings.

However, the Taiyuan massacre meant that the allies might attack the city in revenge. The court therefore moved southwest in early October, reaching Sian on 26 October after a journey of some 700 miles. This erstwhile capital of the Tang dynasty, deep in the territory of the Moslem general Tung Fu-hsiang, whose troops had joined the Imperial procession, was considered a safe haven. The court in exile now prepared to sit out the winter. It

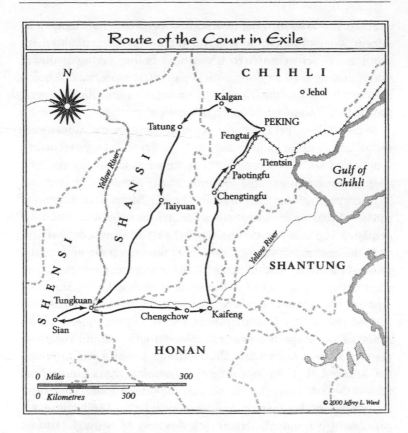

Route of the Court in Exile

needed funds, and messengers were sent out to the viceroys and governors with orders that tribute be sent to Sian at once.

The Empress Dowager brooded over what was happening to her beloved palaces and, even more important, her treasure. Meanwhile, according to Wu Yung, her nephew the emperor was being treated as a semi-idiot. 'The sound of his voice was light and thin like the hum of a mosquito' and, unless he had ceremonial engagements, he spent his days sitting on the floor amusing himself with the eunuchs. He liked to draw pictures of demons and spirits and sometimes he would sketch a large tortoise, inscribing the name of Yuan Shih-kai on its back. The tortoise was a symbol of homosexuality and hence intended as a grievous insult to the enemy who had betrayed his attempts at reform. Kuang Hsu would stick the picture on the wall and then shoot at it with a small bamboo bow before taking it down again, cutting it to ribbons with a pair of scissors, and scattering the pieces into the air 'like a swarm of butterflies.' It was probably the poor man's only consolation.

Meanwhile in Peking the news that the Imperial Court had slipped away came as little surprise. As Sarah Conger recorded simply and without comment: 'The Imperial Court left the city through the north gate the morning of the fifteenth. The armies did not pursue.' As early as July, Luella Miner had shrewdly predicted that 'that old lady is so smart that she will probably manage to be safe outside the city before the army gets here.'

In the absence of instructions from their governments, eagerly awaited down the field-telegraphs, the foreigners were uncertain what policy to pursue and therefore did nothing. Lenox Simpson raged at the impasse, knowing how quickly the court would be beyond reach. 'The mountain-passes would protect them. There could be no vengeance exacted; no retribution could overtake the real authors of this debacle. Nothing. It was a strange end.' He believed that, by one ingenious stroke, the Chinese had turned the tables on the allies and made them look ridiculous. No doubt thinking of the emperor's flight in 1860 and even perhaps of Napoleon's arrival in a deserted Moscow, he grumbled: 'Anyone might have anticipated something of this – there is a precedent in the histories. Yet history is only made to be immediately forgotten.'

Something else had also been forgotten. The foreign legations had been relieved on 14 August. The Empress Dowager and her retinue had decamped on 15 August. However it was not until 16 August that the horrific ordeal of the besieged community in the Peitang Cathedral was finally brought to a close.

16
THE ISLAND OF THE PEITANG

*Poor young man! He was flayed and the Boxers exposed
his skin and head within a few yards of our own walls.*
– Bishop Favier

ONE PERSON IN the Peking legations had remembered the beleaguered Peitang Cathedral. An elderly Catholic priest, Father
d'Addosio, set out alone and on donkey-back to bring the news
of the relief of the legations to his bishop. According to Dr
Martin, his eyes were streaming with joy and he was exclaim-
ing, 'Te Deum, Te Deum, Laudamus!' Father d'Addosio had
been rescued from the burning South Cathedral and it was said
that his shocking experiences had turned his hair white and
disturbed his mind. Yet he was 'so quiet and docile', according
to Polly Condit Smith, that no one had thought to restrain him.
The frail old man was murdered less than halfway to the
Peitang and his severed head impaled on a lance and displayed
outside a yamen.

The defence of the Peitang, the only Christian building within
the Imperial City, was regarded by contemporaries as little short
of a miracle. Dr Gilbert Reid wrote: 'If the siege of Peking is a

story of marvellous preservation, the story of the siege of the North Cathedral is still more marvellous.'[1] With what Morrison called 'wonderful foresight',[2] Bishop Favier had read the danger signals clearly, writing his famous letter of 19 May to Monsieur Pichon requesting help. He was convinced that the Imperial government and the Boxers were conspiring and, with a sinking heart, had watched the small red balloons loosed by the Boxers, their 'signals for assembling', waft ominously over the city.

The commander of the thirty French marines sent by Monsieur Pichon on 1 June to help guard the Peitang was Sub-Lieutenant Paul Henry. This young man of twenty-three was their commanding officer and, according to Bishop Favier, 'as pious as he is brave – a true Breton.' Henry quickly examined the sprawling compound, which encompassed not only the great Gothic-style cathedral but a chapel, convent, bishop's house, orphanage for some 500 children, dispensary, museum, printing press, several schools and a number of stables and other outbuildings. There were nearly 1,400 yards of wall, twelve to fifteen feet high, to be defended – a formidable task with so few troops. The southern approaches to the Peitang looked particularly vulnerable, and the young officer set about digging trenches, throwing up parapets, and loopholing the perimeter wall. He decided that in the event of an all-out attack, all must withdraw into the cathedral itself. Everyone was put to work building barricades, checking weapons and bringing in provisions. Favier shut his ears to the siren words of the city governor, who told him 'You have nothing to fear: the Boxers will not dare to attack the Pei-tang,' writing bluntly: 'This great mandarin is perhaps sincere, but, for my part, I believe his assertion to be absolutely false.'

By the end of the first week in June the sense of menace was growing. Fires were burning throughout most of the night, the firing of guns was heard constantly, and the French marines were keeping watch till dawn. On 11 June, Bishop Favier climbed to the top of his cathedral and watched smoke rising from the summer residences of the Europeans in the Western

Hills. Parties of Boxers, banners aloft, were parading openly through the city, and on 13 and 14 June the other churches and cathedrals of Peking went up in flames. A despairing Bishop Favier described how 'at half-past eleven o'clock the old cathedral of the Immaculate Conception in Nan-tan, the residence, the college, the hospital, the orphanage, all took fire; it is a horrible sight!' Like the diplomats, he wondered whether the Seymour relief expedition was close. However, unlike them he was not pinning his hopes on a swift deliverance.

The numbers in the Peitang Cathedral compound swelled as panic-stricken converts fled there. On 15 June all the Sisters were given Holy Communion because they expected imminent death. In the evening a group of frightened Catholic Sisters and children reached the cathedral in the very nick of time, a group of Boxers hard on their heels. Favier described the frightening scene: 'Their leader, on horse, is a lama or bonze [priest]; he precedes an immense red flag, surrounded by young Boxers who have undergone the incantations and are likewise dressed in red. They burned perfumed sticks, prostrated themselves on entering our street to the south, and then advanced in compact bands.'

The marines let them approach to within some 200 yards and then loosed a volley directly into them, wounding nearly fifty and putting the others to flight. They redoubled 'their noise and ferocious yells' but did not dare attack again. It was the first serious encounter between the defenders of the Peitang and the Boxers and it gave Favier some hope 'in manifesting the cowardice of our enemies.' However, the situation was deteriorating with each passing day. Reports of burning Christian shops and houses poured in. By 18 June Henry was further strengthening the Peitang's fortifications against a possible artillery attack, having noticed several Chinese cannon positioned to the south of the compound.

On 20 June a messenger brought news of von Ketteler's murder and the ultimatum to the ministers to leave Peking within twenty-four hours. The next day, as Favier noted bleakly in his diary, was the thirtieth anniversary of the massacres of

Christians in Tientsin and brought the last formal communication from the legations. A brave convert dodged through the tense streets with a short note from Monsieur Pichon. In characteristically depressed vein, Pichon informed the bishop that the ministers had abandoned any thought of leaving Peking and were taking sanctuary in the British Legation. Pichon concluded with a halfhearted attempt at cheerfulness: 'Let us prepare ourselves for the last journey but let us still hope.' Favier was in a fatalistic mood, writing: 'The situation is grave. Are we going to join the martyrs of Tientsin? We are preparing ourselves for all things.'

The community of the Peitang was now completely blockaded and as isolated from the outside world as the people in the legations. Bishop Favier conducted a census. He found he was responsible for 3,420 souls, of whom about two-thirds were women and children. There were seventy-one Europeans. The defence force was absurdly small for the task. In addition to Henry and his thirty French marines, a dozen Italian marines, including their twenty-two-year-old commander, Lieutenant Olivieri, had arrived on 5 June bringing the overall number of guards to forty-three. However, the able-bodied Chinese converts were formed into a volunteer force by the Catholic fathers, who made spears for them by fastening knives to the end of long poles. They also had the rifles of the marine detachments, seven or eight muskets, and a few old swords. Bishop Favier anxiously reviewed the food stores and calculated that, with a ration of a pound per person per day, there were enough provisions for a month.

Friday, 22 June was the Feast of the Sacred Heart. Early that morning, just as a priest was kneeling at the foot of the altar to begin the consecration service, a cannon-shot burst through a window on the east side, killing a woman. There was panic as people stampeded across to the west side of the cathedral, crowding into the chapels and sacristies. It was the beginning of a wholesale attack as the Peitang came under fire from Krupp guns firing 'the latest improved Schrapnel bombs.' Brick columns and windows shattered. The façade of the cathedral was damaged and its steeples were already in ruins. The attacks became so violent that by 3.30 in the afternoon, Favier believed their last hour had come. By 5.00 the Chinese had positioned 'an ordinary cannon' some three hundred yards from the main gate. One of its first shots blew in a panel. 'Greatly excited by so great audacity,' Lieutenant Henry and Favier's colleague Bishop Jarlin, a man of martial tendencies, acted together. They led a sortie of four marines and thirty converts and managed to seize the gun at the cost of two converts killed and two wounded.

Next day the artillery attack resumed unabated. Favier sat on a bench near the compound's Great Gate watching the beautiful marble façade of his church being blown to smithereens. A lucky shot toppled the marble cross that Bishop Favier had fixed to the apex of the cathedral thirteen years earlier. He vowed to replace it if he survived. Chinese troops sheltering behind the walls of nearby ruined houses were also aiming thousands of rounds from their Mauser repeating rifles into the compound. Sometimes the besieged could hear the sound of heavy firing coming from the legations and wondered what was happening there. On 25 June, Favier wrote: 'It seems that a great battle is being fought on the side of the Legations.'

The attacks on the Peitang varied in intensity but were almost constant. Stress was acute as defenders wondered when the next attack would begin, how strong it would be, and whether it would overwhelm the garrison. On 26 June, Favier wrote that the Boxers had set fire to all the houses adjoining the compound and were placing ladders and scaffolding against the Imperial City walls 'so as to be able to shoot more conveniently.' Defenders were regularly being wounded, but unlike in the legations, there was no doctor or surgeon at hand. On 27 June, Henry's second-in-command, Jouannic, was mortally wounded in the shoulder during a sortie near the south entrance to collect rifles abandoned by the Chinese. He did not die until after midday on 30 June, but by the time he was buried at 5.30, simply and quietly in the cathedral garden amid a hail of cannon balls, his body was already decomposing in the heat. All funerals had to be prompt to prevent the spread of disease.

Earlier that day the besieged had been surprised to see what appeared to be an Imperial sight-seeing party some twelve hundred yards away in the middle of one of the palace lakes. An indignant Bishop Favier thought he could make out 'Prince Tuan, the Empress and other High personages,' who had come to look on the bombardment 'as upon a display of fireworks.' The incensed marines wanted to fire on the group but Favier dissuaded them from such a provocative act 'in order not to excite an already too violent hatred.'

Quite apart from the hazards of shot, shell and incendiary attacks, living conditions were becoming very unpleasant in the Peitang. On 1 July, the inmates had their first taste of ass's flesh. Favier noted grimly that horses and mules would follow but that there were only eighteen of them. All the vegetables and salted greenstuff had been eaten and the heat and humidity were making everyone feel depressed. There was not even the solace of smoking. The tobacco had run out and people were trying to make a substitute from the dried and powdered leaves of pear trees. In addition, smallpox had broken out among the children. By 3 July as many as fifteen were dying each day.

As the siege wore on, the prisoners of the Peitang became more resourceful at defending themselves. The marines used dolls dressed in French marines' hats to draw fire so they could pick off snipers. Watchmakers among the Chinese converts made excellent cartridges for the Mausers and other guns. The besieged were also able to manufacture powder for a cannon they managed to seize from the enemy. Pierre Loti, a French naval officer who visited Bishop Favier after the siege, described how 'the seminarians made powder from the carbonized branches of trees in the compound and from saltpeter, which they discovered in a Chinese arsenal after climbing over the walls during the night.'[3] Nevertheless, Henry kept a careful record each day of the number of rounds fired by his men and of the number remaining. The men were very sparing. Usually fewer than 100 rounds were fired per day. On 5 July, for example, Henry noted only 13 rounds fired and 7,678 remaining. On 14 July, after firing 74 rounds, 7,024 remained.

Unlike the situation in the legations, famine was probably a greater danger than shortage of ammunition. On 6 July all the stores – rice, wheat, beans, and millet – were carefully weighed and checked. Favier was relieved that nearly 60,000 pounds remained. If they maintained the daily ration of a pound per person, there would be supplies for a further twenty days, by which time, he reckoned, they would have either surrendered or been relieved.

Soon, though, the defenders were facing a new hazard. The Boxers began to manufacture exploding missiles, which they hurled into the cathedral. Bishop Favier called the device a '*pot à feu*', or 'fire-pot'. It was 'a kind of casserole filled with two or three pounds of gunpowder and inflammable stuff, and caused to explode by a long fuse.'[4] They also launched fire rockets consisting of a hammered-copper tube about two feet long, tipped with a strong conical point. A wooden stick about ten feet long was fixed to one end. The rockets could penetrate a roof as easily as a loaded ball and brought a dangerous risk of fire. On one day alone the Boxers sent more than 250 of these devices crashing into the Peitang but the besieged again proved their resilience, positioning casks, bathtubs, and buckets full of water at strategic points, ready to douse any fires.

However, the artillery shelling continued as relentlessly as before. The cathedral's clock tower was completely demolished. Everyone was becoming exhausted and Favier wondered how much longer they could hold out. Life had become precarious. On 11 July a Mauser bullet passed through Bishop Jarlin's hat and Favier attributed his survival to divine intervention. There was also a very real danger of being undermined. The defenders found and destroyed a number of unfinished mines beneath their compound but were unnerved by the sound of heavy blows coming from the west side. Their suspicions were further aroused when they saw lamas evacuating a nearby temple. 'Is the army of relief approaching, or do the lamas think that the neighbourhood is going to be blown up?' wondered Favier in his diary.

The defenders began to dig countermines but on 18 July their fears were confirmed when a huge explosion left twenty-five dead and twenty-eight wounded. A horrified French marine described a scene resembling a butcher's shop 'where bits of waste meat were being dragged out';[5] fragments of flesh and severed limbs were spattered about and part of someone's chest was smashed against a wall. Enemy soldiers up on the Imperial City wall fired down on the rescuers as they tried to collect the remains in baskets. Lieutenant Henry wrote less emotionally, simply recording the number of deaths and calmly noting that 'the defensive state had not changed.'[6] However, the young man chose that day to pen his will, bequeathing, among other legacies, 100 francs to the Catholic missions in China.

Provisions were now starting to run low and on 28 July the already reduced ration was cut again to a meager eight ounces a day. Even on that basis there was food for just ten more days. Hard on the heels of this discovery came one of the most demoralizing events of the whole siege. On 30 July, the Chinese fiercely attacked the north wall, throwing blazing brands on to the cathedral roof. Henry raced over there and climbing quickly on to a firing platform built against the wall began to direct return fire. Suddenly a Chinese bullet went straight through the shoulder of a marine called Callac, who was standing at his post in front of Henry, and hit Henry in the neck. Almost immediately a second bullet hit him in the side. Slipping down from the platform, Henry staggered some fifty paces before collapsing into the arms of his men. Callac, although wounded himself, vainly tried to staunch the blood pumping from the gash in Henry's neck by pushing two fingers into the wound. A Chinese priest called Tso gave Henry the last rites – Favier had positioned his priests at strategic points in the defences so that they could administer the last sacrament to the mortally wounded.

Twenty minutes later Henry died in the priest's arms. His wound prevented him speaking but all the accounts note that he had a smile on his lips. 'We shed tears but once during the siege, and it was on this day. Never before have we been so low,' wrote Favier. Henry was buried beneath a statue of Our Lady of Lourdes in the cathedral gardens. The defenders tried to console themselves by remembering Henry's serene smile as he died and recalling, as an omen, how that very morning Henry had said: 'When God has no more need of me to defend the Peitang, he will come for me.'[7] The command of the defences was now shared. The Italian lieutenant Olivieri was appointed military commander while Favier took overall charge.

As if sensing the defenders' depression and despair, the attackers resorted to psychological blackmail. Boxers shot arrows into the compound with messages for the converts. They urged the Christians to abandon the foreigners and return to the old ways. 'You, Christians, shut up in the Pei-tang, reduced to the greatest misery, eating leaves of trees, why do you resist? We have levelled cannon and set mines against you, and you will be destroyed in a short time. You have been deceived by the devils of Europe; return to the ancient religion . . . deliver up Bishop Favier and the others, and you will have saved your lives, and we will give you to eat. If you do not do so, you, your wives and children will all be cut into pieces.'

The Boxers believed that Bishop Favier was the dominant foreign devil in the Peitang. They saw him as a demonic prince and were convinced he could render himself invulnerable by smearing his face with menstrual blood. They believed that the reason their attacks on the Peitang were failing was that the defenders had draped the skins of women from the cathedral spires and nailed naked women and foetuses torn from the bellies of pregnant women to the façade. They also thought that the foreigners had a powerful weapon in a so-called ten-thousand-women flag, woven from female pubic hair, which sapped the power of the Boxer gods.[8]

Favier was proud that none of the converts were seduced by the Boxers' blandishments and propaganda despite the worsening conditions. By 2 August the besieged were facing starvation.

The dogs that gathered to feed on the dead bodies of Boxers and Imperial soldiers were hunted, killed and eaten. Favier later described how 'we were obliged to cook the leaves of trees, and roots of dahlias and cannae, stems and the bulbs of lilies; these, stewed together, increased the small pittance of food allowed to each.' The suffering of the children was hard to bear – for Favier it was an experience he would never forget. 'At night all the children occupied the one place,' he wrote, 'trying to protect themselves against bullets and, especially, mines. Two or three hundred children were crying for hunger; the intense heat kept me from sleeping and I felt as though I were listening to the bleating of a flock of little lambs destined for sacrifice.'

By 5 August, the bishop was writing that 'we can resist balls, bullets and bombs' but that there was 'no defence against famine.' Only 7,000 pounds of food remained. He decided to distribute this at a rate of 1,000 pounds a day to the 3,000 or so inmates of the Peitang. In seven days the stocks would be exhausted. On 9 August, Olivieri described how 'the Chinese Christians dispute over the skins of the last asses which they butchered . . . We are in extreme distress, and yet no signs of the European troops.'9 A few Christian converts, unable to bear the hunger pains, ventured out. Three were captured by Boxers and hacked to pieces.

On 10 August, with only two days' food supply remaining, there were difficult choices to be made. Some 400 pounds of rice and a mule were set aside to enable the defence force to survive a further ten days. The question now was 'whether anything shall be reserved for ourselves [the European priests] and the Sisters,' as Favier wrote. Until this point the food had been distributed equally between the foreigners and the Chinese, unlike the practise in the legations. The idea was unanimously rejected, although someone pointed out that 'we deserved greater pity than the poor people, since they could eat the leaves of trees, and we could not.' Each of the foreigners was, therefore, given a two-pound loaf of bread as a last reserve. At the same time, rations were reduced to two ounces per person per day. At that rate supplies could be stretched to last six more days.

It was a desperate situation and the bishop decided he must try to communicate with the legations, from which, though only several miles away, he was separated 'as completely as if they had been situated at the North Pole.'[10] Favier had already tried several times to send messages to the legations. On each occasion, however, his courier had been caught and killed. The head of one unfortunate young man was displayed before the walls of the Peitang garnished with his own entrails. Now the bishop felt he had no option but to ask one more of his converts to run what he knew was a terrible risk. 'On the 10th of August, one of them again sacrificed himself to inform the minister of our being in the last extremity of need.' Again the attempt failed. 'Poor young man! He was flayed and the Boxers exposed his skin and head within a few yards of our own walls,' wrote Favier.

Yet worse followed. Early in the morning of 12 August, a violent explosion shook the Peitang when 'a mine more terrible than the others burst under the nuns' quarters where the children's crèche was.' It blasted a crater seven yards deep and forty yards wide, burying five Italian marines with their officer Olivieri and over eighty Chinese, including fifty-one babies. After three-quarters of an hour's frantic digging among the rubble, Olivieri was brought out alive: 'They succeeded in uncovering one of my hands, and finding it still warm, redoubled their efforts until my whole body was free,'[11] he later wrote, astonished at his own survival among the nest of beams that had crashed around his bed. Protected from inhaling the worst of the dust by his mosquito net, which had wrapped itself around his face, he had only been slightly wounded in the head and the right foot. However, the rest of his men were dead or dying and all 'horribly mutilated',[12] as he wrote sadly in his report. Sister Vincenza, a tiny Neapolitan nun and a skilled pharmacist who had tried to care for the babies in the suffocating heat, carrying them out in batches of six for a daily airing in an umbrella, said that after that day she never felt young again.

The explosion of the mine had left an enormous breach in the wall and at that moment, given all the confusion, the Peitang could easily have been overrun. 'We appeared to be lost,' wrote Olivieri. 'But true to their character the Chinese did not advance to the assault.'[13] The next day another mine was discovered. No one was injured, but as Olivieri recalled, 'the native Christians went almost mad with terror; they fled away from the wall screaming and wailing. Their minds were over-excited, they imagined every sound to be an explosion. The confusion was indescribable and it required all our efforts to calm the natives.'[14]

It seemed like the end. But then the Boxers began to cry out: 'The devils from Europe are approaching!' They promised to annihilate the converts before they could be rescued, but in the early hours of 14 August, the starving and despondent inhabitants of the Peitang themselves heard the sound of distant firing from the east. Olivieri remembered how 'all rushed to the open, regardless of the shot which still continued to fly. All wished to hear more distinctly the roar of the guns of our deliverers. Then the joy, the immense joy, it produced a choking sensation and found expression in a convulsive cry which burst forth like an impetuous wave of sound on all sides. The hunger, the terror, the tears, all were forgotten.'[15] The jubilant defenders could see Chinese banners being lowered from the walls and Boxers and Imperial soldiers beginning to slip away. By 5.00 in the afternoon they could see five strange foreign officers up on the walls, a marine signalling to the east, and an American flag being waved. 'We are again able to speak, smiles come to our lips,' wrote a grateful Favier.

The next day, 15 August, the community waited expectantly. 'Until nine o'clock in the evening we hoped that they would come to deliver us,' wrote Favier. But no one came. Olivieri began to worry that the allies had, after all, been repulsed. However, the following day the bishop, who had just celebrated Mass, heard heavy firing from the south. Excited converts ran to tell him they could see foreign soldiers. The bishop had already hoisted a large

French flag with the signal 'We ask for immediate relief.' Now he sounded a bugle three times. The reaction was not encouraging: 'No response, no hurrah, came back . . . but . . . a rain of projectiles poured down upon us. A bomb exploded at my feet.' He just had time to shelter behind a brick column. Soon, however, Japanese troops were forcing their way in. A Japanese captain climbed over the wall with the help of a ladder passed down to him and shook hands with Bishop Jarlin. An Italian marine rushed up to Olivieri shouting joyfully, 'We are saved!'[16]

The action of the Japanese had, in fact, taken the other allies by surprise. The Peitang was seen as a French responsibility and on 15 August a small French rescue party had attempted but failed to get through. The following day, French troops, supported by British and Russian contingents, had moved through the deserted streets to capture a gate in the Imperial City wall close to the Peitang compound, preparatory to relieving it. However, a curious sight had then met the affronted gaze of General Frey: 'What was our surprise to see ahead of us between 250 and 300 Japanese whose presence nobody could explain.'[17] The Japanese had simply slipped out early, without fuss, and done the deed. However, the fact remained that the relief of the Peitang had been very tardy.

The cathedral was an awesome sight. 'What a wreck!' wrote the journalist A. Henry Savage-Landor. 'Hardly a foot square of its façade had not been hit by shell or bullet. The greater portion of the upper part had collapsed and the handsome marble ornamentations of the doors and windows were badly damaged, while the coloured glass . . . was broken and shattered in a pitiable manner.'[18] He believed that the defence of the Peitang had been truly heroic. Many shared his view. Sarah Conger visited the Catholic Sisters of the Peitang and 'heard their sad bitter story, and saw the fearful wrecks.' Morrison was moved, writing in his diary of 'the miracles of the Peitang,' while Luella Miner was shown around by a 'bright sweet-faced Portuguese nun' and saw the 'great yawning pit' left by the mine that had exploded under the babies. She realized that 'we at the British Legation experienced few of the horrors of those two months.'

Over 400 people, including 166 children, had died during the siege of the Peitang, which, unlike the attack on the legations, had been relentless and continuous. There had been no truces. The defenders had also been completely cut off, unlike the legation community, who after mid-July had begun to receive reliable messages from the outside world. A weary Bishop Favier assessed the damage of the past weeks to his community: 'In Pekin, three churches, seven large chapels, the colleges, hospitals – all are destroyed . . . The Peitang . . . damaged by shells, is the only building undestroyed . . . In short, the ruin is almost entire, the work of forty years is nearly annihilated; the courage of missionaries, nevertheless, is not on the wane; we shall begin over again.'

17

THE FAITH AND FATE
OF THE MISSIONARIES

The horror of it seems too great to realize. – Luella Miner

BISHOP FAVIER COULD, at least, reflect that he had saved his people
from the dreadful fate meted out to converts and missionaries in
the rural areas during what Luella Miner called the 'summer's
carnival of crime.' News of this was now trickling through. Sarah
Conger described how 'most heart-rending reports are coming in
from different quarters.' She recounted the tale of a four-year-old
Christian child, Paul Wang, who was stabbed with swords and
spears and thrown three times into a fire, but who 'manifested
such tenacity of life that the leading Boxers bowed to him, and
turned him over to the village elders, saying that Buddha was
protecting him.' A shocked Luella Miner wrote that 'the horror
of it seems too great to realize.' She found it difficult to sleep as
her mind resonated with tales of convert children whose heads
had been pulled off; people buried alive in coffins; others
wrapped in cotton, saturated with oil, and set alight. 'One is
taken back to the time of Nero,' she wrote. Thousands had been
murdered. Bishop Favier later estimated the number of Catholic
deaths alone at 'not less than 30,000.'[1]

However, it was the news of the murder of well over two hundred foreign nuns, priests, and missionaries and their families, including many children, that evoked the greatest horror among the foreign community.[2] Arthur Smith catalogued the fate of many missionaries. He described how for days and weeks in succession they were 'confronted by mobs, chased from village to village, into mountains and swamps, obliged to take refuge in abandoned huts, in grave-yards and often in caves of the earth. They were hunted by armed bands like wild beasts, and when caught were beaten, dragged on the ground . . . tied hand and foot, and carried to Boxer altars that it might be decided by the spirits when, where and how they should be murdered. Sometimes they were saved because the villagers were afraid to have them killed in their village, sometimes by a timely fall of rain, and again by the instinctive pity of Chinese for the poor suffering children and the agony of their mothers.' A. Henry Savage-Landor recorded women killed by impaling, flaying or suffering such torments as the unfortunate Mrs Cooper, whose breast and shoulders became so blistered by the sun as she was driven half-naked like a sheep from village to village 'that great ulcers formed, which became filled with maggots before death came to her relief.'[3]

Far from the sanctuary of Peking or Tientsin, vulnerable, isolated and often with their children to protect, many missionaries in northern China had lived through terrifying times. Among the greatest trials were the lack of communications and the uncertainty. Should they stay in their missions and try to protect their flock? Should they flee to the coast or seek sanctuary in the hills? Some, like the Yale-educated Horace Pitkin in Paotingfu, some seventy-five miles southwest of Pcking, were resigned: 'We can't go out to fight – we have no soldiers. We must sit still, do our work – and then take whatever is sent us quietly.'[4] Luella Miner recalled the brave letters this young man sent to her mission in Tungchow when he was already 'living face to face with death.' In early July, after fighting until his ammunition was exhausted, he was killed together with all the remaining Catholic and Protestant missionaries in Paotingfu.

Luella Miner later heard that one of the missionary women had been stripped and dragged to a temple, where she was raped before being beheaded. She wrote: 'It is the first case I know . . . for unlike the Turks the Boxers have not as a rule been swayed by lust as well as savage cruelty.'

For many, the psychological torture was the worst. Eva Jane Price, a strong-looking, lantern-jawed woman, left one of the most moving accounts of a missionary family's ordeal, a true 'letter from the dead.' She and her husband, Charles, both from Des Moines, Iowa, had left America for China in 1889 as members of the American Board Mission. They settled at a mission in Shansi where life was already stressful, given the isolation. Nervous breakdowns and depression were commonplace among the mission community. One of Eva's friends had gone mad and another had committed suicide. In the summer of 1900, however, the province became a death-trap because of the malign influence of its governor, Yu Hsien. As events escalated around their mission station in late June 1900, Eva decided that 'it may be well to keep notes of these troublous times.' She found it difficult at first to grasp what was happening, writing: 'It is hard to realize we are the same persons who, for more than ten years, have lived here in peace and quiet.'

Her diary captures the atmosphere of mounting anxiety, the effort of 'trying not to talk about the danger,' and the impact of 'disturbing letters or rumours' that arrived at nightfall, making it impossible to sleep. The Prices heard that all the foreigners in Peking had been massacred but had no way of authenticating the reports since all lines of communication, post and telegraph, had been cut. They were dependent for their lives and that of their daughter on the goodwill of the local magistrate. He seemed well disposed towards them personally but had to bend with the prevailing wind. One day he was issuing notices favouring the Boxers and on the next insisting that the foreigners be respected. The Prices took the precaution of packing several trunks with necessities and secreting them in the chicken house together with most of their money.

One evening as Eva was putting her daughter, Florence, to bed she heard another missionary cry out, 'They have come!' A Boxer mob was looting the nearby house of another missionary, Mr Atwater, and he and his family had fled. The Prices now prepared for the worst. Their servants bound up their heads with dark cloth to make it harder to be seen or grabbed by the queue and sharpened knives to use as weapons of defence. Charles Price, an American Civil War veteran, grabbed a gun. Eva dressed her daughter again and packed another box of clothes. Everyone waited, quiet but on tenterhooks. Then Elizabeth Atwater arrived with her little girls seeking sanctuary for the night. She told of a terrifying attack but of how the local magistrate had saved them in the very teeth of the mob. He sought out the chief instigators of the rioting and had them savagely punished. However, the missionaries knew that his attitude might change at any moment.

Again it was a question of waiting and praying but the mental strain of the uncertainty and alternating hope and fear was terrible. Eva wrote: 'If we are to be murdered, one can but pray that it may come quickly and end our terrible suspense.' On 30 June she wrote: 'Nights are continual hours of anxious suspense, starting at every sound, and imagining an unruly mob surrounding us and taking our lives.' She was so afraid that 'the heart refuses to act properly and knees and legs shake in spite of all effort to be brave and quiet, trusting in God.'

On 29 July, the Prices and all the foreign missionaries at their station were told that by order of the emperor they were to be escorted out of Shansi to the coast. They suspected this was a ruse to kill them and attempted to escape into the mountains but their plans were betrayed. On 1 August, Eva Price penned her last letter. Addressed to 'Dear, dear Home Folks,' it spoke of her belief that 'the wicked Governor' of Shansi, Yu Hsien, intended to exterminate all the foreigners. She wrote of their continued hopes of surviving but also that 'we are all expecting to die.' Her letter was carried beyond the city gates by a devoted Chinese convert and teacher, Fei Chi-hao, who passed it on to a network of other converts before returning to the Prices. Two days later, Elizabeth Atwater wrote her letter of farewell to her family in America, which also eventually reached its destination: 'We have tried to get away to the hills, but the plans do not work. Our things are being stolen right and left, for the people know we are condemned . . . I have loved you so much, and know you will not forget the one who lies in China . . . I am preparing for the end very quietly and calmly . . . I do not regret coming to China, but I am sorry I have done so little. We will die together, my dear husband and I. I used to dread separation.'[5]

On 15 August the Prices, the Atwaters and a small group of fellow missionaries climbed into two carts. With their baggage following behind, the small convoy, escorted by twenty Chinese troops, wound its way through the city. The entire population had turned out to watch their departure. Fei Chi-hao was with them, but Charles Price had made him promise to escape and tell their story should anything happen to the missionaries. Unknown to them, a further twenty Chinese soldiers were travelling a few miles ahead. At each village through which they passed their commanding officer offered the village elders a choice – to pay him a large sum or to enjoy the dubious privilege of having the foreigners slain in their village. Some twenty miles from the city a village at last refused to pay. The soldiers took up position in a sorghum field and waited. The missionaries had no means of defending themselves when the attack came. A few days earlier they had been forced to hand over their little arsenal of weapons, which included two revolvers, a shotgun and a Winchester. Fei Chi-hao fled for his life but was told by eyewitnesses that all the missionaries, men, women and children were cut down with swords and bayonets and their bodies stripped and buried.

In late July, the Prices and the Atwaters had heard stories of a massacre of missionaries in Taiyuan some fifty miles away, which had greatly added to their mental distress. If true it meant that thirty-three of their friends – including the Atwaters' two eldest girls, Ernestine and Mary, who were at school there – had been killed. The stories were, in fact, entirely true. The largest single massacre of foreign missionaries had taken place in Taiyuan on 9 July under the personal direction of Yu Hsien. According to Arthur Smith, the horrible events were witnessed by a Baptist convert swept along with the crowd. A group of foreign missionaries with their wives and children, some Catholic priests and nuns, and several Chinese converts were taken to the yamen of Yu Hsien, stripped to the waist, and slaughtered in the courtyard.

According to the convert's famous account: 'The first to be led forth was Mr Farthing (English Baptist). His wife clung to him, but he gently put her aside, and going in front of the soldiers knelt down without saying a word, and his head was struck off by one blow of the executioner's knife. He was quickly followed by Mr Hoddle, and Mr Beynon, Drs. Lovitt and Wilson . . . Then the Governor, Yu Hsien, grew impatient and told his bodyguard, all of whom carried heavy swords with long handles, to help kill the others.'

Once the men were dead it was the women's turn. 'Mrs Farthing had hold of the hands of her children who clung to her, but the soldiers parted them, and with one blow beheaded their mother. The executioner beheaded all the children and did it skilfully, needing only one blow, but the soldiers were clumsy, and some of the ladies suffered several cuts before death.' One woman, Mrs Lovitt, held her little boy Jack tightly by the hand and pleaded: 'We all came to China to bring you the good news of the salvation by Jesus Christ; we have done you no harm, only good, why do you treat us so?' It had no effect. A soldier removed her spectacles and cut off her head with two blows of his sword.

It was then the turn of the Catholics. An elderly bishop with a long flowing white beard tried to remonstrate with the governor but received a cut across his face for his pains before being decapitated. The nuns and priests were then quickly killed. Then a further group of Protestants were led out and murdered.

In all, forty-five foreigners – thirty-three Protestants and twelve Roman Catholics – met their deaths in that hot, crowded courtyard, together with a number of Chinese converts. According to the Baptist witness, 'All were surprised at the firmness and quietness of the foreigners, none of whom, except two or three of the children, cried or made any noise.' The bodies were left where they had fallen and were stripped that night of clothing, rings and watches. The next day some of their heads were displayed in cages on the city wall.

The massacre made Yu Hsien hugely popular. When he left the city he was escorted by thousands of people who had prepared wine and refreshments. His 'boots of honour' were hung on the city gate to commemorate his virtues, and a stone tablet was erected 'to glorify his achievements in clearing the province of the hated foreigners.'[6]

There were, however, some miraculous escapes. A party of American missionaries joined forces with ten Swedish missionaries and succeeded in escaping across the Gobi desert. Their remarkable caravan consisted of twenty camels, nineteen horses and six camel carts. As one of them later recalled, 'The heat was intense, and the air was like that of an oven.'[7] After thirty-eight days in the desert they reached the Mongol city of Urga to find that a religious festival was about to begin and that thousands of wild and hostile Mongol soldiers were converging on the area. Only when they reached the Russian frontier town of Kiatka did they finally feel safe.

The Reverend Archibald Glover's account of his family's escape captured the popular imagination. Together with his heavily pregnant wife, Flora; their children, Hedley and Hope; and a young companion, Jessie Gates, he was a member of the China Inland Mission. In early July they decided to flee their station in Shansi, packing their mule litters by lantern light. Soon, however, they were overtaken by a mob and put on trial, accused of poisoning wells, causing the drought, even using babies as fish bait. They were sentenced to death, stoned, carried in litters 'in a kind of sacrificial procession,'[8] and spattered with excrement. At one stage their macabre cortege was joined by a sinister calico-clad figure symbolizing mourning. They managed to flee uninjured but before long were 'surrounded by a following of evil men . . . and a crowd from a village we were nearing, all of whom were armed with agricultural implements. For several hours we sat by the roadside near a little food-shop, hemmed in by these people, who freely discussed our death, sharpening their instruments on stones before our eyes. At last the long suspense was ended by their suddenly seizing us and with cruel violence tearing the clothes from our bodies. Where garments did not readily give way, it was as if we were being torn in pieces. Flora and Miss Gates were stripped of their upper garments, the dear children had nothing left to them except their combinations, while I myself was stripped naked, my socks only being left to me and a flannel binder.'

At another village they were stoned again but managed to get away, stumbling at night along a rocky riverbed. 'Two things were against us,' Glover wrote, 'the superb brilliance of the moon and the whiteness of the ladies' undergarments . . . To this hour I can never look at the full moon in the glory of its radiance without a shudder going through me. Instinctively and invariably it recalls that night of nights, and I live again the fear and trembling of our race for life.'[9]

Eventually, after an astonishing catalogue of events, including an attempt to poison them with sulphur fumes and many days of forced marching harassed by howling, jeering mobs, they finally reached safety. Mrs Glover's baby was born and christened 'Faith' but survived just a few days. She herself died a few weeks later.

As these harrowing stories began to reach the wider world, they strengthened the hand of those who believed that China must now be taught a lesson.

18

THE SPOILS OF PEKING

Every nationality accords the palm to some other in respect to the art of plundering, but it remains the fact that each and all of them went in hot and strong for plunder. – Count von Waldersee

IN PEKING a reign of terror had begun. The local population panicked and more than half had fled the city at the approach of the foreign troops. Dr Martin described how, 'in their haste, they left behind them wardrobes filled with costly furs, their floors were strewn with the richest silks; and in some cases the whole ground was covered with nuggets of silver. What a temptation to plunder!' Luella Miner climbed the tower of the Chienmen on 15 August and saw 'party after party of poor refugees, men, women and children, fleeing from the doomed city.' 'War is hell,' she wrote sadly. Rumours spread that the foreign troops intended to blow up the city, adding to the terrible confusion.

Some grandees who had backed the Boxers chose suicide. The antiforeign Imperial Tutor was discovered 'swinging high now from his own rafters, he and his whole household – wives, children, concubines, attendants, everyone.' Others set themselves alight or threw themselves into the moat, which became so choked with bodies that the water ceased to flow. Many Chinese women, unable to flee on their tiny bound feet, killed themselves. Roger Keyes was shaken by the discovery in a palace of 'five pretty, dainty-looking young girls, aged about twelve to twenty, of the highest manchu class, in lovely clothes, lying dead in a row.' Through an interpreter he learned that they had committed suicide the day the legations were relieved. The special correspondent of the *Daily Telegraph*, Dr E. J. Dillon, was shocked that 'Chinese women honestly believed that no more terrible fate could overtake them than to fall alive into the hands of Europeans and Christians' but added: 'It is to be feared that they were right.'[1] He saw the corpses of women raped and then bayoneted to death, some 'with frightful gashes in the breast, or skulls smashed in.'[2] The stories disturbed Polly Condit Smith, safe within the diplomatic quarter. She wrote that 'each legation, closed up in its little compound, feels like a little question-mark of respectability, surrounded by a whole page of wicked, leering horrors.'

Luella Miner had no doubt who was most to blame: 'The conduct of the Russian soldiers is *atrocious*, the French are not much better, and the Japanese are looting and burning without mercy . . . Women and girls by hundreds have committed suicide to escape a worse fate at the hands of Russian and Japanese brutes. Our American soldiers saw them jumping into the river and into wells, in Tungchow. Twelve girls in one well, and one mother was drowning two of her little children in a large water jar.' She added in despair: 'It is easy to say that . . . this is not war but punishment – but when we *can* distinguish the innocent from the guilty why stain the last pages of the century's history by records which would disgrace the annals of the dark ages?' Roger Keyes was also appalled: 'Every Chinaman . . . was treated as a Boxer by the Russian and French troops, and the slaughter of men, women, and children in retaliation was revolting.' A British officer, Major Luke, told Keyes that 'he had never seen anything more horrible, and some of his young Marines were literally sick.'

According to the journalist George Lynch, the French commander, General Frey, was challenged about 'the frequent occurrence of disgraceful outrages upon women' by his men. His dismissive response was: 'It is impossible to restrain the gallantry of the French soldier.'[3] Some British troops also behaved badly. Lenox Simpson claimed he came across 'a whole company of savage-looking Indian troops' molesting a group of female converts 'green-white with fear' while a lady missionary vainly tried to beat them off with an umbrella. Their officers had the soldiers flogged. The Japanese resorted to a different expedient to control their men's lust. According to Roger Keyes, 'their Government had wisely taken the precaution of sending their "regimental wives" [prostitutes] with them, and they were established in houses at Tientsin and Peking directly the troops settled down.'

Lynch was deeply angered by what he saw, lamenting that 'there are things that I must not write, and that may not be printed in England, which would seem to show that this Western civilization of ours is merely a veneer over savagery.'[4] His words contrast uneasily with the complacent newspaper headlines as news of the relief spread around the world. *The Times* rejoiced that 'history has repeated itself. Once more a small segment of the civilized world, cut off and surrounded by an Asiatic horde, has exhibited those high moral qualities the lack of which renders mere numbers powerless.'[5]

Those 'high moral qualities' were now conspicuously lacking. Shortly after the relief, the allied commanders met to discuss what should be done about the looting, which was, of course, banned under the Hague Convention. According to Polly, the great question was whether 'there should be a unanimous effort to stop all looting and sacking, or whether it should be continued. The Japanese, French and Russians were absolutely *pro*, English and Americans, *con*, the latter having the strictest orders from President McKinley against any looting. The English, although giving their vote for no looting, added they should continue to place "in safe-keeping all valuable things" found in the district given them to police.' As she observed, this effectively gave them the right to loot but, as the goods were later auctioned off and some of the proceeds distributed to the officers and men, 'they are really doing just what the other nations are doing, only in a somewhat more legalized way.'

Whatever the case, the early days after the relief saw indiscriminate, often brutal looting by all nationalities. The allied commander in chief von Waldersee, who did not arrive in China until late September, later wrote: 'Every nationality accords the palm to some other in respect to the art of plundering, but it remains the fact that each and all of them went in hot and strong for plunder.'[6] Lenox Simpson caught the terrified atmosphere: 'Everything was closed, tight shut; there was not a cat or a dog stirring abroad. Near the Legations and the Palace where the fear lay the heaviest, it seemed like a city of the dead.' He sensed people hidden away behind barred doors, nervously watching and waiting while foreign troops ran riot, wresting loot from 'blanched and trembling' shopkeepers. In desperation people hung out the flags of the conquering powers and nailed pathetic notes to their doors protesting their loyalty: 'We please all most noble foreign armies protection';[7] 'We be good people – no makee bobbery! Please, don't shoot';[8] 'Noble and good Sir . . . please do not shoot us. We are good people.'[9] One shopkeeper begged an American soldier to write a sign keeping out looters. He obliged, scribbling: 'USA boys – plenty of whiskey and tobacco in here.'[10] An American marine captain later admitted with honesty that he and his men had looted but pleaded the age-old justification: 'Some allowance should be made for the fact that during the excitement of a campaign you do things that you yourself would be the first to criticize in the tranquil security of home.'[11]

The looting was accompanied by casual brutality. Entering one house, British soldiers found an old Chinaman hiding in a corner shivering with fear. They told him that unless he unearthed his treasure they would kill him. When he said that he had no treasure, one of the soldiers decided to bayonet him, but his comrade intervened saying: 'No, not that way! I'm going to shoot him. I've always had a longing to see what sort of a wound a dum-dum will make and by Christ, I am going to try one on this blasted Chink!' He fired and the result was gruesomely spectacular. The soldier remarked with awe: 'Christ, the dum-dum has blown out the back of his bloody nut!'[12] There was a sense that the Chinese were less than human. Dr Dillon was appalled by the attitude of a man he described simply as a 'European physician' who refused to treat a Chinaman shot through the chest by looting French soldiers. 'Don't look so glum,' the doctor said, 'it is not nearly so bad as it seems. Those Chinese die like dogs. Their feelings are less intense than ours by fifty percent at least.'[13]

Neither was there any understanding of Chinese art or culture. Lenox Simpson watched French soldiers and Russian Cossacks carelessly ransacking warehouses in search of silver and gold. 'Rich silks and costly furs, boxes of trinkets, embroideries, women's head-dresses, and hundreds of other things, were flung to the ground and trampled under foot into shapeless masses in a few moments, raising a choking dust which cut one's breathing. They wanted only treasure, these men, gold if possible, something which possessed an instant value for them – something whose very touch spelt fortune. Nothing else.' British soldiers took a similar view. Some Royal Welch Fusiliers complained it was hard to know what was valuable or to find objects small enough to carry off in a haversack. Priceless items of porcelain and jade were wantonly smashed by soldiers searching for more readily disposable plunder. Some Fusiliers were lucky enough to lay their hands on some exquisite black pearls, which later fetched high prices in Hong Kong. Many filled their bags with silver dollars, which they knew would be too heavy to carry when they were back on the march. The luckiest were those who had friends in the Transport Corps. Several officers with a good eye for curios were rumoured to have 'managed to get away some priceless ornaments in the Officers' Mess-cart.'[14]

Some of the allies competed to seize the greatest prizes for their respective governments. Lenox Simpson hoped to make his own fortune by passing information about the location of the treasure of the Chinese Board of Revenue to the Russians. General Lineivitch promised him a share and eagerly dispatched two companies of infantry to search the cellars, only to find the Japanese had beaten him to it. Dr Martin wrote: 'Of the public treasures, the Japanese, knowing the exact points to seize on, succeeded in getting the lion's share.' On 16 August, Morrison watched 'a continuous chain of mules' carrying the treasure into the Japanese Legation.

The French were similarly opportunistic. Immediately after the siege of the legations was raised, Peking had been divided into sectors under the control of the respective allies. The French knew that the palace of Prince Li – 'a great plum,' in Morrison's words, reputedly filled with silver bullion – lay just within the American sector. General Frey 'blandly' asked the unworldly and unsuspecting Edwin Conger for a slight adjustment to the sector lines. Conger agreed, whereupon the French immediately helped themselves to £60,000 in silver bullion. Morrison wrote that the 'Americans are mad.' When the news broke, the French excused their action by claiming that the money would be used to fund the reconstruction of the Peitang.

Some weeks later, to Morrison's disgust, the French and the Germans appropriated the priceless bronze astronomical instruments of the Imperial Observatory. The French claimed them because they had been made in France and presented to the Chinese Emperor in the reign of Louis XIV. The Germans demanded them because they were in their sector. In the end they agreed to divide the spoils. Sarah Conger was also distressed at such naked banditry: 'One of the most heartrending acts to me is the removing and carrying away of the exquisite bronze instruments at the Peking Observatory. These old, historic treasures were more than valuable and beautiful. They have stood on their sentinel watch between four and five hundred years [sic]. They belong to China and can never act as honourable and beautiful a part elsewhere.' She added with quiet pride that the American government had forbidden looting and 'recognizes no spoils of war.'

Many foreign civilians also profited handsomely. Overcoming his disappointment that the Board of Revenue's silver had escaped him, Lenox Simpson helped himself to a few dozen magnificent sable coats. He also purchased for a paltry few coins a gold belt buckle set with diamonds and rubies brought to China by Jesuits in the reign of Louis XIV. He justified his purchase on the grounds that he was not robbing a private individual but acquiring an Imperial possession. 'Who would not rob a fleeing Emperor of his possessions?' he asked cheerfully. Not his employer, Sir Robert Hart, apparently. The austere old gentleman accused Lenox Simpson of being no better than a 'latter-day robber-chief'. Lenox Simpson defended himself by pointing out that everyone was engaged in the same activity and that 'some of the biggest people in the legations are so mean and so bent on covering up their tracks that *they are using their wives to do their dirty work*.' He may have been referring to Lady MacDonald. According to a British officer, she 'devoted herself most earnestly to looting.'[15] Morrison, dining in the First Brigade Mess, heard similar remarks: 'All condemned the way Sir Claude and Lady MacDonald had looted . . . 185 boxes at least.' However, she and her family later denied this and according to George Lynch she protested when 'burglariously-inclined people'[16] from the legations tried to loot from the Imperial palaces.

Polly Condit Smith certainly acquired some pleasing mementos during her last days in Peking. She was approached by a big Sikh who, 'whacking his chest, which was bulging in tremendous curves,' said, 'Mem-sahib give me two dollars, I give mem-sahib nice things.' She obliged and in return received 'an exquisite gold-mounted cloisonné clock and two huge struggling hens.' Baron von Rahden offered her a fine sable coat but she declined, thinking it too valuable to be quite proper to accept. It cost her some pangs. Not only did the baron, as a Russian, know good sables when he saw them but, within the hour, she saw him 'present it to another woman, who accepted it without a qualm, and without giving him, I thought, very many thanks.' Polly had learned her lesson. When, a little later that day, a Belgian admirer offered her a handsome tortoise-shell bracelet set with pearls taken from a Chinese officer he had killed, she surprised herself 'by promptly accepting it . . . I took it rather than have a repetition of the sequel to the sable-coat episode.'

However, Baron von Rahden was able to be of material help to Polly, albeit not in the matter of sables. Within days of the relief, the first convoys of women, children and wounded began to depart for Tungchow. Polly Condit Smith was to be among them but was eager to see the Forbidden City first. When she asked General Chaffee for permission, he struck the table and replied that 'there were sights of war there which no American girl should see.' However, Baron von Rahden offered to conduct her and off they set on horseback 'lickety split' with an escort of Cossacks. She was entranced by the exquisite gardens and wonderful views from Coal Hill. The piles of corpses apparently worried her not a jot. She did not record whether she returned with any further souvenirs.

Morrison had moved into the palace of a wealthy Chinese prince and was looting everything worth having. As he candidly admitted, 'I have left him the glass in the windows, but nothing else.'[17] On 26 August he recorded with obvious satisfaction that 'this morning I worked at arranging my silks and furs [and] find that I have many of considerable value also porcelain and bronzes perhaps £3,000 in all.' His friend Edmund Backhouse was actually arrested by Russian soldiers in their sector 'on a charge of blackmailing, looting and robbery.'[18] Backhouse later claimed in his *Decadence Mandchoue* that 'with the aid of trusty Manchus' he removed various possessions of the Empress Dowager to a place of safety for her, 'not my own house, as I did not wish my name to appear, knowing as I do the inveterate calumnious suspicions of my unctuous hypocritical compatriots.' However it seems more likely that, like so many others, he was scouring the city on his own account, perhaps acquiring some of the manuscripts he was later to donate or try to sell to the Bodleian Library in Oxford.

Young Lancelot Giles wrote gleefully to his mother: 'Every day looting parties go out and get what they can. I have done some splendid looting already.' It is unclear whether he felt constrained to hand his booty over to the common pool for auction. However, Lieutenant Richard Steel, the young man who had nearly 'catted' at the gruesome scenes on the relief expedition and was clearly still squeamish, heard that a party of marines was going to loot Prince Kung's house. He accompanied them along a road '*horrible* with Chinese corpses in all stages of decomposition.' He was nearly sick but it was worth it. 'Kung's palace is a perfect wonder of wealth, and we carried away any amount of treasure for the common fund.'[19]

Like many others, Roger Keyes soon realized that the British arrangements for 'a common fund' were flawed. 'On more than one occasion I particularly wanted to bid for some of the things I had deposited in the morning, but found by the afternoon, when the auctions were held, that they had already disappeared. Looting is certainly a most demoralizing pastime!' He reflected that 'but for a tiresome conscience' he might have returned to Britain several thousands of pounds richer. As it was, his share of the prize money amounted to just £15.

The auctions were open to all and were held under the colonnade in front of the British Legation. Those with ready money could do well but prices were too high for many. Delicate enamels, miniatures, jewelled snuff boxes, porcelain, jade goblets, watches set with pearls, all came under the hammer. Sir Claude was a frequent bidder, together with General Gaselee and General Barrow. Lieutenant Steel bought some cloisonné and bronze items for Lord Curzon, viceroy of India, who was taking a keen interest in the spoils of Peking and who had sent £1,000 'to invest in curios.'[20] Nigel Oliphant, still recovering from his wound, did less well; he acquired 'a very shabby squirrel-skin coat' and went home in disgust. As he and others soon realized, the best bargains were to be had on the streets. An officer of the Royal Welch Fusiliers saw a Russian drinking at a well from a magnificently carved green jade goblet. When he asked the price, 'the Russian held up one finger, meaning one dollar . . . and the deal took place to the satisfaction of both.'[21]

Missionaries also dealt in looted goods but usually for less venal motives. They had large numbers of dispossessed converts to care for and their missions had been completely destroyed. Arthur Smith described the hopeless scenes that greeted them when they set out to see what had become of mission property. The city was desolate and 'huge pools of stagnant water were reeking with putrid corpses of man and beast; lean cats stared wildly at the passer-by from holes broken in the fronts of shops boasting such signs as "Perpetual Abundance", "Springs of Plenty", "Ten Thousand Prosperities".' Dr Lillie Saville was distressed to find the London Mission 'just a bit of waste ground – not a whole brick anywhere – walls all gone – trees burnt down!'[22]

The missionaries' tactics consisted of hoisting flags over the houses of wealthy inhabitants to protect them from the soldiers and fastening notices on the doors saying this was the property of such-and-such a mission. In some cases wealthy Chinese actually offered the missionaries their homes in the hope of saving them from complete destruction. The missionaries would then move in and hold a sale of the contents. When the goods were exhausted they would move on to another house.

Luella Miner was afraid that she and her comrades would be ordered to leave Peking at any moment, wondering 'what would become of our Christians?' The energetic Mr Tewkesbury, however, found a highly 'desirable' deserted palace in the Russian sector, which they requisitioned. Luella thought it strange for penniless missionaries and converts to be living among such 'exquisite bric-a-brac' but Mr Tewkesbury organized sales of the furs and silks they discovered for the benefit of destitute Chinese converts. Herbert Squiers was 'a large purchaser'.[23] Morrison noted with envy that he had purchased 'all best things at Tewkesbury's 1/5 the value.' Dr Martin had few qualms about doing 'a little looting'[24] on behalf of missionary friends anxious about feeding their flock. He raided a deserted grain shop, and all he took for himself was a goatskin rug. However, he had to leave the comfortable house his servants had found for him because it was constantly being raided by 'straggling soldiers of various nationalities – Hindoo, Russian or American.'[25]

On 18 August, a joint meeting of diplomats and military commanders at the Russian Legation had discussed formal reprisals against the Chinese. One faction, led by the Germans, who felt they had particular rights because of von Ketteler's murder, wished to punish the Chinese severely and argued for a series of punitive military operations, as well as razing the Imperial City. The Russians favoured a more conciliatory line in northern China, hoping to extract further concessions in Manchuria, where they were pursuing their ambitions with brutal savagery. (When news of the Boxer troubles had first reached St Petersburg, the Russian war minister apparently declared in delight, 'I am very glad. This will give us an excuse for seizing Manchuria.')[26] In the absence of the commander in chief, von Waldersee, the conference could make little progress.

While Peking was being ransacked, the diplomats and military commanders did agree that a victory parade through the Imperial City would be a salutary lesson for the Chinese. The allied forces would march through the city, the largest contingents first. The Russians claimed to have the most troops in Peking (it was actually the Japanese who had the greatest number), and so led the great procession, on 28 August. At first attempts were made to exclude journalists from the event, but General Lineivitch allowed A. Henry Savage-Landor to ride by his side. His irreverent description spared few: 'In front stood prominent the lumbering, bony figure of Sir Claude MacDonald, in an

ample grey suit of tennis clothes and a rakish Panama slouch hat
. . . He walked jauntily and with gigantic strides, moving his arms
about as if preparing for a boxing match. To his right the Russian
Minister seemed quite reposeful by contrast. He was clad in dark
clothes, and bore himself with dignity. Next to him came the
Representative of the French Republic, in a garb which combined
the requirements of the Bois de Boulogne on a Sunday with the
conveniences of tropical attire on a weekday. Mr Conger, the
American Minister, strode ponderously behind, dressed in white
cottons and military gaiters . . . The march through the Palace
being a military affair, it seemed as if the Ministers were sulky
and attached no importance to the occasion.'[27] Savage-Landor
thought some of them looked quite bored.

Neither did all the military contingents cut a dash. Lynch was
disgusted by the appearance of the French troops, complaining
that there was every excuse for their uniforms to be dirty 'but
that the faces of many of the men should be so too was quite
inexcusable.'[28] Morrison agreed, writing that the French looked
'singularly decadent in blue dungaree' and that their commander,
General Frey, was small and pot-bellied. He thought the
Cossacks were 'heavy' and 'rough' but that the Germans looked
'splendid' and the Japanese officers 'very smart'. The British, by
contrast, looked rather 'rag tag and bobtail'. The dignity of the
occasion was further undermined by the ineptitude of the
Russian band, which could not keep pace with eight successive
national anthems and found itself blasting out the 'Marseillaise'
as the Italians marched past the saluting base.

Afterwards, wrinkled and impassive eunuchs escorted the
senior officers and diplomats around the palaces of the
Forbidden City. This provided yet another occasion for looting.
A number of small but rare and expensive items were unobtru-
sively appropriated as the foreigners passed through the richly
carpeted chambers. According to Dr Dillon, the 'diplomatist's
euphemism' was 'One cannot go without a souvenir. That word
"souvenir" was the formula which everyone had been seeking
for.'[29] Richard Steel thought it 'rather poor form from an

English point of view'[30] and Roger Keyes was disgusted. He was convinced that nothing was looted by a British officer but wrote that the foreign officers 'looted in the most barefaced way, as did many of the various legation diplomats and ladies . . . General Barrow was lifting the cover off the Imperial throne in order to look at it, when a German officer took the scepter – a priceless piece of jade – right under his eyes!'

The Russians were even worse. According to Keyes, when they came out of the palace their baggy trousers were 'simply bulging with loot.' Luella Miner observed that many 'were more corpulent when they came out than when they went in.' One reporter showed her his haul of two exquisite tablets from the throne room, one jade and one serpentine, inscribed with characters by an emperor; two carnelian cups; and five tiny yellow porcelain cups of Tung Chih's reign. Morrison himself appropriated 'a beautiful piece of jade splashed with gold and carved in the form of a citron.' He noted with regret that it had a blemish and was hence of no value.

Lynch watched a Frenchman make off with a gold vase by crushing it with his knee and concealing it under his coat. He also saw a minister examine a carved and inscribed tablet of jade in one of the emperor's rooms. After a moment the diplomat replaced it and walked on, but 'then he seemed curious to examine it again, and did so carefully for a few moments. Then he put his hands in his pockets, and seemed intent on contemplating the pattern of the ceiling. He apparently got so interested in it that he must have forgotten that he had not put back that bit of jade in its stand.' Lynch felt there was something symbolic about greedy foreigners penetrating to the very heart of this ancient empire and laying bare a 'fistula of cankerous decay.' The grandeur and the honour of the Manchus now seemed as tarnished as the moth-eaten Imperial banners, 'down which the five-clawed dragon writhed in gold.' How would it all end?[31]

V

Another Country?

China in the Wake of the Boxer Rebellion

19
THE TREATY

The city has been turned inside out, like the fingers of a glove, but whose hand shall ultimately fill it remains still to be settled. – Arthur Smith

BY THE CLOSE OF August, many foreigners had already left the 'ancient Empire'. Regimental bands played as long caravans of carts, sedan chairs, and stretchers set out under the shadows of the Tartar Wall for Tungchow. Departing US Marines presented a curious picture that their captain ruefully described: 'Not a man was completely clad in American uniform. As they lined up for inspection, some of them wore blue or rose Chinese trousers, others mandarin coats, and almost all of them were shod in Chinese silk boots.'[1]

Life began to regain some kind of normality for those that remained. After the relief, a weary Jessie Ransome described how the besieged had 'fondly hoped the troops were going to supply us, but, on the contrary, these hungry hordes of men have poured into a city panic-stricken by terror, whence many peaceful folk have fled, and into which the country market folk dare not come.' One of her convert boys managed to find some eggs but they were promptly stolen from him by Russian soldiers. Gradually, however, the situation was improving.

Sarah Conger had quickly moved back into her 'dilapidated Legation home' and was out and about buying curtain fabric to replace the hangings she had destroyed to make sandbags. Her daughter Laura now seemed completely cured of her nervous condition. Journalist Wilbur Chamberlin was amused that she had returned to Peking on the eve of the siege under doctor's orders to avoid excitement and be careful with her diet: 'She was reduced to a diet of horsemeat,' he wrote, 'and as for excitement, maybe you think it wasn't exciting to have rifle bullets whistling about you every minute and occasionally a shell exploding in the house you were in!' He marvelled that, despite her fragile constitution, she had worked ceaselessly through the siege, nursing the sick and sewing sandbags, 'and hasn't been sick a day since.'[2] Chamberlin was also amused by tales of back-biting among the legation women now that the siege was over. It had apparently become so bad in one legation, he does not specify which, that the minister lined them up and 'told them there was important work to be done in Peking and that the men had their hands full, without being constantly worried with the cackling of a lot of jealous women who didn't know what they were talking about.'[3]

Sir Robert Hart had found two rooms behind Kierulff's store and rented a tiny temple under the walls of the Tartar City as an office. All he had been able to salvage from the ruins of his former dwelling was 'the head of a pretty little Saxe shepherdess.'[4] Everything else – his letters from 'Chinese' Gordon and all his beloved photographs – had been burned. Morrison was busily calculating the compensation he intended to claim for the destruction of his house and possessions and writing up his reports for *The Times*.

Baron von Ketteler's body had been found close to the site where he had been murdered. To the foreigners' surprise, it had been buried in 'a respectable coffin' and had not been mutilated. A majestic memorial service was held in the German Legation.

Several months later von Ketteler's killer was to be arrested by the Japanese and decapitated by the Germans on the precise spot where he had shot down the baron.

Officers and civilians went on sight-seeing trips. Thousands of visitors streamed through the palaces of the Forbidden City. It was de rigueur to sit on the Imperial throne and bounce on the royal beds until more stringent rules were introduced. Lenox Simpson was among those to visit the Empress Dowager's bedroom. Looking eagerly around, he saw a large bed draped with wonderfully embroidered hangings; some handsome, carved wooden furniture with European chairs; and some noisily ticking jewelled clocks. His greatest discovery, however, was 'nothing less than a magnificent silver *pot de chambre*,' hidden modestly away in a corner. 'She was here evidently very much at her ease, the dear old lady. That little detail delighted me.' After sitting on her bed he joined a friend in rummaging further. They found a delicately flavoured compote of rose petals, which they promptly ate, and some Russian cigarettes.

Others found opium. A French naval officer described how during his visit to one of the Imperial palaces he reclined on golden cushions and had a good long smoke. 'It goes without saying,' he wrote, 'that it was opium of exquisite quality, the smoke from which rose in small rapid spirals, immediately making the air heavy with its fragrance. By degrees it brought us Chinese ecstasy, oblivion, languor, mystery, youth.'[5]

There were picnic expeditions to the Summer Palace, which the Russians had systematically looted. 'Every article of value is packed and labelled,'[6] wrote Morrison, who thought that this 'grabbing of palaces does not add to the dignity of nations,' adding, with some chagrin: 'In the competition we [the British] have grabbed nothing.' He felt that the Russians, by dint of superior numbers, had Peking in a stranglehold, writing furiously that he could 'go nowhere without seeing Russians.' Count Witte, then Russia's finance minister, later wrote in his memoirs: 'It was rumoured that Russian army officers took part in the looting, and I must say to our shame, that our agent in

Peking unofficially confirmed these rumours to me. One lieutenant general [presumably Lineivitch], who had received the
Cross of St George for the capture of Peking, returned to his
post in the Amur region with ten trunksful of valuables coming
from the looted Peking palaces.'7

Such thoughts did not disturb most other visitors to the
Summer Palace. Captain Casserly was enchanted and thought
the Empress Dowager's fabled white marble junk 'quaint and
graceful' and not unlike 'a white house-boat at Henley.'8 That
indefatigable and generous hostess Harriet Squiers organized a
lunch party on the boat with many courses, including ice cream.
Luella Miner, who was one of her guests, thought that the exquisite covered walkway running then, as now, along the artificial
lake would make 'an unsurpassable bicycle path.'

Luella also visited the British military camp in the Temple of
Heaven and was struck by the paradox of British officers 'feast-
ing in the Temple . . . where the Emperor spends the night in
fasting and prayer.' There were other examples of British philis-
tinism. An article published in Britain railed that 'the Temple of
Heaven, one of the most sacred edifices in China, was selected
by an amateur dramatic troupe of British officers as the theatre
for performing a burlesque, in which the Dowager Empress was
caricatured, put up for auction, and knocked down for five
dollars to an Indian officer impersonating Prince Tuan, who was
declared to have purchased the honour of China for that sum.
This combination of vulgarity and indecency,' it concluded
angrily, 'is one of the things which make the English so much
detested by other races.'9 To American Wilbur Chamberlin it
was 'as full of fun as it could stick'10 but, he agreed, it was tact-
less. Luella thought she might have encountered another example of British crassness when she saw the temple's magnificent
ancestral tablets being removed. However, she was mollified to
discover that they were, in fact, being packed up for the British
Museum, writing that 'if they could not remain in this lovely,
historic spot, I am glad that they will be preserved there.'

*   *   *

If life for the foreigners was improving, life for the Chinese was not. Existence was precarious and humiliating. Dr Dillon saw 'a vulgar little ruffian in military uniform point a revolver at the head of a highly-educated Chinamen, and call him off to do work as a scullion.'[11] He also described 'Boxer hunts' reminiscent of 'The Terror' of the French Revolution, writing that 'the word "Boxer" was fatal to him to whom it clung.'[12] Within just twenty-four hours no outward trace of the Boxers remained in the city. They had torn down their altars, abandoned their weapons, and shed their distinctive red and yellow garb. A temple that had served as a Boxer headquarters was renamed, with more speed than accuracy, 'God Christianity Men.' The allies, however, were determined to flush them out. One man suggested an ingenious way of discovering whether a Chinaman had once been a Boxer: 'Let suspected men . . . be stripped to the waist, and if their right shoulder is blue or bruised it may be safely asserted that that man carried a rifle as a Boxer and deserves death.'[13] Dr Dillon also noted that at night 'every Chinaman, Boxer or no Boxer, was shot down like a dog.'[14]

In fact, there were almost daily executions. Soldiers of the Royal Welch Fusiliers sometimes had to escort between fifty and a hundred prisoners to the execution place before breakfast. Their heads were cut off 'like greased lightning' by a Chinese executioner using a double-handed sword. But at that time of the morning it turned the stomachs of some of the soldiers. 'It was the way the blood spouted up,'[15] wrote one. An Australian sailor found the experience disturbing and distasteful: 'We are growing callous – this is part of the Eastern Education. Until you can bring yourself to regard the Chinaman as something less than human, considerably less, you are at a disadvantage.'[16] Morrison captured the scenes graphically: 'The execution and the long drawn out neck. The butcher with his apron. The executioner tearing open his long coat – the grunt as he brought down the knife – the dogs lapping up the blood – the closeness of the head to the ground, the face nearly touching.' He also wrote that the Germans made their prisoners dig their own trench and then shot them on the edge.

As August drew to a close, some parts of the city were beginning to become more populous again. Morrison noticed a marked contrast between the Russian sector, where a 'half-panic' reigned, and the Japanese, where there was 'contentment and quiet'. Sarah Conger was struck by the same phenomenon. 'For some reason the Chinese are opening their shops in the Japanese quarters and not in other parts of the city,' she wrote thoughtfully in September. The Japanese had prudently offered protection to the traders in their sector from the first days. The British and Americans followed suit but more tardily and their sectors too became relatively peaceful.

Outside Peking the situation remained dreadful. The smell of death – what one French naval officer called *'une odeur de cadavre'*[17] – seemed to hang over the empty fields. Reverend Allen, travelling to Tientsin in late August, passed deserted farms with untended crops ripening in the fields. 'We went into house after house, broken cups and plates lay upon the floor, an evil stench warned the intruder from corners, the water from the wells had a strange taste savouring of disease and death.' Emma Martin, who had nursed in the legation hospital, was similarly revolted, writing of 'bodies left to rot in the sun or be eaten by dogs and worms. Many of the bodies were in the water and sometimes the stench was dreadful. We had to use this river water for cooking and I had to drink it once.'[18]

US Commissioner William W. Rockhill, who travelled to Peking in September to take part in the peace negotiations, described how 'between Tientsin and Pekin the country for several miles on either side of the highroad has been abandoned by the Chinese . . . A few peasants may now and then be seen hiding in the fields of corn or sorghum, trying to cut some of the now ripe grain, but when their presence is detected by the foreign soldiers travelling along the road or on the river, they are exposed to being shot at. I saw several corpses along the road.'[19]

Major General James H. Wilson, who had commanded General Sherman's cavalry in the march through Georgia and was travelling to Peking to serve as General Chaffee's second in command, was also shocked. He later told von Waldersee that 'while our forebears appeared to have left the customs of the Middle Ages behind when they came to America, their racial kinsmen from European countries, greatly to my surprise, seemed to return naturally to the cruelties of primitive man.'[20] He was shortly to have further experience of European crudeness.

During September, while the allies were still awaiting von Waldersee's arrival, a number of military operations were mounted against remaining Boxer strongholds southwest of Tientsin and south and north of the capital. As Lenox Simpson cynically observed, foreign troops were still flooding into Peking. They had to be given something to do. On 16 September, Wilson was ordered to lead a combined American and British expedition to drive off a force of Boxers occupying a famous temple complex in the Western Hills. Wilson had visited the temples as a tourist in 1885 and was anxious to damage nothing of cultural interest. He was particularly keen to preserve the marvellous shimmering White Pagoda, built of porcelain, and over a thousand years old.

The military operation was quickly accomplished. However, the senior British officer present, General Barrow, then asked Wilson's permission to blow up the pagoda as a punitive measure. Wilson refused to contemplate it, whereupon Barrow asked him to give up his command of the British troops. Wilson had little choice and returned to Peking, leaving Barrow a free agent. He promptly exploded a charge of gunpowder under the pagoda's base and 'toppled the world-famed structure over in irretrievable ruin.'[21] When news of this vandalism reached the wider world, odium was heaped on the heads of the perpetrators. Poor Wilson was blamed initially and had to struggle to clear his name. Barrow claimed it had all been at Sir Claude's instigation 'as retribution for the destruction of the missions, chapels and Legation buildings.'[22]

When Field Marshal von Waldersee finally arrived in Peking in October to assume command, he quickly established himself in Tzu Hsi's palace in the Forbidden City. Like von Ketteler, he had an American wife but this did not deter him from installing a beautiful Chinese courtesan. He was delighted that the emperor and the Empress Dowager had fled, writing: 'Had they been taken prisoners in Peking there would have been no trouble about making peace, I should have arrived too late, and probably we should have been able to play no decisive part in the Peace negotiations.'[23] He too had been shocked by the terrible devastation of the countryside during his journey to Peking and worried that the conditions had 'created more Boxers than were killed in battle.'[24] He decided that punitive expeditions would exercise a wholesome moral influence.

Under his direction, Germany took the lead in several dozen expeditions, including one to Paotingfu. Their stated purpose was to flush out remaining Boxers. The kaiser wrote of his delight that German howitzers were going into action. However, his views were not universally shared. General Chaffee thought such activities inhumane and pointless, telling a journalist that 'where one real Boxer has been killed since the capture of Peking, fifteen harmless coolies . . . including not a few women and children, have been slain'.[25] In fact, the American government had specifically ordered its troops not to participate in the raids of the winter of 1900–1901. The British did take part but again there were misgivings. One British officer wrote uneasily: 'We fired about 2,000 rounds, mostly at inoffensive people I believe, and killed about fifteen of them.'[26] According to Luella Miner, the Germans became 'very indignant' at General Gasclee's leniency.

Some of the German attacks were particularly brutal. About one thousand German troops arrived at a city south of Peking in February 1901 and opened fire without warning, killing some two hundred Chinese soldiers and civilians. A local magistrate was viciously beaten with rifle butts and made to kneel in the snow while the German troops prepared to execute the city's four hundred remaining residents. With great bravery he pleaded for their lives and his request was finally granted. As the months, advanced von Waldersee found himself vilified in the foreign press. He blamed Morrison for reports in *The Times* accusing him of brutality and 'pillaging systematically people who were already conquered before the Germans arrived in China.'[27] Von Waldersee concluded that Morrison 'with the true English reporter's megalomania apparently is of the opinion I ought to take notice of him.'[28]

A far harder task than subduing the already cowed population of northern China, or dealing with the press, soon faced von Waldersee. He must smooth relationships among the allied powers while peace negotiations got under way. In November 1900 he wrote in his journal: 'The interests of the European Powers are entirely different and a co-operation between them on plain dealing lines is quite impossible.'[29] When a lady remarked to him that 'during the siege we did not talk about German soldiers, or British, or American, they were all *our* soldiers,' he gravely replied: 'It is not so now.'[30] International rivalries were intense. Luella Miner overheard a general 'of another nation' being asked whether he thought 'there would be fighting this winter.' He replied 'Yes, but not with the Chinese.'[31] Britain and Russia came close to armed conflict over railway lines financed by British bondholders but over which the Russians claimed operational control.

Young Lieutenant Hirshinger of the US Marines summed up the position succinctly in a letter to his mother: 'Our friends, the British, are hungrily watching every move made by any nation; the Japs say nothing, but I imagine that they are warring in secret; the Russians have withdrawn practically all their troops from this section, to Manchuria, in the north . . . while we sit on the fence, and say we don't want anything, but we'd like to see order restored . . . What there is to be gained by staying here, I can't see; we can't get territory, and even if we could, we don't want it.'[32] Von Waldersee observed the rapprochement between the British and the Americans, writing sourly: 'They are declaring themselves to be of the same race and that they are bound to each other by mutual interests. If England had not made such a fearful military fiasco in South Africa she would not be so keen on this American friendship.'[33]

If there was mutual distrust at the political level, there were also more basic rivalries. Fights flared up in the street and it was not unknown for soldiers of various nationalities to take potshots at one another. A British army doctor, Lieutenant Archibald Currie MacGilchrist, wrote with apparent relish: 'There is lots of national jealousy out here. Lately seven French soldiers attacked a British officer quite alone and unarmed as he was going home from the Club one night. The Americans, Japs and ourselves have been great friends all through. The best of it is that both French and Germans get the worst of it in all fights even with Indian coolies.'[34] Captain Poole overheard two sepoys of the Seventh Rajputs making disparaging remarks about some French soldiers who straggled by 'dirty' and 'unkempt'. The first sepoy remarked, 'Without doubt they are Europeans,' to which the second replied, 'Without doubt but of the sweeper caste.' Morrison recorded a number of mischievous anecdotes in his diary: 'Leitch says: "I sent my servant on a message. He was robbed by a Russian, buggered by a Frenchman, killed by a German. In my dismay, I made complaint to a British officer. He looked at me, put his eye-glass into his eye, and said, "Was he really? What a bore!!"'

Still, von Waldersee knew that the foreigners' alliance, however riven by tension and rivalry, must be held together until a suitable peace settlement had been negotiated. At present there was a vacuum. As Arthur Smith shrewdly put it: 'The city has been turned inside out, like the fingers of a glove, but whose hand shall ultimately fill it remains still to be settled.' Li Hung-chang, appointed Imperial plenipotentiary together with Prince Ching, did not arrive in Peking until October and it was not until Christmas Eve that the first meeting was held between the foreign ministers representing the allied powers and the Chinese.

On that occasion Li Hung-chang was not even present due to illness.

The delays had less to do with Chinese intransigence than with allied squabbling about the conditions to be imposed on China. At one stage, linguistic arguments threatened to reduce the negotiations to farce. There was fevered debate about the use of the word *irrevocable* in case it sounded too strong when translated into Chinese. Edwin Conger was ordered by the American government to adamantly oppose its use. Owing to a mistake in deciphering the instruction from Washington, he did the precise opposite. When the mistake was discovered, it prolonged the arguments still further.[35]

Delays were also caused by worries over protocol rather than substance. The allies demanded to know on whose authority the Chinese plenipotentiaries were acting – were they agents of the emperor or of the Chinese government? It was eventually agreed that their credentials would be scrutinized when presented at the meeting. Prince Ching duly handed them over to the foreign ministers. However, he then caused consternation by asking to inspect the allies' own authorizations to negotiate. Only the German minister could produce any paperwork and the meeting closed in confusion.

Sir Robert Hart believed that three choices faced the allies – partition, which was unworkable in the long term because the Chinese would never acquiesce; a change of dynasty, which was also impossible since 'there is no man of mark all China would accept'; or 'patching up the Manchoo (*sic*) rule' and, 'in a word, mak[ing] the best of it.' Common sense dictated that the Manchu dynasty should remain on the throne, and this became the allied policy. Once that point of principle had been agreed, the peace negotiations hinged on two issues – punishment of the guilty, which the allies insisted was a prerequisite before meaningful negotiations could take place, and the size of the indemnity to be extracted from China.

Wrangling over the size of the indemnity to be paid by China lasted into the summer of 1901. A figure of £67,500,000 (about

$335,000,000 at the 1900 rate of exchange, or $4,355,000,000 in current values) was calculated from the combined allied demands and estimated occupation costs. America objected that this was too high and would bankrupt China; they wanted the sum reduced by a third. As early as 3 July 1900, while the siege was still at its height, the American secretary of state John Hay had sent a circular telegram to the Powers making clear that America's policy was to bring 'permanent safety and peace to China' and to preserve China's territorial integrity.[36] An irritated von Waldersee grumbled that the United States 'seems to desire that nobody shall get anything out of China.'[37] However, on 26 May an Imperial edict announced that payment of £67,500,000 would be made in full. It would take thirty-nine years.

The negotiations over who was to be punished and how severely were almost more complex and difficult. The allies had initially sought the deaths of twelve prominent pro-Boxer officials. The Empress Dowager had hoped to avoid such extreme measures. However, when it became clear that her counterproposals were not acceptable, she decided that at least some of her followers must fall on their swords. Yu Hsien, orchestrator of the massacre of missionaries in Taiyuan, received a delicate hint that 'the price of coffins is rising.'[38] He ignored it and was reputedly executed, although there is some doubt whether the sentence was ever carried out. Others were ordered to die by their own hand and did so in a variety of unpleasant ways. One official, Ying Nien, was said to have choked himself to death by swallowing mud. Another had his nostrils and mouth stuffed with twists of rice paper by eunuchs after successive drafts of poison failed to kill him. As members of the Imperial family, Prince Tuan and his brother escaped the death penalty but were exiled to Turkestan. The allies reluctantly conceded that Tung Fu-hsiang, whose Moslem army was still deployed around Sian, was too powerful to be touched. He merely suffered the indignity of dismissal. Over a hundred minor officials were also subsequently punished, usually by death, for crimes in the interior.

*   *   *

A peace treaty containing twelve articles and nineteen annexes was finally signed in the Spanish Legation, the residence of the most senior diplomat, Señor Cologan, on 7 September 1901. In addition to the payment of the indemnity, it included stipulations that the emperor's regrets for the death of Baron von Ketteler would be conveyed to the kaiser and that a monument should be erected on the site of his murder; that official examinations should be suspended for five years in all cities where foreigners had been abused; that an apology was to be delivered to the emperor of Japan for the death of Mr Sugiyama; that the Legation Quarter be placed under foreign control and protected by an enlarged legation guard and that no Chinese be permitted to reside within it; that the Taku forts be razed; that twelve points between Peking and the coast should be garrisoned by foreign troops to maintain lines of communication with the legations; that membership of any antiforeign society should be punishable by death; and that the Tsungli Yamen should become a full-fledged ministry of foreign affairs where foreign diplomats would be received with greater dignity and less inconvenience and discomfort than hitherto. Ten days later the international garrison left Peking.

The path had been cleared and the Imperial Court could return.

20

THE COURT RETURNS

Something told us that the return of the Court to Peking marked a turning-point in history. – Don Rodolfo Borghese

THE EMPRESS DOWAGER had been agreeably surprised by the terms of the treaty. She was not to be punished personally. Neither was China required to surrender any territory. Some members of the exiled court had urged her to continue the war, arguing that Peking and Tientsin had fallen because of traitors, that the allies could never penetrate the interior of China, and that if Tung Fu-hsiang were allowed to increase his force to 50,000 he could chase the foreigners out. It is impossible to know exactly how the arguments ebbed and flowed during those months. However, Tzu Hsi was nothing if not a pragmatist. She was also an old woman who enjoyed her comforts. If the allies would allow her and the emperor to return to her capital with honour, there was little to lose. She was also shrewd enough to read between the lines of the settlement – the allies believed it was in their interest to maintain stability by supporting the Manchus.

The Empress Dowager had therefore been quietly working to

promote her rehabilitation. She sent detailed instructions to Li Hung-chang, who had been entrusted with mediating with the foreign powers before the siege had even ended, ordering him to spare no efforts in re-establishing relations with the foreign governments. She ensured that decrees and edicts in which she had praised the Boxers were expunged from the official records while a penitential decree, issued in the emperor's name, deftly laid any blame for the recent unfortunate events at his door. Conversely, she made sure that the gifts to the besieged of ice and melons and vegetables were attributed to her generosity. She rehabilitated the moderate ministers beheaded during the siege and heaped posthumous honours on the Pearl Concubine, who, she said, virtuously committed suicide because she was unable to catch up with the court. She also disinherited the Heir Apparent, son of the exiled Prince Tuan, whom she anyway heartily disliked. Luella Miner, a thoughtful observer of the political scene, noticed that 'some of the recent edicts bear a little of the flavour of the reform edicts of 1898' and wondered whether they prefigured the Empress Dowager's return.

The answer soon became clear. Even before the peace treaty was formally signed, an Imperial decree in the name of the emperor announced: 'Our Sacred Mother's advanced age renders it necessary that we should take the greatest care of her health, so that she may attain to peaceful longevity; a long journey in the heat being evidently undesirable, we have fixed on the 19th day of the 7th Moon [1 September] to commence our return journey and are now preparing to escort Her Majesty.'[1]

The return of the Imperial Court was to be a most successful public relations exercise. However, the 700-mile journey did not finally begin until October 1901 because heavy summer rains had damaged the roads. The Imperial family were borne in yellow sedan chairs and escorted by cavalry. Some three thousand baggage carts lumbered behind. As George Morrison reported in *The Times*, no expense was spared: 'Along the frost-bound uneven tracks which serve for roads in northern China, an unending stream of laden wagons croaked and groaned through the short winter's day and on, guided by soldier torch-bearers through bitter nights to the appointed stopping places. But for the Empress Dowager and the Emperor there was easy journeying and a way literally made smooth. Throughout its entire distance the road over which the Imperial palanquins were carried had been converted into a smooth, even surface of shining clay, soft and noiseless under foot; not only had every stone been removed but as the procession approached gangs of men were employed in brushing the surface with feather brooms. At intervals of about ten miles, well-appointed rest-houses had been built.' He added disapprovingly: 'The cost of this King's highway, quite useless of course for the ordinary traffic of the country, was stated by a native contractor to amount to fifty Mexican dollars for every eight yards – say, £1,000 per mile – the clay having to be carried in some places from a great distance. As an example of the lavish expenditure of the Court and its officials in a land where squalor is a pervading feature, this is typical.'

Nevertheless, it was a beautiful sight. Wu Yung described the scene as the cortege approached the Yellow River: 'Banners flew in the air. Everyone was silent. The only sounds were the steps of the horses and the grinding of the wheels of the carts in the sand. A city of silk stretched for miles along the river bank and the accoutrements of a thousand soldiers flashed like fire. It was like ten thousand peach trees in full bloom in the springtime.'[2] After offering wine and burning incense to the River God, the Empress Dowager crossed the Yellow River in a gilded, lacquered, dragon-shaped barge. Garlands of flowers floated on the waters.

The last lap of the journey was completed more prosaically by train. The Empress Dowager seemed at ease, even excited, to be bowling along for the first time in a luxuriously appointed 'iron centipede' provided by the Belgians. Her compartment was upholstered with yellow silk, equipped with a European-style bed and opium pipes. There were even two Imperial thrones. She was so pleased that she decorated a Belgian railway official with the Order of the Double Dragon (second class). At Fengtai, the station that Polly Condit Smith and Harriet Squiers had seen burning from their temple in the hills, the Imperial party transferred to a British train. It drew into Peking on 7 January 1902 at the very moment deemed most auspicious by the royal astrologers. The first to descend was the chief eunuch Li Lienying, soon busily fussing among the baggage and bills of lading. The Imperial cortege then alighted and entered the Chinese City, passing through the gate where Mr Sugiyama had been dragged from his cart and hacked to death. They proceeded on to the Chienmen, where a group of foreigners stood clustered on a balcony jutting out above the entrance. An Imperial decree had graciously given permission for them to watch the return of the Imperial Court.

It was an unprecedented honour and the remarkable scene was described by an awestruck young Italian midshipman, Don Rodolfo Borghese: 'First to arrive were the Manchu Bannermen on their fiery little horses. Next came a group of Chinese officials in gala robes, and finally the imperial palanquins, which advanced at an almost incredible speed between the two lines of kneeling soldiers. The higher the rank of the person carried in a palanquin, the faster he should go. The Court chairs, on that memorable occasion, seemed to move as fast as the Tartar cavalry.' The chairs halted and the emperor and empress stepped down to perform the sacred rites of homecoming in a tiny temple with a shrine dedicated to the gods of the Manchus. 'As she got out of her chair, the Empress glanced up at the smoke-blackened walls and saw us: a row of foreigners . . . and, looking up at us, lifted her closed hands under her chin, and made a series of little bows.'[3]

The effect was mesmerizing, as Tzu Hsi, with her love of theatricals, no doubt intended. According to Don Rodolfo the foreigners forgot that here was 'the terrible Empress, whom the West considered almost an enemy of the human race . . . Something told us that the return of the Court to Peking marked a turning-point in history, and in our breathless interest, we forgot our resentment against the woman who was responsible for so much evil. That little bow . . . took us by surprise. From all along the wall there came an answering, spontaneous burst of applause. The Empress appeared pleased.' Morrison was also impressed, writing in his diary: 'Curious sight. Well dressed. Manchu head-dress. Uncoloured with missing teeth. Brave and undeterred. Unprepossessing face. Could not but admire courage.'

The foreigners' reaction reassured Tzu Hsi. Safe within her palace a little while later, she made another satisfactory discovery. Her personal treasure, hidden behind a silk screen, was untouched. Elsewhere in the palace grounds eunuchs were digging up other valuables that had been hastily concealed before her flight.

The work of reconciliation continued. Within days, foreign ministers were summoned to present their credentials to the emperor and allowed for the first time officially to enter the Forbidden City. On 1 February, Tzu Hsi invited the ladies of the diplomatic corps to call on her there. The MacDonalds had by now left Peking, leaving Sarah Conger as 'dean' of the little group. She rehearsed her ladies carefully, advising them to wear white embroidered petticoats so that, should they trip while curtseying, the Chinese would be spared the sight of stockinged leg. Sarah had great expectations of a closer bond between the women of the diplomatic missions and those of the Imperial Court. She had no problem with allowing bygones to be bygones and made a speech heartily congratulating the Empress Dowager that: 'The unfortunate situation which led you to abandon your beautiful capital has been so happily resolved, and that you are now permitted to return to it in freedom and in peace . . . The events of the past two years must be as painful to you as they are to the rest of the world . . . The world is moving forwards. The tide of progress cannot be stayed, and it is to be hoped that China will join the great sisterhood of nations in the grand march.'

The Empress Dowager, whose views on a 'sisterhood of

nations' can readily be imagined, replied that she regretted and grieved over the recent troubles, saying: 'It was a grave mistake, and China will hereafter be a friend to foreigners.' Tzu Hsi seems quite frequently to have used the word *mistake* when talking of the Boxer troubles and it has an interesting ambiguity. However, Sarah Conger was the last person to detect irony in the Empress Dowager's dulcet words and was completely seduced. Others were less charitable, about both Sarah and the Empress Dowager. Writing to Morrison, *The Times'* Shanghai correspondent, John Bland, dismissed 'Mother Conger's' address as 'a cold douche of imbecile fatuity'[4] and doubted the wisdom of allowing women to meddle. According to Princess Der Ling, the Empress Dowager herself thought Sarah lacked finesse, finding her well-intentioned but too hearty.

The audiences continued. American and European cigarettes were handed around amid general bonhomie, even horseplay. On one occasion Sarah and the wife of the Japanese minister were invited to lie side by side on the empress's bed. One account even tells of the emperor placing his hand on a lady's breast out of curiosity and of a eunuch raising the skirt of another lady. The Empress Dowager allowed the Imperial princesses to take luncheon at the British Legation. Sir Robert Hart's band played European music and the princesses were 'playful as kittens,'[5] giggling at their reflections in the backs of the silver spoons and filling their wide silken sleeves with cakes for the Empress to taste.

The princesses also visited the American Legation, and Sarah Conger persuaded Tzu Hsi to have her portrait painted for the St Louis Exposition by an American artist, Katherine Carl. Tzu Hsi had a traditional Chinese view of art and would not allow any shading of her face. She also insisted that both sides of her face be painted identically. When the portrait was finally completed, any subjects who saw it, including the emperor, were required to prostrate themselves. It was dispatched to the St Louis Exposition with instructions that, to protect the Imperial dignity, it must be carried vertically at all times.

Against this background of rapprochement with the foreigners, Tzu Hsi had been acquiescing in a programme of long overdue reforms. Manchus and Chinese were now allowed to intermarry; discrimination between Manchu and Chinese officials was abolished; China's legal code was revised; and the army was organized under foreign instructors. By 1904 the Baptist missionary Robert Forsyth was writing of 'the marvellous change now passing over China'[6] with the extension of the postal system and the telegraph, the growth of the railway system and of inland steam navigation – in short, everything the Boxers had feared and resisted. Also, arrangements were made for Chinese students to study in America, Europe, and Japan, hastening the influx of new ideas into China. In 1908 the US Congress decided to remit the surplus from the American share of the Boxer indemnity to pay for educating Chinese scholars there.[7]

It was Yuan Shih-kai, the general who had betrayed the reformers of 1898, who guided the Empress Dowager through this reform process. He had benefited from the deaths of Li Hung-chang in November 1901 (after eating 'a large quantity of doughcakes')[8] and of Jung Lu in 1903 to become one of her most trusted advisers. He even gave her a car fitted with a throne. Sadly, she could not use it because it would have been unthinkable for a chauffeur to sit in her presence.

In 1908, a curious and sinister coincidence occurred. On 14 November the emperor died. By the following day his aunt, the Empress Dowager, too was dead. It was of course immediately rumoured that the emperor had been murdered. However, Reginald Johnston, who saw the medical reports some years later, was convinced that he had died a natural death. A courtier told him a touching tale of how the emperor had staggered into the presence of his aunt to perform his ritual obeisance. His head was drooping and his limbs were trembling. It was clear that he was dying. Bystanders were astonished to see tears on Tzu Hsi's cheeks and to hear her tell him he need not kneel. He replied: 'I will kneel. It is for the last time.'[9]

While the emperor lay close to death, Tzu Hsi herself fell ill. A bad cold caught on her seventy-third birthday, compounded by dysentery from excessive eating of crab apples and clotted cream, apparently brought on a seizure. She died at 3.00 p.m. on 15 November. Tzu Hsi's funeral in the Eastern Tombs was a magnificent spectacle with bearers and priests in robes of yellow and red. Tzu Hsi had chosen the tiny two-year-old Pu Yi, son of Prince Chun and Jung Lu's daughter, as the new emperor. During his lifetime, the magnificent anachronism of the Manchus would pass into insignificance. He would be deposed within a few years and end his life as a gardener at the height of the Cultural Revolution.

The Empress Dowager could not have foreseen such an end for her house. She undoubtedly bore some responsibility for it.

21

. . . AND THE
FOREIGNER DEPARTS

*The starlight shone . . . softening all harsh outlines, hiding
all the horrors of destruction, glorifying the . . . sordid
surroundings in soft mystery.* – The Reverend Roland Allen

BY THE TIME OF Tzu Hsi's death, many of the foreigners who had
experienced the strange events of the Boxer Rebellion were long
gone. Within weeks of the relief, Sir Claude MacDonald had
exchanged places with Sir Ernest Satow in Tokyo. He became
the first British ambassador, as opposed to minister, to Japan. A
few days before Sir Claude left Peking, Morrison wrote to
Moberley Bell of *The Times*: 'I, personally, am very sorry. He
acted exceedingly well during the siege and was an example to
all the other Ministers, especially to the French Minister who
was a craven-hearted cur.'[1] Sir Claude died of heart failure in
London in 1915.

The Congers left Peking in 1905. Sarah felt deep sympathy
for the country she was quitting. She could not condone the
excesses of the Boxer rising but she understood the frustration
that had led to it, maintaining that China belonged to the
Chinese and that the foreigner was 'an obnoxious invader' who

The sluice or watergate under the Tartar wall through which allied troops entered to relieve the Peking Legations. Many complained about having to wade through sewage.

Fortified wall and mine defences within the Legations.

Major General Chaffee,
Commander of the US relief force.

General Gaselee the British
Commander-in-Chief of the allied
force which finally relieved the Peking
Legations.

The Peking Legations are relieved at last – scenes of joy in the British Legation gardens.

The Food Supply Committee posing proudly outside the British Legation gatehouse after relief. They had been responsible for doling out the rations of ponymeat and rice.

The gatehouse to the former British Legation in August 1998. The royal coat of arms which once surmounted the arch has been removed and the arch itself now houses a business selling security equipment.

The world's media took a close interest in the events of the Boxer rising. Some commended the way the allied powers were working together to overcome superstition and savagery. Others suggested that there was little to choose between the bloodthirsty behaviour of the Chinese and the allies and that the predatory powers were impatient for the chance to dismember China.

Bad for the Dragon! (*News of the World*)

For once the Powers seem really to be working together. (*Chicago Record*)

Barbarism and Civilisation.
(*Cri de Paris*)

Too Many Cooks.
PIG: "I ain't going to be eaten!"
(*Sydney Bulletin*)

After the siege was raised the allies extended the railway line through the walls of Peking and into the heart of the city.

The Catholic Peitang Cathedral where Bishop Favier successfully defended thousands of Chinese converts during a siege possibly even more harrowing than that of the Legations, pictured in August 1998.

The eagle lectern presented to the British Legation by the Americans who took refuge there during the siege. The lectern was damaged during an attack on the British Embassy during the Cultural Revolution. Repaired, it now stands in the entrance to the British Ambassador's residence in Peking.

The well in the Forbidden City down which the Emperor's favourite, the Pearl Concubine, was reputedly thrown on the orders of the Empress Dowager as she prepared to flee from the invading allies, pictured in August 1998.

The Empress Dowager's beloved marble boat built at huge expense on the lake of the Summer Palace where allied troops feasted after the relief. One British officer wrote approvingly that the boat looked like a houseboat at Henley, pictured in August 1998.

had forced his way in. She also believed she had established a 'genuine friendship' with Tzu Hsi, whose farewell gift to her was the lucky bloodstone she had carried with her during her flight from Peking. Her husband, Edwin, died just two years later. His friend President McKinley had become another victim of the anarchist's bullet in 1901.

Using her influential connections, Polly Condit Smith managed to quit Peking almost immediately after the siege. She regretted the necessity of having to travel in 'an antiquated Chinese boat,' rather than a train, to reach the coast but was grateful that her journey would allow time for quiet reflection. 'Floating down the river, I will have much time to think quietly about this wonderful siege, to forget the disagreeable and the bad, and to remember the great and the good,' she wrote.

Polly's hosts, Herbert and Harriet Squiers, left in September 1901, taking with them a magnificent collection of Chinese porcelains, bronzes and carvings. According to the *New York Times* of 3 September 1901, they intended to present them to the Metropolitan Museum of Art in New York. Asked whether the museum accepted 'loot', the curator replied that it did not. He added, however, that 'it would be presumed by the Museum that Mr Squiers' collection had been honestly got, he being a gentleman without question.'[2] Squiers had certainly started his collection well before the siege and frequently bought goods at official auctions after the relief. Whether he indulged in more clandestine purchases remains conjecture. Squiers became US Minister to Cuba and Peru; he apparently told Morrison that he would have become minister to Peking had it not been for spurious press reports of his looting, reports that also prevented him from running for governor of New York. He also told Morrison that he had made so much money that his failed political prospects were immaterial. Proof of this was the elegant 400-ton steam yacht *Invincible*, which he kept in England, moored at Cowes. He died in 1911, barely into his fifties.

The American second secretary, William Bainbridge, also died young, in Paris in April 1909. His wife, Mary, blamed it on overwork. His experiences in China had convinced him that, however unforgivable the attack on the legations, the foreigners had brought their troubles on themselves and that the Boxer rising was 'the spontaneous outburst of an injured people's wrath.'

The much-derided, and in many ways underrated, Monsieur Pichon returned to his true love – politics. He served as France's foreign minister and played a leading role in the negotiations leading to the Treaty of Versailles after the First World War.

The young British volunteer and bank official Nigel Oliphant left Peking in October 1900, having enlisted Sir Claude MacDonald's help in applying for compensation for his knee wound, which was still troubling him. He spent his last weeks planning a golf course on the grounds of the Temple of Heaven, the British headquarters, so that by the time he left China, he should 'have the pleasing recollection of having introduced at least one branch of civilization into Peking.'[3] He asked for a golfing trophy to be dedicated in memory of his brother, David, killed during the siege, whose possessions he was now sadly sifting through. His task was made more melancholy by the arrival in Peking of four delayed letters to his brother expressing concern for his welfare.

Sir Robert Hart finally left China some seven months before Tzu Hsi's death. After the siege, he had reassumed his autocratic but conscientious control of the Imperial Chinese Customs, writing philosophically to a colleague: 'I am horribly hurt by all that has occurred, but there it is and we can only try and make the best of it!'[4] 'Too big for resentment,'[5] according to his niece, and unwilling to waste time in pointless recriminations, he determined to have everything 'in apple-pie order'[6] again within three years – and he succeeded. Conscious of his advancing years and increasingly sensitive to Peking's cold winters, Hart retired to England in April 1908, loaded with honours and an exceedingly rich man. He died in 1911, aged seventy-six, just three weeks before the overthrow of the Manchu dynasty and the establishment of the Chinese Republic.

His erstwhile employee, Bertram Lenox Simpson, had quickly fallen out with the authorities. Sir Claude MacDonald and General Gaselee became so incensed by his looting that they issued a warrant for his arrest. He evaded capture by shunning those areas of Peking under British control. His *Indiscreet Letters from Peking* caused an uproar when published in 1906 under the nom de plume 'Putnam Weale'. The pseudonym was based on the names of his maternal grandfather, John Weale, and his grandmother, Sarah, daughter of the American revolutionary General Putnam. Lenox Simpson stayed on in China, leading a shadowy, raffish life first as a journalist, editing the *Far Eastern Times*, and then as political adviser to various of the warlords who tussled over China in the 1920s.

This was the era of men like the military governor of Shantung, nicknamed the 'Dog-Meat General' or 'Old Sixty-Three' because his erect penis supposedly equaled a stack of sixty-three silver dollars. Foreigners like Lenox Simpson and the mercenaries 'One-Arm Sutton' and 'Two-Gun Cohen' were useful to them. Sutton killed a general in single combat, defending the mint at Chungking against mighty odds; he also trained the forces of the most powerful warlord of all, Marshal Chang Tso-lin. Cohen was Sun Yat-sen's bodyguard in Canton, saving him three times from assassination. Lenox Simpson was less fortunate. He was placed in charge of the Tientsin Customs Service by one of his patrons but was murdered in 1930. Three Chinese drove up to his house in Tientsin and asked for an interview. As he was conducting them to his study, one of them drew a gun and shot him in the spine. Lenox Simpson's obituary in *The Times* was guarded. It described him as 'an entertaining writer' but dropped some disapproving hints about a career spent amid 'the chaos of military brigandage.'

The Allied commander-in-chief, von Waldersee, was grateful, despite his Chinese mistress, when the kaiser allowed him to leave China in June 1901. He had had a narrow escape when his headquarters in the beautiful Ying-tai pavilion in the Forbidden City were destroyed by fire after silken draperies caught light.

Von Waldersee managed to climb out of a window, but his chief of staff burned to death. The count died three years later convinced that Britain and Germany would shortly be at war. His last words were: 'I pray to God that I may not have to live through what I see coming.'[7]

Of the British forces, Vice-Admiral Sir Edward Seymour and Captain John Jellicoe of the Royal Navy were decorated for their respective roles. Seymour became an Admiral of the Fleet, dying in 1929 at nearly ninety years of age. Both Jellicoe and David Beatty had highly distinguished careers. At the battle of Jutland in 1916, Jellicoe commanded the British Grand Fleet and Beatty served under him, commanding a battle cruiser squadron. Despite taking fewer casualties than the British, the German fleet retreated to port and never sought battle again. Jellicoe soon went on to become First Sea Lord and was succeeded by Beatty as Commander of the Grand Fleet. Jellicoe died in 1935, Beatty in 1936.[8]

Roger Keyes also continued his successful career. Vice-Admiral Seymour initially reprimanded him for having pressed General Gaselee to take him to Peking, but relented, admitting that in Keyes's shoes he would probably have done the same thing. In April 1918, already an admiral, Keyes led a combined operation to storm German batteries and sink blockships across the harbour at Zeebrugge in Belgium. He became Admiral of the Fleet and then an MP before being appointed the first Director, Combined Operations, in 1940 at the age of sixty-eight. He died in 1945.

Although he rose to rear admiral, Commander Cradock, who led the storming of the Taku forts, was less fortunate than Keyes. At the Battle of the Coronel off South America in November 1914, he turned his outgunned, obsolete cruiser squadron to face a superior German force and went down with his flagship, HMS *Good Hope*.

Of the legation guards, Captain Halliday of the Royal Marines received the Victoria Cross and fought through the First World War to become a general. The acerbic Captain

Poole, who had been in Peking as a language student and had volunteered during the siege, was awarded the Distinguished Service Order. His brother Wordsworth, the British Legation doctor, died in Peking only two years after the siege, aged just thirty-four.

Among the Americans, General Chaffee became an army chief of staff. Captain McCalla, Vice-Admiral Seymour's second-in-command during the abortive relief expedition, became a rear admiral. Lively young Oscar Upham was one of over two dozen US Marines who defended the legations to be awarded the Congressional Medal of Honour. He died in Oklahoma in 1949 at the age of seventy-seven. In a curious episode, one of Upham's officers, Captain Newt Hall, was charged with cowardice and a range of other offenses, including abandoning his position on the Tartar Wall without orders from his commanding officer, Captain Myers. Herbert Squiers was one of his accusers but Hall was vigorously defended by Captain McCalla. McCalla had not, of course, been present in Peking but seems to have blamed events on tensions caused by interference from diplomats like Squiers, Conger, and MacDonald. He noted that Hall had refused to accept 'threats from diplomatic sources.'[9] The Court of Inquiry held in the Philippines gave Hall an honourable acquittal and the American press likened the case to the Dreyfus affair, which had recently rocked France.

Captain McCalla also did his best to help Clive Bigham's brave servant, Chao Yin-ho, who had carried the message from Seymour's beleagured relief column to Tientsin. After Bigham returned to England, McCalla arranged for Chao to enlist in the American navy on board his own ship the USS *Newark*. However, after giving up command a year later Captain McCalla received a letter from Chao reading: 'I beg to inform you that I am very sorry leave US Navy but the Japanese steward he sarcasm me very hard so I had to apply off position.' He added that he now had a job as a clerk in the Imperial Chinese Post Office.

The Hoovers left China in September 1901 – their claim for

the losses they had sustained amounted to over $50,000. Herbert Hoover, of course, went on to become the thirty-first president of the United States (1929–33). He died at age ninety, in 1964.

The dashing Chamots returned to San Francisco in 1903 with a fortune. Auguste Chamot had received $200,000 compensation for damage to the Hôtel de Pékin. He had also been a conscientious and gifted looter. The Chamots built two magnificent houses; set up a private and exotic menagerie of pythons, bears, panthers and monkeys; and bought a sailing yacht. However, Auguste Chamot took to drinking and gambling, and the great San Francisco earthquake of 1906 destroyed both their houses. Annie Chamot divorced Auguste, who died penniless in 1909, aged forty-three. He married his manicurist mistress, Betsy Dollar, on his deathbed, leaving her just fifteen cents.[10]

For many foreigners, the compulsion to leave China had been strong. They wanted to be reunited with family and friends and to forget the trauma and uncertainty of months of siege and privation. Yet their feelings were often ambivalent. The Reverend Roland Allen rejoiced that it was good to be on the way home 'free from the horrors of Peking' but China still moved him deeply. He described his evacuation to Tientsin by boat in elegiac terms: 'There was no moon, but it was one of those lovely starlight nights which we enjoy in North China, and we could see the course of the river perfectly clearly . . . The stars were reflected in splashes of gold on the dark water, and the morning star, which shone with a splendid brilliancy, cast a long stream of light on the river like a little moon . . . We moved in perfect silence; only a ripple seemed to make the universal stillness more profound. When we reached the junction of the Grand Canal with the Peiho, where stood the great Roman Catholic Cathedral, only the west front and tower were standing, and cast a long shadow on the water . . . and when we got directly opposite to it the starlight shone through the empty doorway and windows and crowned it with the tenderest light, softening all harsh outlines, hiding all the horrors of destruction, glorifying the squalor of its sordid surroundings in soft mystery. We were in raptures.'

Many members of the religious community elected to stay in China, eager to begin the work of reconstruction. Young Jessie Gates, who had suffered with the Glovers on their terrible journey, was, like many other missionaries, back within the year at the station from which she had fled, Luan in Shansi. It was heart-rending work, at first, as the missionaries tried to discover what had become of their converts, who was dead and who was alive, and to comfort the survivors. One Chinese Christian, forced to flee into the mountains, told Luella Miner with breaking voice how he had returned to discover that his wife, son, mother, and several other relatives had all been killed, 'leaving him only a little deaf and dumb daughter.'

The shock and fatigue of recent events proved too much for some. The seventy-six-year-old sister superior of the Peitang collapsed and died within days of the relief, while Bishop Scott's wife succumbed to dysentery not long after her ordeal in Tientsin. However, Bishop Favier summoned the energy to travel to Rome for a papal audience and then to France to raise money to rebuild his churches and his missions. He died in Peking in 1905, still lauded as the saviour of the Peitang.

A number of British missionaries received awards. Jessie Ransome was personally decorated by King Edward VII for her work in the siege hospital. Dr Lillie Saville was presented with the Royal Red Cross at the British legation, together with the American Abbie Chapin, who had run the hospital kitchen. Luella Miner thought that Abbie thoroughly deserved it 'for the appetizing ways in which she served up horse meat!' Luella herself put the 'bitter grief' of the Boxer uprising behind her and went on to a distinguished career as a teacher and writer, pioneering the higher education and emancipation of Chinese women. She was responsible for the establishment of Yenching College in Peking. She died in China in 1935, aged seventy-four.

Frank and Mary Gamewell left Peking, never to return, a few

days after the siege. Appointed executive secretary of the Open Door Commission in New York by the Missionary Board of the Methodist Episcopal Church, Frank Gamewell travelled all over America addressing conventions and conferences. Mary died in New Jersey, in 1906.

The missionary movement itself received a fillip from the events of 1900 and the resulting publicity. The Yale-in-China Mission, set up to commemorate the unfortunate Horace Pitkin, sent a thousand energetic new missionaries to China within the decade. The China Inland Mission, which had suffered the highest death toll among the Protestants, gained its highest number of recruits. By the time of a missionary conference in Shanghai in 1906, there were some 3,500 Protestant missionaries working in China with 180,000 converts, compared with some 2,800 missionaries and 85,000 converts in 1900.

Not everyone approved of this upsurge in missionary activity in the immediate aftermath of the Boxer rising. Mark Twain, who vehemently opposed what he saw as America's growing imperialism, argued that the missionaries were nothing more than debt collectors, squeezing reparation money out of an already oppressed people. He also accused them of demanding the life of a Chinese for every Christian killed during the rising, summing up his view of the missionaries' position with a bitter pun: 'Taels I win, Heads you lose.' (Taels were silver currency.)

Several notable personalities stayed on. George Morrison remained as *The Times*'s Peking correspondent, writing passionate and idiosyncratic dispatches and ridiculing the efforts of lesser journalists. He dismissed Captain Elliot Lockhart, sent out as 'special correspondent' by *The Times* to cover the punitive expeditions against the Chinese, as 'a thoroughly incompetent dull-witted ass.' Morrison devoted much of his energy to highlighting the dangers of Russian expansionism and was delighted when war broke out between Russia and Japan in 1905. Indeed he had openly worked for it and some even called it 'Morrison's war'. His relationship with Edmund Backhouse turned sour as he began to realize Backhouse's penchant for manipulating the truth. Morrison became deeply involved in bitter internal politics at *The Times*. At one stage there was talk that he might become foreign editor in London. However, he also nursed an ambition to be British minister in Peking. It irked him that he had never been given the knighthood or other honours he considered his due. The only formal recognition he received was the street named after him close to the Imperial City.

Morrison married at last in 1912 after years of womanizing and of decrying and cataloging in his diaries the infidelity and deceit of women. His bride was an attractive twenty-two-year-old New Zealander, Jennie Wark Robin, whom he had brought out from England to work as his private secretary. A month later Morrison began an extraordinary career as political adviser to Yuan Shih-kai at triple his former salary. Yuan had become president after the revolution of 1911, shouldering aside Sun Yat-sen. The shrewd Yuan had cultivated Morrison over the years. Morrison in turn was impressed with his political acumen, believing him to be the strongman China needed. He apparently believed Yuan's only flaws to be excessive copulation, overeating, and lack of exercise. Yuan died in 1916 aged fifty-six, gross and disappointed, after an abortive attempt to become emperor.

Morrison continued to advise the Chinese government after Yuan's death and went to Paris to help China prepare for the Versailles Peace Conference. However, he contracted acute pancreatitis. This vigorous man who had worried perennially about his weight was soon under 100 pounds. He died in England in 1920, aged fifty-eight. His heartbroken young wife survived him by only three years, dying at thirty-four.

The seemingly fragile and timorous Edmund Backhouse proved to be of more enduring stuff. He was also to exercise an influence over interpretations of the Boxer rising that far outweighed his very minor role in the events themselves. He claimed that after the relief of the legations he moved into the house of a court official, Ching-shan, and there discovered the man's secret diary. Its sensational contents and the insight they apparently offered into Chinese court politics during the Boxer period influenced scholars for generations. In particular it portrayed the Empress Dowager as a ruthless woman bent on murdering the foreigners and her adviser Jung Lu as the voice of moderation.

It was some years before the Ching-shan diary actually saw the light of day. Backhouse had gradually been transferring his allegiance from Morrison to John Bland, *The Times*'s Shanghai correspondent, who, unlike Morrison, was fluent in Chinese. In 1910 Bland and Backhouse published *China under the Empress Dowager*, based heavily on the Ching-shan diary. Morrison initially praised the book but grew suspicious. Soon he was conducting a furious dialogue with Bland, accusing Backhouse of inventing the diary. He was unable to prove it and wary of making formal accusations, but he had set hares running in the literary world. Backhouse never forgave Morrison, later writing joyfully of his hope that his dead former patron was 'howling in the deathless flames of hell.'[11]

Bland had continued to trust in Backhouse. Indeed, in 1914 Backhouse and Bland had published a further book, *Annals and Memoirs of the Court in Peking*. A review in the *New York Times* described some of the material as 'repellent and even shocking' but conceded it was essential reading for the scholar of Chinese affairs. Despite the controversy, the two books became the primary lenses through which subsequent genera-tions of westerners viewed the behaviour of the Chinese court and, in particular, the Empress Dowager, who was vividly portrayed. A typical description read: 'When she sent a man to death, it was because he stood between her and the full and safe gratification of her love of power . . . Among the effete classical scholars, the fat-paunched Falstaffs, the opium sots, doddering fatalists and corrupt parasites of the Imperial Court, she seems indeed to have been . . . a cast back to the virility and energy that won China for her sturdy ancestors. Imbued with a very femi-nine love of luxury, addicted to pleasure, and at one period of her life undoubtedly licentious . . . she combined these qualities with a shrewd commonsense and a marked penchant for . . . amassing personal property.'[12]

Source material in the *Memoirs* appeared to vindicate and reinforce the Ching-shan diary, the translated sections of which Bland had sensibly deposited in the British Museum, but scholars continued to debate its authenticity. In 1924 the Dutch sinologist Professor Duyvendak declared it genuine. Ten years later the British scholar William Lewisohn came to the opposite view, concluding that the Ching-shan diary was inaccurate, incredible, and a pastiche of sources. Backhouse defended himself but failed to produce the untranslated sections, which, if genuine, would have helped resolve the debate. He claimed he had had to sell them in 1932 and that the agent who had arranged the sale had been murdered. Professor Duyvendak reluctantly and rather ungraciously now changed tack, declaring that while Backhouse was undoubtedly gifted he was also undoubtedly a fraud. The issue hung fire and, with the passing of the years, the arguments became obscured and Backhouse again became accepted as a reputable scholar.

He was, in fact, a fantasist on a monstrous scale whose fraudulent activities extended far beyond academia. It was Hugh Trevor-Roper of Oxford University who, in his famous study *Hermit of Peking*, at last exposed Backhouse in 1976. In 1910, Trevor-Roper tells us, Backhouse was appointed Peking agent of the shipbuilding firm John Brown, with the task of persuading the Chinese to purchase battleships. With the outbreak of the First World War, Backhouse also became a British secret agent. Using his position with John Brown as cover, he was asked to negotiate a huge supply of rifles and arrange their shipment to Britain through his supposedly extensive contacts among the high-ranking Chinese. Needless to say, John Brown never saw any ship contracts. Neither did the British government ever see the massive quantities of rifles and other munitions so persuasively promised them by Backhouse. He also persuaded the American Bank Note Company of New York to allow him to negotiate a contract for the company to print money for China.

Again, it was some time before the unfortunate company discovered that Backhouse was nothing but a con.

Backhouse had also been keeping in frequent contact with the Bodleian Library in Oxford, donating thousands of documents and offering to procure others. While researching this book in the Bodleian, I noticed his name, 'Edmundus Backhouse, baronettus' (he inherited his father's baronetcy in 1918), inscribed on a white-marble honour roll of the library's greatest benefactors. However, he never achieved his heart's desire – the Oxford University Chair of Chinese. There were simply too many doubts, unfulfilled promises and hints of scandal. He would disappear for months when most needed and there were unexplained financial irregularities. Books for which the Bodleian had advanced him the freight costs failed to arrive. There were tales that he was trying to sell a nonexistent string of pearls that he claimed had once belonged to the Empress Dowager. Some of the documents procured by Backhouse with Bodleian money were found to be forgeries. The legacy of confusion and frustration persisted well into the 1920s.

In 1921, Backhouse returned to Peking, moved into a house in the Tartar City, and began to dress in white silken Chinese robes. He let his beard grow long and shunned the company of Westerners. In 1939, frightened by the anti-British attitude of the Japanese then occupying Peking, he took refuge in the compound of the former Austrian Legation. In December 1941, with the outbreak of the Pacific War, he refused repatriation and was allowed to live in a house in the British Legation compound. The Swiss honourary consul, Professor Reinhard Hoeppli, took him under his wing. Backhouse felt ill and depressed. To distract him, Hoeppli suggested he write down some of the fascinating stories with which he had been entertaining him. The result was two remarkable texts.

The first was the 'Decadence Mandchoue', an extraordinary and at times pornographic catalogue of Backhouse's supposed contacts with the Manchu Court. It included graphic accounts of sadomasochistic encounters in Peking's brothels and a detailed description of his supposed affair with the Empress Dowager from 1902, when he was twenty-nine and she was sixty-seven, until her death. 'I felt for her a real libidinous passion such as no woman has ever inspired in my pervert homosexual mind before or since,' he wrote. A typical passage describes how the Empress Dowager told him: 'You are now permitted to have me, but just before you are coming let me know. I want you to take your tool out and put it in my mouth, so that I may swallow the semen and thus enjoy a tonic.' Backhouse added as an aside that 'Oscar Wilde used to say that male sperm, if swallowed, was beneficial to the system,' and that 'he should know!' Afterwards the Empress Dowager told Backhouse that his semen tasted sour, adding, 'Don't apologize. I like it and enjoy the tart flavour.'

Backhouse claimed that court eunuchs obtained sexual gratification from male fowls, ducks or goslings, that ladies of the court shared the passion of women in the legations for having their private parts licked by dogs, and that the Empress Dowager liked to watch her ladies copulating with foxes. He recalled a visit to Tzu Hsi's tomb, after its looting by Nationalist Chinese troops in 1928. True to form but not to fact, he dwelt on Tzu Hsi's 'once beautiful pudenda which I had formerly (to her pleasure and mine own) so playfully fondled . . . displayed before us in their full sacrilegious nudity, the pubic hair still abundant.' He added with characteristic self-righteousness that he and his companions found a strip of matting and 'covered up Her Majesty's secret parts from the gaze of the vulgar.' He also described the circumstances of the deaths of the emperor and empress in 1908, claiming that the emperor was murdered by eunuchs on Tzu Hsi's orders and that she, in turn, was shot by Yuan Shih-kai, adding the spurious detail that he only used three shots from a six-chambered revolver.

The second text, 'The Dead Past', depicted Backhouse's early life. In it he claimed to have been taught by Verlaine at preparatory school; to have slept with Lord Alfred Douglas at

Winchester; to have known Oscar Wilde and Max Beerbohm at
Oxford; to have acted with Sarah Bernhardt; to have been the
intimate of such literary lions as Mallarmé in Paris and Henry
James, Edmund Gosse and Joseph Conrad in London; to have
been a friend of the Romanoffs; and to have worshipped Ellen
Terry. He also claimed to have had a passionate affair with the
Prime Minister, Lord Rosebery.

Even in these late works of fantasy Backhouse married invention, plausibility and circumstantial detail. He cocooned his
fabrications in a cunningly spun web of accepted facts, current
gossip and wide scholarship, and thereby gave them credence.
For example, Max Beerbohm's letters certainly refer to
Backhouse, but as a subject for financial exploitation rather
than friendship. Backhouse's claims to have been taught by Paul
Verlaine are also plausible. Verlaine did indeed teach for a
period at English private schools. The time when Backhouse
claims Verlaine instructed him was a blank in the biographies of
the poet to which Backhouse would have had access. However,
scholars have since discovered that during the period cited by
Backhouse Verlaine was, in fact, engaged in quite different activities in Paris.

Similarly, the private life of Lord Rosebery, with whom
Backhouse claims to have enjoyed 'slow and protracted copulation,' was the subject of much malicious speculation at the time.
His private secretary, Lord Drumlanrig, was the brother of Lord
Alfred Douglas, the cause of Oscar Wilde's trial for homosexual
acts. Drumlanrig shot himself in 1894, perhaps accidentally,
perhaps to escape his own exposure in a homosexual scandal. It
was whispered that Rosebery himself indulged in homosexual
practices at his villa in Naples, which, it was hinted, was rather
too close to Capri.[13] After meeting him, Morrison wrote in his
diary, probably as a result of Backhouse's influence, that
Rosebery had 'the same kind of mouth as Oscar Wilde's' and
that his name had been closely associated with the disgraced
writer.

However, the fact that Backhouse enjoyed weaving elaborate

and plausible fantasies does not mean that everything he wrote was a lie. Sir Claude MacDonald accepted much of what he wrote in the Ching-shan diary. Backhouse was a gifted and erudite scholar and genuinely knowledgeable about China. It was he who, in 1913, warned Bland that the recently published memoirs of Li Hung-chang, authenticated by former American secretary of state John W. Foster, were in fact a fake. The problem with Backhouse lies in distinguishing reality from fantasy. Perhaps he did not always know the difference himself.

Backhouse died in the French St Michael's Hospital in Peking in January 1944, the year he completed the texts. Hoeppli preserved them, aware of their possible historical importance but equally of their salacious content. He had been particularly struck by an incident that occurred before he ever read 'Decadence Mandchoue'. An elderly Manchu rickshaw man seeing Backhouse go by remarked casually to Hoeppli that the Englishman was said to have been the Empress Dowager's lover. Hoeppli was concerned that after his death the papers should pass into reputable academic hands. He died in 1973 and his colleagues duly submitted them to Professor Trevor-Roper for arbitration. He established beyond any reasonable doubt that Backhouse had indeed fabricated the Ching-shan diary. It had been the most brilliant deception of a brilliant deceiver, throwing dust in the eyes of future generations.

22

THE BOXER LEGACY

This episode of today is not meaningless – it is the prelude to a century of change and the keynote of the future history of the Far East: the China of the year 2000 will be very different from the China of 1900! – Sir Robert Hart

THE EVENTS OF 1900 puzzled people well before Backhouse added to the confusion. Even while the fighting was still at its height, the beleaguered foreigners struggled to make sense of their predicament. What had caused the 'unprecedented occurrences of a Peking summer,' as Hart called them? Why did the siege go on for so long? What was the reason for the extraordinarily schizophrenic behaviour of the court – attacks punctuated by unexplained cease-fires, gifts of ice and melons, and unctuous and conciliatory messages? Why didn't the Chinese overrun the foreigners while they had the opportunity? They also asked some deeper questions. Was the Boxer Rebellion just another spasm in China's fractured relations with the outside world or would it have more lasting significance? Put bluntly, did it matter?

Although the Boxer rising is one of the best-documented

episodes in the history of the Far East, it is also one of the most perplexing. One problem is that most of the available diaries and accounts were written by Westerners. Sir Robert Hart wrote wistfully to Arthur Smith: 'It would be interesting to get a really reliable Chinese account of Palace doings – and Peking doings – during 1900. As it is, we are all guessing and inferring and putting this and that together.'[1] As time has gone by, fires, deaths, forgeries and revolutions – cultural or otherwise – have rendered finding such an account ever more unlikely.

Backhouse sought to remedy the deficiency, of course. In the Ching-shan diary he makes a bellicose Empress Dowager declare: 'The foreigners are like fish in the stew-pan. For forty years have I lain on brushwood and eaten bitterness because of them, nursing my revenge.'[2] Disregarding the colourful imagery, Backhouse was probably correct in depicting the Empress Dowager's deep antipathy to the foreign encroachers. However, antipathy alone does not explain why the Imperial Court took such a suicidal course. The Reverend Allen ascribed it to 'the deep unfathomed abyss of Chinese mind and policy.'[3] He understood very well the resentments and superstitions that had sparked and then ignited the Boxer rising, but admitted: 'How far they affected the Court it is much more difficult to say.'[4] Fifty years later Chester Tan made an exhaustive study of the available Chinese sources, but was forced to conclude that 'while it is evident that the attack . . . was authorized by the Imperial Court, it is not so clear why such an attack should have been made.'[5]

Nevertheless, it is possible to make an informed guess. Wishful thinking no doubt played a part. The Empress Dowager and some of her advisers appear to have believed there was a real prospect of using the Boxers to banish the foreigners. The Chinese had thwarted Italian ambitions in Sanmen Bay without disaster, prompting the thought that the foreigners might be resisted successfully. Britain's poor performance against the Boers may have given further cause for hope. Writing in 1901, Professor Russell of the Imperial

University in Peking suggested that 'doubtful friends of England had kept the Chinese well posted in the history of the South African War. If a small republic numbering not more than 40,000 men could keep England at bay for so many months, what could not a nation like China numbering 400,000,000 souls accomplish, even if all Europe were arrayed against her?'[6] The prospect of flushing the detested foreigners with their insatiable demands out of China must have seemed highly tempting.

However, the Empress Dowager was not, on the evidence of a remarkably long and successful career, a natural risk-taker. Other factors beyond mere opportunism must have guided her. One of these could have been a sincere belief in the invulnerability of the Boxers and the 'spirit soldiers' they could conjure. The Empress Dowager was deeply superstitious and had a strong sense of theatre. Thus she was impressed by the Boxers' rituals and claims of otherworldly powers. Her belief in them gave her sufficient confidence to take a gamble.

The Reverend Allen believed, in another sweeping generalization, that 'the Eastern mind seems to feel that when all is lost it is better to die dramatically than to live tamely' and that the court 'preferred a momentary vengeance and annihilation to slavery.'[7] Yet in the circumstances the decision to attack the foreigners may not have seemed so insane to the court as it did to outsiders. It may have appeared a less dangerous strategy than seeking to suppress the Boxers. They had real social and economic grievances and could as easily have become anti-Manchu as antiforeign. Robert Hart understood this, writing in May 1900 that 'if the attempt to suppress them is made, this intensely patriotic organization will be converted into an antidynastic movement!'[8] The court felt it infinitely preferable that the Boxers should wage war against the foreigners than against the ruling house.

Ignorance and confusion contributed to the decision to go to war. Isolated in the Forbidden City and cushioned from everyday reality by the sycophancy and self-interest of her reactionary advisors, the Empress Dowager was ignorant of the true strength of the foreigners' forces and the power of their technology. In any case, the Imperial Court rarely had a complete picture of events. It was forced to make decisions based on partial knowledge, often acting on rumour alone. Events frequently outpaced the speed with which information travelled. For example, the court learned of the allies' ultimatum demanding the surrender of the Taku forts on 19 June, two days after the forts had been taken. Yet it was this report, which did not even mention that hostilities had broken out, that convinced the Empress Dowager to order the foreigners out of Peking. In the days that followed, the Empress Dowager was further misled by overfavourable reports from officials anxious to please her. On 21 June she received a memorial from the viceroy at Tientsin. Instead of admitting that the forts had fallen, he reported that shells from the forts had hit two foreign warships, that allied troops in Tientsin had been repulsed, and that the Boxers were helping Imperial forces. That very day Tzu Hsi issued the Imperial edict declaring war against the foreign powers and announced the incorporation of the Boxers into the militia. Had she known on 17 June that the forts were already lost she might have acted differently.

Yet could the foreign powers have somehow prevented the fighting? From the Chinese perspective, the muscular diplomacy of the Powers was both insensitive and inflammatory in its flagrant disregard of Chinese sovereignty. Guards were summoned to the legations in May with the late and grudging permission of the court. In early June, more than twenty foreign warships had massed uninvited off the Taku bar. On 10 June, Vice-Admiral Seymour set out from Tientsin with a 2,000-man armed relief force. The Imperial Court had not sanctioned his doing so. It must have looked like a precipitate foreign invasion. Then, a week later, came the attack on the Taku forts. The military justification was the need to keep allied communication and supply lines to Tientsin and Peking open. The worrying messages from the ministers in Peking also contributed greatly. Remembering General Gordon at Khartoum, British officers, at least, ignored such pleas for help at their peril. The American General Wilson, however, believed that the storming of the forts was 'doubtless considered by the Chinese as tantamount to a general declaration of war, and as such was made the occasion, if not the excuse, for giving a free hand to the Boxers against the entire foreign colony in Peking.'[9] George Lynch asked, reasonably enough, how British public opinion would have reacted if foreign ships had bombarded forts at the mouth of the River Thames. Herbert Hoover agreed that it was an act likely to provoke the Chinese government, which was then wavering between two factions.

Muscular diplomacy was not uncommon then (nor is it now), but news of the attack on Taku also perturbed some ministers, including Sir Claude MacDonald, when it finally reached them during their tense negotiations with the Chinese in Peking. There is an argument, however, that the ministers themselves could have prevented the crisis from escalating in the first place. Many of their contemporaries certainly thought so. Luella Miner blamed them for their inclination 'to pooh-pooh all that the missionaries said about the seriousness of the Boxer movement.' Since the missionaries lay 'outside the charmed military and diplomatic circles,' in Luella's words, their views perhaps counted for less. Nigel Oliphant, looking back immediately after the relief, wrote: 'Everybody except the diplomatists . . . knew that big trouble was bound to come, and for a full month before it broke out several people thoroughly cognizant of the Chinese . . . told their several Ministers exactly what was going to happen, and were sneered at for their pains.'[10]

Robert Coltman agreed. He thought it 'marvellous that with the information so readily obtainable as to the Boxer movement, its aims and intentions, and after having it forced almost upon them, as the British, the American and the French ministers certainly have had by their missionaries and others, the diplomatic corps should have blindly allowed themselves to be penned up in Peking with only a handful of guards, to endure treatment as disgraceful as it has been unpleasant.' He hoped that the ministers' successors would be 'common-sense kind of men, who have eyes and ears.' Certainly the oft-reviled Monsieur Pichon's was the lone warning voice in the diplomatic wilderness.

Sir Claude MacDonald later defended the diplomats on the grounds that even experienced China hands had failed to see the coming storm. How, he asked lamely, could ministers as mere 'birds of passage'[11] have been expected to understand the significance of what was happening in northern China? He cited in his defence a comment by Arthur Smith that 'the indisputable fact that men who knew so much about China did not see the Boxer movement on the horizon nor yet apprehend it when it was at their doors, is one of the most remarkable psychological facts of modern times, but it is, nevertheless, a fact.'[12] In a letter of 27 May 1900, on the eve of the outbreak, Sir Robert Hart had written philosophically and accurately to a colleague: 'We have been crying "Wolf" all the last fifty years and still life goes on as before, but some day or other there is bound to be a cataclysm but as none can say *when*, it will probably be unprovided for and so will work very thoroughly and disastrously. The frontier line between *Before* and *After* is what history can record very exactly: but our Prophets can give no exact indications, and we have to go on living as if it were always to be in the Before period.'[13]

Sir Claude also pointed out that both Sir Robert Hart and Bishop Favier believed that once the extra guards arrived, 'the Empress Dowager would see the error of her ways' and matters would quiet down. In fact, almost the reverse was true. The summoning of guards to the legations in late May was seen by the court as an aggressive and provocative act. It prompted an almost immediate reversal of the orders that had been given on 29 May for the suppression of unruly Boxers.

It is hard to escape the conclusion that the ministers did fail to interpret and anticipate events intelligently. Thus they failed both their governments and, more important, their nationals isolated in northern China. Part of the problem was their preoccupation with other issues. Their role in Peking was to monitor one another's activities and ambitions just as much as, if not more than, it was to represent their governments to the Chinese. At the same time, their governments were, in some instances, not particularly interested in what was happening in China and consequently unreceptive. The British were preoccupied with fighting the Boers and the Americans were engaged in the Philippines. When Queen Victoria pressed Lord Salisbury about progress in assembling a relief force, he replied that Russia, not China, seemed to him the greatest danger of the moment.

In the circumstances, ministers were afraid of annoying their foreign offices by appearing alarmist. In early 1900, Sir Claude wrote a dispatch to London warning of rising Boxer activity, but sent it by sea – hardly an indication of urgency! They were also, perhaps, in the wrong mindset themselves. Attacks on missionaries, although regrettable, were nothing new and, to some extent, explicable. Conversely, an attack on the diplomatic community seemed almost inconceivable. As William Bainbridge, the American second secretary, wrote: 'China had for more than half a century sat at the council board of nations and had shown herself not unskilled in the arts of diplomacy. We had hoped that she would still respect the immunities guarantied by international law to the representatives of friendly powers.' It seemed fantastic that the court would not only tolerate but also actively orchestrate an attack on the legations.

When it became clear that this was, unfortunately, the case, the ministers' ability to act decisively and effectively was hampered, even more than the Imperial Court's, by poor communications. It was even unclear to them for a while whether the foreign Powers were actually at war with China. William Bainbridge wrote of the diplomats' bafflement on the eve of the siege: 'War, if war existed, changed our status to that of enemies. We were prisoners in an enemy's Capital, in the very seat of his power and pride.' Cut off as they were from their governments, the ambiguity of their situation made it all the more difficult to know how to act, although as shot and shell began to fall such finer points became academic.

Many believed that the crisis could have been averted had Vice-Admiral Seymour reached Peking in mid-June and criticized him for taking his relief force by train. The flat terrain between Peking and Tientsin was infested with Boxers and he must have known that there was a strong possibility they would sabotage the line and leave him stranded. On the other hand, he was responding to an urgent request for help from the ministers in Peking and this modern technology was quickest. In normal circumstances the train journey should have taken less than four hours, whereas attempting to march would have taken at least a week, by which time the foreigners might well have been dead. He would also have had to wait to assemble a suitable baggage train of carts, horses, oxen and provisions. He therefore took a gamble and lost, but it was not a foolish one. In setting out he was not acting simply on what the *Spectator* described as 'the assumption that any force of Europeans however small can beat any force of Chinamen however large.'[14]

Seymour has also been criticized for retreating to Tientsin, rather than advancing to Peking, once his trains became immobilized. Sir Robert Hart, cooling his heels in the legations, certainly believed he should have tried to get through, and Squiers called his actions 'unutterable folly'.[15] Seymour considered going on but was, rightly, afraid of losing his lines of communication with Tientsin. He also had a large number of sick and wounded men to think of. Tellingly, none of the senior officers of various nationalities who accompanied him disagreed. They would all have been conscious not only of the recent reverses suffered by overeager British commanders against the Boers, but of such disasters as Isandlwana, twenty years earlier, where the Zulus had overwhelmed a major British column,[16] and the Little Big Horn, where Custer and his US cavalry had been surrounded and killed. In the circumstances, marching on across country and risking guerrilla attacks, encirclement, or a pitched battle with Imperial troops before the gates of Peking was not a sensible option. However, Seymour's subsequent difficulties and the long time it took him to regain the relative safety of the foreign settlements had one unfortunate long-term consequence: It convinced the allies that an enormous force would be needed to relieve the legations – a logistical nightmare of a task not achieved until early August.

The delay caused the besieged to wonder whether their governments had abandoned them. However, against the background of mutual suspicion, hostility and nationalism, what is surprising is not that the Powers argued about the composition, objectives, and command of the relief expedition but that they managed to put it together at all and reach Peking. The relief force and its successor, the occupation force, constituted probably the first major international police force. One commentator was moved to remark: 'The outbreak of nationalism in China has had as its immediate result the precipitation of the latent internationalism of Europe and America into the visible concrete shape of an international navy and an international army. Japan also takes her place in the international ranks. The presence of a common danger menacing the common interests of all Western Powers has brought about a practical federation of the West, the like of which has never been seen . . . The fact is that international force is police force, whereas national wars are always more or less of a retrogression to the savage lust of sheer barbarism . . . the great formula of progress is to substitute the policeman for the soldier.'[17] The pope believed that there had been nothing like it since the Crusades.

This experiment in international collaboration had to weather the problems of a divided command, sometimes succeeding only by the skin of its teeth. As Clive Bigham wrote, 'The numerous discrepancies of training, language, and method always rendered combined action slow and uncertain.' He might also have referred to the problems of unashamed nationalism, bigotry and stereotyping that enliven all the accounts.[18]

In addition, the relief force survived incompatibility of equipment and incidents of 'blue on blue' or 'friendly' fire. The latter quite often resulted from the British and American use of yards and the Continental use of meters when giving firing ranges.

The fact remains that the ill-prepared legations had to endure a protracted siege of fifty-five days. One of the most puzzling aspects is why the Chinese failed to overrun them. Admittedly, the besieged had a reasonable supply of food, at least for the foreigners who no more thought of sharing on equal terms with the natives than Baden-Powell did at Mafeking.[19] They were also fortunate that the weather, though oppressive, was not as hot and wet as it might have been, which helped limit the spread of disease. More crucially, they had the help of the starving Chinese converts, without whom, most agreed, the legations would not have survived. All the same, it should have been no contest – the foreigners should have been massacred.

They were not facing untrained peasants – most of the Boxers had been pulled back from the siege. Captain Hall later wrote that from his position on the Tartar Wall 'I never saw a yellow-sashed, fist-shaking Boxer . . . during the entire siege . . . But, I did see a large number of Chinese soldiers with various uniforms, and numerous armed coolies and thugs.'[20] Yet, although at times the assault seemed terrifying, at others it had a strangely feeble quality. Arthur Smith wrote that 'there were occasions when it would have been easy by a strong, swift movement on the part of the numerous Chinese troops to have annihilated the whole body of foreigners,' for example, by 'following up initial successes' or making 'a sudden and violent attack at a weak point . . . but the opportunities were not seized.' Another defender reflected that had they been facing Zulus or Sudanese dervishes they would not have lasted a day.

Lenox Simpson believed that the Chinese failed to take the legations because their commanders were not united. This was certainly true. Sir Robert Hart suspected 'that somebody intervened for our semi-protection.' Looking back after the siege, he realized that 'attacks were not made by such numbers as the

Government had at its disposal – they were never pushed home, but always ceased just when we feared they would succeed – and, had the force round us really attacked with thoroughness and determination, we could not have held out a week, perhaps not even a day.' Similarly, much of the available modern artillery, from Krupps and elsewhere, was never brought into action.

Hart attributed this to 'a wise man' who understood that the annihilation of the legations would cost the Chinese Empire and the Manchus dear and who intervened 'between the issue of the order for our destruction and the execution of it, and so kept the soldiery playing with us as cats do with mice, the continued and seemingly heavy firing telling the palace how fiercely we were attacked and how stubbornly we defended ourselves, while its curiously half-hearted character not only gave us the chance to live through it, but also gave any relief forces time to come and extricate us.' Sir Robert probably had Jung Lu in mind. As a senior commander, he had the military power to frustrate, even if he could not alter, court policy.

Hart's theory cannot be proved conclusively. Again the 'mysterious Backhousian twilight',[21] as Hugh Trevor-Roper called it, obscures the picture. The Ching-shan diary portrays Jung Lu as consistently pro-foreign and anti-Boxer and ascribes to him Talleyrand's well-known phrase that the siege 'is worse than an outrage, it is a stupidity.'[22] Yet the evidence of Chinese officials who knew him well suggests he was an ambitious and ruthless political animal who in the early stages, at least, supported the attacks on the legations. However, as the situation developed it seems likely that he recognized the dangers and began to oppose the Boxers. On 9 July he wrote: 'If we save the foreign ministers, it will be good for the future.'[23] While it seems unlikely that he conducted a thoroughgoing campaign to sabotage Imperial policy, evidence suggests that he prevented the deployment of high-explosive shells and heavy guns and sought to restrain the excitable Tung Fu-hsiang, keeping him short of artillery. After the relief, a quantity of Krupp guns, of which he must have been aware, were discovered in warehouses still in their packing cases.

Another factor in the failure to overrun the legations was that the Chinese were not particularly good or committed soldiers. Even Sir Robert Hart, always quick to acknowledge Chinese talent and achievement, wrote that they did not shine as soldiers. Lancelot Giles disparagingly described one attack in the early days of the siege: 'The attack was severe, but as the Chinese never bother to take any aim, no casualties were reported. One death for every 15,000 bullets fired is a poor percentage.' Even allowing for exaggeration and for the considerable use by the Chinese of firecrackers to add to the din, this was not good shooting. The Reverend Forsyth wrote: 'Strange as it may seem, the fire of the Chinese artillerymen was invariably too high. Thus the greater part of the shot and shell cleared the buildings at which they were directed, and fell harmlessly on the other side.'[24] Arthur Smith described the wild and erratic firing of the Chinese, adding that 'no one wished at the time to criticize it on that account.' In the case of the artillery it was probably difficult, even with the use of ramps, to achieve the correct elevation among the tightly packed Chinese houses.

Certainly soldiering had a low social status in China. Clive Bigham wrote of 'the military career being always held in contempt and confined to the lower and illiterate classes.' Soldiers were 'a necessary evil', not to be compared with the great and learned Chinese bureaucracy founded on the teachings of Confucius. The net result was that many of the Imperial troops besieging the legations were underpaid, poorly trained, and badly led. Although the Chinese had purchased large quantities of foreign weapons, their soldiers were seldom instructed in their proper use. Thus, although the allies were confronted by vastly superior forces, a high proportion were ineffective.

Panic and vacillation at court also contributed to the failure to pursue a consistent and wholehearted campaign against the legations. Launching the attack in a spirit of optimistic bravado was one thing; prosecuting it single-mindedly was another. Despite the vociferous antiforeign faction at court, there were those brave enough to point out the probable dreadful consequences of a massacre of foreign diplomats. Some paid with their heads, but they must have sown seeds of doubt. However, once committed to the conservative strongmen and their allies, the Boxers, the Empress Dowager would have found it difficult to draw back. But at the same time, she must have been uneasily aware that key officials elsewhere in China, particularly in the south, did not support her antiforeign policy. In fact, the declaration of war and the court's legitimization of the Boxers caused grave misgivings to those viceroys of southern and eastern China who believed the Boxers should be suppressed. Most turned a discreetly deaf ear to Imperial demands for troops and money and continued to protect foreigners. The reaction of Chang Chih-tung, viceroy at Hankow, was typical and correct: 'Since the dawn of history there has been no case where one country can fight all the Powers.'[25] Very significantly, Yuan Shih-kai, then governor of Shantung, did not allow his foreign-drilled army to join the forces engaged against the allies.

Such action not only helped prevent war's spreading to the southern and eastern provinces. It also created an illusion that what was happening was beyond the control of the throne, thus leaving the door for peace open and incidentally strengthening the position of the southern viceroys in the future negotiations. Shrewd elder statesman Li Hung-chang, then viceroy at Canton and trusted by the other southern viceroys, certainly sought to stave off disaster. He telegraphed urgently to Chinese ministers abroad that 'fighting at Taku was not ordered by the Throne' and asked them to make this clear to foreign governments. Li also disregarded the frequent and peremptory Imperial decrees summoning him to Peking.[26]

The siege of Tientsin raises interesting questions. Again there was no all-out attack on the foreigners. Lou Hoover later wrote: 'We all wonder what might have been the outcome of that Siege if they had come from the North at the same time they came from the South, East and West.'[27] Her husband described their survival as a miracle, particularly since, unlike the Peking legations, they had faced foreign-drilled and foreign-equipped troops with modern rifles, machine guns and artillery – 170,000 artillery shells landed in an area just over a quarter-mile wide and a mile long. However, once again the attacking forces were not united. Imperial troops tangled with the Boxers and the assault on the foreign settlements lacked coordination. Also, the death of General Nieh on 9 July was a blow – he was killed on the battlefield the very day an Imperial decree was issued dismissing him for his anti-Boxer actions. Apparently, he deliberately exposed himself to danger, believing he had been placed in an impossible position by contradictory commands from the court.

The attack on the Peitang came into a different category. This was left largely to the Boxers, who were united in their hatred and contempt for the Christian converts sheltering inside. They would have got in if they could have and the massacre of the defenders would have been easier for the court to excuse than if the entire diplomatic community had been slaughtered. The Peitang defenders were fortunate that the cathedral was in a good defensive position and that Bishop Favier had had the forethought to bring supplies within its lines. They were also lucky that the Boxers' fear of the Christians' supposed supernatural powers sometimes made them falter. However, had the siege lasted very much longer, there was a strong possibility that the defenders would have been starved out, died of disease, or been blown up by mines. Of all three events – the siege of the legations, the attack on the foreign settlements in Tientsin, and the siege of the Peitang – the last was perhaps the most harrowing, the most consistently prosecuted, and the closest the Chinese came to success.

In the aftermath of all the bloodshed and the drama, many foreigners, particularly experienced China hands, sensed that the Boxer rising had been a watershed. Hart was convinced that 'this episode of today is not meaningless – it is the prelude to a century of change and the keynote of the future history of the Far East: the China of the year 2000 will be very different from the China of 1900!' The missionary Robert Forsyth hoped that 'the sufferings, so patiently and bravely borne, may be looked upon as but the birth-pangs of a new era in China.'[28] Certainly the events of 1900 and their aftermath precipitated reforms that, albeit late and grudging, were far-reaching and laid the foundations for a modern state. In so doing they may have created an environment that evolved too quickly for the Manchus themselves and hence contributed to their destruction.

The tandem deaths of the emperor and the Empress Dowager in 1908 brought the problems facing the dynasty into sharp relief. As one recent historian put it, 'The Manchu leadership left behind by the Empress Dowager was thoroughly unmemorable: a child emperor, a venal regent, vainglorious young princes, effete courtiers, all of them together just smart enough to inhibit change but quite incapable of leading it . . . The end of the dynasty was only a question of time.'[29] Many believed that Tzu Hsi should never have been allowed to resume her position and that if the process of reform had been entrusted to the emperor the outcome for China might have been different.

As China underwent her metamorphosis, the events of 1900 continued to resonate. The Boxers were lauded and indeed 'reinvented' for propaganda purposes. They achieved deeper significance as a metaphor for Chinese pride and patriotism than their activities in 1900 deserve. In 1903 the republican Sun Yat-sen praised the Boxers for rising up in the face of an impotent court to prevent China's dismemberment by the foreigners. During the 1920s the Chinese Communists depicted the Boxers as anti-imperialist patriots. In 1949, after the Communist takeover, elderly former Boxers were actively encouraged to describe their experiences. Collections of 'improving' Boxer tales were published for young people. In 1955 Chou En-lai called the Boxer revolt 'one of the cornerstones of the great victory of the Chinese people fifty years later.'[30] In 1960, to coincide with the sixtieth anniversary of the rising, a play was written about the Boxers by a Manchu whose father had been in the Imperial Guard at the time.

During the Cultural Revolution of the 1960s and 1970s, the Boxers enjoyed fresh popularity, hailed as valiant patriots fighting against both foreign aggressors and a corrupt, decadent Imperial Court interested only in saving its own neck. In 1967 a series of incidents occurred that in many ways paralleled events during the siege of the legations. On 9 June, the British chargé d'affaires held a champagne reception in the British Embassy, by then in new premises, to mark the queen's birthday. Sir Robert Hart and his Chinese band might have been present in spirit. Crowds of angry Red Guards prevented most of the guests from getting through. Meanwhile, Chinese who had contacts with the foreign community were being persecuted and victimized.

A few weeks later, on the night of 22 August, the British Embassy was sacked and burned by Red Guards. In truly British style, the chargé d'affaires, Donald Hopson, was playing bridge. He described how 'I had just bid three no-trumps when I heard a roar from the crowd outside. Just like the Boxers they were shouting "Sha! Sha!" "Kill! Kill!"' The eighteen men and five women pushed a piano against a door while the wireless operator sent a final message that the mob was breaking in. The diplomatic staff were then hauled by their hair, half-strangled, kicked and beaten on the head with bamboo poles, and the women were sexually molested. An angry crowd waved posters of Harold Wilson, then British prime minister, that proclaimed that 'Wilson must be fried.' The Britons were next forced to stand in a 'circle of hate'. As in the Boxer rising, however, it seems that someone in authority decided they should not be killed, and after a while they were ushered to safety.[31]

By a quirk of fate, one of the few things to survive the Red Guard's attack was a silver cigarette box that had lived through the original siege of the legations. It was inscribed 'Tennis Tournament, Peking, September 1899. Presented by H. O. Bax-Ironside Esq. Won by A. D. Brent.' The nephew of the winner of the tournament had sent it to the chargé d'affaires as 'a symbol of resistance' just a few weeks earlier. Trampled flat, it was repaired, and a new inscription added: 'This box having survived the Boxer rebellion was damaged by Red Guards when they sacked and burned the Office of the British Chargé d'Affaires on 22 August 1967.'[32]

That the Boxer rising was a kind of harbinger of the people's revolution was part of the official folklore of the Cultural Revolution. The rhetoric in one booklet published towards the tail end was typical: 'Armed with swords and spears and shouting anti-imperialist slogans, they [the Boxers] stood erect before the imperialists and their lackeys. Bold, dignified and without a trace of sycophancy, they made the foreign aggressors shake in their boots and demolished the arrogance of the Ching official, high and low.'[33] Articles in the press quoted old Boxer slogans and demonized von Waldersee and Seymour. The Red Lanterns were praised for rising up for the rights of women. Mao's wife wrote an opera lauding the achievements of a railway worker's daughter who became a Red Lantern.

Even as recently as the mid-1980s, a memorial was erected to a Boxer leader in his home village in Chihli. During the democracy demonstrations in Tiananmen Square in 1989, young protesters told foreigners they felt like the Boxers of old, invulnerable against bullets. In the aftermath of the Tiananmen Square killings, the authorities sought to justify their actions by harking back to atrocities committed by foreigners in 1900, claiming that they exposed Western society's claims to be civilized as a sham.

The memory of Chinese weakness persists, and Li Hungchang remains a despised symbol of China's humiliation. In rejecting a proposed British compromise during discussions in the 1990s about the future of Hong Kong, Chinese leader Deng Xiaoping told the British delegation that he did not wish to go down in history as a second Li Hung-chang by making territorial concessions to foreigners.

*   *   *

If the Boxer incident caught the Chinese popular and political imagination, it also achieved an enduring significance in Western eyes by feeding the idea of the 'Yellow Peril'. The Boxers, indeed all Chinese, seemed the personification of alien superstition, xenophobia and cruelty. One Australian wrote: 'The future of the Chinese is a fearful problem. Look at the frightful sights one sees on the streets of Peking . . . See the filthy tattered rags they wrap around them. Smell them as they pass. Hear of their nameless immorality. Witness their shameless indecency and picture them among your own people – ugh, it makes you shudder!'[34] Sir Robert Hart anticipated such reactions, asking in August 1900, 'What is this "Yellow Peril"?' and defending the Chinese as 'an intelligent, cultivated race, sober, industrious and on its own lines civilized.' However, he also thought it 'as certain as that the sun will shine tomorrow' that 'the future will have a "yellow question" – perhaps a yellow "peril" – to deal with.' The Chinese would become strong enough to fulfil their desire to rid themselves of 'foreign intercourse, interference and intrusion.' To him China was a creature that had long been hibernating but was now waking, 'its every member . . . tingling with Chinese feeling.' He predicted that the Boxer movement would spread as a patriotic volunteer movement.

Anticipating China's emergence as a superpower, he wrote that in the future it would be armed not with spears and swords but with Mauser rifles and Krupp guns. Hart sympathized with Chinese aspirations but feared that, unless checked, China would one day 'pay off old grudges with interest, and will carry the Chinese flag and Chinese arms into many a place that even fancy will not suggest today.'[35]

Others saw the Yellow Peril as a more immediate threat. Far from simply seeking to keep China for the Chinese, they would soon overrun the earth. Japan had shown China the way. Captain Casserly wrote that 'Japan now ranks among the Great Powers of the world . . . All that Japan has become, China may yet be.'[36] There was also a real fear that the Chinese and Japanese would combine. In 1902 Hart told Morrison of a conversation with a Russian journalist who believed that 'England and Russia ought to combine, otherwise the Yellow Peril – Japan and China – will work mischief.'[37] (The journalist would have found it hard to credit that, after defeating Russia, Japan would, in fact, become China's dominant foreign aggressor.)

The Centenary of the Boxer Rebellion in the summer of 2000 was judged by both the Western and Chinese governments to be too sensitive to mark. They were searching again to dispel the mutual misunderstanding and myopia that had blighted 1900. On a pragmatic level both were eager to avoid giving offence as the protracted negotiations to bring China into the World Trade Organization drew to a close. The German Embassy in Beijing simply stated that they had no plans to mark the event and Baron von Ketteler's death. The French explained, 'It would be seen as a bit provocative by the Chinese side.' The British spokesman was more evasive: 'The relatives and decendants of those involved have not approached the embassy about commemorating the centenary.' The Chinese too in their desire to secure Western investment remained silent about the Boxers who are nevertheless still lauded as patriotic proto-Communists in the nation's schoolbooks. They may also have thought that praise for the Boxers, as a secret society claiming powers of healing and invulnerability, would jar with the government's campaign to suppress the Fulan Gong, an entirely peaceful sect but which also claims mystic healing powers.

Similarly, the Communist-controlled 'Patriotic' Catholic Church of China, which does not recognize the Pope, held no commemoration or mass at the Peitang Cathedral, which it now operates. Liu Bainian of the Catholic Patriotic Association took the party line that in 1900 Christianity was no more than a device of the imperialists. He commented, 'China's door was forced open. Some foreign missionaries were truly religious but others entered China with an evil purpose. They bullied and oppressed the Chinese people and collected useful information for their own countries. Ordinary Chinese people hated them very much.'

In fact, the only commemoration was planned by the Vatican. The Pope announced plans to canonize a group of Chinese Catholic victims on 1 October 2000. Catholics in Taiwan had long pressed for such canonization but the Vatican had held back in hopes of improving relations with the Chinese government. Liu Bainian refused to comment but Chinese Catholics loyal to Rome were believed to be delighted. It would not have escaped their notice or that of the Chinese government that 1 October is also Chinese National Day.

Whatever their view of the long-term consequences, those who lived through the Boxer rising knew that they had experienced something extraordinary, even unique. The events of that hot, uneasy summer of 1900 and their aftermath fully justified the Chinese aphorism 'There are things which could never be imagined, but there is nothing which may not happen.'[38]

EPILOGUE

To HELP RESEARCH this book, my husband and I visited China in August 1998. I wanted to be there at the same time of year that the international relief force fought its way through to Peking so I could experience and understand something of the conditions described so vividly in the accounts.

Our journey began in the former international settlement in Tientsin (Tianjin), along the banks of the Peiho River. We sat on the veranda of the handsome Astor Hotel, where Russian officers once noisily toasted each other with vodka and which Herbert Hoover called his 'home from home'. The veranda has been enclosed but otherwise the old part of the hotel, with its wood-panelled corridors, brass fittings, service bells and antique lift, is little changed.

In fact, Tientsin's former foreign quarter still has a very distinct identity. Many turn-of-the-century customs and commercial buildings have survived, together with some later, very sumptuous Art Deco ones. In a way it did not seem strange to walk across the wide, tree-shaded road from the Astor to find Gordon Hall largely intact but somewhat truncated. Wedged between two modern buildings, it looks a little cramped, but

with its neat masonry, pointed Gothic windows, and crenela-
tions it is unmistakable. I remembered how women and children
had flooded into it for refuge and thought of Mrs Scott, the
bishop's wife, and her dismay at finding herself living cheek-by-
jowl with a troupe of circus performers in the basement.

The nearby Victoria Park, opened in honour of Queen
Victoria's Jubilee, was where nurses once wheeled foreign children in perambulators under parasols. It too is still there,
complete with its cast-iron bandstand. We sat for a while on a
bench, watching local people play Ping-Pong or chess under the
trees, before walking on past the grand former Tientsin Club
through the old British concession to find a former residence of
the British consul. I thought of Mr Carles sitting down in his
study to write his well-meaning but obscure message of comfort
to the besieged community in Peking.

Turning our back on the old international settlement, we
crossed the Peiho by an iron bridge where tanned Moslem
hawkers from Uruqami sell sticky confections of honey, nuts
and dried fruit from mobile stalls converted from bicycles. I was
struck by how narrow the Peiho is there and how close the
opposing forces must have been. We walked on to catch our
double-decker train to Peking. Tientsin's railway station lies
close to the terminus where Seymour's men embarked for their
abortive rescue mission amid scenes of chaos, and which the
Russians later struggled to defend.

Like Seymour we anticipated a short journey. Today the trip
from Tientsin to the capital takes under three hours. Kept cool
by air-conditioning and well plied with cups of fragrant Chinese
tea by the carriage attendants, we looked out as the train passed
over the flat, hot, and parched plains. There were the same high,
waving stalks of maize that made the march to Peking so
irksome. I thought of parties of Bengal Lancers and Imperial
Chinese cavalry passing within feet of each other in the dense,
suffocatingly airless foliage, and of soldiers collapsing in the
heat along the ridged and dusty roads meandering towards
Peking. We passed through the same stations the Boxers

attacked, among them Fengtai, which Polly Condit Smith and Harriet Squiers watched go up in smoke.

Unlike the foreigners of 1900, we did not arrive at a little terminus outside the city. Instead we drew into one of Peking's new stations – a glittering structure of metal and glass – in one of the commercial districts. The Beijing of today is not the exotic culture shock it was to the visitor of 1900. It is a huge, sprawling, increasingly modern city. Of its ancient encircling walls only traces remain. Instead, it is dominated by scaffolding as yet another high-rise building – probably a bank or hotel – sprouts up.

I remembered another arrival in 1979, the first time I visited China, when there was hardly a car to be seen, and drab neonless streets were clogged with bicycles ridden by people identically dressed in blue Mao suits. At that time foreigners were allowed to travel only in groups and I never forgot the strangeness of gazing through the window of our coach to be met by a sea of faces staring back at me in equally frank surprise and with no point of contact between us. Perhaps that experience was closer to how it might have felt to the stranger of 1900 arriving in the 'capital of capitals' for the very first time.

At first the search for relics of the Boxer era seemed less promising here than in Tientsin. The face of Beijing is changing so very rapidly and the Chinese have no reason to preserve and protect buildings associated for them with shameful foreign aggression. We knew, however, that the Peitang Cathedral, northwest of the Forbidden City, still stands, and so we began our journey there.

It was a Sunday morning when we walked into the compound. I had read that the building had been restored after the Boxer rising, that a new cross had been installed to replace the one mourned by Bishop Favier, and that new statues had replaced the shattered ones in the niches in the façade. But I also knew that the cathedral had been used as a store during the Cultural Revolution, so I was not prepared for how perfect the Peitang looks today. The outside is washed in pale blue, with features picked out in white, like icing on a cake. The great carved red doors have the sheen of lacquerware. Walking around it we saw vines curling thickly along the external walls and strings of garlic hanging out to dry in well-tended gardens full of roses.

We had arrived during Mass. Glancing in through the open doors and windows, we saw a large congregation praying among scarlet, green and gold painted pillars and heard their voices resonating under the high-vaulted roof. Later, we were shown the pockmarks left by shot and shell, both inside and outside the cathedral, and delicate designs of tiny flowers painted directly on to the plaster of the interior walls.

The narrow lanes abutting the Peitang compound look much as they did in 1900 when they seethed with angry Boxers. Ancient, worm-eaten wooden doors guard the entrances to minuscule courtyards full of plants and caged songbirds. The smell of garlic, mingling occasionally with a whiff of sewage, still fills the air, a reminder that the foreigners once called the city *Pékin-les-Odeurs*. Taxi drivers now offer tourists trips around these alleys. Perhaps this means that they will soon be gone.

A fifteen-minute walk through hot, sticky streets brought us to the northern entrance to the Forbidden City. Street noises faded. The air seemed cooler. It is still the fairy-tale palace described by Polly Condit Smith, a place of fabled magnificence. The marble bridges with their motif of writhing dragons, the immense courtyards, the massive ceremonial buildings with scarlet pillars, built to awe and impress, draw the visitor on. But the real life of the Forbidden City went on in the secluded nest of courtyards and pavilions east and west of the main thoroughfare. Labyrinthine paths led us through sculpted pleasure gardens planted with orange trees and silent courtyards dotted with brass incense burners. They also led past ochre-walled pavilions with yellow-tiled roofs supported by beams of vivid blues and greens, picked out in gold leaf.

These were the living quarters of the Imperial house. We were shown the ornate theatre with its elaborate trapdoors and cunning devices where Tzu Hsi loved to watch plays and operas, the pavilion where she slept, and the silken screen behind which she sat to pronounce on matters of state. In one small courtyard we found the well down which the Pearl Concubine was supposedly thrown the night the Imperial Court fled from Peking. The notice to visitors maintains that it certainly happened. Whatever the case, I could picture an agitated Tzu Hsi listening to the booming of the allied guns and worrying what the outcome would be.

We left the Forbidden City by the great gate through which the victorious allied troops marched during their victory parade of August 1900 and went in search of the old Legation Quarter. We knew it lay close by to the southeast, but were unsure quite what we would find. After the Communist regime took over in 1949, they decided to empty the quarter of foreign missions and organizations and progressively moved them into new compounds beyond the former city walls. We had been told that some of the old legation buildings had been torn down or rebuilt and a number had been converted into Chinese government buildings – for example, the Japanese Legation is now the Beijing City Offices while the Austrian Legation has become part of the Ministry of Foreign Affairs.

Taking the underpass that goes beneath the dual carriageway running into Tiananmen Square, we found our way into what was once Canal Street. A narrow park now covers the Jade River, the noisome, fetid canal that carried sewage from the Imperial City down to the sluice gate and was a hazard to late-night wanderers. We walked along it in search of the old British Legation. The compound now belongs to the ministries of State and Public Security but we could make out the gatehouse, still set in its high grey wall. The entrance has been filled in with what looks like a shop or offices. From the writing around the door, it seems to be a shop selling security equipment such as burglar alarms, perhaps a piece of police private enterprise. The occupants politely but firmly prevented us from penetrating further. Our best view of the old British Legation was from one of the upper galleries of the adjacent Museum of History. By surreptitiously tweaking the thick net curtains, we could see the tiled roofs of old buildings and pavilions, including the chapel, dotted about the leafy grounds. I could imagine Lady MacDonald strolling under the trees with her little girls in their starched white pinafores and eager young consular officials heading for the tennis court.

The British finally quit their old legation in 1959 but were allowed to take a number of relics of the siege. These were given a new home in the ambassador's residence, which we were later shown. In a tranquil, shady corner of the ambassador's garden we saw the stone laid to mark the spot where poor David Oliphant of the Consular Service fell while cutting down a tree, together with a large plaque inscribed to the memory of, among others, Captain Strouts and Professor Huberty James. Also saved was the bell cast for Queen Victoria's Diamond Jubilee that sounded the alarm during the siege – it looks suitably battle-scarred. The brass lectern in the form of an eagle, presented by the Americans who sheltered in the British Legation, stands in the entrance to the ambassador's residence. There is no sign that it was badly damaged when it was used to barricade a door during the attack on the British Embassy in 1967.

However, we spent most of our time wandering the old Legation Quarter, trying to identify what is still there and what has vanished. Kierulff's store, which once sold European luxuries to epicurean Manchu princes, has gone, together with Auguste Chamot's magnificently provisioned Hôtel de Pékin. Many of the compound walls are still there, however, painted dark grey and still concealing private, rarefied worlds. Through open gateways we glimpsed handsome, solidly proportioned buildings standing in fine gardens, looking little changed since 1900, as well as more modern buildings. It was interesting to find that the stone lions that flanked the entrance to the former French Legation are still there, guarding what is now the Peking residence of Prince Sihanouk.

Most interesting of all was the discovery that the topography of the quarter is relatively unchanged. It was surprisingly easy to peel back the layers and reconstruct that vanished world of 1900. For example, I could trace the route taken by missionaries Frank and Mary Gamewell and their long crocodile of frightened converts when the marines escorted them into the legations for safety. I could understand how easy it must have been for Imperial troops to fire into the compounds from the nearby walls of the Imperial City. I could calculate where the first allied troops entered through the sluice gate, even though a multilane highway now runs over the spot. I could appreciate how vulnerable and exposed the Fu must have been, across the canal from the British Legation, and what a desperate struggle Colonel Shiba had to defend it. Walking the narrow twisting lanes that link the main boulevards, I could picture how they must have looked in 1900.

Yet one thing stands out for me. After much searching we found the only surviving street name from the Boxer period. It is carved on a wall near the old Imperial Customs and has, incredibly, outlived revolution and war, as durable and integral a part of the history of Peking as the elderly gentleman who inspired it. I brushed the omnipresent dust away and the lettering stood out sharp and clear – *Rue Hart*.

NOTES AND SOURCES

THE BOXER STORY is rich in personal accounts and reminiscences, particularly on the Western side. Many of the foreigners kept detailed diaries, wrote copious letters or subsequently published books. I was intrigued by the extent to which the writers were influenced by such factors as background, nationality and reasons for being in China. Another issue was how far their own prejudices and preconceptions, and their view of those of their readers, show through in what they wrote.

It was also interesting to look at their motivation for wanting to record their experiences. Were they writing for themselves, perhaps as a kind of catharsis, enabling them to express privately fears and anxieties they could not share in public? Was it a release valve in a besieged community where people under stress were packed closely together? Were they writing for friends and family, to comfort and to reassure? If so, did this produce a nonchalance of style like the 'stiffening of the lip' of British officers who underplayed their experiences in letters home? Were they writing to tell the world what had happened to them, like some families who wrote farewell letters and locked them in the safe of the British legation in case they were killed? Were they writing with a view to publication? Were they writing to justify their own actions, or perhaps to criticize and denigrate the actions or behaviour of others? I realized that criticisms in some private accounts had to be treated with as much caution as praise in some of the works written specifically for publication. I was struck, too, by the difference between those who were recording events as they happened when they did not know the outcome – like Oscar Upham – and those who were writing after the event, with all the benefits and comforts of hindsight.

Whatever the case, I asked myself whether the writers could really have known as much about what happened, and why, as they claimed. Most were, after all, only eyewitnesses to a part of the events they recorded. They had to rely on others to fill in the wider picture. The 'fog of war' effect was particularly true where writers with the relief force spoke of what happened in the siege of the legations, but also where those actually in the legations were writing about events in other parts of the compound. Similarly, what was really going on in the Imperial Court could only be guessed at by Westerners, who often recorded rumours as fact. There were also considerable differences among the writers in their level of understanding of China and her customs. I found it surprising how relatively few of the residents spoke Chinese. Yet, as the accounts show, limited knowledge was not allowed to inhibit critical expression! In assessing them I became wary not only of self-justification on the part of long-term residents but also of ignorance, misunderstanding or excessive generalization from visitors, military men or journalists arriving during the crisis.

Because this book is intended primarily for the general reader, I have tried to keep the number of textual references to manageable proportions and have not referenced the numerous quotations from the following primary sources, except where I thought the source might be unclear in the context. For complete publishing information on the following (as well as for all the sources used in the book), refer to the Bibliography.

Allen, R., *The Siege of the Peking Legations*
Bainbridge, M. and W. Bainbridge, Journals and Papers
Bigham, C., *A Year in China*

Brown, F., *From Tientsin to Peking with the Allied Forces*
Coltman, R., *Beleaguered in Peking*
Conger, S. P., *Letters from China*
Drew A., and E. B. Drew, Notes and Journals
Hall, Capt. N., Papers
Hart, Sir R., *These from the Land of Sinim*
Hooker, M. (P. Condit Smith), *Behind the Scenes in Peking*
Hoover, H. and L. Hoover, Letters and Papers
Keyes, Sir R., *Adventures Ashore and Afloat*
Marchant, L. R., ed., *The Siege of the Peking Legations, Diary of Lancelot Giles*
Martin, W. A. P., *The Siege in Peking*
Miner, L., Diary and Papers
Morrison, G. E., Diary and Papers
Oliphant, N., *Siege of the Legations in Peking*
Poole, F. G., Diary
Ransome, J., *The Story of the Siege Hospital*
Seymour, Sir E. H., *My Naval Career and Travels*
Smith, A. H., *China in Convulsion*
Tuttle, A. H., *Mary Gamewell and Her Story of the Siege*
Upham, O., Journal
Weale, B. L. Putnam (B. L. Simpson), *Indiscreet Letters from Peking*

I have included below a few notes, often anecdotes or sidelights, that I found interesting and relevant but that might have interrupted the flow if included in the main text.

PROLOGUE

1. *Daily Mail*, 16 July 1900.
2. *New York Times*, 16 July 1900.
3. Letter from Lord Salisbury to Queen Victoria, 20 July 1900, *Letters of Queen Victoria*, Vol. III, p. 573.

   By 1900, the sixty-nine-year-old Lord Salisbury had been prime minister twice previously. In his third term of office, which began in 1895, he was combining the roles of foreign secretary and prime minister. A Conservative patrician to the core, he was a direct descendant of Robert Cecil, adviser to Queen Elizabeth I. Educated at Eton and Oxford, he regarded democracy as somewhat at odds with individual freedom and was strongly critical of radical ideas about 'progress'. As prime minister he chose not to live in Downing Street. Perhaps understandably, given his family history, he had a strong faith in the historical continuity of government. In foreign policy he was a relatively benign imperialist. Salisbury was also an amateur scientist and fellow of the Royal Society and very enamoured of new inventions such as the telephone and electricity. In 1881 his home, Hatfield House in Hertfordshire, had been one of the first two in England to have electricity installed. Because there were no fuses, his electric lights and their wiring often sparked, igniting wooden beams and panelling. He and his family extinguished incipient fires by throwing cushions and, quite unperturbed, just carried on talking. He had always been absentminded, but towards the end of his life a combination of myopia and detached aloofness meant that Salisbury frequently failed to recognize people, even members of his cabinet and his butler. After he left office in 1902, King Edward VII gave him a signed photograph of himself. Salisbury looked at it carefully, shook his head sadly, and said 'Poor Buller.' (Sir Redvers Buller was one of the generals defeated on several occasions during the early stages of the Boer War.)

4. *Whitaker's Almanack* for 1998 gave populations as follows: United Kingdom, 56 million; United States, 249 million; Japan, 125 million; France, 58 million; Germany, 81 million; Italy, 57 million; Russia, 148 million; and China, 1,208 million. Writing in *The North American Review* of January 1900, the director of the US Census described the arrangements. In addition to himself there was an assistant director; five statisticians; 2,800 enumerators; 300 supervisors; 3,000 clerks, messengers and others; and 50,000 people actually to take the census. The results in terms of 'race, sex, colour, age, conjugal condition etc.' were to be put on punch cards. Although individually a mere seven thousandths of an inch thick, it was estimated that the cards used would, if stacked up, be about nine miles high and weigh 200 tons. The

director mistakenly expected the US population to be no more than 73 to 74 million.

5. William Thomas Stead, *Review of Reviews*, December 1900, Vol. 22, p. 536.

William Stead (1849–1912) was probably the most prominent journalist of his age, with self-confidence equal to his energy. His telegraphic address was 'Vatican London' because he thought of himself as the pope of journalism. A campaigning journalist, he edited the *Pall Mall Gazette* in the 1880s. Among the issues he embraced were the conditions of Siberian convicts, slavery in the Congo, and, closer to home, village libraries and decent housing. However, his most famous campaign was against child prostitution. He claimed to have purchased a thirteen-year-old virgin, Eliza Armstrong, for £5, publicizing his exploit under the title *The Maiden Tribute of Modern Babylon*. His story made headlines around the world and was a major influence in raising the age of consent from thirteen to sixteen in the United Kingdom. It also led to his being sentenced to three months in prison for abduction. On his release, Stead continued to work at the *Pall Mall Gazette* until he founded the *Review of Reviews*. He subsequently campaigned for 'sane imperialism', arms limitation, the use of arbitration to settle international disputes (he was a strong supporter of the Hague conference) and a closer union of the English-speaking world – as well as for the regeneration of Chicago. After a visit, he wrote a book called *If Christ Came to Chicago* and formed a civic federation to orchestrate change. The confidant of politicians and princes, he was strongly opposed to the Boer War and lost Cecil Rhodes's friendship as a result. Like Arthur Conan Doyle, he became a spiritualist in his later years and believed himself to be a reincarnation of Charles II sent back to make amends for previous misdemeanours. His spiritualism did not help him foresee that the *Titanic*, on which he perished, would sink.

6. Review of *Anglo-Saxons and Others* by Aline Gorren, *Review of Reviews*, July 1900, Vol. 22, p. 90.

7. Ada Mateer, *Siege Days*, p. 373.

8. Albert Beveridge's comments on American imperialism are

quoted in Barbara Tuchman's *The Proud Tower*, pp. 153–4.

9. In 1900, the fifty-six-year-old William McKinley (1843–1901) was in the final year of his first term as the twenty-fifth president of the United States. He had fought in the Civil War, beginning as a private in the Ohio Volunteer Infantry, but ending as a major. After studying law, this devout, teetotalist Methodist entered politics as a Republican. He was a believer in high tariffs to build business and was instrumental in related tariff reforms. He was nominated for the presidency by the Republicans in 1896 as something of a compromise candidate. Some in his own party considered him spineless – one Republican even declared that 'McKinley had no more backbone than a chocolate eclair.' In office he presided over growing imperialism and rising prosperity. In the 1900 presidential campaign he and his running mate, Theodore Roosevelt, campaigned on the promise of 'the full dinner pail' and an expansionist policy.

10. Quoted in *Expansion in the Pacific*, Small Planet Internet Site.

11. *Life* magazine, 15 November 1900.

12. Warming to the theme of sporting versus academic prowess in January 1900, one British magazine suggested that Oxford and Cambridge universities seemed to the foreign observer little more than a federation of sporting clubs. However, Lord Curzon thought sport rather commendable, writing in his *Problems of the Far East*: 'It is his passion for games, which keeps him healthiest of all the foreign settlers in the East, while the German grows fat, and the Frenchman withers, the Englishman plays lawn tennis under a tropical sun.'

13. Britain's reaction to the defeats was, however, generally stoical, causing the *New York Evening Post* to praise one virtue of their fellow Anglo-Saxons: 'Englishmen have, on the whole, taken their unexpected disasters in South Africa in manly fashion. One can imagine what would have happened in France under similar circumstances.'

14. Quoted in Walter Lord's *The Good Years*, p. 1.

15. Extracts from Hague Conventions quoted in Barbara Tuchman, op. cit, p. 267.

16. *The Times*, 17 July 1900.
17. This rhyme by a woman from Iowa, published in *The Independent* in August 1900, is quoted in Paul Cohen's *History in Three Keys*, p. 235.
18. Quoted in introduction to *The Siege of the Peking Legations, Diary of Lancelot Giles*, ed. L. R. Marchant, p. 9. It is surprising for how long and by whom theories on racial origins and characteristics have been held. For example, prompted by a note in Patrick French's book *Liberty or Death* I found in the Public Record Office, London, the following letter dated 6 August 1942 from an official in the British Embassy in Washington reporting an astonishing conversation with President Franklin Roosevelt:

> 'Dear Cadogan,
>
> Amongst many other thoughts thrown out by the President when I saw him on August 2 was the following: – He had set one Prof. Hrdlicka of the Smithsonian Institute to work on a private study of the effect of racial crossing. A preliminary report had been given him, with all of which he by no means agreed. But it seemed to him that if we got the Japanese driven back within their islands, racial crossing might have interesting effects particularly in the Far East. For instance Dutch-Javanese crossings were good, and Javanese-Chinese. Chinese-Malayan was a bad mixture. Hrdlicka said that the Japanese-European cross was bad and the Chinese-European equally so. It was here he disagreed with the Professor. Experience the President said, had shown that unlike the Japanese-European mixture, which was he agreed thoroughly bad, Chinese-European was not at all bad.
>
> The President had asked the Professor why the Japanese were as bad as they were, and had followed up by asking about the Hairy Ainus [*sic*]. The Professor had said the skulls of these people were some 2000 years less developed than ours (this sounds very little doesn't it?). The President asked whether this might account for the nefariousness of the Japanese and had been told it might as they might well be the basic stock of the Japanese.

As far as I could make it out, the line of the President's thought is that an Indo-Asian or Eurasian or (better) Eurindasian race, could be developed which would be good and produce a good civilization and Far East "order" to the exclusion of the Japanese languishing in Coventry within their original islands.'

19. A. H. Smith, *China in Convulsion*, Vol. I., p. 8.

20. Story of encounter between the Reverend Timothy Richard and a Chinaman is from T. Richard, *Forty-Five Years in China,* pp. 156–57.

21. Anarchists also turned their attention to the British royal family. In April 1900 the Prince of Wales was shot at by a sixteen-year-old anarchist in Brussels but was unhurt.

22. Quoted in R. O'Connor's *The Boxer Rebellion*, p. 176.

23. When Colis P. Huntingdon, the American railroad builder, died on 13 August 1900 his obituary said that 'he and his associates reduced the time from New York to San Francisco from six months to six days.'

24. W. A. P. Martin, *The Siege in Peking*, p. 74.

25. In 1900 France was the biggest manufacturer of cars, producing some 1,500 that year.

26. Quoted in Barbara Tuchman, op. cit., p. 268.

27. A novel product (to the British at least) at the Paris Exposition was the yoghurt on show in the Bulgarian pavilion. One British organizer dismissed it as 'a mixture of cheese and cream appreciated locally but requiring a special palate to judge it.' Other innovations or introductions during 1900 included the paper clip designed by Johann Waaler, a Norwegian based in Germany, and the box 'Brownie' camera invented by George Eastman. It was sold in the United States for one dollar and advertised as the first camera 'anyone' could use. It had no viewfinder, just a mark showing where to aim.

28. In 1900, a tourist guidebook described Le Moulin Rouge as resembling 'a railway station miraculously transformed into a ballroom . . . On each side of the room is a raised platform, a broad open gallery from which you can watch the dancing . . .

and enjoy a general view of all the women in full regalia, strolling about and parading before you in this veritable marketplace of love . . . A few English families . . . are scandalized by the sight of these women who dance by themselves . . . and whose muscular elasticity, when they spread their legs wide apart [in the splits] betokens a corresponding elasticity of morals . . . Through the lace ruffles of drawers or the transparent gauze of silk stockings, you can often catch glimpses of pink or white skin, displayed as samples by these pretty vendors of love.' (From *Guide des Plaisirs à Paris*, quoted in J. Frey's *Toulouse-Lautrec – A Life*, pp. 261–62).

29. Oscar Wilde went to Paris after serving a sentence in Reading Jail for homosexual practices and died there, in 1900, aged forty-six, probably from syphilis caught from a female prostitute during his student days at Oxford University. Henri de Toulouse-Lautrec, also probably syphilitic, died on 9 September 1901.

30. E. Sellon's *The Ups and Downs of Life* (1867), quoted in D. Judd's *Empire*, p. 179.

31. B. L. Putnam Weale, *Indiscreet Letters from Peking*, p. 246.

My great-aunt was fond of telling a story that when her husband was appointed a magistrate in Burma in the 1920s the local Burmese leader brought him a teenage boy and a teenage girl so that he could choose whichever he preferred as a companion. However, my aunt would never say which, if any, he selected.

32. Quoted in S. Hyne's *The Edwardian Turn of Mind*, p. 152.

Only in 1884 did the UK Parliament rescind the law that allowed men to have their wives jailed for refusing sexual intercourse. In 1891 a British court ruled that a man could no longer imprison his wife at home to enforce restitution of conjugal rights, causing *The Times* to lament that one fine morning in England marriage was suddenly abolished.

33. At the beginning of 1900, George Nathaniel Curzon was forty years old and had been viceroy of India for one year. He had previously journeyed extensively through the East and Far East and his subsequent writing had gained him a reputation as a leading authority on Asiatic affairs. He was capable of telling

stories against himself, of which the following say much both about Curzon and his times. The sight of private soldiers bathing in a swimming pool apparently caused him to exclaim, 'Good heavens, I never knew that the working classes had such white skins.' Describing the experience of taking a bus, he famously remarked: 'This omnibus business is not what it is reported to be. I hailed one at the bottom of Whitehall and told the man to take me to Carlton House Terrace. But the fellow flatly refused.' These quotes are given on p. 181 of the *Oxford Book of Political Anecdotes*.

34. The self-governing colony of New Zealand was the first country to give its female citizens full rights to vote. It did so in 1893 with no qualification other than attaining the age of majority. In the United Kingdom in 1900, about 1 million women had the right to vote in municipal elections. In the United States, women's suffrage had made inroads before 1900 in four thinly populated Western States: Wyoming (1869), Colourado (1893), Utah and Idaho (both 1896). Britain had, however, had her first Asian MP when, in 1892, Dadabhai Naoraji, the son of a Parsee priest from Bombay, was elected Liberal MP for Central Finsbury, despite various racial slurs during the campaign by his Conservative opponents including Lord Salisbury. I recently saw his statue, which still stands in central Bombay.

   Sir Claude MacDonald, when serving in West Africa in 1891, appointed the first woman to preside over a court within British jurisdiction. Her name was Mary Mitchell Slessor. She sat in judgment shoeless and stockingless but was entirely in control. One official described her as 'unhampered by legal technicalities' in her judgments. Once, when a man sued another for debt, she found in favor of the creditor, but, because she thought him a bad man who treated his mother disgracefully, she ruled that he could be paid only after the debtor had given him a caning in her presence.

35. Quoted in Vincent Cronin's *Paris on the Eve 1900–1914*, p. 316.

36. The comments of the Duchesse d'Uzes and Max Nordau on women and sport are quoted in the British *Review of Reviews* of

July 1900, in turn quoting an article of July 1900 in the French *Revue des Revues* on women and modern sports.

37. George Lynch, *The War of the Civilisations*, p. 142.

1. A THOUSAND DEATHS

1. The various uncomplimentary remarks about the smells of Peking are drawn from Captain Poole, Lady Susan Townley, Clive Bigham, and Lord Curzon but can be found in most accounts of the period.

2. B. L. Putnam Weale, *Indiscreet Letters from Peking*, p. 23.

3. Lord Curzon, *Problems of the Far East*, pp. 245–46.

4. Ibid., p. 245.

5. Ibid., p. 251.

6. Juliet Bredon, *Peking*, p. 67.

7 . Footbinding had been introduced about 800 years earlier. At the age of three or four, little girls had their feet tightly bound with bandages so that all the toes except the big one were folded under the sole to make the foot slender and pointed. The sight of a woman teetering on her little points, moving her hips from side to side 'like a tender young willow in a breeze' to keep her balance, was believed to have an erotic effect on men. The ideal length was three inches. In 1980 during a visit to Sian I saw a group of old ladies whose feet were still bound and was told that releasing them would be more painful than leaving them bound at this stage in their lives.

8. Lord Curzon, op. cit., p. 252.

9. Mary Hooker (Polly Condit Smith), *Behind the Scenes in Peking*, p. 3.

10. Juliet Bredon, op. cit., p. 62. Chinese men had their heads shaved at the front while the hair at the back was plaited into a long pigtail or queue that hung down their backs, sometimes as far as their knees. While working, many curled their queues around their heads for convenience.

11. B. L. Putnam Weale, op. cit., p. 26.

12. A. H. Smith, *China in Convulsion*, Vol. I, p. 127.

13. B. L. Putnam Weale, op. cit., p. 28.

14. The references to the Empress Dowager's sexual proclivities are from Edmund Backhouse's typescript 'Decadence Mandchoue'.
15. Princess Der Ling, *Old Buddha*, p. 229.
16. Lord Curzon, op. cit, p. 279.
17. Sir Meyrick Hewlett, *Forty Years in China*, p. 4.
18. A. H. Smith, op. cit., Vol. I, p. 27.
19. Ibid., pp. 8–9.
20. The Chinese would argue rightly that the 1898 agreement was an 'unequal treaty'. When Britain surrendered this lease in 1997, Hong Kong itself became unviable. Consequently the whole territory was returned to China. Some Hong Kong officials blamed Claude MacDonald for the handover! One recently retired British senior official from the Hong Kong Government Service told me, somewhat ruefully, that Sir Claude was responsible for the Hong Kong lease's being only 99 years rather than in perpetuity, since he thought 99 years 'as good as forever'.
21. Sir Claude MacDonald's lecture to the Royal United Services Institution (RUSI), 25 March 1914, published in the *Journal of the Royal United Services Institute*, Vol. 59, 1914.
22. Letter from Francis Younghusband to *The Times*, 19 July 1900. In his youth, Younghusband (1863–1942) was a leading player of the 'Great Game', seeking intelligence about Russian movements and aspirations in the mountains of central Asia on the borders of Britain's Indian Empire. In 1900 he was an imperialist to the core and adviser to and admirer of Lord Curzon. In 1903 Younghusband turned a small British diplomatic mission into an invasion of Tibet. Later he became the organizer of early British attempts to climb Mount Everest. Following a spiritual conversion in Tibet, he became a mystic and freethinker.
23. In 1900, according to *Whitaker's Almanack*, 363 of the 672 foreign companies in China were British, 99 were German and 87 were Japanese.
24. John Hay (1838–1905) was born in Indiana. He was one of Abraham Lincoln's private secretaries. After Lincoln's death, he served in the US legations in Paris, Vienna and Madrid, but also wrote very successful short stories, the most famous of which

were entitled 'Little Breeches' and 'Jim Bludso' from a collection called *Pike County Ballads*. He was also a poet and co-author of a major biography of Lincoln. When President McKinley came into office, he first made Hay US ambassador to Great Britain and then appointed him secretary of state in 1898. It was Hay who coined the phrase 'a splendid little war' to describe the fighting with Spain. He took a major role in the peace settlement with Spain. In addition to the Open Door policy in China, achievements of his years in office concerned the construction of the Panama Canal and the settlement of the boundary between Alaska and Canada.

25. Li Hung-chang (1823–1901) played a pivotal role in China over many years. He rose to prominence as governor of Kiangsu province during the Taiping Rebellion. He was instrumental in making arrangements with the western governments to raise the Ever Victorious Army led, most famously, by Gordon and in other measures leading to the rebellion's suppression. After the massacre of Christians in Tientsin in 1870, the Imperial Court appointed him governor of Chihli, the province in which Tientsin was located. From then on he became a major figure in China's relations with the West. He played the relatively weak Chinese hand well, while at the same time trying to encourage gradual reform. Although usually acting in China's best interests, as he saw them, he was considered pro-Russian and Tsarist archives have revealed that he took a large bribe from the Russians during the negotiation of the Sino-Russian Treaty in 1896. China's defeat by Japan caused him to be dismissed as viceroy, but he remained active in foreign relations. In December 1899, at age seventy-six, he was appointed viceroy of Kwangtung and Kwangsi and, with other southern viceroys, helped confine the fighting to the north. He was then given a leading role in the peace negotiations.

Li Hung-chang and Sir Robert Hart had known each other for over thirty-five years by 1900 and their relationship was close, though not always friendly. Sir Robert once said of him that he had 'lots of ability, but no honesty or veracity'. On another occasion he remarked that Li was 'overrated and not necessary' to Chinese foreign policy. In a remark typical of his time and underlining the difference between Eastern and Western customs, Hart wrote spitefully that 'the great man dines out when asked and he was at MacDonald's Fancy Dress Ball on New Year's Eve – very much out of place with his pocket spittoon to the fore always.' George Morrison was disgusted by Li's habit of blowing his nose into a teacup. He also reacted indignantly in 1897 to Li's attempt to bribe him to advocate increased import duties in *The Times*.

26. Quoted in Chester Tan, *Boxer Catastrophe*, p. 8.
27. Imperial edict of 21 November 1899, quoted in P. H. Clements, *The Boxer Rebellion: A Political and Diplomatic Review*, p. 105.
28. George Lynch, *The War of the Civilisations*, p. 310.
29. Lord Curzon, op. cit., p. 237. Many of his political rivals and even some of his cabinet colleagues would have considered these words to apply equally well to Curzon. His undergraduate colleagues at Balliol College, Oxford, coined the following lines: 'My name is George Nathaniel Curzon, I am a most superior person.' The 17th Earl of Derby observed that 'he makes one feel so terribly plebeian' (*Oxford Book of Political Anecdotes*).
30. Quoted in Chester Tan, op. cit., p. 17.
31. A. H. Smith, op. cit., Vol. I, p. 125.
32. W. A. P. Martin, *Siege in Peking*, p. 59.
33. Reginald Johnston, *Twilight in the Forbidden City*, p. 41.
34. Edmund Backhouse, op. cit.
35. Princess Der Ling, *Two Years in the Forbidden City*, p. 171.
36. A distinguished Frenchman quoted in Katherine Carl, *With the Empress Dowager of China*, p. 101.
37. Ibid., p. 164.
38. After leaving China, Kang Yu-wei organized political movements and founded newspapers among the Chinese community abroad. He travelled avidly around the world and was a keen student of astronomy with a great interest in the emerging genre of science fiction. His political philosophy became more extreme and he favoured the abolition of all distinctions between and within

nations. Property and the family would all be abolished in a kind of egalitarian Utopia.

39. Reginald Johnston, op. cit., p. 38.

40. J. H. Wilson, *Under the Old Flag* Vol. II, p. 517.

41. C. Pearl, *Morrison of Peking*, p. 90.

42. Lady MacDonald, *Empire Review*, April 1901. In *Boxers, Blunders, and Bullets or the Crisis in China*, the missionary Frederick Brown wrote bitterly of the success of Tzu Hsi's overtures to the gullible diplomatic ladies who were 'all united in the opinion which they doubtless communicated to their husbands that "she is a nice old lady."'

43. Princess Der Ling, *Two Years in the Forbidden City*, p. 144.

44. A. H. Smith, op. cit., Vol. I, p. 114.

45. Sir Robert Hart, *These from the Land of Sinim*, p. 51.

2. BOXERS AND DEVILS

1. Quoted in J. W. Esherick, *The Origins of the Boxer Uprising*, p. 231.

2. Quoted in Ibid., p. 243.

3. Quoted in Pat Barr, *A Curious Life for a Lady*, p. 317.

4. Robert Coltman, *Beleaguered in Peking*, p. 37.

5. Quoted in Princess Der Ling, *Two Years in the Forbidden City*, p. 179.

6. Wen Ching, *The Chinese Crisis from Within*, p. 325.

7. Ibid., p. 327.

8. Lord Curzon, *Problems of the Far East*, p. 314.

9. Wilbur Chamberlin, *Ordered to China*, p. 48.

10. The bellicose missionary is described in A. H. Savage-Landor's *China and the Allies*, Vol. I, p. 241.

11. Quoted in Princess Der Ling, op. cit., p. 177.

12. The numbers of nuns, priests, missionaries, and Christian converts are quoted in P. Cohen, *History in Three Keys*, pp. 93 and 322.

13. G. Lynch, *The War of the Civilisations*, p. 106.

14. Letter from Luella Miner, 4 May 1900, quoted by P. Cohen, op. cit., p. 149.

15. Charles Price's diary between 15 and 23 June, quoted in E. J. Price, *China Journal 1889–1900*.

16. A. H. Savage-Landor, op. cit., Vol. I, p. 23.

17. Rev. Allen, *Cornhill Magazine*, November 1900.

18. William Bainbridge in his typescript journal, 'Besieged in Peking.'

19. Letter to G. E. Morrison from G. Owen, 24 May 1897, quoted in *Correspondence of G. Morrison 1895–1912*, ed. Lo Hui-min.

20. W. A. P. Martin, *Siege in Peking*, p. 141.

21. Journal of Anna Drew.

22. G. Lynch, op. cit., p. 196.

23. Report of the Reverend Henry Mathews quoted in Victor Purcell, *The Boxer Uprising*, p. 290.

3. THE APPROACHING HOUR

1. S. Conger, *Letters from China*, p. 67.

2. P. Clements, *Boxer Rebellion*, p. 106.

3. Sir M. Hewlett, *Forty Years in China*, p. 6.

4. G. E. Morrison's diary, quoted in C. Pearl, *Morrison of Peking*, p. 83.

5. Letter from R. Coltman to G. E. Morrison, 16 January 1900.

6. Ibid.

7. S. Conger, op. cit., p. 189.

8. G. E. Morrison quoted in C. Pearl, op. cit., p. 83.

9. C. Bigham, *A Year in China*, p. 41.

10. Comments on the Tsungli Yamen are from C. Bigham, Ibid., pp. 42, 43.

11. Ibid., p. 48.

12. Ibid. Clive Bigham was right. The Westerner's consumption of dairy products like milk and butter accounted at least in part for what the Chinese discerned as an unpleasant sweetish smell.

13. The edict of 11 January 1900 is quoted in British Parliamentary Papers in a dispatch from Sir Claude MacDonald of 17 January 1900.

14. A. H. Smith, *China in Convulsion*, Vol. I, p. 189.

15. At this time it had become quite common for titled European men

like von Ketteler to seek wealthy American brides. The heiress Jennie Jerome married Lord Randolph Churchill. Their son was Winston Churchill. Others in the Victorian and Edwardian era with American wives included Lord Curzon, Rudyard Kipling, Joseph Chamberlain, and the Duke of Manchester. The Americans sometimes went to great lengths to woo aristocratic sons-in-law. The Vanderbilts were said to have laid out $2.5 million to marry their daughter Consuelo to the Duke of Marlborough. The Earl of Yarmouth was arrested for debt on the morning of his wedding to American heiress Alice Thaw and consequently upped his dowry demands, delaying the ceremony for forty-five minutes. The marriage was later annulled on the grounds that he had failed to consummate it.

16. Letter from R. Coltman to G. E. Morrison of 16 January 1900, quoted in *Correspondence of G. E. Morrison*, ed. Lo Hui-min, p. 130.

17. Ibid.

18. Quoted in P. Clements, op. cit., p. 114.

19. Sir C. MacDonald, op. cit., p. 5.

20. A. H. Smith, op. cit., Vol. I, p. 195.

21. William Bainbridge, Journals and Papers.

22. The rude comments about internal rivalries in the legations are from B. L. Putnam Weale, *Indiscreet Letters from Peking*, pp. 3-5.

23. W. Townsend's diary for 6 May 1900, quoted in his *In Memoriam*.

24. S. Conger, op. cit., p. 75.

25. C. Bigham, op. cit., p. 45.

26. L. Miner's diary for 5 June 1900.

27. R. Allen, *Siege of the Peking Legations*, p. 12.

28. Letter from E. Backhouse to G. E. Morrison of 23 January 1900, quoted in Lo Hui-min, ed., op. cit.

29. Mrs C. Goodrich's letter of 30 May, quoted in A. Mateer, *Siege Days*, p. 38.

30. Miss G. Smith's letter of 25 May 1900, correspondence of the London Missionary Society.

31. G. Casserly, *The Land of the Boxers*, p. 99.

32. P. Loti (pseudonym of Louis Viaud, an officer in the French navy), *Les Derniers Jours de Pékin*, p. 244.

33. Quoted in P. Fleming, *Siege at Peking*, p. 64.

34. All quotes in this part of the paragraph are from Dr Lillie Saville's pamphlet *Siege Life in Peking, May to August 1900*, correspondence of the London Missionary Society.

35. J. Stonehouse's letter of 16 May 1900, correspondence of the London Missionary Society.

36. R. Allen, op. cit., p. 42.

37. Mrs C. Fenn's letter of 29 May 1900, quoted in A. Mateer, op. cit., p. 54.

38. G. E. Morrison's letter to his mother, quoted in C. Pearl, op. cit., p. 87.

39. Morrison was fascinated throughout his life by the vagaries of his fellow human beings. Travelling through Morocco some years later he observed: 'Hemorrhoids are the commonest non-venereal disease which afflict the suffering ladies of the harem. Their life is sedentary and voluptuous . . . they habitually over-feed . . . everything conduces to that unladylike complaint – piles.'

40. Letter from G. E. Morrison to V. Chirol of 21 March 1899, quoted in Lo Hui-min, ed., op. cit.

41. *Hansard*, 4th Series, Vol. LV, cols. 1244–45.

42. Quoted in C. Pearl, op. cit., p. 69. In China thousands of girls were sold by their impoverished parents into prostitution. A concubine could be purchased for a handful of coins. There was also every type of brothel. In 1900 Tientsin had five grades of establishment, including thirty-five male brothels served by 800 boys. In Shanghai there were estimated to be some 40,000 prostitutes, catering to every need.

43. G. E. Morrison's diary for 17 April 1900.

44. H. Hoover, *The Memoirs of Herbert Hoover*, p. 48.

45. B. L. Putnam Weale, op. cit., p. 1.

46. G. E. Morrison for 14 May 1900.

47. Sir R. Hart, *These from the Land of Sinim*, p. 1.

48. *The Times*, quoted in C. Pearl, op. cit., p. 83. The Chinese Imperial
    Maritime Customs was set up in 1853 by agreement between
    China and Great Britain, the United States, and France, partly
    because of disruption to the Chinese collection of customs dues
    resulting from the Taiping and other risings. Staffed by Westerners
    (mainly British, but also Americans, French, and others) and about
    4,500 Chinese, all under the direction since 1863 of Sir Robert
    Hart, the Imperial Maritime Customs provided the Chinese
    authorities with a more efficient, less corrupt means of gathering
    customs dues than any previous arrangements. It produced about
    one-third of Manchu revenues but gave Western governments
    considerable influence.

49. Sir Robert often spoke of his acquaintance with Charles George
    Gordon (1833–1885), who ranks among the most frequently
    written about and more controversial British 'heroes.' He trained
    as a Royal Engineer and took part in the Crimean War. He was
    second-in-command of the Royal Engineers who, on Lord Elgin's
    orders, burnt Peking's magnificent Summer Palace in 1860. He
    also first laid out the British concession at Tientsin. However, he
    achieved fame as commander of China's 'Ever Victorious Army',
    which helped put down the Taiping rebels in 1862–63. The
    Taipings were led by the 'Heavenly King', Hung Hsiu-ch'uan,
    who blended Old and New Testament Christian beliefs with
    Chinese religion. His men kept the Ten Commandments and sang
    hymns and Hung claimed Jesus as his elder brother. Launching a
    revolution against the Manchus from southern China in 1851,
    the Heavenly King was initially very successful, capturing great
    tracts of China, including Nanking, which he made his capital.
    After a number of ups and downs Taiping forces even threatened
    Shanghai.

    The Western nations had, at first, favoured the Taipings but
    became disillusioned with them. At the request of Li Hung-
    chang, then embarking on his distinguished career, they agreed to
    help form a well-drilled army officered by Europeans and
    Americans to fight the Taipings on behalf of the Manchu
    dynasty. The first two commanders of the army were American

adventurers – F. T. Ward and, after Ward's death in action, Henry Burgevine. Their successes earned the army the name 'Ever Victorious', but Li Hung-chang found Burgevine 'full of intrigues and stubborn' and successfully intrigued for his dismissal. Li then persuaded the British government to second the then major Gordon to command the Ever Victorious Army temporarily. Gordon was a great success, keeping ruthless discipline among his men and marching into battle at their head carrying nothing but a cane. He soundly defeated the Taipings but soon fell out with Li Hung-chang. When Li executed a group of rebel leaders whom Gordon had promised to spare if they surrendered, he called Li an 'asiatic barbarian' and demanded his dismissal. It required the diplomatic skills of Robert Hart to smooth things over.

After the suppression of the Taipings, Gordon's career eventually took him to the Sudan. In 1884, having successfully withdrawn the Egyptian garrisons from the country in the face of a rebellion led by a Moslem prophet, the Mahdi, and his dervish followers, Gordon himself held on to Khartoum against orders. The Mahdi promptly besieged the city. The British government, blackmailed into sending a relief force, delayed too long, and on 26 January 1885, two days before Gordon's fifty-second birthday and the 320th day of the siege, the Mahdi's forces stormed the city. According to the heroic legend, Gordon met his death at the top of the palace steps, armed only with his deep Christian faith.

Gordon immediately became a flawless Christian hero in the popular imagination. His very human failings – bad temper, overwhelming conceit, sudden mood swings, and occasional bouts of heavy drinking – were forgotten until twentieth-century biographers, beginning with Lytton Strachey in *Eminent Victorians*, began to rake through the ashes. However, in 1900 Gordon's status as a Christian hero was still unchallenged. The outcry that followed his death was a cautionary reminder of the perils of delay to any British military leader who, like Vice-Admiral Seymour, was contemplating the relief of a besieged British community.

50. Sir R. Hart, op. cit., p. 8.
51. Ibid., p. 9.
52. Quoted in P. Fleming, op. cit., p. 64.

4. RATS IN A TRAP

1. Dispatch from Sir Claude MacDonald, 21 May 1900, quoted in British Parliamentary Papers, 1900.
2. S. Pichon, quoted in G. E. Morrison's diary, May 1900. The Paris Commune had been a traumatic event. During the Franco-Prussian War, Paris was besieged from September 1870 to January 1871. The defenders were reduced to eating rats but held out with great gallantry. They used hot-air balloons to communicate with the provinces. After the armistice with Prussia, there was widespread unrest and dissatisfaction in Paris with the French National Government, which was thought to be proposing the disbandment of the National Guard, which had for so long resisted the Prussians. On 18 March 1871 there was a mass rising and the Commune was proclaimed. The national government retreated to Versailles, from whence it organized a second siege of Paris. There was brutality on both sides. The Commune was finally suppressed on 28 May after heavy fighting (for which the Communards organized female as well as male militias), and the burning of much of Paris including the Tuileries. In the massacres that followed, between 20,000 and 30,000 Parisians were killed on the flimsiest suspicion of having been Communards. Many surviving Communard leaders fled to London, two of whom married daughters of Karl Marx.
3. G. E. Morrison's report in The Times of 13 October 1900.
4. M. Hooker, Behind the Scenes in Peking, p. 6.
5. R. Coltman, Beleaguered in Peking.
6. A. H. Smith, China in Convulsion, Vol. I, p. 209.
7. Sir E. Seymour, My Naval Career and Travels, p. 342.
8. 'G. E. Morrison's diary, May 1900.
9. Ibid.
10. A. H. Smith, op. cit., Vol. I, p. 211.
11. Hoover, Letters and Papers.

12. Sir R. Hart's letter to Mr Campbell of 27 May 1900, quoted in *The I. G. in Peking – Letters of Robert Hart*, ed. by J. K. Fairbank, K. F. Bruner, and E. M. Matheson Vol. II, p. 1230.

13. W. Lord, Good Years, p. 12.

14. R. Pelissier, *Awakening of China*, p. 217.

15. Sir R. Hart's letter to Mr Campbell of 3 June 1900, quoted in Fairbank, Bruner, and Matheson, eds., op. cit., Vol. II, p. 1231.

16. M. Hooker, op. cit., p. 15.

17. Quoted in R. O'Connor, *Boxer Rebellion*, p. 60.

18. G. E. Morrison's report in *The Times* of 13 October 1900.

19. Quoted in R. O'Connor, op. cit., p. 60.

20. Sir C. MacDonald, *Journal of the Royal United Services Institute*, p. 8.

21. Sir R. Hart's letter to Mr Campbell of 3 June 1900, quoted in Fairbank, Bruner, and Matheson, eds., op. cit., Vol. II, p. 1231.

5. 'SHA! SHA!'

1. Quoted in P. Fleming, *Siege at Peking*, p. 69.

2. F. Brown, *From Tientsin to Peking with the Allied Forces*, p. 21.

3. M. Hooker, *Behind the Scenes in Peking*, p. 20.

4. Quoted in P. Fleming, op. cit., p. 71.

5. Sir M. Hewlett, *Forty Years in China*, p. 14.

6. B. L. Putnam Weale, *Indiscreet Letters from Peking*, p. 30.

7. Quoted in P. Fleming, op. cit., p. 66.

8. M. Hooker, op. cit., p. 22.

9. Quoted in F. Laur, *Le Siège de Pékin*, p. 215.

10. Mrs C. E. Ewing, quoted in A. Mateer, *Siege Days*, p. 38.

11. E. G. Terry, quoted in Ibid., p. 81.

12. M. Hooker, op. cit., p. 24.

13. B. L. Putnam Weale, op. cit., p. 31.

14. Quoted in G. Lynch, *The War of the Civilisations*, p. 119.

15. American Presbyterian missionary Mrs C. Fenn, quoted in P. Cohen, *History in Three Keys*, p. 178.

16. B. L. Putnam Weale, op. cit., p. 37.

17. G. E. Morrison's report in *The Times* of 13 October 1900.

18. Ibid.

19. Ibid.
20. B. L. Putnam Weale, op. cit., p. 53.
21. N. Oliphant, *Siege of the Legations in Peking*, p. 17.
22. Sir Claude MacDonald to Baron von Ketteler, quoted in P. Fleming, op. cit., p. 98.
23. B. L. Putnam Weale, op. cit., p. 54.
24. Quoted in C. Tan, *Boxer Catastrophe*, p. 72.
25. A. H. Tuttle, *Mary Gamewell and Her Story of the Siege.*
26. During what the British called 'The Great Mutiny' in 1857, the British community at Cawnpore on the Ganges was besieged by Indian mutineers from the British Army led by the Nana Sahib, son of the deposed local ruler. The besieged totaled less than 1,000, of whom around 400 were women and children and another 100 male civilians. After a harrowing siege in baking temperatures, the British commander, General Wheeler, agreed to surrender on the promise of a safe passage down the Ganges to Allahbad. The Nana Sahib broke his word and the whole party was attacked as people began to board the boats. Many were killed there and then but about 125 surviving women and children were imprisoned in a house known as the Bibighar. They were later murdered on the Nana's orders by butchers from the bazaar and their mutilated bodies thrown down a well, some apparently still alive according to reports reaching the British. The Nana was supposed to have spent an evening of celebration singing and dancing. Once they had retaken the city, the British took wholesale revenge, making prisoners break caste by licking the blood-stained flooring of the Bibighar before they were hanged or blown from cannon. Giving someone 'a Cawnpore dinner' became a euphemism for bayoneting him in the stomach. Cawnpore became a touchstone for the unreliability of the 'native' word and the need to protect that other white man's burden – his women and children – from falling into 'native' hands. In 1900 Cawnpore was still an awful, resonating memory and many of the British besieged saw parallels with their own situation.
27. Quoted in P. Fleming, op. cit., p. 103.
28. G. E. Morrison's report in *The Times* of 13 October 1900.

29. *The Times* of 18 June 1900 carried a news agency report from Berlin dated 17 June stating that the German minister had been killed.
30. Miss J. G. Evans quoted in A. Mateer, op. cit., p. 124.
31. Estimates of the number of nationalities vary. In addition to the eleven nationalities with diplomatic representation in Peking and the Chinese converts there were Portuguese, Swedes, Norwegians, Finns, Danes and 'Boers'. There were also Irish, Canadians and Australians, like Morrison, who were sometimes counted as British but sometimes treated as nationalities in their own right.
32. Quoted in F. Laur, op. cit., p. 237.

6. A FAILED RESCUE

In this chapter quotes from Captain Lieutenant Paul Schlieper are from his account 'The Seymour Expedition' and all quotes from Vice-Admiral Seymour are from his book *My Naval Career and Travels*.

1. G. E. Morrison's diary, 27 June 1900.
2. Earl Jellicoe, Papers, 9 June 1900.
3. Diary of Lieutenant Fownes-Luttrell in Jellicoe Papers for 1900, British Library.
4. Commander Mori's report, July 1900.
5. H. Harper, *The Handyman in China*, p. 1.
6. Quoted in P. Fleming, *Siege at Peking*, p. 77.
7. Sir R. Hart, *These from the Land of Sinim*, p. 12.
8. Quoted in Papers of Captain McCalla, US Navy Historical Centre.
9. C. Bigham, *Year in China*, p. 179.
10. Report by midshipman in *The Times* of 17 September 1900.
11. C. Bigham, op. cit., p. 181.
12. Quoted in R. H. Bacon's *The Life of John Rushworth, Earl Jellicoe*, p. 111. The will made by John Jellicoe is among the Jellicoe Papers for 1900 held by the British Library. He wrote it in pencil on a wafer-thin scrap of paper, now mottled with age. It was addressed to his mother and asked to give remembrances to his sisters and others, including his faithful coxswain, who

returned the will to him over twenty years later. During a visit to the historical museum in Peking in the 1980s his son happened to mention to his Chinese guide that his father had been badly wounded by the Boxers. 'A thin smile crossed his features. I then happened to add that the Boxer bullet had remained lodged in one lung and might well have contributed to his later death. On this the thin smile widened into a grin of very evident pleasure. Thereafter our nice guide went out of his way and befriended me': Quote from Earl Jellicoe's Fifth Wellington Lecture, p. 29.

13. Sir E. Seymour, op. cit., p. 351.

14. C. Bigham, op. cit., p. 182.

15. Jellicoe Papers for 1900.

16. C. Bigham, op. cit., p. 186. Chao Yin-ho had already served in two navies – the Chinese and the British – before becoming Clive Bigham's servant. As a reward for his bravery in carrying the message to Tientsin, he received $1,000.

17. Captain Bayly's journal, p. 14.

18. Quoted in W. S. Chalmers, *The Life and Letters of David, Earl Beatty*, p. 48.

19. Report by midshipman in *The Times* of 17 September 1900.

20. Commander Mori, op. cit.

21. C. Bigham, op. cit., p. 188.

22. Letter from Mrs Scott to Commodore E. H. Burrows of 27 June 1900. Mrs Scott's dying day was not far off. She died of dysentery in September 1900.

23. Quoted in paper on Captain McCalla, US Navy Historical Centre.

7. CITY OF MUD AND FIRE

1. A. H. Smith, *China in Convulsion,* Vol. II, p. 571.

2. Anon., Boxer chain letter, British Library.

3. Translated and quoted in P. Cohen, *History in Three Keys*, p. 138.

4. Quoted in Ibid., p. 149.

5. All quotes in this paragraph are taken from journal of David Beatty (later Earl Beatty).

6. F. Brown, *'Boxer' and Other China Memories*, p. 74.

7. C. C. Dix, *The World's Navies in the Boxer Rebellion*, p. 31.

8. Ibid., p. 32.

9. Ibid., p. 35.

10. Ibid., p. 30.

11. As they sailed past the noncombatant USS *Monocacy*, Keyes and his men recalled a previous British naval attack on the Taku forts in the summer of 1859, when the United States had officially been neutral. Then, British landing parties had tried to seize the forts by landing on shore under heavy fire and rushing them. However, the sailors and marines had begun to sink in the soft slime of mudflats exposed by a receding tide and to take numerous casualties. The American naval commander on the spot was a Southerner, Commodore Josiah Tatnall, in his ship *Toeywan*. He could not bear to see the suffering of the British. Ignoring his American neutrality, he joined in the action with the comment that he could not stand aside because 'this is the cause of humanity . . . blood is thicker than water.' (Quoted from C. Hibbert's *The Dragon Wakes*, p. 245.) Although his actions did not lead to the capture of the forts, they helped the British withdraw. Without his help casualties would have been even greater than the 89 killed and 345 wounded. The commodore's actions were later officially approved by the US Secretary of the Navy. The British eventually took the forts with the French in 1860 by making a landing some distance away and attacking from the rear.

12. Sir R. Keyes, *Adventures Ashore and Afloat*, p. 255.

13. C. C. Dix, op. cit., p. 42.

14. Midshipman's report in *The Times* for 3 September 1900.

15. Anon., *The Boxer Rising*, reprinted from the *Shanghai Mercury*, p. 21.

16. C. C. Dix, op. cit., p. 48.

17. Hoover, Letters and Papers.

18. H. Hoover, *The Memoirs of Herbert Hoover*, p. 49.

19. Mrs Scott's letter of 18 June 1900 to her father.

20. Journal of David Beatty.

21. H. Hoover, *The Memoirs of Herbert Hoover*, p. 51.

22. All quotes in this paragraph are from Captain Bayly's Journal.

23. F. Brown, *From Tientsin to Peking with the Allied Forces*, p. 41.

24. H. Hoover, 'History of the Inside Circle.'

25. H. Hoover, *The Memoirs of Herbert Hoover*, (Hoover's Letters and Papers), p. 50.

26. Ibid., p. 52.

27. F. Brown, *Boxers, Blunders and Bullets or the Crisis in China*, Lecture.

28. Letter of Mrs Scott to Ste and Belle, 24 June 1900.

29. Journal of Anna Drew.

30. Journal of David Beatty.

31. C. C. Dix, op. cit., p. 62. Watt's efforts prompted Bayly's characteristically waspish comment that his ride 'did not hasten the reinforcements one minute, nor save one life in Tientsin. Much exaggeration as regards this ride has been shown.' Nevertheless Watt was awarded a medal by the kaiser and made a Chevalier of the Order of Leopold by the Belgians and a Companion of St Michael and St George by the British.

32. Ibid., p. 63.

33. Sir R. Keyes, op. cit., p. 239.

34. Letter from George Herbert to Mrs E.V. Young of 2 July 1900.

35. *Morning Post*, 12 September 1900.

36. A. A. S. Barnes, *On Active Service with the Chinese Regiment*, p. 29.

37. Journal of David Beatty.

8. BEHIND THE TARTAR WALL

1. Miss E. G. Leonard, diary for 20 June 1900, quoted in A. Mateer, *Siege Days*.

2. J. Bredon, *Sir Robert Hart*, p. 208.

3. G. E. Morrison's report in *The Times* on 15 October 1900.

4. Quoted in W. A. P. Martin, *Siege in Peking*, p. 119.

5. W. Lord, *Good Years*, p. 27.
6. Frank Gamewell quoted in M. Hooker, *Behind the Scenes in Peking*, p. 113.
7. Miss A. D. Gloss, quoted in A. Mateer, op. cit., p. 33.
8. S. Goodrich, quoted in A. Mateer, op. cit., p. 161.
9. B. L. Putnam Weale, *Indiscreet Letters from Peking*, p. 84.
10. G. E. Morrison's report in *The Times* on 15 October 1900.
11. Ibid.
12. A. H. Smith, *China in Convulsion*, Vol. II, p. 474.
13. M. Hooker, op. cit., p. 50.
14. R. Allen, *Siege of the Peking Legations*, p. 118.
15. Ibid., op. cit, p. 122.
16. Ibid., p. 125.
17. Sarah Goodrich, quoted in A. Mateer, op. cit., p. 162.
18. Miss F. Andrews, quoted in A. Mateer, op. cit., p. 139.
19. Quoted in C. Pearl, *Morrison of Peking*, p. 119.
20. Sterling Seagrave argues in *Dragon Lady* that the main Hanlin Library building was not burned down by the Chinese. He suggests that they set fire to some buildings in the compound in retaliation for a sortie into the Hanlin by Captain Poole. However, this fire was brought under control and, on the evidence of Arthur Smith's account, Seagrave suggests that the library was still standing when the wind changed direction, that there was no subsequent outbreak of fire, and that it was purposely looted and destroyed by the foreigners who subsequently mounted a cover-up. However, many accounts, including those of Gilbert Reid and other missionaries and academics who had no axe to grind, as well as Monsieur Pichon and other officials, suggest that the Chinese did indeed make a determined attempt to restart the fire using such methods as dousing the trees in the compound with kerosene and were certainly responsible for the spread of the fire to the main Hanlin building in an attempt to set fire to the adjacent British Legation buildings such as the student interpreters' quarters. Lizzie Martin, for example (Mateer, op. cit., p. 139) says of the Hanlin that it was 'their

treasure house of literature and had been left unmolested by our men because they did not wish to bring down on our heads more wrath than was necessary from the Chinese, yet so anxious were the enemy to burn us out that . . . they themselves set this place on fire.' It is difficult to see why so many accounts should be wrong or why so many disparate interests (rival diplomats, missionaries, soldiers, and academics) should have united in a conspiracy.

21. Robert Coltman quoted in M. Hooker, op. cit., p. 79.
22. L. Miner's Diary.

9. THE DRIFTING HORROR

1. Quoted in C. Tan, *Boxer Catastrophe*, p. 95.
2. B. L. Putnam Weale, *Indiscreet Letters from Peking*, p. 113.
3. In 1900 the standard of female beauty was the S-shaped body, with waists corseted so tightly they could easily be encircled with two hands. The corseting made both breasts and bottoms more prominent. The shirtwaister blouse was a favourite garment. According to an American salesman this was 'because they are comfortable, because they can be made to fit any form and because they are mannish'. While some wearers might have disagreed with the latter, they would not have doubted his assertion that 'the shirtwaist has come to stay.' Skirts were cumbersome, just touching the ground at the front and four inches longer at the back, so that the 'brush binding' had to be frequently cleaned and replaced due to constant contact with the ground.
4. B. L. Putnam Weale, op. cit., p. 124.
5. X rays had first been used clinically by Franz Exner in Vienna on 28 December 1895 to x-ray a gunshot wound in a forester's hand. In 1898, British surgeons were the first to use them in the diagnosis of war wounded in the Tirah campaign.
6. Sir M. Hewlett, *Forty Years in China*, p. 25.
7. Quoted in P. Fleming, *Siege at Peking*, p. 142.
8. G. E. Morrison's report in *The Times* on 15 October 1900.
9. Typescript Journal of Oscar Upham.

10. W. Townsend, *In Memoriam*, p. 3.
11. M. Hooker, *Behind the Scenes in Peking*, p. 91.
12. Extracts from Sir C. MacDonald's journal, quoted in R. O'Connor, *Boxer Rebellion.*, p. 166.
13. Sir Claude MacDonald, op. cit., p. 31.
14. R. Allen, *Siege of the Peking Legations*, p. 194.
15 S. Pichon, *Dans la Bataille*, p. 256.
16. P. Pelliot, *Carnets de Pékin*, p. 23.
17. Sir C. MacDonald, op. cit., p. 26.
18. Quoted in C. Pearl, *Morrison of Peking*, p. 123.
19. Commandant Darcy, quoted in F. Laur, *Siège de Pékin*, p. 335.
20. Sir M. Hewlett, op. cit., p. 28.
21. Captain F. G. Poole's Diary.
22. G. E. Morrison's Diary.
23. Quoted in M. Hooker, op. cit., p. 88.
24. P. Pelliot, op. cit., p. 33.
25. A. H. Smith, *China in Convulsion*, Vol. I, p. 308.
26. Edmund Backhouse in his 'Decadence Mandchoue' claimed that the Empress Dowager was disturbed by the noise of the gun.
27. Quoted in P. Cohen, *History in Three Keys*, p. 178.
28. J. Ricalton, *China through the Stereoscope*, p. 163.
29. Quoted in R. O'Connor, op. cit., p. 146.
30. C. Aspinall-Oglander, *Roger Keyes*, p. 57.
31. G. E. Morrison's Diary.
32. Queen Victoria's journal for 5 July 1900, Third Series, Vol. III, p. 570. Queen Victoria's journal for early July is peppered with references to her fears for her 'good Minister.' She wrote instantly to Lord Salisbury that she believed the report to be true but adding unhappily 'we are urging troops forwards with all rapidity in our power, but we cannot diminish the distance.' Her nephew the German kaiser wrote to her: 'This means serious business.'
33. Quoted in C. Tan, op. cit., p. 86.

10. THE DARKEST NIGHT

1. Sir. M. Hewlett, *Forty Years in China*, p. 30.
2. T. Piry, in charge of the Secretariat of the Imperial Customs,

quoted in A. Grigoratz, *Siège de Pékin*, p. 145.

3. A. H. Smith, *China in Convulsion*, Vol. I, p. 339.

4. Sir C. MacDonald, *Journal of the Royal United Services Institute*, p. 33.

5. The poem mentioned is *The Defence of Lucknow*. During the Great Mutiny, the British community in the city of Lucknow was besieged in the residency buildings at the beginning of July 1857. The defenders numbered no more than 1,700 men, including Indian troops loyal to the British. Those sheltering behind them included about 500 British women and children. An initial relief force managed to reach the besieged enclave but was not strong enough to break the siege. Rescue eventually came in mid-November with the arrival of forces spearheaded by turbaned Sikhs and kilted Highlanders. The residency was preserved as a revered museum site. When I was there last, over thirty-five years after Indian independence, the rebel lines in the model panorama still bore the neatly inscribed word 'mutineers'. Lucknow became well known throughout the world as a symbol of heroic resistance. There were several books on Lucknow in the legation libraries so the besieged of Peking could compare their experiences with what had happened in India. Perhaps they compared diet – at one stage the besieged of Lucknow, who did not have the luxury of a supply of ponies and donkeys, were reduced to eating sparrow curries. However, both sieges were remarkable for the quantities of alcohol, particularly champagne, available throughout.

Many of Tennyson's lines would have struck a chord with the besieged – not only the descriptions of horrible living conditions amidst heat and flies but hints about the 'fate worse than death' that might await women who fell into enemy hands and the duty to kill them first:

> *There was a whisper among us but only a whisper that past*
> *Children and wives – if the tigers leap into the fold unawares*
> *Everyman die at his post and the foe may outlive us at last*
> *Better to fall by the hands that they love, than fall into theirs.*

6. R. Coltman, *Beleaguered in Peking*, p. 104.
7. L. Miner's diary.
8. S. Conger, *Letters from China*, p. 131.
9. Quoted in A. Grigouratz, op. cit., p. 150. The reckless schoolboy bravado of some of the young Britons is a recurring theme – and complaint – in many of the accounts of other nationalities.
10. Quoted in P. Fleming, *Siege at Peking*, p. 161.
11. R. Allen, *Siege of the Peking Legations*, p. 211.
12. *The Times*, 17 July 1900.
13. The obituaries of Morrison, MacDonald, and Hart were published in *The Times* on 17 July 1900.
14. *New York Times*, 2 August 1900.
15. Quoted in P. Fleming, op. cit., p. 139.

11. A TRUCE AND A TRIUMPH

1. N. Oliphant, *Siege of the Legations in Peking*, p. 108.
2. M. Hooker, *Behind the Scenes in Peking*, p. 108.
3. Ibid., p. 110.
4. M. Gamewell, quoted in A. Tuttle, *Mary Gamewell and Her Story of the Siege*.
5. Mrs C. Ewing, quoted in A. Mateer, *Siege Days*, p. 199.
6. Comments made to Lu Wantian, a Chinese Methodist serving as a labour recruiter, quoted in P. Cohen, *History in Three Keys*, p. 198.
7. Ibid.
8. Quoted in A. Tuttle, op. cit.
9. Quoted in A. Mateer, op. cit., p. 347.
10. B. L. Putnam Weale, *Indiscreet Letters from Peking*, p. 146.
11. A. H. Smith, *China in Convulsion*, Vol. I, p. 302.
12. Herbert Hoover, Hoover Letters and Papers.
13. 'The Ninth Is on the "Logan"' was one of the songs sung by the men of the US Ninth Infantry and was written down by Anna Drew.
14. Captain Bayly's Journal.
15. Ibid.
16. H. Hoover, *Memoirs of Herbert Hoover*, p. 53.

17. Quoted in M. Glover, *That Astonishing Infantry*, p. 4.

18. Quoted in W. S. Chalmers, *Life and Letters of David, Earl Beatty*, p. 68.

19. Captain Bayly's Journal.

20. Letter from H. J. Hirschinger to his father of 8 December 1900.

21. Dr J. Matignon, *Revue Philomatique de Bordeaux et du Sud-Ouest*, 1902. According to Frederick Brown, the Japanese recognized that the glory belonged to them. He described how, when the Japanese had stormed in through the south gate: 'The officer called his buglars, sent them on the wall, and they played the Japanese National Anthem.' (*From Tientsin to Peking with the Allied Forces*, p. 39.)

22. Quoted in P. Cohen, op. cit., pp. 156–7.

23. J. Ricalton, *China through the Stereoscope*, p. 41.

24. Ibid.

25. H. Kinman, letter to his sister of 24 July 1900.

26. H. Harper, *Handyman in China*, p. 71.

27. H. Kinman, letter to his sister of 24 July 1900.

28. All quotes in this paragraph are taken from C. C. Dix, *World's Navies in the Boxer Rebellion*, pp. 188–92.

29. H. Hoover, *Memoirs of Herbert Hoover*, p. 54.

30. Letter from Lou Hoover to college friend Evelyn Wight Allen, 8 August 1900.

12. THE HALF-ARMISTICE

1. R. Allen, *Siege of the Peking Legations*, p. 213.

2. M. Bainbridge, Journals and Papers.

3. Quoted in B. L. Putnam Weale, *Indiscreet Letters from Peking*, p. 159.

4. Quoted in ibid.

5. The references to Imperial edicts and memorials from the viceroys in this paragraph are from C. Tan, *Boxer Catastrophe*.

6. R. Allen, op. cit., p. 227.

7. Ibid., p. 226.

8. G. Casserly, *Land of the Boxers*, p. 53.

9. Sir C. MacDonald, *Journal of the Royal United Services Institute*, pp. 38-39.

10. B. L. Putnam Weale, op. cit., p. 158.

11. A. H. Smith, *China in Convulsion*, Vol. II, p. 394.

12. L. Giles, p. 163.

13. L. Miner's Diary, 21 July 1900.

14. A. H. Smith, op. cit., Vol. II, p. 390.

15. R. Allen, op. cit., p. 229.

16. L. Miner's Diary, 25 July 1900.

17. M. Hooker, *Behind the Scenes in Peking*, p. 139.

18. G. E. Morrison's report in *The Times* on 15 October 1900.

19. *'notre sacrifice'*: S. Pichon, *Dans la Bataille*, diary for 28 July.

20. The reference to men moving out of the hearing of the women is from *The Times* report of 15 October 1900.

21. R. Hart, *These from the Land of Sinim*, p. 36.

22. N. Oliphant, *Siege of the Legations in Peking*, p. 154.

23. L. Miner's Diary, 1 August 1900.

24. R. Allen, op. cit., p. 237.

25. Mrs Inglis, quoted in A. Mateer, *Siege Days*, p. 284.

26. L. Miner's Diary, 3 August 1900.

27. A. H. Tuttle, *Mary Gamewell and Her Story of the Siege*.

28. Sir C. MacDonald, op. cit., p. 39.

29. Ibid., p. 40.

30. Quoted in C. Tan, op. cit., p. 105.

31. Ibid., p. 106.

32. P. Fleming, *Beseiged at Peking*, p. 178.

33. P. Fleming, op. cit., p. 179.

34. All quotes in this paragraph are from Count A. von Waldersee, *A Field-Marshal's Memoirs*, p. 207.

35. R. Keyes, *Adventures Ashore and Afloat*, p. 304. The speech was rendered all the more ridiculous because by the time Count von Waldersee arrived in China the siege of the legations was over. Waldersee left for China on 18 August after a great deal of pomp and ceremony at which the kaiser handed him the field-marshal's baton. Just the night before, news had reached the kaiser that the allies had entered Peking and that the Imperial court had fled.

The count later wrote: 'Naturally this was at first a great disappointment for the Kaiser. He had got it fixed firmly in his head that the Ministers and their personnel had been murdered long ago, and it was only after my arrival that the combined march on Peking – which had been regarded as impracticable during the rainy season – was to begin under my Supreme Command, thus winning for me the fame of having taken Peking.' Count A. von Waldersee, op. cit., p. 209.

36. C. C. Dix, *The World's Navies in the Boxer Rebellion*, p. 196.
37. All quotes in this paragraph are from G. Casserly, *The Land of the Boxers*, p. 51.
38. A. Savage-Landor, *China and the Allies*, Vol. I, p. 327.
39. All quotes here are from C. C. Dix, op. cit., p. 198.
40. H. G. Vaughan, *St George and the Chinese Dragon*, p. 33.
41. Report of the US Secretary of War (Elihu Root) 1900, quoted in H. B. Morse, *The International Relations of the Chinese Empire*, p. 267.
42. General Barrow's Campaign Diaries.
43. R. F. Gartside-Tipping papers.
44. Letter from Archibald Currie Gilchrist to his sister May, 22 April 1901, quoted in the *Journal of the Society for Army Historical Research*, 1968 No. 40, pp. 113–115.
45. R. Steel, *Through Peking's Sewer Gate*, p. 1.
46. S. D. Butler, *Old Gimlet Eye*, p. 67. Butler also noted that the Royal Welch Fusiliers were wearing the ribbon awarded for their valour at Bunker Hill and that they became firm friends with the US Marines on the march, presenting them with a handsome loving cup. The modern British army still contains one remnant of the British Indian Army. This is the regiment of Gurkhas, recruited from the mountain kingdom of Nepal. Among the toughest soldiers in the British army, they have, in 1999, formed an important part of both the British contribution to NATO peacekeeping in Kosovo and the UN peacekeeping effort in East Timor. A Gurkha was the first NATO soldier killed in Kosovo, when attempting to defuse unexploded bombs.

47. Letter from H. Kinman to his sister of 3 August 1900.

13. HORSEMEAT AND HOPE

All quotations in this chapter from Lieutenant Steel are from *Through Peking's Sewer Gate;* all quotations from Colonel Daggett are from *America in the China Relief Expedition* and all quotations from Lieutenant-Colonel Vaughan are from *St George and the Chinese Dragon.* References to them are given below only where they may not be clear in the context.

1. W. Townsend, *In Memoriam.*
2. Some foreign children had managed to bring their pets with them into the legations and food was found for them. Little Dorothea Goodrich wrote: 'They said that if any dog was loose they would shoot it. I was scared for fear that Dinger would be shot. I was afraid too that some day there would not be even a little scrap of food for little Dinger but that time never came.' Quoted in A. Mateer, *Siege Days*, p. 182.
3. A. H. Smith, *China in Convulsion*, Vol. II, p. 424.
4. L. Miner's Diary.
5. King Umberto was an inoffensive monarch who was killed on 29 July 1900 while handing out prizes from his carriage to athletes at his summer residence of Monza. He was shot four times at very close range by Gaetano Bresci. The thirty-year-old Bresci was an anarchist and silk weaver from Paterson, New Jersey. He had travelled steerage from New York to Le Havre and thence to Italy. Sentenced to life imprisonment (Italy had abolished the death penalty), he killed himself after a few months in prison where he was to have served the first seven years in solitary confinement. The American newspaper accounts of the assassination were read again and again by Leon Czolgosz, giving inspiration to his murder of President McKinley in 1901.
6. Sir C. MacDonald, *Journal of the Royal United Services Institute*, p. 40.
7. B. L. Putnam Weale, *Indiscreet Letters from Peking*, p. 185.
8. L. Giles, p. 174.
9. Quoted in C. Pearl, *Morrison of Peking*, p. 120. Not only did Sir

Robert's note get through, he received his new clothing on 26 October 1900.

10. W. A. P. Martin, *Siege in Peking*, p. 103.

11. R. Hart, *These from the Land of Sinim*, p. 47.

12. W. Townsend, op. cit., p. 126. August 12 is the beginning of the grouse shooting season in Britain.

13. Quoted in N. Oliphant, *Siege of the Legations in Peking*, p. 164.

14. C. C. Dix, *World's Navies in the Boxer Rebellion*, p. 209.

15. A. A. S. Barnes, *On Active Service with the Chinese Regiment*, p. 111.

16. Hoover, Letters and Papers.

17. A. H. Savage-Landor, *China and the Allies*, Vol. I, p. 363. Throughout the century the difference has remained between the Americans, who bring the bodies of their dead troops home, and the British, who generally bury their dead in the countries in which they fall in the superb cemeteries of the Commonwealth War Graves Commission.

18. C. C. Dix, op. cit., p. 219.

19. S. D. Butler, *Old Gimlet Eye*, p. 69.

20. R. Keyes, *Adventures Ashore and Afloat*, p. 278.

21. R. Steel, op. cit. According to *The Classical Dictionary of the Vulgar Tongue* by Captain Francis Grose (1731–91), first published in 1785, to 'cat' (or to 'shoot the cat') meant to vomit from excess of liquor. Here Lieutenant Steel presumably meant that he nearly vomited from disgust.

22. F. Brown, *From Tientsin to Peking with the Allied Forces*, p. 76.

23. A. H. Savage-Landor, op. cit., Vol. I, p. 365.

24. It is probably true that both British and American forces were less implicated than those of other nations in acts of violence against the local population and killing those assumed on the flimsiest of evidence to be Boxer suspects. However, neither country had a spotless record then or in the recent past. British reprisals against captured mutineers in the Indian Mutiny of 1857 had been savage. Inflamed by the massacre of British women and children at Cawnpore and elsewhere, the British had blown some prisoners from the mouths of cannon. After the battle of Omdurman in the

Sudan in 1898, the victorious British allegedly shot wounded dervish prisoners. Although this has not been fully substantiated, Kitchener and his men certainly neglected the dervish wounded. (Fewer than 400 of the British forces were wounded so there was no excuse that the British doctors had been overwhelmed.) Kitchener also removed the body of the Mahdi from his tomb, intending to use the skull as a souvenir, possibly to be mounted in silver and used as an inkstand. However, Queen Victoria made clear her lack of amusement with this scheme and the skull was buried.

US forces had massacred Indians, including women and children, during their campaigns in the second half of the nineteenth century. One such occasion was the fight at Wounded Knee in December 1890 at which Herbert Squiers was present as a cavalry officer. US troops also shot prisoners in the Philippines. Mark Twain's address of 1901 'To the Person Sitting in Darkness' quoted a letter from a soldier in the Philippines to his mother. Published in an Iowa newspaper, it described the finish of a victorious battle: 'We never left one alive, if one was wounded we would run our bayonets through him.'

Perhaps what distinguished Britain and America from some of the other participants was the extent of press coverage and subsequent public concern about such actions when they occurred.

25. A. H. Savage-Landor, op. cit., Vol. I, p. 365.
26. F. Brown, op. cit., p. 89.
27. Sir G. K. Scott-Moncrieff's Notes on Experiences in the Boxer Rebellion.
28. G. Lynch, *The War of the Civilisations*, p. 38.
29. F. Brown, op. cit., p. 88.
30. S. D. Butler, op. cit., p. 71.
31. G. Lynch, op. cit., pp. 46–47.
32. F. Brown, op. cit., p. 104.
33. Quoted in C. Tan, *Boxer Catastrophe*, p. 110.
34. Ibid.
35. According to another story, Russian scouts came across a group of Welch Fusiliers heading towards Peking and when they heard them conversing in Welsh decided a plot was afoot for them to

be first to enter Peking. This is an implausible if engaging story, but a number of accounts do tell of half a company of Welch Fusiliers who became lost and unwittingly arrived within sight of Peking. Whatever the case, the Russian rush to best NATO to Pristina airport in Kosovo in 1999 reminds one strongly of their rush to Peking!

36. Sir C. MacDonald, op. cit., p. 41.
37. M. Bainbridge, Journals and Papers.
38. Quoted in R. O'Connor, *Boxer Rebellion*, p. 234.
39. Sir C. MacDonald, op. cit., p. 41.
40. N. Oliphant, op. cit., p. 168.

14. IN THROUGH THE SLUICE GATE

As in the previous chapter, all quotations from Lieutenant Steel, Colonel Daggett, and Lieutenant-Colonel Vaughan are from their respective accounts and are referenced below only where they may not be clear in the context.

1. R. Keyes, *Adventures Ashore and Afloat*, p. 288.
2. Quoted in Daniele Varè, *The Last Empress*, p. 239.
3. G. E. Morrison's report in *The Times* of 15 October 1900.
4. Ibid.
5. W. A. P. Martin, *Siege in Peking*, p. 106.
6. Quoted in H. Keown-Boyd, *The Fists of Righteous Harmony*, p. 102.
7. A. H. Smith, *China in Convulsion*, Vol. II, p. 433.
8. S. Conger, *Letters from China*, p. 161.
9. De Courcy, quoted in G. Lynch, *The War of the Civilisations*, p. 133.
10. General Barrow's Campaign Diaries.
11. Sir G. K. Scott-Moncrieff, Notes on Experiences in the Boxer Rebellion.
12. Quoted in A. H. Smith, op. cit., Vol. II, p. 485.
13. *Daily Graphic* correspondent's letter of 14 August 1900.
14. The quotes from G. Lynch in these two paragraphs are all from op. cit., pp. 63–73.

15. 'TOUR OF INSPECTION'

All quotations from Wu Yung in this chapter are taken from his account *The Flight of an Empress*.

1. A. H. Savage-Landor, *China and the Allies*, Vol. II, p. 195.
2. A. S. Daggett, *America in the China Relief Expedition*.
3. The Empress Dowager apparently later told Princess Der Ling that she did not flee in disguise and that it was a story maliciously put about to degrade her.
4. S. Conger, *Letters from China*, p. 353.
5. R. F. Johnston, *Twilight in the Forbidden City*, p. 48.
6. J. O. P. Bland and E. Backhouse, *China under the Empress Dowager*, p. 18.
7. In her book, *My Chinese Note Book,* Lady Susan Townley, the wife of a British diplomat who arrived in Peking just after the siege, decided to take a ride in a 'Peking cart' and reflected on how the Empress Dowager must have felt: 'Helpless in the depths of that horrible cart I was bumped from this side to that like a parcel of oats; down went one wheel into a rut, my hat got knocked off, I endeavoured to adjust it, oh my poor funnybone! I began to get angry.' She vowed she would never ride in such a conveyance again.
8. Quoted in *New York Times*, 8 January 1902.
9. J. O. P. Bland and E. Backhouse, op. cit., p. 349.

16. THE ISLAND OF THE PEITANG

All quotations on the siege of the Peitang are from *The Heart of Peking*, Bishop Favier's diary of the siege, edited and translated by J. Freri, unless otherwise stated. The information on amounts of rations remaining at various times is taken from the same source. To make the figures tally exactly, one must assume that not all the ration reductions were mentioned by the bishop, or else that further food was discovered at certain stages.

1. Quoted in Anon., *The Boxer Rising*, reprinted from the *Shanghai Mercury*, p. 111.
2. G. E. Morrison's report in *The Times* of 15 October 1900.
3. P. Loti, *Derniers Jours de Pékin*, p. 247.

4. A. H. Savage-Landor, *China and the Allies*, Vol. II, p. 233.

5. R. Bazin, *L'Enseigne de Vaisseau Paul Henry*, p. 245.

6. Ibid., p. 246.

7. Ibid., p. 260.

8. The references to the Boxers' superstitious beliefs are from P. Cohen, *History in Three Keys*, pp. 132–33.

9. Olivieri's diary is quoted in S. Townley's *My Chinese Note Book*, p. 83.

10. W. A. P. Martin, *Siege in Peking*, p. 79.

11. Olivieri's diary quoted in S. Townley, op. cit., p. 84.

12. Olivieri's report quoted in R. Bazin, op. cit., p. 265.

13. Olivieri's diary, quoted in S. Townley, op. cit., p. 84.

14. Ibid.

15. Ibid.

16. Ibid.

17. Quoted in P. Fleming, *Siege at Peking*, pp. 220–21.

18. A. H. Savage-Landor, op. cit., Vol. II, p. 224.

17. THE FAITH AND FATE OF THE MISSIONARIES

All quotations in this chapter from Eva Price are from her *China Journal 1889–1900*.

1. Quoted in W. A. P. Martin, *Siege in Peking*, p. 66.

2. P. Cohen, *History in Three Keys*, p. 310, discusses the detailed numbers.

3. A. H. Savage-Landor, *China and the Allies*, Vol. I, p. 262.

4. Quoted in P. Cohen, op. cit., p. 206.

5. Quoted in R. C. Forsyth, *The China Martyrs of 1900*, p. 72.

6. The Baptist convert's account of the Taiyuan massacre is quoted in full in A. H. Smith, *China in Convulsion*, Vol. II, pp. 614–15.

7. Quoted in R. C. Forsyth, op. cit., p. 88.

8. Quoted in ibid., p. 128.

9. Letter from A. Glover to his parents of 17 August 1900, quoted in *Martyred Missionaries of the China Inland Mission*, ed. M. Broomhall, p. 83. Jessie Gates was back at her mission station within a year.

18. THE SPOILS OF PEKING

1. E. J. Dillon, *Contemporary Review*, January 1901.
2. Ibid.
3. G. Lynch, *The War of the Civilisations*, p. 140.
4. Ibid., p. 142.
5. Quoted in W. Lord, *The Good Years*, p. 38.
6. Count A. von Waldersee, *A Field-Marshal's Memoirs*, p. 207.
7. G. Lynch, op. cit., p. 145.
8. W. A. P. Martin, *Siege in Peking*, p. 138.
9. A. H. Smith, *China in Convulsion*, Vol. II, p. 521.
10. W. Lord, op. cit., p. 38.
11. S. D. Butler, *Old Gimlet Eye*, p. 77.
12. F. Richards, *Old-Soldier Sahib*, p. 150. Dumdums were soft-nosed expanding bullets, called after the village of the same name near Calcutta where there was a large arsenal. At the Hague conference of 1899 the British and Americans argued that they were needed to stop the onrush of fanatical natives.
13. E. J. Dillon, op. cit.
14. F. Richards, op. cit., p. 149.
15. Quoted in P. Fleming, *Siege at Peking*, p. 243.
16. G. Lynch, op. cit., p. 186.
17. H. Trevor-Roper, *Hermit of Peking*, p. 54.
18. G. E. Morrison, quoted in ibid., p. 53.
19. R. Steel, *Through Peking's Sewer Gate*, pp. 18–19.
20. Quoted in C. Pearl, *Morrison of Peking*, p. 131.
21. G. Lynch, op. cit., p. 185.
22. Dr L. Saville's letter of 20 August 1900, London Missionary Society Correspondence.
23. W. A. P. Martin, op. cit., p. 136. Arthur Smith told George Morrison the tale of Harriet Squiers's acquisition of a box of silks from the missionary Mr Tewkesbury, who was 'cheerfully hoping to sell it for untold treasures.' Mrs Squiers, after glancing at the contents, said, 'I'll give you $20 for it. I don't want to see it. I buy it in the interests of the poor Christians. Take it right away.'

24. Ibid., p. 135. Mark Twain directed a tirade at missionary Dr Ament in the *North American Review* as being 'simply beneath contempt' for going out with armed expeditions.

25. Ibid., p. 137.

26. Count Witte, *Memoirs of Count Witte*, p. 107. Russia was the only power to achieve substantial territorial acquisitions, profiting from the Boxer rising to pursue her ambitions in Manchuria. However, this led directly to the war of 1904 with Japan in which she was roundly beaten.

27. A. H. Savage-Landor, *China and the Allies*, Vol. II, p. 367.

28. G. Lynch, op. cit., p. 158.

29. E. J. Dillon, op. cit.

30. R. Steel, op. cit. Although there is no suggestion that General Barrow acquired any 'souvenirs' on this occasion, he recorded in his journal that during a visit to the Imperial carriage park the day after the relief 'I picked up the pair of big brass Dragon claws which now adorn my Drawing Room fire place in lieu of fire dogs. I ascertained afterwards that they were the heads of the shafts of the Empress's state elephant carriage.'

31. All the descriptions of looting in this paragraph are from G. Lynch, op. cit., pp. 160–61.

19. THE TREATY

1. S. D. Butler, *Old Gimlet Eye*, p. 78.

2. W. Chamberlin, *Ordered to China*, p. 149.

3. Ibid.

4. J. Bredon, *Sir Robert Hart*, p. 217.

5. P. Loti, *Derniers Jours de Pékin*, p. 236.

6. Quoted in C. Pearl, *Morrison of Peking*, p. 131.

7. Count Witte, *Memoirs of Count Witte*, p. 108.

8. G. Casserly, *Land of the Boxers*, p. 127.

9. *Review of Reviews*, 1901, Vol. 23, p. 21.

10. W. Chamberlin, op. cit., p. 213.

11. E. J. Dillon, op. cit., p. 14.

12. Ibid., p. 13.

13. Ibid., p. 14.
14. Ibid.
15. F. Richards, *Old-Soldier Sahib*, p. 153.
16. Assistant Paymaster G. Wynne, quoted in B. Nicholl's *Blue-jackets and Boxers*, p. 104. An Australian naval brigade had reached China immediately after the Boxer rising.
17. P. Loti, op. cit., p. 140.
18. Quoted in P. Cohen, *History in Three Keys*, p. 180.
19. Ibid., p. 350.
20. J. H. Wilson, *Under the Old Flag*, Vol. II, p. 523.
21. Ibid., p. 530.
22. General Barrow's Campaign Diaries.
23. Count A. von Waldersee, *A Field-Marshal's Memoirs*, p. 210.
24. Ibid., p. 217.
25. Quoted in P. Fleming, *Siege at Peking*, p. 253.
26. Ibid.
27. Quoted in C. Pearl, op. cit., p. 132.
28. Count A. von Waldersee, op. cit., p. 254.
29. Ibid., p. 232.
30. L. Miner's Diary.
31. Ibid.
32. Lieutenant H. Hirschinger's letter to his mother.
33. Count A. von Waldersee, op. cit., p. 268.
34. A. C. MacGilchrist's letter to his sister May of 22 April 1901, quoted in the *Journal of the Society for Army Historical Research*, 1968, No. 40, pp. 113–15.
35. The embarrassing mistake in deciphering the telegram from Washington is discussed in P. Fleming, op. cit., p. 247.
36. The circular telegram from John Hay of 3 July 1900 is described in C. Tan, *Boxer Catastrophe*, p. 148.
37. Quoted in P. Fleming, op. cit., p. 250.
38. Ibid., p. 238.

20. THE COURT RETURNS

1. Quoted in P. Fleming, *Siege at Peking*, p. 257.
2. Wu Yung, *Flight of an Empress*, p. 281.

3. Don Rodolfo Borghese's account of the Empress Dowager's return is quoted in D. Varè, *The Last Empress*, pp. 259-61.

4. J. O. P. Bland's letter of 12 February 1902 to G. E. Morrison: From *Correspondence of G. E. Morrison*, Lo Hui-min, ed., Vol. I, p. 178.

5. Lady S. Townley, *My Chinese Note Book*, p. 290.

6. R. C. Forsyth, *China Martyrs of 1900*, p. 492.

7. The traditional view of America's handling of the Chinese indemnity is basically that the US government made reasonable indemnity demands, took China's part in the peace negotiations by urging other powers to scale down their indemnity claims, and, when American claims fell short of the amount China had agreed to pay, spontaneously and unconditionally returned the surplus to China. The Chinese government then decided of its own volition and out of gratitude to use the money to educate young Chinese in the United States. However, analysis by Michael Hunt of Yale University suggests a somewhat different picture. Writing in the *Journal of Asian Studies* in May 1972, he argued that the American indemnity claims were in fact excessive and that Secretary of State John Hay knew this, that the administration of Theodore Roosevelt ignored Chinese claims on the surplus for as long as possible and only agreed to remit the funds provided they were used as America wished. The educational project was genuinely seen as beneficial to China. However, there was also a degree of self-interest, since America hoped to benefit from the creation of a cadre of American-educated Chinese leaders. The Chinese, on the other hand, deeply resented the American attitude, seeing the educational project as interference and an assault on Chinese values. They wished to use the money to fund a bank in Manchuria. A Chinese editor wrote in 1908: 'It is truly as if our country were a guest whose affairs were to be managed by those nations which made arrangements together.'

The reality about the American decision is that altruism and self-interest blended, as in very many 'aid deals' before and since.

8. Lady S. Townley, op. cit., p. 87.

9. R. F. Johnston, *Twilight in the Forbidden City*, p. 74. Princess

Der Ling maintained that he was murdered by the Chief Eunuch Li Lien Ying, who feared Kuang Hsu would kill him immediately on the Empress Dowager's death. She claims the 'savage neuter' told Tzu Hsi that the Emperor believed that he would outlive her and that the Empress Dowager tacitly authorized his murder by poison. She paints a macabre picture of the eunuch hovering above his bed 'like a bird of ill omen' and dressing him for the tomb while he still breathed.

21 . . . AND THE FOREIGNER DEPARTS

1. G. E. Morrison's letter to M. Bell of 20 October 1900: *Correspondence of G. E. Morrison*, Lo Hui-min, ed., Vol. I, pp. 148–50.
2. Quoted in S. Seagrave, *Dragon Lady*, p. 369.
3. N. Oliphant, *Siege of the Legations in Peking*, p. 217.
4. Letter to Campbell, 18 September 1900.
5. J. Bredon, Sir Robert Hart, p. 214.
6. R. Hart's letter to Mr Macoun of 13 November 1901: From *The I. G. in Peking – Letters of Robert Hart*, J. K. Fairbank, K. F. Bruner, and E. M. Matheson, eds.
7. Count A. von Waldersee, *A Field-Marshal's Memoirs*, p. 286.
8. During the crucial battle of Jutland in May 1916, two of Beatty's battle cruisers, hit by German shells, blew up and others were severely damaged. As Beatty ordered his flag captain to continue to turn towards the enemy, he is said to have remarked casually: 'Chatfield there seems to be something wrong with our bloody ships today': From *Oxford Dictionary of Quotations*, p. 35.
9. From McCalla's unpublished correspondence, quoted in Keown-Boyd, *Fists of Righteous Harmony*, p. 248.
10. Among other returning Americans may have been Tom Mix. Olive Stokes Mix in her book *The Fabulous Tom Mix* suggests that Tom Mix, the famous cowboy film star of the 1920s, took part in the fighting around Tientsin with the US Army and was badly wounded. The book also states that he had fought with Teddy Roosevelt at San Juan Hill, that he was wounded in subse-

quent operations on the island, and that he fought in the Philippines. However, most oddly, the book suggests that after being wounded at Tientsin, presumably in July 1900, he was invalided out of the US forces but, after recovering, sailed to South Africa with a consignment of horses for the British and took part in the siege of Ladysmith. The chronology here at least seems a little awry since Ladysmith had been relieved on 28 February 1900, well before the Tientsin fighting. This makes me a little dubious about the whole story, although it is a colourful one.

11. This charitable wish is from E. Backhouse's 'Decadence Mandchoue.'

12. J. O. P. Bland and E. Backhouse, *China under the Empress Dowager*, p. 480.

13. Capri was rumoured to be a nest of homosexuality. Krupp, the German industrialist who had sold so many guns to China, was accused in a German newspaper in November 1902 of debauching Italian boys with his friends on the island. Krupp was dead within days, officially of a stroke, but much more likely a suicide victim of a prejudiced age.

22. THE BOXER LEGACY

1. A. H. Smith, *China in Convulsion*, Vol. II, p. 596.

2. J. O. P. Bland and E. Backhouse, *China under the Empress Dowager*, p. 274.

3. R. Allen, *Siege of the Peking Legations*, p. 160.

4. R. Allen, *Cornhill Magazine*, November 1900, No. 53, New Series.

5. C. Tan, *Boxer Catastrophe*, p. 239.

6. S. M. Russell, *The Story of the Siege in Peking*.

7. R. Allen, *Cornhill Magazine*, November 1900, No. 53, New Series.

8. Sir R. Hart's letter to Campbell of 27 May 1900, quoted in *The I.G. in Peking – Letters of Robert Hart*, J. K. Fairbank, K. F. Bruner, and E. M. Matheson, eds., Vol. 2, p. 1230.

9. Quoted in G. Lynch, *The War of the Civilisations*, p. 305.

10. N. Oliphant, *Siege of the Legations in Peking*, p. 177.

11. Sir C. MacDonald, *Journal of the Royal United Services Institute*, p. 8.

12. Ibid., quoting A. H. Smith in *China in Convulsion*.

13. Sir R. Hart's letter to Campbell of 27 May 1900, quoted in Fairbank et al., op. cit., Vol. 2, p. 1230. Writing in September 1900, the Reverend T. Biggins of the London Missionary Society thought that few had recognized the extent of the danger: 'No one suspected how deep and powerful "the forces of reaction" were until they broke loose upon us, when hatred for foreigners and Christians turned into lead bullets we appreciated its force more, or at least I did.': Correspondence and Reports, London Missionary Society.

14. *Spectator*, 9 June 1900.

15. Quoted in G. E. Morrison's Diary.

16. At Isandlwana, on 22 January 1879, 20,000 warriors of a Zulu impi surprised the camp of General Chelmsford, who was advancing into Zululand. Of the 1,800–strong British force (950 Europeans and 850 Africans) only 55 Europeans and at most 300 Africans survived. Over 2,000 Zulus died. Later that same day, as depicted in the film *Zulu*, a British force of 140, mostly from the 24th Regiment of Foot, held the mission station at Rorke's drift, the ford over the Buffalo River, against a Zulu impi, winning a record eleven Victoria Crosses.

17. *Review of Reviews*, July 1900.

18. There are numerous examples of stereotypes that the authors at least believed to be true. Captain Hall noted that his men resented the patronizing tones of the British diplomats. One parodied them 'using a highly accentuated British pronunciation "My mon" do this, "My mon" do that etc., and concluded by saying that he was "no one's damn man!"' The other Europeans were often irritated by what they considered the exaggerated coolness of the British officers. Conversely, in a letter to Bacon included among the Jellicoe papers, Captain Jellicoe thought the French he encountered were 'a poor lot always having a meal when wanted to do anything!' Interestingly, though, the Japanese were praised as fighting men by all, but often in terms of unflattering surprise.

Jellicoe, J. I., Papers Relating to the Boxer Rebellion, letter to Bacon, 31 July 1935.

19. Thomas Pakenham, in *The Boer War* (p. 406 et seq.), makes a convincing case based on Baden-Powell's confidential staff diary of the siege of Mafeking that 'the white garrison took part of the rations of the black garrison. And part of the black garrison was accordingly given the choice of starving to death in the town or running the gauntlet of the Boers.'

20. Capt. N. Hall's account of the siege of the legations.

21. H. Trevor-Roper, *Hermit of Peking*, p. 322.

22. Ibid., p. 247; Trevor-Roper points out that the phrase is Talleyrand's.

23. Quoted in C. Tan, op. cit., p. 113.

24. Quoted in R. C. Forsyth, *China Martyrs of 1900*, p. 111.

25. Quoted in C. Tan., op. cit., p. 77.

26. Chester Tan makes the point forcefully that the refusal of the southern viceroys to respond to Imperial edicts actually strengthened the court's position when the time came for negotiations: Ibid., p. 78.

27. Lou Hoover's letter to Lucy Drew, 9 August 1932, Hoover Letters and Papers.

28. Quoted in R.C. Forsyth, op. cit., p. 497.

29. J. K. Fairbank, *The Great Chinese Revolution: 1800–1985*, p. 158.

30. Quoted in P. Cohen, *History in Three Keys*, p. 10.

31. The report of the attack on the British Embassy is from J. Hoare's article in the *Pacific Review* and from the *Daily Telegraph* of 1 January 1999, quoting from recently released UK government papers for 1967.

32. The account of the strange fate of the cigarette box is from A. Grey's *Hostage in Peking*.

33. Anon., *The Yi Ho Tuan Movement of 1900*, p. 35.

34. Assistant Paymaster G. Wynne of the Australian Navy, quoted in B. Nicholls, *Bluejackets and Boxers*, p. 105. In addition to his naval duties, Wynne was a correspondent for the *Telegraph* in Sydney, which published these words.

35. The references in these paragraphs to Sir Robert Hart's hopes and fears for China's future are all from pp. 50-55 of *These from the Land of Sinim*.

36. G. Casserly, *Land of the Boxers*, p. 292.

37. Sir R. Hart's letter of 17 March 1902 to G. E. Morrison: From *Correspondence of G. E. Morrison*, Lo Hui-min, ed., Vol. I, p. 184.

38. A. H. Smith, op. cit., Vol. I, p. ix.

EPILOGUE

We knew that the white memorial arch to Baron von Ketteler, promised in the peace settlement and dutifully constructed on the site of his murder, was long gone. It was apparently a monument of some beauty but was knocked down in 1917 when the Chinese Republic entered the First World War and sided with the Allies against Germany. The stone was used to construct a memorial commemorating the 'Victory of Right Over Might'. Until that time, curious tourists were apparently told by their guides that the arch honoured a soldier who killed the baron. The concluding sentences of the inscription in Latin, Chinese and German were suitably elliptical and oblique: 'The monument is erected in order to point out that what is good, is good, and what is evil, evil. Let all Our subjects learn lessons from the past occurrence and never forget them. We order this.'

BIBLIOGRAPHY

UNPUBLISHED SOURCES

Anon. Miscellaneous Chinese Papers and Posters. British Library, Oriental manuscripts 5896, 7451, 7690, 8143.

Backhouse, Sir E. 'Decadence Mandchoue' and 'The Dead Past'. Bodleian Library, Oxford University.

Bainbridge, M. and Bainbridge, W. Journals and Papers. Herbert Hoover Library, West Branch, Iowa.

Barrow, General E. G. Campaign Diaries and Journal. European Manuscripts, Oriental and India Office Collection, British Library.

Bayly, Captain E. H. Journal. Manuscript Collection of Jean S. and Frederick A. Sharf.

Beatty, D. (later Earl Beatty). Correspondence and Journal. National Maritime Museum.

Campbell, R. I. Letter to Sir Alexander Cadogan, 6 August 1942. Public Record Office, File: PREM 4/42/9/1008.

China Inland Mission. Correspondence of the Mission and Its Members. Special Collection of the School of Oriental and African Studies, University of London.

Connor, E. R. Papers. Mitchell Library, Sidney, New South Wales, Australia.

Drew, A. and Drew, E. B. Notes and Journals. Herbert Hoover Library, West Branch, Iowa.

Fownes-Luttrell, Lieutenant J. L. Correspondence and Journal. Jellicoe papers for 1900, Manuscript Department, British Library.

Gartside-Tipping, Lieutenant-Colonel R. F. Papers. National Army Museum, Chelsea, London.

Hall, Captain N. Papers including Records of Court Inquiry. US Marine Corps Historical Centre, Washington, D.C.

Herbert, G. Correspondence. US Marine Corps Historical Centre, Washington, D.C.

Hirschinger, H. J. Correspondence. US Marine Corps Historical Centre, Washington, D.C.

Hoover, H. and L. Hoover. Letters and Papers. Herbert Hoover Library, West Branch, Iowa.

Jellicoe, J. I. (later Earl Jellicoe). Papers Relating to the Boxer Rebellion. Jellicoe papers for 1900, Manuscript Department, British Library.

Kinman, H. Correspondence. US Marine Corps Historical Centre, Washington, D.C.

London Missionary Society. Correspondence and Reports of the Society and Its Members. Special Collections, School of Oriental and African Studies, University of London.

McCalla, Captain B. Papers. US Navy Historical Centre, Washington, D.C.

Miner, L. Diary and Papers. The Houghton Library, Harvard University, Cambridge, Massachusetts.

Mori, Commander. Translation of a report by Commander Mori of the Imperial Japanese Navy in the *Japan Weekly Mail,* July 1900. Collection of Jean S. and Frederick A. Sharf.

Morrison, G. E. Diary and Papers. Mitchell Library, Sydney, New South Wales, Australia.

Poole, F. G. Diary. National Army Museum, Chelsea, London.

Satow, Sir E. Diaries and Related Correspondence. Public Record Office, London.

Schlieper, P. 'The Seymour Expedition.' English translation. Edward

H. Seymour Collection, Phillips Library, Peabody Essex Museum, Salem, Massachusetts.

Scott, E. Correspondence for 1900. Jellicoe papers for 1900, Manuscript Department, British Library.

Scott-Moncrieff, Sir G. K. Notes on Experiences in the Boxer Rebellion. European Manuscripts, Oriental and India Office Collection, British Library.

Upham, O. Journal. US Marine Corps Historical Centre, Washington D.C.

PUBLISHED SOURCES

BOOKS

Allen, R. *The Siege of the Peking Legations*. London: Smith, Elder and Co., 1901.

Anon. *The Yi Ho Tuan Movement of 1900*. Peking: Foreign Languages Press, 1976.

Anon. *The Boxer Rising*. Reprinted from the *Shanghai Mercury*, Peking: Shanghai Mercury Ltd., 1900.

Arlington, L. C. and W. Lewisohn. *In Search of Old Peking*. Peking: Henry Vetch, 1935.

Aspinall-Oglander, C. *Roger Keyes*. London: Hogarth Press, 1951.

Backhouse, E. and J. O. P. Bland. *Annals and Memoirs of the Court of Peking*. Boston: Houghton Mifflin, 1914.

Bacon, R. H. *The Life of John Rushworth, Earl Jellicoe*. London: Cassell and Co., 1936.

Baker, H. *Chinese Family and Kinship*. London: Macmillan, 1979.

Barnes, A. A. S. *On Active Service with the Chinese Regiment*. London: Grant Richards, 1902.

Barr, P. *A Curious Life for a Lady*. London: Macmillan/John Murray, 1970.

Barr, P. *To China with Love*. London: Secker and Warburg, 1972.

Bazin, R. *L'Enseigne de Vaisseau Paul Henry*. Tours: Maison A. Mame et Fils, 1905.

Bell, S. *Hart of Lisburn*. Lisburn, Ireland: Lisburn Historical Press, 1985.

Bigham, C. *A Year in China*. London: Macmillan, 1901.

Bland, J. O. P. and E. Backhouse. *China under the Empress Dowager*. London: Heinemann, 1910.

Bloodworth, D. *The Chinese Looking Glass*. London: Penguin, 1969.

Bodin, L., and C. Warner. *The Boxer Rebellion*. London: Osprey, 1979.

Bredon, J. *Peking*. Shanghai: Kelly and Walsh, 1922.

———. *Sir Robert Hart*. London: Hutchinson, 1909.

Briggs, A. *Victorian Cities*. London: Pelican, 1968.

———. *Victorian People*. London: Pelican, 1965.

———. *Victorian Things*. London: Batsford, 1988.

Broomhall, M., ed. *Martyred Missionaries of the China Inland Mission*. London: Morgan and Scott, 1901.

Brown, D. *Bury My Heart at Wounded Knee*. London: Arena, 1987.

Brown, F. *'Boxer' and Other China Memories*. London: A. H. Stockwell, 1936.

———. *From Tientsin to Peking with the Allied Forces*. London: C. H. Kelly, 1902.

Butler, S. D. *Old Gimlet Eye*. New York: Farrar and Rinehart, 1933.

Cameron, R. *Barbarians and Mandarins*. Chicago: University of Chicago Press, 1976.

Carl, K. A.. *With the Empress Dowager of China*. London: Eveleigh Nash, 1906.

Carr, E. H. *The Bolshevik Revolution 1917–1923, Vol 1*. London: Pelican, 1966.

Casserly, G. *The Land of the Boxers*. London: Longman, Green and Co., 1903.

Chalmers, W. S. *The Life and Letters of David, Earl Beatty*. London: Hodder and Stoughton, 1951.

Chamberlin, W. J. *Ordered to China*. London: Methuen, 1904.

Clements, P. H. *The Boxer Rebellion: A Political and Diplomatic Review*. New York: Columbia University, 1915.

Cohen, P. A. *History in Three Keys*. New York: Columbia University Press, 1997.

Coltman, R., *Beleaguered in Peking: The Boxers' War against the Foreigner*. Philadelphia: F. A. Davies, 1901.

Conger, S. P. *Letters from China*. London: Hodder and Stoughton, 1909.

Cronin, V., *Paris on the Eve 1900–1914*. London: Collins, 1989.

Curzon, Hon. G. N. *Problems of the Far East*. London: Longman, Green and Co., 1894.

Dagget, A. S. *America in the China Relief Expedition*. Kansas City: Hudson-Kimberley, 1903.

Der Ling, Princess. *Old Buddha*. London: The Bodley Head John Lane, 1929.

——. *Two Years on the Forbidden City*. New York: Dodd, Mead and Co., 1925.

Dix, C. C. *The World's Navies in the Boxer Rebellion*. London: Digby, Long and Co., 1905.

Esherick, J. W. *The Origins of the Boxer Uprising*. Berkeley: University of California Press, 1987.

Evans, H. *The American Century*. London: Jonathan Cape, 1998.

Fairbank, J. K. *The Great Chinese Revolution: 1800–1985*. New York: Harper and Row,1986.

Fairbank, J. K., K. F. Bruner and E. M. Matheson, eds, *The I.G. in Peking – Letters of Robert Hart* (two vols.). Cambridge, Massachusetts: The Belknap Press, Harvard University Press, 1975.

Fairbank, J. K. and Kwang Ching-Lu. *Cambridge History of China*, Vol. II. Cambridge University Press, 1980.

Fleming, P. *The Siege at Peking*. London: Rupert Hart-Davis, 1959.

Forsyth, R. C. *The China Martyrs of 1900*. London: The Religious Tract Society, 1904.

French, P. *Liberty or Death*. London: Harper Collins, 1997.

Freri, J., ed. *The Heart of Peking – Bishop Favier's Diary of the Siege*. Boston: Marlier and Co., 1901.

Frey, J. *Toulouse-Lautrec*. London : Weidenfeld and Nicolson, 1994.

Furnas, J. C. *The Americans – A Social History of the United States 1587–1914*. London: Longman, 1969.

Gipps, G. *The Fighting in North China*. London: Sampson Low, Marston and Co., 1901.

Glover, M. *That Astonishing Infantry*. London: Leo Cooper, 1989.

Gray, J. *Rebellions and Revolutions*. Oxford University Press, 1990.

Grey, A. *Hostage in Peking*. London: Michael Joseph, 1970.

Grigoratz, A. *Le Siège de Pékin*. 1900.

Grose, Captain F. *The Classical Dictionary of the Vulgar Tongue*. London: [n. p.], 1785.

Haldane, C. *The Last Great Empress of China*. London: Constable, 1966.

Harper, H. *The Handyman in China*. Hong Kong: Kelly and Walsh Ltd. 1901.

Harrington, P., and F. A. Sharf. *'A Splendid Little War.'* London: Greenhill Books, 1998.

Hart, Sir R., *These from the Land of Sinim*. London: Chapman and Hall, 1901.

Hewlett, Sir M. *Forty Years in China*. London: Macmillan, 1943.

Hibbert, C. *The Dragon Wakes*. London: Penguin, 1984.

Holdsworth, A. *Out of the Dolls House*. London: BBC Books.

Hooker, M. (Polly Condit Smith). *Behind the Scenes in Peking*. New York: Brentano's, 1911.

Hoover, H. *The Memoirs of Herbert Hoover – Years of Adventure 1874–1920*. London: Hollis and Carter, 1952.

Hyam, R. *Empire and Sexuality*. Manchester University Press, 1900.

Hynes, S. *The Edwardian Turn of Mind*. Oxford University Press, 1968.

Irwin, W. *Herbert Hoover*. London: Elkin Mathews and Marrot, 1929.

Jellicoe, Earl. *Fifth Wellington Lecture*. University of Southampton, 1993.

Johnson, P., ed. *The Oxford Book of Political Anecdotes*. Oxford University Press, 1986.

Johnston, R. F. *Twilight in the Forbidden City*. Oxford University Press, 1985.

Judd, D. *Empire*. London: Harper Collins, 1996.

Kent, S. K. *Sex and Suffrage in Britain*. Princeton, New Jersey: Princeton University Press, 1987.

Keown-Boyd, H. *The Fists of Righteous Harmony*. London: Leo Cooper, 1991.

Keyes, Sir R. *Adventures Ashore and Afloat*. London: Harrap, 1939.

Kieser, E. *Als China erwachte: der Boxeraufstand.* Esslingen and Munich: Bechtle, 1984.

Laur, F., ed. *Le Siège de Pékin: Récits Authentiques des Assiégés.* Paris : Société des Publications Scientifiques et Industrielles, 1904.

Lo Hui-Min, ed. *Correspondence of G. E. Morrison 1895–1912* (2 vols.) Cambridge University Press, 1976.

Lord, W. *The Good Years.* London: Longman, 1960.

Loti, P. (Louis Viaud). *Les Derniers Jours de Pékin.* Paris: Calmann Lévy, 1902

Lynch, G. *The War of the Civilisations.* London: Longman, Green, 1901.

Lynch, G. *Impressions of a War Correspondent.* London: George Newnes, 1902.

Marchant, L. R., ed. *The Siege of the Peking Legations, Diary of Lancelot Giles.* University of Western Australia Press, 1970.

Martin, W. A. P. *The Siege in Peking.* London: Oliphant Anderson and Ferrier, 1900.

Mateer, A. H. *Siege Days.* San Francisco: Chinese Materials Centre, Inc., 1975, reprint.

Mitford, A. B. *The Attaché at Peking.* London: Macmillan, 1900.

Mix, O. S. *The Fabulous Tom Mix.* New York: Prentice-Hall, 1957.

Morris, J. *Pax Britannica.* London: Faber paperback, 1975.

Morse, H. B. *International Relations of the Chinese Empire* (3 vols.) London: Longman, Green, 1910–18.

Morton, W. S. *Japan.* Newton Abbot, England: David and Charles, 1973.

Narbeth, C. *Admiral Seymour's Expedition and the Taku Forts, 1900.* London: Picton Publishing, 1980.

Nash, G. H. *The Life of Herbert Hoover.* London: W. W. Norton and Co., 1983.

Neillands, R. *The Dervish Wars.* London: John Murray, 1996.

Nicholls, B. *Bluejackets and Boxers: Australia's Naval Expedition to the Boxer Uprising.* Allen and Unwin, 1986.

O'Connor, R. *The Boxer Rebellion.* London: Robert Hale, 1973.

Oliphant, N. *Siege of the Legations in Peking.* London: Longman, Green, 1901.

The Oxford Book of Political Anecdotes. P. Johnson, ed. Oxford University Press, 1986.

The Oxford Book of Quotations. Oxford University Press, 1979.

Packenham, T. *The Boer War.* London: MacDonald Futura, 1982.

Page, N. *An Oscar Wilde Chronology.* London: Macmillan, 1991.

Pearl, C. *Morrison of Peking.* Sydney, Australia: Angus and Robertson, 1967.

Pearsall, R. *The Worm in the Bud.* London: Penguin, 1983.

Pelissier, R. *The Awakening of China.* London: Secker and Warburg, 1967.

Pelliot, P. *Carnet de Pékin: 1899–1901.* Paris: Imprimerie Nationale, 1976.

Pichon, S. *Dans la Bataille.* Paris: Albert Méricant, 1908.

Pratt, K. *Europeans in Nineteenth-Century China.* London: Macmillan, 1968.

Price, E. J. *China Journal 1889–1900.* New York: Charles Scribner, 1989.

Purcell, V. *The Boxer Uprising.* Cambridge University Press, 1963.

Ramelson, M. *The Petticoat Rebellion.* London: Lawrence and Wishart, 1967.

Ransome, J. *The Story of the Siege Hospital.* London: SPCK, 1901.

Ricalton, J. *China through the Stereoscope.* New York, Edward Mellon Press, 1990.

Richards, F. *Old-Soldier Sahib.* London: Faber, 1965.

Richard, T. *Forty-Five Years in China.* London: T. Fisher Unwin, 1916.

Robinson, P. *The New Shell Book of Firsts.* London: Headline, 1994.

Russell, S. M. *The Story of the Siege in Peking.* London: Elliot Stock, 1901.

Savage-Landor, A. H. *China and the Allies* (2 vols.). London: Heinemann, 1901.

Seagrave, S. *Dragon Lady.* New York: Vintage, 1992.

Seymour, Sir E. H. *My Naval Career and Travels.* London: Smith, Elder and Co.,1911.

Shiel, M. P. *The Yellow Danger.* London: Grant Richards, 1898.

Smith, A. H. *China in Convulsion* (2 vols.). New York: Fleming H. Revell, 1901.

Smith, A. H. *Village Life in China*. London: Oliphant, Anderson and Ferrier, 1900.

Smith, R. J. *Mercenaries and Mandarins*. New York: KTO Press, 1978.

Spence, J. D., and Annping Chin. *The Chinese Century*. New York: Random House, 1997.

Steel, R. (ed. G. W. Carrington). *Through Peking's Sewer Gate*. New York: Vintage, 1985.

Strachey, L. *Eminent Victorians*. London: Penguin, 1979.

Sullivan, M. *Our Times – The United States 1900–1925*. New York: Charles Scribner, 1926.

Tan, C. *The Boxer Catastrophe*. New York: Columbia University Press, 1955.

Taylor, A. and H., eds. *Stuart Papers at Windsor.* (includes Letters of Queen Victoria, Third Series, Vol. III, and extracts from Queen Victoria's Journal). London: John Murray, 1939.

Thomson, H. C. *China and the Powers*. London: Longman, Green, 1902.

Townley, Lady S. *My Chinese Note Book*. London: Methuen, 1904.

Townley, Lady S. *'Indiscretions' of Lady Susan*. London: Thornton Butterworth, 1922.

Townsend, W. E. *In Memoriam*. Printed for private circulation, 1901.

Trevor-Roper, H. *Hermit of Peking*. London: Penguin, 1978.

Tuchman, B. *The Proud Tower*. London: Macmillan, 1980.

Tuttle, A. H. *Mary Gamewell and Her Story of the Siege*. New York: Eaton and Mains, 1907.

Varè, D. *The Last Empress*. New York: Doubleday, Doran and Co., 1938.

Vaughan, H. G. *St George and the Chinese Dragon*. London: C. Arthur Pearson, 1902.

Wagenknecht, E. *American Profile 1900–1909*. Amherst, Massachusetts: University of Massachusetts Press, 1982.

Waldersee, Count A. von. *A Field-Marshal's Memoirs*. London: Hutchinson and Co., 1924.

Weale, B. L. Putnam (Bertram Lenox Simpson). *Indiscreet Letters from Peking*. London: Hurst and Blackett, 1906.

Wen Ching. *The Chinese Crisis from Within*. London: Grant Richards, 1901.

Whittle, T. *The Last Kaiser*. London: Heinemann, 1977.

Wilson, J. H. *Travels and Investigations in the Middle Kingdom*. New York: D. Appleton and Co., 1887.

Wilson, J. H. *Under the Old Flag* (2 vols.). New York: Appleton and Co., 1912.

Witte, Count (trans. and ed. A. Yarmolinsky). *The Memoirs of Count Witte*. London: Heinemann, 1921.

Woodcock, G. *The British in the Far East*. London: Weidenfeld and Nicolson, 1969.

Wu Yung. *The Flight of an Empress*. London: Faber and Faber, 1937.

NEWSPAPERS (for the period of the book)

Daily Express
Daily Graphic
Daily Mail
The Daily Telegraph
Morning Post
New York Evening Post
New York Times
North China Herald
North China Daily News
Shanghai Mercury
The Times

MAGAZINES, PERIODICALS, AND JOURNALS (for the period of the book unless otherwise indicated)

Blackwoods Magazine
Century Magazine (1898)
Contemporary Review
Cornhill Magazine
Empire Review

Fortnightly Review
Hansard
Illustrated London News
Japan Weekly Mail
Journal of Asian Studies (1972)
Journal of the Royal United Services Institute (1914)
Journal of the Society for Army Historical Research (1968)
Lady's Realm
Life Magazine
North American Review
Pacific Review (1994)
Review of Reviews
Revue des Deux Mondes
Revue des Revues
Revue Philomatique de Bordeaux et du Sud-Ouest (1902)
Scribner's Magazine
The Spectator
Temple Magazine
Whitaker's Almanack

OTHER PUBLISHED SOURCES

Beijing International Society: Note on the Old Legation Quarter by
    Susan Pares, 1992
British Parliamentary Papers: Correspondence respecting the distur-
    bances in China (1900–1901)
Brown, F. *Boxers, Blunders and Bullets or the Crisis in China*, lecture
    printed by A. G. Wood (undated)
The Small Planet Internet Site

INDEX

Other titles in this series available from Robinson

A Brief History of The Tudor Age   Jasper Ridley   £7.99 [ ]

From the arrival of Henry Tudor and his army, at Mitford in 1485, to the death of the great Queen Elizabeth I in 1603, this was an astonishingly eventful and contradictory age. All the strands of Tudor life are gathered in a rich tapestry by this highly acclaimed historian and biographer.

A Brief History of The Druids   Peter Berresford Ellis   £7.99 [ ]

This compelling history explores who the Druids really were and what role they played in the Celtic world. A fresh and convincing interpretation, based on both archaeological and etymological findings.

A Brief History of Fighting Ships   David Davies   £6.99 [ ]

This is the story of the beautiful but deadly battleships that waged the war at sea during the Napoleonic Wars. Here are the construction and armaments, the daily life of the men, and the problems faced by the commanders in battle.

Robinson books are available from all good bookshops or can be ordered direct from the Publisher. Just tick the title you want and fill in the form below.

TBS Direct
Colchester Road, Frating Green, Colchester, Essex CO7 7DW
Tel: +44 (0) 1206 255777
Fax: +44 (0) 1206 255914
Email: sales@tbs-ltd.co.uk

UK/BFPO customers please allow £1.00 for p&p for the first book, plus 50p for the second, plus 30p for each additional book up to a maximum charge of £3.00.

Overseas customers (inc. Ireland), please allow £2.00 for the first book, plus £1.00 for the second, plus 50p for each additional book.

Please send me the titles ticked above.

NAME (block letters) . . . .

ADDRESS . . . .
. . . .

POSTCODE . . . .

I enclose a cheque/PO (payable to TBS Direct) for . . . .
I wish to pay by Switch/Credit card

Number . . . .
Card Expiry Date . . . .
Switch Issue Number . . . .